Emperor Alexander Severus

Emperor Alexander Severus

Rome's Age of Insurrection, AD 222–235

John S. McHugh

Pen & Sword
MILITARY

First published in Great Britain in 2017 by
Pen & Sword Military
an imprint of
Pen & Sword Books Ltd
47 Church Street
Barnsley
South Yorkshire
S70 2AS

Copyright © John S. McHugh

ISBN 978 1 47384 581 7

Printed and bound in Malta by Gutenberg Press Ltd.

Pen & Sword Books Ltd incorporates the Imprints of Pen & Sword
Aviation, Pen & Sword Family History, Pen & Sword Maritime,
Pen & Sword Military, Pen & Sword Discovery, Pen & Sword Politics, Pen & Sword
Atlas, Pen & Sword Archaeology, Wharncliffe Local History,
Wharncliffe True Crime, Wharncliffe Transport, Pen & Sword Select,
Pen & Sword Military Classics, Leo Cooper, The Praetorian Press,
Claymore Press, Remember When,
Seaforth Publishing and Frontline Publishing.

For a complete list of Pen & Sword titles please contact
PEN & SWORD BOOKS LIMITED
47 Church Street, Barnsley, South Yorkshire, S70 2AS, England
E-mail: enquiries@pen-and-sword.co.uk
Website: www.pen-and-sword.co.uk

Contents

List of Illustrations

List of Maps

Maps

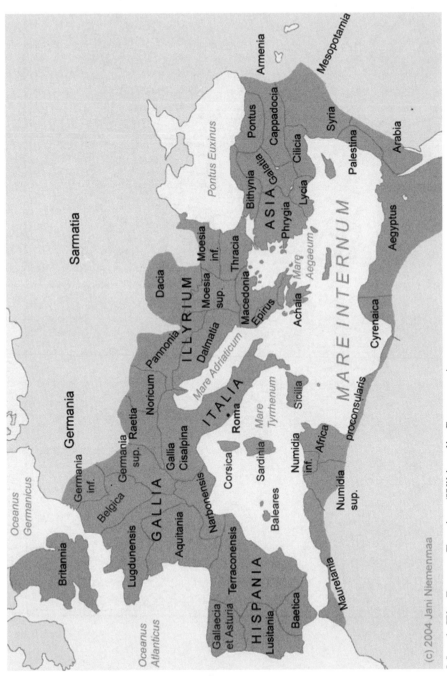

Map 1. The Roman Empire. (Wikimedia Commons)

(c) 2004 Jani Niemenmaa

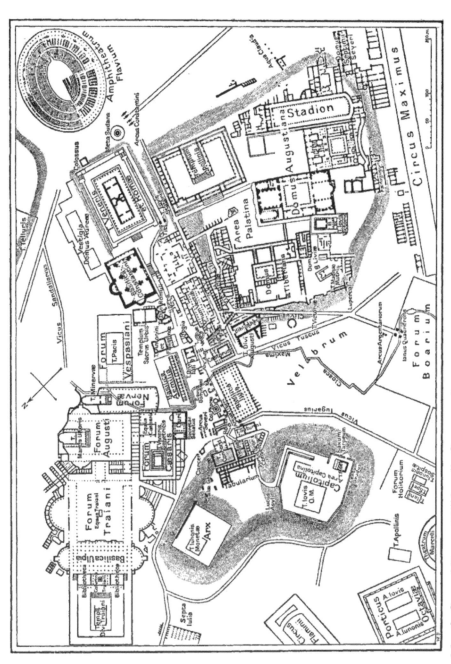

Map 2. Central Rome. (Wikimedia Commons)

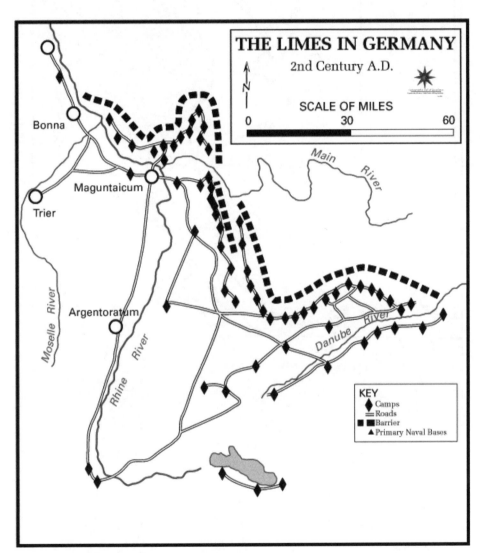

Map 3. The Limes in Germany, Second Century AD. (Wikimedia Commons)

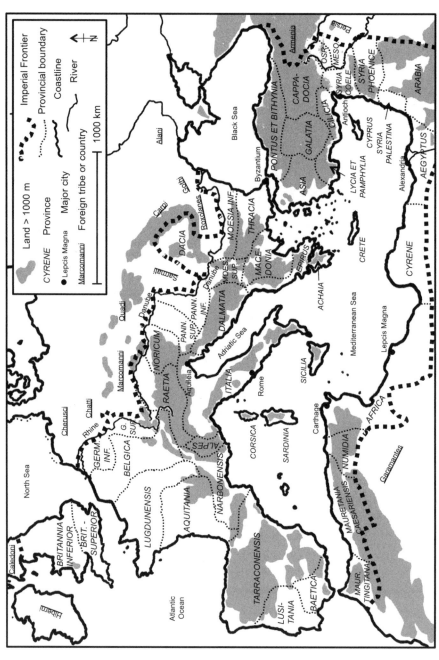

Map 4. Sketch Map of the Roman Empire in the Early Third Century, Based on Birley (1988). (Paul Pearson)

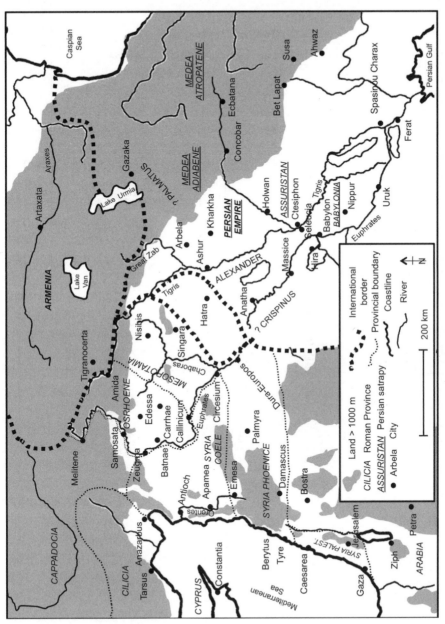

Map 5. Sketch Map of the Eastern Frontier of the Roman Empire c. AD 230. (Paul Pearson)

Family Tree

The family of Alexander Severus

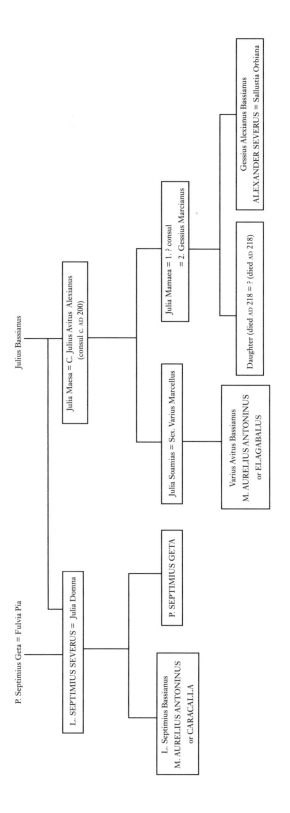

Chapter 1

Murderers and Usurpers AD 192–211

'... the lot of all Emperors is necessarily wretched, since only their assassination can convince the public that conspiracies against their lives are real'[1]

These prophetic words were uttered by the Emperor Domitian, murdered in AD 96 by his own friends, his *amici*, and imperial freedman in a palace conspiracy that probably included his wife and Praetorian Prefects. As the desperate emperor was stabbed repeatedly by his assailants, he attempted to reach the dagger that he kept under his pillow, but he found that its blade had been removed by his closest advisor. His successor, M. Cocceius Nerva, one of his closest *amici*, was named emperor on the same day, suggesting, at the very least, prior knowledge of the plot.[2]

This reign heralded the 'Antonine Age' of stability, peace and prosperity that ended with the Marcomannic Wars from AD 166, the outbreak of the 'Antonine Plague' and the murder of Commodus in AD 192. Nerva and his successors, Trajan, Hadrian, Antoninus Pius, Lucius Verus and Marcus Aurelius, all died of natural causes. Commodus, however, was the victim of another well-planned palace plot involving his closest *amici*, including the Praetorian Prefect tasked with ensuring his personal safety, his consort Marcia and his *cubicularius*, the freedman responsible for the imperial bedchamber. The Antonine emperors had faced plots, barbarian incursions and military revolts, but, apart from Commodus, had survived and prospered. Yet from AD 192 until the reign of Diocletian in AD 284, there were thirty-one emperors, of whom only three – Septimius Severus, Claudius Gothicus and possibly Carus – did not die violently. In this age of insurrection, placing power into the hands of a capable commander or politician provided them with the opportunity for revolt or murder. Yet at the same time the empire faced invasions along its considerable borders. An emperor could only be in one place at once. In this period of nearly 100 years, twelve emperors were murdered either by their own troops or the Praetorian Guard, whilst six were assassinated in what can loosely be termed 'palace conspiracies', three executed by successful usurpers, two killed in battle with rivals, another two either killed or captured by external enemies, one committed suicide, and of the three who died 'naturally', one died of the plague. One wonders why the imperial throne appeared so attractive.

One of the main problems for all these emperors is commented on only in passing by the historian Cassius Dio. When summing up the murder of Commodus, the senatorial historian laments that, 'with him the line of the genuine Aurelii ceased to rule'.[3]

The Antonine emperors had adopted their successors, and so in Roman eyes were legitimate members of the imperial family and clearly designated successors. This was not a deliberate policy, simply a failure until the reign of Marcus Aurelius to produce male offspring who survived to adulthood. Commodus was the son of Marcus Aurelius and, as such, his nobility, ancestry and right to rule were never questioned, even by the senatorial elite who despised him. These views are represented by the contemporary historian Herodian, who composed a fictive speech for Commodus after the death of his father that was delivered before the assembled legions on the Danube:

> 'Fate has given the empire to me as his successor, not as an adopted heir like my predecessors ... but as the only one of your emperors to be born in the palace. No commoner's swaddling clothes for me; the imperial purple lay waiting for me the moment I was born. On that day I was both man and emperor.'[4]

Commodus took immense pride in his ancestry and nobility, his coins promote the legend *nobilitas*, milestones were erected carrying the superlative *nobilissimus* (most noble) and inscriptions carried the grand title *nobilissimus omnium princeps*, the most noble emperor.[5] The senatorial aristocracy prided themselves on their own lineage; some families like the Acilii Glabriones and Aviolae traced their ancestry back to the Roman Republic, whilst others like the Claudii Pompeiani, the Bruttii and Claudii Severii could point to connections with the imperial family of the Antonines. Pertinax, Commodus' successor and a leader of the successful conspiracy against him, was a man of senatorial status but not noble birth,[6] and anticipating the problems this may cause, he first offered the throne to Acilius Glabrio, 'the most nobly born', who turned it down, settling instead on being the hand behind the throne and sitting alongside the new emperor in the Senate.[7] These aristocrats are described in the senatorial sources as being 'the best men', and their pride can be seen in their attitude to the new emperor, who would send treats from the imperial table to the homes of senators, yet 'for this the wealthy and vain glorious made great sport of him'.[8] The elite senatorial families had to rely on the emperor for offices of state, influence, power, honours, favours, gifts and other forms of *beneficia*, and yet would resent dealing with a man who was not their social equal. However, once the last of the Antonine emperors was dead, there were many who felt they had the ancestry and nobility to become emperor.

Pertinax's reign lasted three months before members of the Praetorian Guard, many angered by the murder of Commodus, burst into the palace and stabbed him to death. With no legitimate successor to turn to, they simply put the empire up for sale, which had the added benefit of lining their own pockets.

Two members of the senatorial aristocracy took part in what must be one of the most unusual auctions in history. Pertinax's father-in-law, the Urban Prefect Claudius Sulpicianus, stood on the walls of the Praetorian camp in a bidding war against Didius Julianus, who was not allowed in but had to stand below next to the gates of the fort. Julianus was reputed to be the wealthiest man in Rome and seen as easily capable of making good the monetary promises he made. To the winner, the empire and allegiance of the Praetorian Guard; the loser could expect a summary execution. The bids rose and rose until Sulpicianus promised the enormous figure of 20,000 sesterces per man, which appeared to carry the day. In desperation, Julianus raised his bid massively, to 25,000. The Praetorians may also have feared that Sulpicianus would avenge his murdered son-in-law, and Julianus wrote on placards that he would avenge the murder of Commodus. This swayed the contest in Julianus' favour and the gates were opened to him. He was declared emperor and acclaimed the new 'Commodus'. The guard then placed the image of the last Antonine on their standards.[9] The soldiers' choice of epithet reflected their loyalty to the extinguished imperial family. The power of the Praetorians and the weakness of Julianus' position is reflected in the appointment of their two Prefects, who were the choice of the soldiers themselves and had openly supported Sulpicianus.[10]

These claimants should have read their history. Tacitus, describing the consequences of the death of Nero and the march of Vespasian on Rome in AD 68–69, commented: 'A well-hidden secret of the principate had been revealed: it was possible, it seemed, for an emperor to be chosen from outside Rome.'[11]

A number of senatorial commanders were now declared emperor by their troops. These acclamations had no doubt been carefully planned by each, two of whom had been *amici* of Commodus. Pescinnius Niger, the governor of Syria, had the support of all the legions in the eastern provinces, but he was the first of his family to enter the Senate and was granted a *suffect* consulship for his military campaign with Clodius Albinus in Dacia in the reign of Commodus. Then he had, along with Septimius Severus, helped to crush the brigand Maternus in the Deserters War before his appointment to Syria. His career is described by Herodian as a 'distinguished record'. Decimus Clodius Albinus, another senator with an exemplary military record, had been an *amicus* of Commodus. He held the governorship of Britain with its three legions. According to the suspect life in the *Historia Augusta*, he came from a noble family, which can be confirmed by Herodian, who refers to him as ' a patrician-born member of the Senate'.[12] However, the first to declare himself emperor was Septimius Severus, who had in all probability been made governor of Upper Pannonia on the recommendation of Commodus' Praetorian Prefect and Pertinax's fellow conspirator, Laetus. Septimius Severus did not have any distinguished record of military service, having only held a legionary command in Syria. The appointment to Upper Pannonia, with its three legions, usually went to men who had previously held a post-consular provincial governorship and, due to its proximity to Italy, to senators of proven loyalty. Septimius Severus' brother, Geta, was appointed at the same time to Lower Moesia on the Danube, with its two legions. Laetus and Pertinax's conspiracy against Commodus was built on firm foundations. The murder of Pertinax and the execution of Laetus by Didius Julianus freed Septimius Severus of his bonds of loyalty to his fellow conspirators and patrons. Additionally, he could now portray himself as the avenger of Pertinax.

Only twelve days after the murder of Pertinax, Septimius Severus assembled the XIV *Gemina* and probably representatives of the other legions that supported him at his headquarters at Carnuntum. In this time he had assured himself of the support not only of the three legions in his province, but those of his brother in Lower Moesia, as well as the governors and legionary commanders, legates, in Lower Pannonia. Once assured of support in the two Pannonias, he sent reliable representatives to Upper Moesia and Dacia, as well as Noricum and Raetia, carrying letters armed with 'extravagant promises to raise their hopes'. He easily won their commitment of support. He also ensured that his two sons, Geta and Bassianus, the latter known to history as Caracalla, were safely spirited out of Rome and the clutches of Didius Julianus. Considering the distances involved and the delicate negotiations that this political manoeuvring must have entailed, it is evident that Septimius Severus was preparing the ground for his revolt long before the murder of Pertinax. He would have won over governors and legates with promises of future offices. The governor of the neighbouring province of Lower Pannonia, C. Valerius Pudens, would become governor of Lower Germany and then Britannia.[13] He would have reminded the legionaries of the I *Adiutrix* that Pertinax had been their commander twenty years previously; some of those listening would have remembered him as the successful general of the Marcomannic Wars. These legions acclaimed their commander 'Imperator Caesar L. Septimius Severus Pertinax Augustus'.

The initial stages of a military revolt are described in much more detail in Herodian's account of Niger's preparations:

> 'As a first measure he summoned the legionary commanders and military tribunes and more distinguished soldiers in small groups to his private residence, where he discussed the subject with them and tried to win them over by telling them the news he was receiving from Rome. In so

doing he intended the news to come to the ears of the soldiers and the rest of the inhabitants of the eastern provinces, once the rumour was current. In this way Niger hoped that no one would have any difficulty in supporting him, if they heard that he for his part was not making any insidious bid for power, but going to assist the Romans in response to their call. And indeed everyone did become excited. Straight away they began to press Niger with requests to be allowed to take a personal part in the campaign.'[14]

It would have taken at least twelve days for the news of Pertinax's murder to reach Antioch, and there is evidence of Niger making preparations before this.[15] Those first conversations would have been extremely dangerous and probably initially involved testing the loyalty of his guests to Didius Julianus. Events in Rome had taken a turn for the worse for the winner of the imperial auction. The treasury was empty and his own personal wealth could not cover the financial donative he had promised to the Praetorians, who now openly insulted him and refused to guard him. Their loyalty to the new regime was further sapped by constant training in preparation for the war against the seasoned soldiers from Pannonia. Didius Julianus attempted to portray himself as the avenger of Commodus, just as his opponents set themselves up as the avengers of Pertinax, by having the conspirators Marcia and Eclectus, Commodus' *cubicularius*, executed. This was not enough, and his support melted away despite his attempt to win over the nobles with lavish banquets 'playing court to the Senate as well as to all men of any influence'. Frequent games were organized to win over the people.[16] Coinage was the main vehicle of propaganda, especially the silver denarius, as it was used to pay the troops. Julianus' coinage proclaims *concordia militum*, the harmony of the soldiers.[17] Nothing could be further from the truth. The populace of Rome both feared and hated the Praetorian Guard for its arrogance and use of violence to impose its control over the streets of the capital: 'and great also was the fear inspired by the rest of the population by the armed troops, because the later hated them.'[18] Now the open contempt of the Praetorians and Niger's own agents meant that the games and shows Didius Julianus organized to win support became a hostile furnace of contempt as the mob, over 200,000 strong in the Circus Maximus, shouted insults at him as he sat in the imperial box. The crowd made jokes at his 'sensuality', it denounced him for sullying the dignity of the empire by buying the imperial throne, and called upon Niger as 'protector of the empire' and 'champion of the sacred office of emperor'. The mob cried out for Niger to march on Rome and oust their present ruler, chanting his name, and acclaimed him with the titles normally awarded to emperors.[19]

The Circus Maximus and Colosseum were regularly used to organize public demonstrations, as the numbers involved gave the mob a certain level of security from arrest or execution. Emperors used these public occasions to win popular approval and also as an open audience to hear popular complaints. The emperor, on entering the imperial box, would be greeted with a rhythmic form of chanting, in the same manner he would be greeted as he entered the Senate. This would need some form of organization. We can imagine that as Didius Julianus entered the arena, he was greeted not by the acclamation of his own name but that of Niger's. This must have been organized by Niger's freedmen, slaves and clients at the connivance of the main circus factions, the blues and the greens. Demands could be communicated to the assembled crowds by writing on large tablets, which were then paraded around the arena, or at a prearranged signal Niger's clients, spread around the stadium, could start a chant, which would then be taken up by those around. Dio describes fingers being raised up as such a signal. The emperor had tried to placate opposition by promising a distribution of money, or *congiaria*, but this only incensed the mob further, so he ordered the guards to kill those nearest to them. Rioting broke out and the streets of Rome ran with blood as the populace and the Praetorians fought, 'but though many were wounded and killed in many parts of the city, they continued to resist'. The mob had managed to seize weapons, probably from the gladiatorial schools and perhaps from the *vigiles*, the urban militia charged with policing the capital and dealing with its regular fires. The stadium of the Circus was used as a temporary fortress, and Niger's supporters were besieged there by Didius Julianus' troops. The besieged called upon the Praetorians to join them and support Niger, the besiegers waiting for the lack of food and water to drive their opponents into submission. A day later, the besieged surrendered and the inevitable retribution was exacted.[20]

Frequent messages would have kept all parties updated on events in Rome and could be used to persuade influential commanders and governors of the hopelessness of Didius Julianus' position. Niger's conversations focused on the call of the people of Rome for his help, the demoralized nature of Didius Julianus' only military force, the Praetorian Guard, and the chaos and bloodshed that reigned in the capital – a situation that he had helped to instigate.[21] Guests attending banquets and subordinates would be instructed to communicate this information to their juniors, and then allow rumour and exaggeration to undermine what loyalty the soldiers had towards the distant emperor in Rome. Niger, like Septimius Severus, also presented himself as the avenger of Pertinax by claiming to be bringing justice to those who had murdered him. He adopted the title *Justus* and issued coins with the legend *justitia*. He also promoted a reputation for fairness and moral rectitude.[22] The problem with this approach was many of the provincial governors and legionary commanders in the East supported Niger's revolt, not through enthusiasm for his cause but in order to avenge the humiliation suffered by the empire at the actions of the Praetorians and Didius Julianus.

Dio describes Niger as 'remarkable for nothing either good or bad' who was 'not a man of keen intelligence in any case, but made mistakes in spite of his vast power. At this time he was more puffed up than ever, so that, when men called him a new Alexander, he showed his pleasure, and when a man asked, "Who gave you permission to do this?" he pointed to his sword and answered, "This".'. However Dio's account of Niger's abilities and actions are not entirely above the suspicion of bias, as his career was promoted by the Severan emperors and he wrote his history under their rule. Herodian, writing his history in the 250s, after the fall of the Severan dynasty, is far more complimentary, describing Septimius Severus' rival as 'quite old with a distinguished record for a number of important activities. He had a reputation for being a gentle, fair man.'[23] The facts, though, speak for themselves: Emperor Commodus used Niger's undoubted military ability in wars in Dacia and in the Deserters War, then appointed him as a loyal and reliable governor to the prestigious province of Syria with its legions, and, if the *Historia Augusta* is to be believed, Commodus included him in a mosaic in his imperial gardens which contained the pictures of his closest *amici* performing the rites of Isis.[24] Like Clodius Albinus, the soldiers would trust this man to lead them to victory. He was a man of proven military experience and courage, defined in the Roman concept of *virtus*.

As in all civil wars, all men had a dangerous choice to make: who to support? Some had little choice, as they were simply caught on the wrong side of the dividing line. A speech made by Cassius Clemens is enlightening. Brought to trial before the victor of the civil war, Septimius Severus, he eloquently defended himself against the charge of treason, having fought on the side of Niger:

'I was acquainted with neither of you, but, finding myself in the midst of his partisans, I was constrained to look to the moment, not with the purpose of fighting you, but of deposing Julianus. I therefore did nothing wrong, either in this respect, since I strove in the beginning for the same ends as you, nor, later, in refusing to desert the master once given me by the will of Heaven and to come over to you. For you would not have liked it either, to have any of these men who are sitting with you here in judgement betray you and desert to him.'[25]

Septimius Severus, much impressed with his honesty and dignity, spared him his life and only confiscated half of his property. Many had similar difficult decisions to make. Asellius Aemilianus, the proconsular governor of Asia, and a man of influence and *dignitas*, was courted by all sides as his support would help add legitimacy to the cause of each usurper. However, Aemilianus understood that to back the losing side would probably mean death and the confiscation of his family's property, wealth and lands. He was a relative of Clodius Albinus, but Septimius Severus, in an astute move to neuter the threat of the British legions, offered his rival the office of Caesar, so acknowledging him as his successor. Aemilianus' province, however, lay in the East, on the boundary of the areas controlled by Niger. He decided the safest course of action was to remain neutral and wait upon events. However, wars, especially civil wars, allow no such latitude, and soon further pressure was placed upon him. Septimius Severus, on his capture of Rome, found Aemilianus' children living there and held them as hostages. Niger, in return, offered the eminent senator a major command in his forces. Forced to make a choice, he made, with hindsight, the wrong one. Aemilianus joined Niger and was given command of a large army. At the Battle of Cyzicus, he met the Severan forces and was comprehensively beaten, captured and put to death.[26]

Civil war brought opportunity for advancement and enrichment, as to the victor went the spoils. Herodian describes the many people who 'began to press Niger for requests to be allowed to take part in the campaign'.[27] The emperor's position was based upon patronal ties to his supporters, who competed with each other for offices, influence, wealth, gifts, honours for themselves and their own clients. This was a reciprocal relationship based on the concept of *amicitiae*, or friendship. In return for loyal service to the emperor, or other powerful politicians with access to the emperor's ear, you could expect to be repaid in a variety of ways, for example financially through gifts of land, politically by appointment to a magistracy, a governorship, a military command or *adlection* into the senatorial or lesser equestrian order, or legally through preferential hearing in a case brought before the emperor, Praetorian Prefect, praetor or governor. This was the foundation of all public life and is found regularly in the ancient sources. Emperor Nerva explained that he became emperor 'in order that I might confer new *beneficia* [gifts and honours] and preserve those already granted by my predecessors'. Pliny, the recipient of this letter, wrote to Nerva's successor, Trajan, on behalf of his clients for grants of citizenship, admission to the equestrian order and access to the water carried in aqueducts. Septimius Severus received senatorial status, the *latus clavus*, from Marcus Aurelius through the patronage of his uncle. Candidacies for magisterial posts of quaestor, tribune, aedile, praetor and consul were appointed at the favour of the emperor, as well as entry to the senatorial order itself. The award of the consulship ennobled the recipient and his family forever, whether the lesser 'suffect' consulship or the more prestigious 'ordinary' consulships, the year being dated by the names of its two holders. There were only about 100 senatorial and equestrian posts available each year, but other forms of *beneficia* were not so restricted. It was vital to have regular access to the emperor or his *amici* and officials. Exclusion from access to imperial favour threatened careers, wealth, status and the ability to satisfy or grant the requests from a patron's client base. Niger was the honey pot that attracted all those whose positions were threatened by the imperial throne being occupied by Didius Julianus, Septimius Severus or Clodius Albinus.[28]

It wasn't just the 'great and the good' who stood to gain or lose in civil conflict. The victorious soldiers of any conflict could expect a generous cash donative from the emperor. Defeat would bring death to many, and demotion or dishonourable discharge from the ranks. The vast amount of money the Praetorians had been promised as their 'reward' for selling the empire would have angered and alienated many soldiers serving in the provinces. Niger and Albinus would have promised such a financial reward on the successful completion of their campaigns. Septimius Severus presented 1,000 sesterces to each soldier, a figure that ensured their future loyalty.[29] Legionaries seldom showed loyalty to the state. The concept of the state would be ephemeral in the minds of the soldiers, who instead personalized loyalty to the figure and actions of the man sitting on the throne. Loyalty was shown primarily to individuals as emperor and his 'Divine House' rather than the idea of 'Rome'. The emperor dominated the army as its supreme commander-in-chief, their pay had his image upon it and their oath of allegiance was to preserve his safety and carry out his commands. This oath is only preserved from the Christian era of the empire: 'by God, Christ, the Holy Spirit, and the majesty of the emperor… to carry out all the emperor's commands energetically, never desert their military service or shirk death on behalf of the Roman state.'[30]

The oath was made on enlistment and yearly on the date of the accession of the emperor. The idea of statehood in the oath is clearly secondary to the expressions of loyalty to the person of the emperor himself. Epictetus, writing in the pagan era, describes this oath as sworn to god 'to value the safety of the emperor above every-thing'.[31] The name of the emperor was probably included to make explicit the personal tie with the soldiers. The oath would have been made in front of a statue of the emperor and was part of a religious ceremony. The English word 'sacred' is derived from the Latin *sacramentum*, meaning oath made before the gods. The contemporary writer Philostratus described how difficult it was for a governor to plan a revolt against the emperor: 'If he intends to use force against the man who appointed him to his command and in whose best interests he swore to give advice and to act, he first of all must prove to the gods that he is breaking his oath without impiety.'[32] Each unit also had its own standard, and these carried the image of the emperor. As Tertullian observed, the soldiers 'venerated the standards, swore by the standards, set the standards before all the gods'. These standards remained in constant view in the unit's fort, and images of the emperor and his family were kept in the fort's temple.[33]

The delay between the accession of Didius Julianus and the final preparations for the revolt would mean that all of Niger's soldiers had performed the oath to Didius

Julianus, as probably had those in the armies of Septimius Severus and Clodius Albinus. The soldiers would need some convincing to break an oath of loyalty that held religious power, and so perjure themselves. Seneca uses the word 'nefas', an act that was against divine law, when a soldier deserted.[34] However, if the legitimacy of the emperor was questioned, either through his actions in attaining the throne or his character defects, then such an oath could be interpreted as invalid. Both Septimius Severus and Niger presented themselves as the avengers of Pertinax, the legitimate emperor, murdered in an act of impiety by the Praetorians, and Didius Julianus was by his actions complicit in this murder. Septimius Severus adopted the name 'Pertinax' in his official title as his soldiers acclaimed him emperor, whilst Niger added 'Justus', the gods' harbinger of justice.[35]

The Antonine emperors were held in awe by the soldiers, their legitimacy stretching back through generations of imperial predecessors. Trajan had conquered Dacia and Mesopotamia; Hadrian crushed the Jewish revolt and toured the empire inspecting his troops and improving the imperial defences; Lucius Verus had defeated the Parthians; and Marcus Aurelius fought the decades-long Marcommanic War, repeatedly crossing the Danube in a war brought to a successful conclusion by his son, Commodus, an emperor who, like Hercules and the soldiers themselves faced death in combat by fighting as a gladiator. The coinage the soldiers used would have borne the names of these emperors, the titles they won for their successful campaigns – Parthicus, Britannicus, Germanicus – and the number of times they had been acclaimed 'imperator' or general by their victorious army. The mystique of the Antonine imperial house had been destroyed with the murder of Commodus.[36] Didius Julianus did have some military success, defeating an invasion of the Chauci across the Rhine into Belgica and repulsing an incursion of the Chatti, but this paled into insignificance when compared to the Antonine emperors. The soldiers would look to the distinguished military reputations of Clodius Albinus, Niger and, after AD 193, Septimius Severus. Senators, military commanders and even some equestrians would look at the man on the throne, compare their own achievements against his and ask themselves why they were not a better imperial candidate. Soldiers would also make the same calculation with their own commanders. Writing over 100 years previously, Tacitus describes how the centurion Clemens managed to sow dissent amongst the mutineers in the Pannonian legions by asking a simple question: would they be happy to follow the commands of the common soldiers leading the rebellion, Percennius and Vibulenus, or take orders from Augustus' successor, Tiberius, and his son, Drusus? Both were members of the Julio-Claudian house and so could claim descent from Julius Caesar, and furthermore had themselves fought a number of successful military campaigns. He continued by asking who provided pay for the soldiers and land for veterans. The revolt fragmented and was crushed.[37]

Niger also needed the support of the provincial elite in the East. His army would require vast amounts of supplies and money. Rome would not now be financing these armies in revolt. Gifts of money and grain would be awarded later, once he was emperor. Yet this would not have met his needs. Septimius Severus enforced confiscation in the areas that supported his rival, but Niger, the epitome of justice and rectitude, had to balance his financial demands made on the elite with the need to retain support for his cause. Niger had attempted to increase his popularity by attending festivals, which would have included athletics events and performances. The winners would have been rewarded from his hands and the festivities paid for by his purse. He would have banqueted the elites of the cities, listening to their petitions and requests, and, where possible, granting them their requests or promising future rewards. He would have toured the province, dispensed justice and ensured taxes were paid promptly. Cities would have had to send golden crowns to him in celebration of his accession. Herodian says 'he had been a mild governor to everyone.' He also provided shows himself in the city of Antioch, no doubt at great expense. Granting Antioch further rights to hold religious feasts and celebrations would help the city raise funds from pilgrims and provincials who came to the city as spectators. He also appears to have built a Plethrion, or wrestling arena, for these games, which would also have provided jobs in the second largest city in the empire. The Syrians, and Antioch in particular, were enthusiastic supporters of his revolt. He made the city his mint and headquarters.[38]

Niger took on the role of emperor in his administrative duties. He received embassies from Parthia and its client state of Adiabenes, and from the Arabs, accepting their gifts but politely refusing offers of alliance. A legitimate emperor could not make alliances with Rome's enemies to finance a war against fellow Romans. However, he did accept a unit of valuable archers sent by the king of Hatra. He officiated at the games in Antioch as emperor, regaled in the trappings of luxury, an expression of imperial power. An imperial court would have consisted of officials appointed as secretary of Latin letters (*ab epistulis Latinis*), Greek letters (*ab epistulis Graecis*), a chamberlain (*cubicualrius*), financial controller (*a rationibus*), administers of the imperial estates (*patrimonium Caesaris*), for the private estates of the emperor (*res privatae*), legal advisors (*a cognitionibus*), officials responsible for petitions (*a libelis*), taxes (*aerarium militare*) and two Praetorian Prefects. Each would have a department of freedmen and slaves to help with administration, another financial drain on limited resources. He toured the legions inspecting his troops, although Herodian is amiss when he criticizes him for failing to visit the Illyrian armies, as these had already indicated their support for Septimius Severus.[39]

Whilst Niger had been making careful but time-consuming preparations, Septimius Severus had organized a rapid march on Rome. His forces entered Italy even before news of his revolt reached Rome. The capital lay about thirty-four days' march away. Immediately the Senate, at Didius Julianus' bidding, declared him a *hostis publicus*, an enemy of the people. Despite this, Aquileia and Ravenna threw their gates open to him. At first, prominent senators were sent to win over Septimius Severus' troops, but they were easily persuaded to change sides through a combination of promises and money. The increasingly desperate Didius Julianus despatched assassins. However, 600 carefully selected soldiers guarded the usurper day and night, and these also deserted the faltering cause of Didius Julianus. Just as Niger had used his clients to stir up popular unrest in the capital, so Septimius Severus prepared for his arrival. On the capture and execution of the Praetorian Prefect Crispinus, Didius Julianus offered the post to the influential equestrian Veturius Macrinus, only to be turned down as Macrinus had already accepted the same post in Septimius Severus' entourage. Secret messages were sent to the centurions and tribunes of the Praetorian Guard, promising that they would come to no harm so long as they arrested the murderers of Pertinax and offered no resistance. Realizing he was losing control of the Praetorians, the emperor raised additional money from his *amici* and clients to try to provide another donative to the troops. However, as he had failed to distribute the full amount he had previously promised, they merely considered this their due deserts. Septimius Severus' letters had won over prominent senators such as Commodus' son-in-law, Plautius Quintillus, and the consuls L. Fabius Cilo and Silius Messalla. Placards appeared on the streets of Rome as the capital descended into anarchy and panic as Severan troops infiltrated the city. The Senate now curried favour with Septimius Severus, passing a death sentence on the emperor they had so recently acclaimed as Augustus. A hundred senators left Rome and went to greet his successor, encamped 50 miles away at Interamna. Didius Julianus died in an empty palace, abandoned by all apart from his son-in-law and one of the Praetorian Prefects. A Praetorian tribune ended his life, his last words being: 'But what evil have I done? Whom have I killed?'[40]

Since the murder of Commodus, the Praetorians had become a law unto themselves. Their loyalty remained suspect and, despite their execution of those soldiers responsible for the assassination of Pertinax, they were all seen as culpable. None had defended the emperor and all had left their posts in the palace. The guard was summoned to meet their new emperor outside Rome, leaving their weapons behind. They clearly expected that they would be asked to give their oath of allegiance, but instead found themselves surrounded by armed legionaries. Septimius Severus then rose to stand on the tribunal, and instead of a formal address to the massed ranks of soldiers, the *adlocutio*, he harangued them for their failure to perform their sworn duties or arrest the murders of Pertinax, for slaughtering their fellow citizens and their humiliation of Rome by auctioning the empire. Although, in the words put into Septimius Severus' mouth by Herodian, they 'deserved to die a thousand times', he acknowledged the promise that they would come to no harm. So their lives were spared, but they were dishonourably discharged, told to leave their ceremonial belts and daggers and not come within 100 miles of the capital. Most acquiesced, but some refused, their belts cut from them by the legionaries surrounding them. One preferred death to suffering such humiliation, and killed himself.[41]

Septimius Severus then entered Rome, surrounded by his army in full armour, preceded by the standards of the Praetorians being dragged through the dirt to symbolize their disgrace. As he was acclaimed Augustus in the Senate, and as he gave the traditional promises of refraining from putting any senator to death, his soldiers fanned out through the city. Interestingly, these men were posted 'in the temples, in porticoes, and in the shrines on the Palatine'.[42] These appear to be the locations where crowds gathered in moments of crisis or celebration. On the death of Commodus in AD 192, people gathered at temples and altars, and in AD 238, crowds 'ran to the altars and the temples' upon news of the death of Maximinus Thrax and his son. Upon receiving such news, the great and the good went to give sacrifice to the gods, either requesting divine assistance to keep their family from danger, to give thanks or to hear the latest rumours. It was there that their clients were summoned, rather than have them gather in the confines of the patron's atrium in his house, where events might get out of hand. The capital's corporations also met regularly in the temples around the forum when they planned for public festivals.[43] In the absence of banks, many of the rich also deposited their valuables within these temples, and it is understandable that in times of unrest they would quickly gather together an armed group of slaves and clients in order to guard their deposits from looting. Such temples and shrines were reasonably close together to allow the elite to communicate with each other, and the open area of the forum allowed large crowds to be addressed from the public rostra. This was also the place where official proclamations were announced and so people could be kept up to date with news of events. Furthermore, the imperial palace on the Palatine Hill loomed large above, placing pressure on the emperor as he looked down upon the gathering crowds below. At night, the torches of the gathered multitude would have lit the darkness.

The situation on the streets of Rome remained volatile; Dio uses the word 'turbulent', with modest understatement. According to the *Historia Augusta*, the army 'inspired both hate and fear, for the soldiers seized goods they did not pay for and threatened to lay waste the city'.[44] As their new emperor attended a meeting in the Senate, protected by armed *amici*, the soldiers demanded 10,000 sesterces each. They based this figure upon the amount Octavian, later named Augustus, gave to soldiers in his army in 43 BC. They were, however, placated with the more modest donative of 1,000 each. These men would now form the nucleus of a reconstituted Praetorian Guard, recruited from the legions in Pannonia, Dacia and Moesia that had supported Septimius Severus, and, in particular, those from his province of Upper Pannonia: the I *Adiutrix* based at Brigetio, the X *Gemina* at Vindobona and the XIV *Gemina* at Carnuntum. It was not an auspicious start for the elite unit of the Roman Army.

The Danubian legions had recruited locals into their ranks since the Marcomannic Wars of Marcus Aurelius and Commodus. These men were from some of the least Romanized provinces in the empire. Their brutalized Latin and fashion offended the delicate sensibilities of the more refined citizens of the capital. Their clothing originated across the border of the empire in '*barbaricum*'; they wore the local attire, consisting of a long-sleeved tunic and trousers, which had gradually spread to other legions and now became the style worn by Praetorians when out of uniform. The idea of serving an abstract Roman state would have become increasingly tenuous in the consciousness of these men. They served their commander, who led them to victory in battle and rewarded them with donatives and promotion to his bodyguard.[45] Many inscriptions from Pannonia show that the majority of the local population were Celtic Illyrians in origin and culture, painted with a veneer of Romanization. However, in the towns attached to the legionary fortresses, there were significant numbers of residents whose origins lay in the eastern half of the empire, encouraged to settle in the cities destroyed in the wars fought under Marcus Aurelius. Many of the defeated Quadi, Marcomanni, Cotini, Osi and Naristae were settled on the lands left vacant by frequent barbarian invasions in the interior of these provinces. Most inscriptions and dedications come from the environs of the major settlements. These regularly refer to the manumission, or freeing, of slaves by soldiers and veterans, many becoming the wives of these men. Some tombstones also refer to interpreters of different local languages, *interprex Dacorum*, an *interprex Sarmatarum* and *Germanorum* denoting regular contact with the inhabitants of *barbaricum* across the Danube.

There is only one inscription from the interior of the two Pannonias, and unlike those near the towns, there is no reference to slaves. An inscription from the reign of Alexander Severus was found near Budapest on the site of Vicus Vindonianus. In it, a clear distinction is made between the owners of land and the peasants who farmed it, suggesting a clear dependence of these landless labourers on more urbanized, higher status land owners. These local elite were often veterans or their descendants who formed a privileged class in the urban centres, or local merchants and traders supplying local garrisons. This diverse population now served as the recruiting ground of the Roman army along the Danube, and in particular the officers and men of the new Praetorian Guard. These were the men who patrolled the corridors of the palace, escorted the emperor to the Senate house and drank in the taverns and brothels of the capital. They exalted in their new status, and they were hated.[46]

The old Praetorian Guard had been mainly recruited from Italy, supplemented by men from Spain, Macedonia and Gallia Narbonensis.[47] Dio laments the ruin of Italy's youth, who, now barred from the guards, turned to brigandage or fighting in the arena. This is an oversimplification, as new legions were recruited from Italy, but Italy increasingly lost its privileged position and became just another province of the empire. What Dio and his fellow senators did disdain was the decision of Septimius Severus that allowed the capital to be filled with uncultured soldiers, barbaric in nature and lacking the embellishments of civilization: '[A] throng of motley soldiers most savage in appearance, most terrifying in speech, and most boorish in conversation.'[48]

The Praetorians would continue to be recruited from soldiers promoted from the legions, in particular those along the Danube, and from the guard many would return to army units as centurions. The 'habits' and 'traditions' of the old members of the guard were to be continued by soldiers in the new guard. Given licence, they would plunder from the civilian population, insult members of the populace and strike the unsuspecting passer-by. Juvenal, writing at the turn of the second century in his sixteenth satire, warns against returning a blow given by a soldier:

> 'A soldier's blow no commoner dare return!
> What! show the judge and hope to be forgiven,
> Those bleeding sockets whence thy teeth were driven!
> What! of thy livid bumps and bruises complain,
> And live to bear such bumps and bruises again.'

Soldiers acted with impunity. A victim could either deny any assault had taken place for fear of receiving worse, or, if the case was brought to trial, the soldiers were subject to military justice and so tried before centurions, who would offer no support or credence to a mere civilian's claim.[49] Soldiers' privileges had grown over the second century, and were to be enhanced even further by Septimius Severus.

On his death bed, Septimius Severus advised his two children, Caracalla and Geta, to 'Be harmonious, enrich the soldiers, and scorn all other men.' The nature of his government was clear from the start; the senatorial historian Dio blames the emperor 'for placing his hope of safety in the strength of his army rather than in the good will of his associates [in the government]'. By that, he meant the senatorial elite.[50] The pay of the soldiers was increased in his reign to 450 *denarii*, paid in three or four monthly instalments, and Caracalla increased it again to around 675 *denarii*, whilst soldiers were also paid increasingly by *annona*, in the form of grain, oil and other basic staples. The Praetorian's pay was increased by Caracalla to 2,250 *denarii* or, according to some estimates, the less likely figure of 3,600.[51] Additionally, they were granted an increased number of donatives. Soldiers were also granted the right to marry, as legally this had been prohibited until retirement; many soldiers were married before they left the service, yet if they died in service, their wife and children were not legally entitled to inherit. An absurd situation that had existed for 200 years was now rectified. At the same time, Septimius Severus improved the married quarters in the *canabae* (local settlements), which now became the best accommodation in the towns associated with each fort. Furthermore, the military establishment had previously frowned upon the *collegia* set up by different grades of soldiers, which provided social and financial benefits in case of death, injury, promotion or retirement. These societies usually had a club house, or *schola*, where meetings, feasts and other forms of entertainment were provided. Septimius Severus appears to have encouraged their development, even allowing for the provision of club houses within the confines of forts themselves.[52]

The opening up of the Praetorian Guard gave all soldiers the opportunity of a career progression from the legions, via the guard and on to the post of a centurion, who could also command separate auxiliary units. The highest grade of centurion, the *primus pilus*, could expect to become a senior officer or a procurator in the imperial administration, or even enter the equestrian order. Centurions and officers were also given the right to wear a gold ring, which was the status symbol of the equestrian order and clearly indicates the opportunities that were now available to the able, ambitious soldier. Since the joint ravages of the barbarian invasions from AD 166–181 and the Antonine plague, the number of recruits to the army had probably dropped significantly. On enlistment, a soldier could expect twenty-five years' service on distant, uncivilized frontiers under harsh and strict discipline, for pay which, due to inflation, can at best be described as inadequate. These were the conditions that threatened the security of the borders, and yet both Dio and Herodian seem blissfully unaware of threats facing the empire. These reforms made service far more attractive and so encouraged a steady supply of new soldiers. However, recruitment was mainly from the less Romanized provinces. The loyalty of these men lay with the person who paid them, granted them regular donatives, provided land on retirement and in whose hands they felt confidence as their commander-in-chief. From the reign of Domitian onwards, it was expected that the emperor would take personal command of the armies on campaign. This is evident in the Arch of Septimius Severus, constructed in AD 204 after his successful campaign against the Parthians, where the emperor is carved supervising sieges, leading soldiers in battle and addressing the assembled legions in an *adlocutio*. So long as the emperor was perceived as a successful military general, such as Septimius Severus or Caracalla, the legions' loyalty remained steadfast.[53]

The total number of Praetorians was increased by Septimius Severus to 10,000, and he later raised three new legions, one of which, II *Parthica*, he stationed outside Rome at Alba. Added to these were the *equites singulares*, a 2,000-strong cavalry guard whose origins lay in the early empire, and the Urban Cohorts, whose

number was increased to 6,000, many being veterans commanded by military officers. He had effectively created a reserve army which could be rapidly deployed in
conjunction with local forces to counter a revolt or deal with an enemy incursion.

With time pressing, Septimius Severus marched in the autumn of AD 193
against Niger with troops consisting of detachments or vexillations from the
legions of Pannonia, Moesia, Dacia and the Praetorian Guard. Niger's forces were
defeated in two battles by the Severan general Claudius Candidus in early AD 194,
the first at Cyzicus leading to the capture of Aemilianus, and the second, in which
Niger had command, in a narrow pass west of Nicaea in Asia Minor. The anni-
hilation of Niger's forces was only prevented by the timely arrival of dusk and
the close proximity of Nicaea itself. Defeat, as always, undermined the confidence
of the army in their commander. Herodian records that: 'The hopes of the eastern forces were shattered at a single blow and the confidence of the Illyrians [the
army of Septimius Severus] grew.' Niger still held most of the East, but his support now ruptured. The provinces of Asia Minor immediately fell to the victor.
Furthermore, a papyrus from Egypt – dated to 21 February AD 194 – shows the
province, after declaring for Niger, now supported Septimius Severus. Its Prefect,
Sabinus, probably instigated this deft change of loyalty, as he did not suffer any
disgrace from the new regime. The governor of Arabia, P. Aelius Severianus, was
rewarded for changing allegiance with the consulship of AD 194, and the VI *Ferrata*
legion in Palestine probably also abandoned Niger's cause after Cyzicus. The final
battle took place in the Cilician Gates, at Issus. This was a narrow pass through the
Taurus Mountains, which reduced the chance of being outflanked but also allowed
Niger the opportunity to force his demoralized soldiers to fight. Behind his lines,
Niger placed baggage-handlers whose presence would prevent his men turning
and fleeing from the enemy. However, after heavy fighting Niger's forces did break
and run, many cut down by a cavalry force sent through forests to attack their rear.
Twenty thousand were slaughtered, and Niger, after fleeing towards Parthia, was
captured and beheaded. After accepting the acclamations of his troops, Septimius
Severus now punished those who had supported his enemy. Fines were imposed,
wealthy senators exiled and their estates confiscated, and cities lost their status
and privileges. Vast sums of money were raised from the vanquished to pay for the
promised donative to his troops and reward his own loyal followers.[54]

To attempt to unify the two armies, a campaign was launched against a shared
enemy. The Roman citadel of Nisibis was besieged by Niger's erstwhile allies of
Adiabene and Arabs. The combined Roman forces invaded the neighbouring territory of Osrhoene, which was annexed, Nisibis relieved and a number of easy victories won. This provided Septimius Severus with the opportunity to be acclaimed
'*imperator*' by Niger's troops, along with the titles *Arabicus* and *Adiabenicus*. This
gave the demoralized soldiers a taste of success under his imperial leadership,

in contrast to the series of defeats they had suffered under the command of Niger. Niger's old province of Syria was now divided in half. Syria Coele was to be the more prestigious province, as it contained two legions, the IV *Scythia* and XVI *Flavia*, and so was governed by a consular senator. Syria Phoenice was to be governed from Tyre, and the *legate* of the III *Gallica* was also to administer the province. A province containing more than two legions placed too much military power in the hands of one man. For this reason, a legion was also transferred from Upper to Lower Pannonia on the Danubian frontier.

Julia Domna, the emperor's wife, accompanied him on his campaign. She was a Syrian from Emesa. The close proximity of her native city and family would have allowed her the opportunity to return home to enable the Emesenes to acknowledge their 'Augusta'. It was at this time that her husband also gave her the title *mater castrorum*, or 'Mother of the Camps'. Septimius Severus was extending the loyalty of his soldiers to his immediate family in order to create a new dynasty. For this reason, he felt his role as avenger of Pertinax had run its course. Military success did confer loyalty, but it did not consign legitimacy. Most of the soldiers in his army had, upon enlisting, sworn to protect and serve the Antonine emperor Commodus, and it was this family that retained the imperial mystique, even though many of its rulers had been adopted into the imperial house. Septimius Severus now declared that he had been posthumously adopted by Commodus' father, Marcus Aurelius, and, on his return to Rome after the defeat of Clodius Albinus, demanded the Senate declare their hated nemesis, Commodus, a god. Septimius Severus' coinage now describes him as 'Son of the deified Marcus Pius'. He was now the son and brother of a god. Soon after, he renamed his 7-year-old son, Bassianus, as Marcus Aurelius Antoninus, known to history as Caracalla, and conferred the title Caesar on him. This was a public pronouncement that Caracalla was the designed heir to the imperial house. Clearly this was a conceit, as the Antonines had been adopted by a living emperor and granted the imperial titles whilst their predecessor was still alive. For this reason, Dio, upon the murder of Commodus, commented that the 'genuine' imperial family had ceased to exist.

Severan coinage issued to the soldiers now carried the old imperial family name, and when each soldier swore the oath of allegiance, it was to the Antonines. Dedications and inscriptions to Septimius Severus refer to his divine ancestry dating back to Emperor Nerva, and confirm his official claim to be the 'brother of the deified Commodus'.[55] On his brief return to Rome in late AD 196, Septimius Severus made a dedication to Nerva as his 'forefather' rather than 'descendant'.[56] The audience for the fictional adoption into the Antonine house was clearly the army.

Caracalla was declared a Caesar in the spring of AD 195; however, there was another Caesar in Britain. The temporary truce between Clodius Albinus and Septimius Severus was now effectively over, and to make a permanent end to their arrangement, assassins were sent by Septimius Severus disguised as imperial couriers with an important message that could only be divulged in a private hearing, and there they were ordered to murder him. Failing that, poison was to be used. Forewarned, the messengers were tortured and the plan revealed. Many senators in Rome, especially the aristocrats, had been in communication with the nobly born Clodius Albinus, urging him to advance on Rome whilst Septimius Severus was absent in the east.[57] Albinus and his legions crossed into Gaul, where they were met in battle in AD 197 at Lugdunum. The Severan forces were drawn into a trap as they attempted to advance across land covered with concealed pits containing sharpened stakes. As his forces began to give way, Septimius Severus advanced with his Praetorians, but they also soon fell into confusion, with the emperor thrown from his horse. As his troops started to flee the battle, he drew his sword and threw himself into the melee, hoping to restore order through his own example or meet death. Some rallied, and cut down some of their own retreating soldiers, thinking they were Albinus' legionaries. These then rallied, fearing similar treatment, and routed the enemy, supported by the Severan cavalry led by Laetus. Dio describes the consequences for the empire:

> 'Roman power suffered a severe blow, inasmuch as countless numbers had fallen on both sides. Many even of the victors deplored the disaster, for the entire plain was seen to be covered with the bodies of men and horses; some of which lay there mutilated by many wounds, as if hacked in pieces, and others, though unwounded, were piled up in heaps, weapons lay scattered about, and blood flowed in streams, even pouring into the rivers.'[58]

This was a foretaste of the horrors to come in the constant civil wars that erupted after the murder of Alexander Severus. Amongst the possessions of Clodius Albinus were discovered the secret correspondence from senators in Rome, many of whom had feigned loyalty to Septimius Severus. In a fury, the victor returned to the capital, preceded by the severed head of Clodius Albinus. Alarm spread. He announced his return as the brother of Commodus, an emperor murdered in a conspiracy that was celebrated in the Senate. The speech delivered in the *curia* denounced the hypocrisy of those sat before him. He praised the men who governed with severity and cruelty, as mildness was perceived as weakness. This can also be seen in his advice to his sons to 'scorn all other men'. He released those senators who had openly opposed him; twenty-nine others were condemned to death.[59] The supporters of Clodius Albinus, like those of Niger, now suffered death or exile and the confiscation of their estates and property. The income of the imperial treasury was massively increased as huge areas of land across the empire now became part of the imperial estates, requiring the expansion in numbers of procurators with responsibility to manage them. A new imperial department was created to administer these confiscations under a *procurator rerum privatorum*.[60] Senatorial governors now found their power undermined by equestrian procurators, who answered directly to the emperor and administered large tracts of land across a number of provinces.

Slaughtering Roman soldiers was not the ideal way to build a reputation as a great general. It was a dubious legacy upon which to found an imperial dynasty. An external foe had to be found to unite the empire and its army, one preferably that was weak enough to provide the opportunity for overwhelming victory. Fate gifted Septimius Severus with a dying superpower, Parthia, which had used his absence from the East to attack Nisibis. Septimius Severus' *comes*, Laetus, was dispatched with an advanced force which relieved the city. The main force, under the personal command of the emperor, advanced down the River Euphrates to sack the Parthian capital, Ctesiphon. The Parthian king escaped, but the royal treasury was captured along with 100,000 prisoners. On 28 January AD 198, Septimius Severus took the title *Parthicus Maximus*, an honorary title once held by the Emperor Trajan, considered by the Romans to be 'the best of emperors'. On the same day, his eldest son, Caracalla, was confirmed as co-ruler, with his youngest son, Geta, as Caesar. This military success was used to build the foundations of the new dynasty. This success was also used to improve Rome's strategic situation between the great rivers of the Euphrates and Tigris. The province of Mesopotamia was added to the empire, with its capital at Nisibis garrisoned by two recently raised legions, the I *Parthica* at Singara and III *Parthica* at Raphanaea. This new strategic province acted as a protective shield to Syria and, with its legions, was too important to be governed by a senator. Instead, it was held by equestrian prefects hand-picked for loyalty and military experience by the emperor. Geographically, the area is extremely difficult to defend, as it is a low, flat plain with few areas of elevation. Included in the territory annexed by Rome were the mountains of Jebel Sinjar, adjacent to the strategic fortress city of Singara, which acted as a southern bulwark of the new province. Defence in depth was centred on the province's cities, which acted as strongpoints. However, control of this area represented a threat to Parthian control of the rest of the Mesopotamian plain, dominated by Hatra and Ctesiphon. This would lead to future conflict with Parthia and its successor state, Sassanid Persia.[61]

A further effect of this campaign was to destabilize the Parthian Empire, which would have serious unforeseen consequences. The military reputation of the Parthian king was shattered with the loss of his capital and his failure to make any effective defence of his heartland.[62] The result was a civil war that Ardashir I and his father would take full advantage of in founding a new dynasty, based initially in the southern Parthian satrapy of Pars – the Sassanids.

Septimius Severus now made two attacks on Hatra which he hoped would further consolidate his control over Mesopotamia, while also exacting vengeance on the city that had supported Niger. The city sat on a ridge surrounded by arid desert, depriving the besiegers of food and water. Herodian refers to soldiers unable to stand the heat, suffering intolerably in the stifling atmosphere, falling ill and dying.[63] Hatran and Arab cavalry archers cut down many men sent on foraging parties. The city was surrounded by a double curtain wall four miles in length, topped with engines that fired missiles and *naphtha* (Greek fire). Many Romans were burnt alive, and in his first siege virtually all of the siege engines were set ablaze. Septimius Severus was forced to retreat, but with defeat threatening military unrest, he attempted to take the city a second time. Finally, towards the end of this second siege, a breach was made in the walls, but the emperor signalled his men to retreat. Inside the city was a great temple to the sun god, which had accumulated a vast amount of wealth in offerings. If the soldiers had entered the city, this wealth would have been plundered and its population slaughtered, leaving an empty husk, strategically useless. Expecting Hatra to sue for terms, the emperor waited overnight, but the morning only brought disappointment. The breach in the wall had been repaired. The elite legions from Pannonia and Moesia refused to attack, angered by being deprived of their opportunity to plunder and rape. The Syrian legions were ordered forward, but were slaughtered. Even a proven commander was only as successful as his last victory. Defeat, as Niger discovered to his cost, undermines morale and confidence. Soldiers are willing to risk all if they feel their commander will not sell their lives cheaply. As the emperor is the commander-in-chief, his ability to rule is based on his military success. Defeat undermines his prestige, and no emperor could survive a number of defeats.

After the failure of the first siege, Septimius Severus found his position threatened by the stirrings of rebellion in the army. A Praetorian was brought before the emperor who accused a tribune called Julius Crispinus of quoting a line from Virgil: 'In order that Turnus may marry Lavinia, we are meanwhile all perishing all unheeded.' (The goddess Juno, an enemy of the Trojans, had urged Turnus, a suitor to Lavinia, to demand war with the Trojan hero Aeneas, to whom Lavinia was betrothed. Juno wanted to ensure that more Trojans died in the fighting.) The tribune was angered by the massive numbers of dead and wounded in what he saw as a pointless attempt to conquer the impregnable city. Even the Emperor Trajan had failed to take this fortress city. Crispinus appears also to have questioned the emperor's ability as a commander as he became 'vexed at the war's havoc'. The tribune was executed and his accuser promoted to his post. A more prominent figure also fell victim to the unrest in the army. The emperor's *comes* and close advisor, Laetus, had acquired an admirable military reputation, based on his decisive arrival with his cavalry at the Battle of Lugdunum and his later relieving of the siege of Nisibis. The soldiers admired him and demanded that he lead them in the assaults. Yet a man of such prestige in the eyes of the soldiers was a threat to the emperor, so he was executed. Both Crispinus and Laetus had probably served in the Pannonian legions, increasing the resentment of these legions. Septimius Severus had employed senatorial generals, whose wealth, influence and status would help him establish control of the political networks in the capital. Once these powerful figures had established a prestigious military reputation, they were quickly 'promoted' away from serving posts to a consulship at Rome and then *amici*, advisors, at court. With military connections and renown, access to money and senatorial connections, they became potential threats.[64] Claudius Candidus, the victor of Cyzicus and Nicaea, also appears to have been executed at this time, his name removed from an inscription carrying his statue at Tarraco.

The second siege of Hatra was clearly a risk, and the refusal of the European legions to fight left Septimius Severus in a very dangerous position. The failure to capture it was seen by his army as a defeat.[65] No source mentions any consequences for the mutinous legionaries, and safety in numbers probably ensured no punishments were enforced. However, the refusal of the Danubian legions to follow imperial orders undermined imperial authority. The Syrian legions had also suffered grievously in their assault. Both were probably on the verge of open revolt. What in all probability saved the emperor was his previous record in capturing the Parthian capital, the loyalty of his subordinates, the lack of a viable alternative and promise of a massive donative financed by the plunder from Ctesiphon. The army was quickly withdrawn from Hatra after a second siege lasting only twenty days and the situation restored, but it clearly indicates the precarious position that even a successful emperor faced when met with a military reverse.[66]

Fittingly, Septimius Severus died on campaign. In AD 209, in conjunction with his co-ruler Caracalla, he advanced beyond Hadrian's Wall and into Caledonia, laying waste to the countryside. Both emperors were acclaimed *imperators* and accepted the title *Britannicus*. However, Septimius Severus was now an old man and the years of campaigning had taken their toll. By AD 210, beset by illness and infirmity, he had to be carried in a litter, and was forced to remain at Eboracum (York) with his wife and youngest son, Geta, whilst Caracalla continued the campaign, as the Maeatae had abandoned the peace treaty they had signed and joined with the Caledonians. Realizing his life was ending, he raised Geta to the rank of Augustus and co-emperor in late AD 210. It was a desperate attempt to give him a fighting chance in the conflict with his elder brother. On 4 February AD 211, Septimius Severus died. According to the late Roman historian Aurelius Victor, he despaired: 'I have been all things, and it has profited nothing.'[67] His two sons were soon at each other's throats.

Chapter 2

Conspiracy AD 211–217

'Thy house shall perish utterly in blood'
(The reply of the oracle of Zeus Belus at Apamea to Septimius Severus,
Dio, 79.8.6)

As the 63-year-old Septimius Severus prepared for the war in Britain accompanied by Julia Domna, his two sons and a multitude of *amici* and imperial administrators, the future emperor Alexander Severus was born on the opposite side of the empire. According to the notoriously unreliable account of his 'life' in the *Historia Augusta*, and the more circumspect Dio, this took place on 1 October AD 208 in the city of Arca, situated 20km north-east of Tripoli in Syria. This seems likely, as his father, Gessius Marcianus, was also from this city and he was probably born in the family villa. Arca, now reduced to a small village, is located on the western slopes of the Lebanese mountain range, commanding spectacular views across the coastal plain to the sea. Marcianus' career is mostly lost to us, but he had held a number of procuratorships and at some point was *adlected* into the Senate.[1]

The mother of Alexander Severus was, however, far more distinguished. Julia Mamaea's first marriage was to an unknown senator of consular status, who died at some point before the sole reign of Caracalla. She married Gessius Marcianus, who was only of equestrian rank, and so she was granted imperial dispensation to retain the higher rank that she had previously acquired through marriage to an ex-consul. She also had a daughter by Marcianus, who was old enough to be married in AD 218, but she appears to have had no children from her first marriage.[2] Mamaea's mother, Julia Maesa, was the sister of Septimius Severus' wife, Julia Domna. Despite the tenuous imperial connection, Julia Maesa was a member of the imperial court throughout the reign of Septimius Severus and Caracalla.[3] Alexander Severus' mother's family were descended from the ancient kings of Emesa, whose last ruler, King Sohaemus, supported Vespasian in his successful attempt for the throne. A funerary inscription at Emesa from the reign of Vespasian refers to a C. Julius Samsigaramus of Roman tribe Fabia, the son of C. Julius Alexio, suggesting the family received Roman citizenship from either Julius Caesar or Augustus. After the AD 70s, it appears this client kingdom was absorbed into the Roman Empire. However, this local dynasty was allowed to retain its hereditary priesthood of the Temple to the sun god Elagabal, and with it local prestige and status, as well as control over the temple resources.

Maesa and Julia Domna's father, Julius Bassianus, bore the names that were associated with the dynasty, and is described as a 'priest of the Sun, whom the Phoenicians, from whom he sprang, call Heliogabalus [Elagabal]'. Alexander Severus was born Gessius Alexianus Bassianus, acquiring Gessius from his father and Alexianus from his grandfather, Maesa's husband, Julius Avitus Alexianus. Alexio and Alexianus were also the ancestral name of the Emesene priesthood. His grandfather was a powerful *amicus* and *comes* of both Septimius Severus and Caracalla, dedicating an altar to the god Elagabal whilst serving as a *legate* (legionary commander) in Raetia before becoming a consul before AD 211, and then attaining the prestigious proconsular governorship of Asia. In AD 208, he accompanied the emperors on their campaign in Britain, and would serve as *comes* to Caracalla in his campaigns in Germany and the East, before his death in Cyprus around AD 217. The name Bassianus was inherited from the priestly line on his maternal side. The name itself was derived from the Phoenician title for a priest, *basus*.[4]

We do not know where Marcianus held his procuratorships, nor whether his wife and children accompanied him or remained on the family estates around Arca and Emesa. Herodian states that Alexander Severus and the son of Mamaea's sister, Soamias, Varus Avitus Bassianus (known to history as the future Emperor Elagabalus), were raised by their mothers and grandmother, Maesa.[5] This might suggest they were both brought up at court throughout this time, or perhaps Herodian is merely commenting on the situation in AD 218 when Maesa had retired with her daughters and their families to Emesa. Maesa was in Rome in December AD 211, comforting her sister on the death of Geta. For most of AD 213, Caracalla had been campaigning beyond the Rhine, which would not have been the ideal environment for a 4-year-old child. The end of the year saw Caracalla wintering at Nicomedia in Bithynia, whose reasonable proximity to Syria and Emesa may have allowed for Mamaea and her children to attend. The presence of his young cousin, Varus Avitus Bassianus (Elagabalus), is attested in an inscription from Thyatira, which was on the route Caracalla would have taken in the spring of AD 215 to reach Antioch from Nicomedia.[6] There are some springs at Thyatira, and the emperor may have spent a few weeks there to relax, and this could have been the time that the extended members of the imperial family were invited to court.

The next time Alexander Severus reappears in the historical record is in AD 218. He is aged 9 and carrying out priestly duties at the Temple of Elagabal in Emesa, in the company of his cousin. Their role is open to conjecture, as the ancient Greek used by Herodian is open to interpretation. Both boys were either 'being trained' in the service of the sun god or were 'dedicated' to the god. The elder cousin was the chief priest and had responsibility for the cult.[7] Varus Avitus Bassianus

(Elagabalus) demonstrated, in all he did, a deep religious fervour for the god, to the extent that this close association led to him being known as Elagabalus. This devotion cannot have developed over a few months, but from childhood over a number of years. This suggests he was not at court for much of his youth, which implicitly implies that Alexander Severus remained around Emesa, serving in the temple and living on the extensive properties the family would have owned.

The temple was a huge construction, decorated in gold, silver and precious stones. Emesene coinage from the reign of Caracalla shows the temple raised up on a podium, approached by a long flight of steps, leading up to the temple itself, which was faced with eight columns. An opening shows the god Elagabal as a conical stone, with the representation of an eagle in front of it with a wreath in its mouth. At the base of the steps appears to be an altar, which is shown in greater detail in Julia Domna's coinage. The altar is built on a massive base approached by two steps. A cornice and two rows of niches contain statues, probably representations of other gods, including Zeus and Helios, who were considered subordinate to the supreme god Elagabal. The god's origins were ancient and rooted in the rich cultural heritage of Emesa itself. The name Elagabal is derived from the Babylonian word El or IL, for god, and a combination of the Arab deities for the morning and evening star, Salman (or Aziz) and Mun'im. The population of the East would have spoken Aramaic, as well as Greek and some Latin. 'Elagabal' has been translated as 'God of the Mountain' in Aramaic, and its size, unusual conical shape and black colour suggest it was seen as a symbolic representation of god dating from long before classical ideas were introduced by the Greeks in the Hellenistic period. These images of god represented as conical, rectangular and circular stones called baetyls are common in Nabataea. Other similar baetyls have been discovered at Nezala (Qaryatayn), between Damascus and Palmyra, with a representation of the same deity labelled in Palmyrene 'LH'GBL. Conical images of the god are also found at the coastal cities of Sidon, Laodicea and Seleucia. The stone was worshipped as a gift from heaven. It seems to have acquired an association with the sun, and so during the Hellenistic period the god was also known as Heliogabalus, deriving from the Greek sun god Helios. The name Samsigeramus, carried by rulers of Emesa, derives from the Semitic word for sun, shamash or shams.[8]

Visiting temples of the gods and sacrificing to them was a key component of ancient religion. Temples were mystical places where the mortal and the immortal met, their location a point in time and place where divinities could be addressed and their intervention requested. The cult image was placed in a prominent location and was the focus of the acts of devotion. Symbolism and ritual added to the religious experience of the worshippers, whose sacrifices or other acts of worship encouraged the gods or god to communicate with them through oracles, dreams or in other forms. There would be grand processions, ritual banquets and incense-burning around the altar and forecourt of the temple. Elagabalus, as he shall now be called, and no doubt his young cousin, is described as 'dancing at the altars to the music of flutes and pipes and all kinds of instruments in the barbarian fashion'. He is portrayed as wearing a long-sleeved gold and purple 'chiton', associated by the Romans with Parthian culture and religious belief, but also with effeminacy. He also wore a form of trousers, and on his head a crown covered in precious stones. Alexander Severus, helping to officiate, would have worn similar garments, but not as elaborate or decorative as those of the chief priest. Carvings of priests from Palmyra show priests wearing conical hats and a long belted tunic, whilst other reliefs from the nearby city of Heliopolis shows the same conical hat decorated with stars and suns, and a tunic with bells and pom-poms attached. Although the Romans would have respected the ancient religious heritage of the god, they would have found it unusual not to symbolize the divine in human form, as they would have found the priests' attire strange. However, the rituals, architecture and plan of the temple would have conformed to Roman conventions. On festival days, the worshippers would have gathered on the courtyard in front of the altars, with the vast facade of the temple itself acting as a backdrop. They would have raised their right palms in the universal act of religious devotion as the sacrifices were performed at the altars. Afterwards, the meat would be divided up amongst those present, wine distributed in large quantities and gifts dispersed. Public performances and competitions would augment these activities on civic festival days. The temple would face east, so ceremonies beginning at dawn could start with the doors of the temple opened to receive the sun and allow the conical stone to be bathed in light. The stone would then leave the temple, carried in a portable shrine built on wheels, in a procession that allowed the thousands of pilgrims the chance to see their god.[9]

The temple was famous throughout the East, drawing not just local pilgrims but also many from neighbouring kingdoms who brought offerings and supplications. The temple and the priestly family that ran it were immensely rich, but their link to the imperial house also drew the curious and inquisitive.[10] The empire was also experiencing a religious transformation in this period as its population started to look beyond the established, state-sponsored cults and religions towards ones that not only tended to be monotheistic but also offered a life beyond death. Into this religious context fell Christianity and Mithraism; the cult of Elagabal, however, failed to spread with the same vigour. As the protector deity of Emesa, soldiers recruited from the area made dedications to their god throughout the empire; at Intercisa on the Danube, an Emesene cohort of mounted archers demonstrated an intense degree of religious fervour, as did another cohort at El Kantara in Africa. In Rome itself, there existed, from the late second century, a shrine to 'Sol Invictus Alagabalus' (The Unconquered Sun Elagabal) with its own college of priests.[11]

In December AD 211, an event of premeditated barbarity transformed the Roman Empire. The feud between Caracalla and Geta grew into deadly proportions as they transported their father's body home. Julia Domna's attempts to mediate had no impact, and the division of the empire was discussed then abandoned. Roman society was divided between those who supported Geta and those who backed his brother. The palace itself was divided in half, and each had their own guards. Caracalla, however, decided to end this division permanently, using his mother's presence to provide the opportunity to strike Geta down. He asked Julia Domna to invite them both to a meeting in her rooms in the palace, and at the appointed time centurions burst in and stabbed Geta to death, even as his mother tried to protect him. Caracalla immediately went to the Praetorian camp defending his actions as self-defence, accusing Geta of conspiring against him and promising untold riches to the soldiers. According to Dio, he announced to the Praetorians: 'Rejoice, fellow soldiers, for now I am in a position to do you favours.' He lavished a multitude of promises on them: 'I am one of you ... And it is because of you alone that I care to live, in order that I may confer upon you many favours; for all the treasuries are yours.'[12] The Alban legion was at first difficult to win over, but its moral scruples were negated by a distribution of 10,000 sesterces per man as a donative and a massive increase in pay. The loyalty of the army was now paramount to Caracalla, and indeed it became devoted to him. He created an emotional bond with his soldiers by eating with them on campaign, sharing the same food, sleeping on the cheap army bed, sharing the same burdens and marching at their side. Borrowing an idea from the reign of Commodus, he bestowed his name upon every legion, so the I *Minervia* became the I *Minervia Antoniniana*. This was a public demonstration of the reliance of the emperor upon the loyalty of the army and Caracalla's increased identification with his 'fellow soldier'. A successful campaign against the Alemanni was launched in AD 213 to cement their loyalty. However, by playing the soldier, Caracalla lowered his status and prestige in the eyes of the senatorial elite, but having purged all supporters of Geta – to the number of 20,000 – it is doubtful the remaining nobility would offer him any more than feigned loyalty. Amongst those executed were the eminent jurist Papinian, who as Praetorian Prefect had tried to mediate between the brothers, and surviving descendants of Marcus Aurelius and Commodus.[13]

Caracalla increased pay to 3,000 sesterces and raised discharge bonuses from 12,000 to 20,000, whilst the bonus for Praetorians was raised to an unknown figure from 20,000 sesterces. To pay for the donatives and pay rise for the army, he was forced to reduce the silver content of the silver denarius from 56.5 to 51.5 per cent. The confidence of the soldiers in the money they were paid with was paramount; consequently the silver 'antoninianus', or 'double denarius', was introduced, which, although weighing a lot more than the denarius, only contained 52 per cent silver. Another consequence of Caracalla's fratricide was the introduction of the Antonine Constitution. It had been thought that the primary reason for the Antonine Constitution – which granted Roman citizenship to the vast majority of the population – had been financial, to pay for the monies now being paid for the army. All new citizens were now liable to inheritance tax and the tax paid on the manumission of slaves, which markedly increased the income of the treasury. However, the consensus of recent opinion is that Caracalla wished to multiply the thanksgiving offered by Roman citizens to the gods on his behalf, having been 'saved' from his brother's 'conspiracy'. Now the majority of the empire's population could take part. Understandably, the emperor was concerned with the divine understanding of his murderous actions. Furthermore, it was traditional for those receiving citizenship to take the name of the person granting it to them, so 'Aurelius' was now included in the nomenclature of the large numbers of newly enrolled citizens. It was a name that linked them to the 'Antonine' imperial house, Caracalla's full official *nomen* being Marcus Aurelius Severus Antoninus. Caracalla was now the great patron.[14]

The grant of citizenship also made virtually all the population subject to Roman law, when previously they had been subject to local laws and customs, particularly in the Greek East. This led to the rise to prominence of a series of gifted lawyers, often working in the imperial administration, who, through their writings, attempted to make Roman law accessible to this newly enfranchised population. Amongst them was Ulpian, who, unlike Papinian, had sided with Caracalla in his feud with Geta, but also the jurists Paul, Tryphoninus, Messius, Menander and Modestinus. All were members of the equestrian order.[15] The Antonine Constitution also had a number of unintended positive consequences. Women across the empire now gained enhanced rights over property from the primacy of Roman law over local customs, and with wealth came increased political power.[16] Most important of all, however, was the unity the extension of citizenship brought to the empire. At a time of immense crisis and the fragmentation of the empire, the commonality of law and culture amongst the elite, the shared citizenship and ultimately the unifying bond of the army preserved it.

Septimius Severus did not trust his senatorial generals, and was weary of anyone who had the status and military prestige to potentially claim the throne. The death of the nobly born Commodus levelled the field for potential imperial candidates. His successor, Pertinax, was the son of a freedman, although raised to consular senatorial status by Emperor Marcus Aurelius; Didius Julianus came from an illustrious senatorial family, as did Clodius Albinus. Niger, like Septimius Severus, started his career as an equestrian and was raised to the Senate and consulship for successful and loyal military service to Commodus, but they were not the offspring of senators themselves. The field had therefore been opened up by the very success of Septimius Severus. His dying words, recorded by Dio, demonstrate an acute suspicion of all men of senatorial status, and the *Historia Augusta* records that 'he was especially suspicious of anyone who seemed qualified for imperial power'.[17] Caracalla took this advice to heart. The Severan generals who had served his father so well were never employed in military commands again. This fear of the potential threat posed by men of senatorial rank is seen in the gradual substitution of senatorial governors, who had significant military forces in their provinces, by equestrians, who held posts as acting governors with the titles *agens vice praesidis* or *agens vice legati legionis*.[18] Yet death, when it came, did not come from the blade of a senator, but a soldier.

In AD 213, buoyed up by his victory against the Alemanni on the Rhine, Caracalla decided to take advantage of the civil war that had erupted in the Parthian Empire on the death of the Parthian King Vologases V. His two sons, the elder Vologases VI and his younger brother, Artabanus V, now contested the throne. Caracalla decided to launch an unprovoked attack, the excuse being a failed marriage proposal with the daughter of the Parthian king.[19] He admired the military prowess of Alexander the Great and wished to establish a comparable reputation for himself. Having narrowly escaped death as he crossed the Hellespont in AD 214, the emperor wintered with the imperial court at Nicomedia. The following spring, he journey to Antioch after visiting Ilium, the site of ancient Troy, the springs at Thyatira – where he was joined by Elagabalus and probably other members of the imperial family – as well as Prusias ad Hypium, Tyana and Tarsus. Emesa was only a short distance from the great metropolis of Antioch, and so it is likely that Julia Mamaea and her children joined the imperial court at this point, if they hadn't done so already at Thyatira. Preparations for a campaign against Parthia were in full swing, and at the end of the year Caracalla decided to visit Alexandria. His visit coincided with rioting, during which he appears to have been insulted by the population. Never one to turn the other cheek, he ordered his troops to massacre the male populace and the city was pillaged. Alexandria was then punished by having walls constructed, dividing the city, and occupied by troops, its festivals cancelled and games forbidden. Another donative was then granted; 25,000 sesterces to the Praetorians and 20,000 to the other soldiers.[20] Sated, he returned north to spend the winter of AD 216/217 in Antioch again. The spring of AD 217 saw the launch of his Parthian campaign. He marched across the Roman province of Mesopotamia to the Parthian palace at Arbella, ostensibly, according to Herodian, to meet with Artabanus V to negotiate an alliance, cemented with the marriage of the emperor to the daughter of the Parthian king. The deceit worked and Caracalla ordered his army to fall upon his unsuspecting hosts. Artabanus was rescued by his bodyguard, but many Parthians were slaughtered.[21]

Dio, however, records that Caracalla's offer of marriage was rejected, providing the excuse to invade. Both historians agree that the Romans marched through the

Parthian territory of Adiabene unopposed, with cities and fortress systematically sacked. In imitation of Alexander the Great, Caracalla ransacked the royal tombs, scattering the remains of the Parthian royal house in the dirt. His 'successes' were enough for him to send a letter to the Senate claiming victory, and he was voted the title *Parthicus*. He fell back to spend the winter at Edessa. Julia Domna, accompanied by Julia Maesa, had remained at Antioch, administering the empire whilst the emperor was on campaign. It was here that Julia Domna received a letter from Flavius Maternianus, Urban Prefect of Rome, that Macrinus, present with Caracalla as one of his two Praetorian Prefects, was the subject of a prophecy that foretold he would ascend to the throne. However, Macrinus was warned directly by Ulpius Julianus, who was in charge of the census in Rome, that he was in danger. The planned conspiracy was already at an advanced stage, as Caracalla had previously become suspicious of Macrinus and removed some of his *amici* from influential positions. Plans were brought forward as the Praetorian Prefect used his position to suborn members of the bodyguard. Two brothers, Apollonaris and Nemesianus, tribunes in the Praetorian Guard, were recruited, along with Julius Martialis, who as an *evocati* had completed his years of service but had voluntarily re-enlisted, probably at the urging of Macrinus. According to Herodian, Macrinus was this soldier's patron. Martialis held a grudge against Caracalla, as, according to Dio, the emperor had not promoted him to the rank of centurion, or, in the slightly different version by Herodian, the emperor had ordered the execution of his brother.

The number of conspirators was enlarged to encompass those who had direct access to the emperor. The prefect of the II *Parthica*, Aelius Decius Triccianus, which was stationed near Apamea, was most importantly in charge of cavalry used to escort the emperor. Martialis had been instrumental in winning over Marcius Agrippa, the commander of the fleet, and many members of his staff. It was important to ensure communications with Rome and the Senate were open, and food supplies for the masses of soldiers in the East were secured. Agrippa was clearly an able and respected senator. He had been born a slave and risen to be an *advocatus fiscus* with responsibility for defending the interests of the treasury, usually in court. He had been promoted by Caracalla to the post of *a cognitionibus*, a legal advisor to the emperor, and then his *ab epistulis* with responsibility for imperial correspondence. However, he had then fallen from favour and was removed from court by being 'promoted' to the Senate with the rank of ex-praetor. His fall from favour appears only temporary, as he was trusted to command the imperial fleet in the Parthian War. He had clearly been honoured and respected by the emperor, but, like Martialis, bore a grudge. Macrinus was himself a skilled lawyer, and the two may have been acquainted when working at court, and so, knowing his past history, Macrinus may have felt Agrippa was amenable to persuasion.

Each conspirator would have been promised lavish rewards for their involvement. Macrinus, on becoming emperor, made Agrippa governor of Pannonia and then Dacia; Triccianus became the governor of Pannonia Inferior, whilst Julianus was rewarded with the Praetorian Prefecture. In both Herodian and Dio, it is clear Macrinus feared for his life, and that was his primary motive to murder the man he had sworn to protect rather than a desire to become emperor himself. His equestrian status, rather than the rank of a senator, appeared to preclude him from the throne.[22]

The opportunity to strike came on 8 April AD 217 with Caracalla's visit to the Temple of the Moon near Carrhae. Agrippa no doubt ensured that members of the conspiracy were added to the escort of Praetorian cavalry, supported by Germans, probably members of the *equites extraordinarii*. The emperor was suffering from a stomach upset and ordered the party to halt whilst he dismounted and headed off into the bushes to relieve himself. The guard turned their backs to allow their sovereign some privacy in his moment of discomfort. Martialis saw his chance and approached the emperor, acting as though he had been summoned by Caracalla. As the emperor's back was turned to adjust his garments, Martialis struck. The assassin had hidden a small dagger in his hand, which he used to stab the emperor near his clavicle. The blow was fatal. Martialis rapidly withdrew, mounted his horse and fled the scene. The German bodyguards who had been standing closer to the emperor than the rest ran to him, only to discover his body. Quickly mounting their horses, they ran down Martialis with their javelins. Dio records that the emperor was critically but not fatally injured by Martialis, but the Praetorian tribunes Apollonaris and Nemesianus finished him off as they had been left with the emperor as the German cavalry chased the assassin.[23]

Two main threats existed to an emperor. Firstly, the army and the threat of an army revolt. Caracalla, however, was immensely popular with the soldiers, who associated him with military victories in Britain with his father, in Germany against the Alamanni and now in the East against Parthia. He lavished donatives and pay increases upon them, and protected their recently won privileges. The other threat came from those who had direct access to his person, including members of his family, his friends and *amici*, imperial freedmen and other important officers of state, including the two Praetorian Prefects. Macrinus could not be associated with the murder of Caracalla, as the army would have killed him as well. As Praetorian Prefect, he was amongst the first to arrive at the scene of the murder. A consummate actor, he wept tears of grief over the emperor's body. The army did not suspect Macrinus, but saw the murder as the result of a bitter and personal grudge held by Martialis against the emperor.[24]

Caracalla had nominated no successor, nor did he have any children. Macrinus would have been aware that any imperial successor would seek the support of the army by seeking to avenge the murder of Caracalla. Macrinus would only be safe if he or another of the conspirators became emperor. However, he could not openly seek the throne as his actions would incite suspicion, and instead advocated his elderly colleague, Adventus, knowing full well he lacked the ability, leadership, support or inclination to manage the empire. Furthermore, the war against Parthia was still ongoing and the campaigning session was about to open with a long-awaited Parthian offensive. The army would need a competent leader, and quickly. For two days, the arguments, offers, promises and compromises were made before Macrinus was acclaimed emperor, supported by his fellow conspirators. The deciding factor for many was Macrinus' promise to end the war quickly. However, raising Macrinus to the imperial throne fatally undermined the status and author-ity of the position of emperor. He was not of senatorial status, but a member of the equestrian order. He was an admired jurist whose skills and abilities had taken him to the very top of the equestrian career ladder, but he lacked the distinction of the 'latus clavus', the broad band of purple worn on the toga by members of the senatorial order. Nor did the new emperor have any significant military experience to appeal to the loyalty of the army. The need to protect his leadership in the plot to murder the legitimate emperor, and the lustre of the imperial purple, had blinded him to the fragility of his position. He would pay dearly for his naivety.

The significance of Macrinus' short reign was a turning point in Rome's his-tory. The murder of Caracalla had ended the male line of the Severan dynasty, despite Macrinus' adoption of the name 'Severus' in his official title and the use of 'Antoninus' for his young son's official nomenclature when he raised him to the lesser position of Caesar.[25] His status as a non-senator further undermined the position of that body and the exclusivity of the imperial throne. In the past, emperors had in theory been appointed by the Senate, although this had merely been a formality, retained to support the status of elite senatorial class. The senator Vespasian, on ascending the throne after a bloody civil war that erupted after the murder of Nero, sought a political compromise by issuing the *lex Vespasiani*. This publically acknowledged that the Senate was the ultimate source of legal authority in the Roman state, and that it was the sole source of authority in the granting of the unlimited powers, honours and titles of the emperor. The purpose of this was to deny legal authority and legitimacy to any usurper raised by acclamation of the troops, just as Vespasian himself had been.[26] Macrinus, an expert jurist, would have appreciated that legal authority for his position derived from the passing of a *senatus consultum* by the Senate rather than the declaration of the troops. However, a letter was sent to Rome, not requesting the granting of the traditional powers and titles, as the law demanded, but announcing his assumption of imperial power and adoption of the titles *Pius Felix*. Initially, the Senate was so relieved that Caracalla had been removed that it was prepared to accept this undermining of its authority.

The new emperor was granted senatorial status with the rank of an ex-consul. However, Caracalla's popularity with the army precluded any attempt to obliterate his memory through issuing a *damnatio memoriae*. Senatorial resentment was to rapidly grow as the lowly born Adventus was appointed Urban Prefect. His lack of etiquette, education and understanding of political correctness seemed to mirror the lack of nobility of the emperor, and only added to Macrinus' unpopularity with the aristocracy in Rome.

To retain the loyalty of the army, Macrinus had maintained his pretence of mourning the death of Caracalla. His predecessor had been given a lavish funeral before the assembled troops, and he may even have had him deified, according to his problematic 'Life' in the *Historia Augusta*.[27] The cremated remains were returned to his mother, Julia Domna, at Antioch before being sent on to Rome, probably with an escort of Praetorians, accompanied by Adventus.[28] Julia Domna knew the truth behind her son's death, and so was probably forbidden to return to the capital, where she could use her extensive connections to raise a revolt. Keeping his friends close and his enemies closer, Macrinus kept Julia Domna and Maesa at Antioch, from where Domna continually reminded Macrinus of his role in the assassination of her son, the legitimate emperor. On receipt of her son's ashes, she had at first attempted to starve herself to death, but had a dramatic change of heart, driven by her hatred of the former Praetorian Prefect. She sent a stream of letters to him from Antioch, full of abuse and invective. Macrinus, fully aware of his delicate situation, sent her sympathetic and benevolent replies. She was allowed to retain her status and court, with its detachment of Praetorians. These men retained their loyalty to her and the memory of her son. She no doubt informed them of Macrinus' treasonable behaviour. There would also be many troops stationed in the area, as food and logistical supplies for the vast army in Syria and Mesopotamia would be channelled through Antioch.

Rumours of Macrinus' role in the murder of Caracalla would spread like a virus from Julia Domna's palace to the military camps and forts in the area, carried by the disaffected Praetorians like spores on the wind. Unfortunately, Dio's account at this point becomes fragmentary, but the historian suggests Julia Domna aspired to become sole ruler, fearing an imminent return to private life at Emesa and a loss of her power and influence. It is likely she would have been permitted to retire to her estates and live in quiet retirement if she had been willing to abandon her imperial ambitions. Macrinus had been attempting to establish the foundations of his rule by building tentative connections to the imperial family of the Severans, and the murder of Julia Domna would have undermined these efforts.[29] However, her attempts to raise revolt at Antioch could not be tolerated; she was ordered to leave the city, but given permission to settle where she wished. A return to Rome was out of the question, as the hostility to Caracalla was now openly expressed by prominent senators, and a life in the backwater of Emesa had little appeal. She was also in pain from a cancerous growth in her breast, which, according to Dio, had been exacerbated by the huge blow she gave her chest on news of her son's death. Declining all food, the disease consumed her and death quickly followed.[30]

Her sister, Julia Maesa, appears to have been allowed to remain to tend to the ailing Augusta, but upon Julia Domna's death she was ordered to leave Antioch for her ancestral home at Emesa. Maesa was allowed to retain all of her estates and wealth which she had accumulated over the reigns of Septimius Severus and Caracalla.[31] These were immense, and the family, as holders of the priesthood of Elagabalus, had numerous clients in the city and the surrounding area. She appeared to meekly acquiesce, living with her two daughters, Soamias and Mamaea, along with their children, Bassianus – the future Emperor Elagabalus – and Alexianus, the future Emperor Alexander Severus.[32] However, like her sister, she had no intention of relinquishing the reins of power, and slowly built up the foundations of a revolt that would send Macrinus to his grave. Yet the fact that Alexianus and Bassianus were allowed to live demonstrates the tenuous connection they had to the imperial house of the Severans. The very existence of a close male relative to Septimius Severus or Caracalla would have constituted a very real threat to the dynasty Macrinus hoped to establish. He clearly perceived that neither Alexianus nor his cousin Bassianus, despite the hereditary name the latter shared with Caracalla, were a threat or might be seen as potential focal points for any opposition to his rule. Both were members of the family of Septimius Severus' wife, and only Maesa and her husband had been closely associated with political power.

The powerful male figures in Julia Domna's family were, by AD 217, already dead. Maesa's husband, Julius Avitus, a close friend and *comes* of both Septimius Severus and Caracalla, had died of old age and sickness in Cyprus in AD 217. Maesa's son-in-law, Sextus Varius Marcellus, husband of Soamias, was originally from the Syrian city of Apamea. He had pursued an illustrious career and became a trusted *amicus* of Caracalla, being appointed to a combined office of *ratio private* and *vice* (ie acting) *praefectorum praetorio et urbi functus*. Although only a temporary appointment, these offices constituted a remarkable concentration of power. The best historical context for this combined post was the period immediately after the murder of Geta. Caracalla turned to men whose loyalty was unquestionable in order to ensure his own survival in the volatile climate that existed after his murder of his brother. Marcellus appears to have been rewarded with *adlection* to the senatorial order at the honorary rank of ex-praetor, followed by appointment as *praefectus aerarii militaris* with responsibility for the military treasury. This suggests Caracalla was having difficulty raising the necessary funds to honour his pay rise to the army. Appointment to the governorship of Numidia followed, but there his career was cut short by death. On the death of her consular husband, Maesa's younger daughter, Mamaea, had married Gessius Marcianus, the father of an unnamed daughter and Alexianus, the future Emperor Alexander Severus. However, we know very little of his career. He held a number of equestrian posts as procurator and, by AD 217, may have been *adlected* into the Senate, but he appears to have been denied the illustrious career of his brother-in-law. Lacking experience, connections and the required *dignitas*, Marcianus was probably retired to his estates with his wife and young children.[33]

As Macrinus attempted to suppress unrest in the army in the East, precipitated by the attempted revolt of Julia Domna, Rome itself was riven by discord. The circus and the games as always provided the opportunity to stir the mob into open dissent. Crisis within the empire was mirrored by crisis within Rome itself. As an integral element in his conspiracy, Macrinus himself appears to have used the mob in Rome to undermine support for Caracalla. Dissent appeared at the Circus Maximus, where the green faction at the chariot races had just been defeated, and then 'as if by pre-arrangement, all cried out "Martialis, hail! Martialis it is a long time since we saw you last."' Martialis was of course the assassin of Caracalla, but this was also a reference to the *ludi Martiales* celebrated on 14 May to commemorate Mars Ultior, the god of war, and the foundation of the temple dedicated to him by Augustus. The crowd was perhaps inferring that Caracalla's victory against the Parthians lacked real substance. Clearly, clients of Macrinus and his fellow conspirators, along with the leaders of the circus factions, had organized this demonstration to raise tension. At the same time, a 'spirit' resembling a man led an ass up to the Capitol whilst predicting the death of Caracalla. This man was arrested but 'disappeared' en route to the East for trial.[34]

Just as Macrinus and his supporters had been ready to use the mob to destabilize Caracalla's government, so were Macrinus' enemies. On 14 September, races were held to celebrate the birthday of Macrinus' son, Diadumenianus. As the assembled members of the senatorial and equestrian orders went through their ritual homage to the absent Macrinus, still campaigning against the Parthians, the crowd 'raised their hands towards heaven and exclaimed: "Yonder is the Roman's Augustus; having him we have everything."' The mob rejected Macrinus due to his lack of nobility, and suggested that the empire had no legitimate sovereign, apart from the divine sovereign, Jupiter. The ringleaders could find anonymity in the huge numbers assembled, whilst the spectators knew their open opposition could not be punished without a wholesale massacre.[35] The Circus Maximus held 250,000, and the coordinated response of the crowd required organization and planning. The hand of the senatorial nobility, resentful of the low-born status of their emperor, hoped to spark a revolt in the city. The aristocracy were further outraged by the raising of their hated nemesis, Caracalla, to the rank of a god.

Macrinus had not only deified his predecessor, but refused to hand over the names of his many spies and informers, the despised *delatores,* who had denounced many eminent men, sending them to an early grave. The repeated senatorial requests met with imperial excuses: none of the official documents identifying these men could be found. Macrinus said Caracalla had destroyed them. These were lame excuses that were not believed. A few token scapegoats had been tried before the Senate and condemned, but many remained unpunished, protected by the hand of their new emperor. No doubt there was the fear that Macrinus intended to utilize the services of these despised men again.[36]

What this group of conspirators lacked was a widely recognized and legitimate replacement for Macrinus. Tellingly, the future emperors Elagabalus and Alexander Severus were not considered as appropriate imperial candidates. They may have been seen as too closely linked to the despised Caracalla, or, more likely, not recognized as members of the imperial house at all. Furthermore, both were mere children and were in the East. Caracalla had been extremely diligent in murdering any noble even distantly related to the old Antonine house of Marcus Aurelius and Commodus. However, two remained. L. Aurelius Commodus Pompeianus, the ordinary consul of AD 209, was the son of Marcus Aurelius' close *amicus* Tiberius Claudius Pompeianus and Lucilla, the daughter of Marcus Aurelius who was executed by her brother, Commodus, for leading a conspiracy to murder him. Pompeianus was executed in AD 211/212, but was survived by at least one son, Tiberius Claudius Pompeianus. The latter's nobility was second-to-none, and would have been readily accepted by the other nobles and aristocrats. Yet he had no military experience and would hold no loyalty amongst the army. The family originated from Antioch and there is no certainty he was even in Rome at the time. The murder of his father in Alexandria by Caracalla would have served as a timely reminder of the pitfalls of playing politics in imperial Rome.[37]

Another potential candidate for the purple was Pomponius Bassus, the consul of AD 211. His prestige was based on his marriage at some point around AD 217 to Annia Aurelia Faustina, the great-granddaughter of Marcus Aurelius. His own family lacked the prestige brought by a long series of consular ancestors, as it was his father's consulship in around AD 193 that had ennobled the family. He was, though, an *amicus* of Septimius Severus. Bassus, however, is unlikely to have been a potential candidate for the throne, as he owed a debt of gratitude to Macrinus, who had recalled him from exile. It is also likely he was governor of either Lower or Upper Moesia at this time rather than present in Rome.[38]

Macrinus' position was becoming increasingly tenuous, even in the provinces. Pergamum had received a number of privileges from Caracalla, including money towards the rebuilding of its temple to Aesculapius. The city's loyalty to the new regime was considered questionable, and Macrinus revoked the previous emperor's *beneficia*. This in itself was not unusual, but the reaction of Pergamum was. In the past, cities in similar situations had attempted to regain imperial favour by sending delegations requesting festivals named in honour of the emperor or expansion of the imperial cult. Not so Pergamum, whose city council 'heaped many extraordinary insults upon him'.[39] The emperor understandably 'dishonoured' the city, probably by lowering its municipal status. This usually occurred after a city had supported a usurper, yet Pergamum clearly felt that gaining the enmity of the present emperor was in its long term interests due to the anger felt at the original loss of privileges. These events support Dio's assertion that Macrinus and his son were held in 'great contempt' by the populace. This was due primarily to his equestrian rank.[40] The members of the ruling council of Pergamum would themselves be powerful landowners in their own right, and some probably senators in Rome. Dio himself was a senator from nearby Nicaea. He would empathize with their resistance to the rule of an emperor whom they clearly considered a usurper.[41] Their actions suggest they felt Macrinus' rule would be merely temporary, and, in the long run, his successor would reward them for their stance.

In the summer of AD 217, the situation went from bad to worse. Macrinus was desperate to return to Rome to consolidate his position on the throne. He would also have wanted to disburse his army to their various permanent stations around the empire. Rumours of his role in the murder of Caracalla would have been diluted by time and distance. As it was, many thousands of men were concentrated in Syria and Mesopotamia. This made it extremely difficult to contain the poisonous rumours of his role in the murder of his predecessor. Furthermore, he had promised a quick resolution to the war with Parthia in return for the support of the soldiers on the death of Caracalla. These men were eager to return to their families.[42] The war against the Parthians, however, forced him to remain in Syria. He had sent an embassy to Artabanus V apologizing for Rome's aggression and the desecration of the Parthian royal tombs, laying the blame for this on his deceased predecessor. Captives were returned and a promise of Roman 'friendship' offered. Artabanus, perceiving the military and political weakness of his new adversary, insisted on recompense for the damage to the cities and forts destroyed by Caracalla's unopposed destruction of Parthian territory. This could have been accepted by Macrinus, but the return of Mesopotamia was Artabanus' central demand, and this issue became the sticking point and the cause of future wars.[43] Such a concession would have fatally undermined the remaining confidence the soldiers had in their emperor. His prestige would have never recovered. Therefore the conflict continued.

In the autumn of AD 217, a massive Parthian army struck deep into the heart of Roman Mesopotamia, heading for the strategic fortress city of Nisibis. The Roman army was mobilized and encamped before the walls of the city. This was Caracalla's army, assembled in AD 214, based primarily on the central reserve created by Septimius Severus. The core of this army was based on the elite Praetorian Guard, composed of promoted soldiers from the Danubian provinces, and in particular Upper and Lower Pannonia. Alongside these were the *equites singularii*, the elite cavalry bodyguard, and a unit of German and Scythian cavalry favoured by Caracalla, the *equites extraordinarii*. The II *Parthica,* based at Alba outside the capital, was also in the East, as well as large detachments from the I and II *Adiutrix*, III *Augusta*, III *Italica*, III *Cyrenaica*, IV *Scythica*, XVI *Flavia* and large numbers of German auxiliaries. Added to these forces were those legions stationed in the East, in particular the I and III *Parthica* in Mesopotamia. Whilst the strength of the Roman army lay with its heavy infantry, the Parthian cavalry were the elite units of their army. Mounted archers offered the mobility to out-flank the enemy line, whilst heavy cavalry, the *cataphracti* and *clibanarii*, were able to overwhelm the enemy formations through the power of their charge, crushing them in a terrifying frontal assault. These were supplemented by large numbers of armoured riders mounted on camels, who used long spears to impale the enemy. The Parthian infantry, however, lacked the armour of their adversaries, but were protected by a vast array of archers.[44]

It is at this point that the accounts of our two main sources, Dio and Herodian, dramatically diverge. Furthermore, much of Dio's account of the Battle of Nisibis is fragmentary, yet both agree that the encounter resulted in a decisive defeat for the Roman forces. Herodian paints the picture of a vast Parthian army approach-ing the Roman forces encamped at Nisibis as the first rays of dawn pierced the dark horizon. As Zoroastrians, the whole army halted to worship the rising sun. Then, as dawn became day, they attempted to undermine the morale of the Romans through orchestrated shrieks and shouts. The attack, when it came, was initiated by the archers firing into the Roman lines, followed by a cavalry charge. Dio, how-ever, suggests both armies had built camps opposite each other, and the battle grew from a struggle to control the water supply. In the arid desert conditions around Nisibis, an army without water would soon suffer in the heat, encased as many were in armour.[45]

According to Herodian, the Romans were deployed with the infantry in the centre and the cavalry on either wing, with the Moors, probably cavalry archers and lightly armed, used as skirmishers. These African soldiers, raised by Caracalla, were immensely loyal to their emperor, as he was also a Moor, and were famous for their bravery and 'complete disregard for death'. It was vital that the enemy, despite their significantly larger numbers, were not allowed to outflank the Roman line. To add cohesion to the line, light-armed skirmishers were deployed in the spaces between the blocks of cohorts. These were elite light infantry troops called *lanciarii*, after the bundles of short spears called *lancea* that they carried into bat-tle. Their role was to advance in front of the Roman lines and disrupt the enemy advance whilst avoiding close combat, for which they were ill-equipped. The killing range of their spears has been estimated as not in excess of 15 metres.[46] After using up their supply of weapons, they retreated to the safety of their own lines, seeking the protection of the heavily armoured legionaries. The Roman soldiers had to initially withstand a hail of arrows. Their shields would have offered some protection, but many would have fallen even before the first contact with the enemy. It is very difficult to imagine the terror of facing a charge by thousands of armoured cavalry armed with long spears. These were the ancient world's equivalent of the tank, and the Roman infantry had to stand firm and face them. The sound of the hooves impacting on the surface would be deafening. The enemy would emerge from the dust cloud to hit the men in the first few lines. The legionaries would have little time to throw their heavy spears, the *pilum*, before the enemy were upon them. It is likely that only the first couple of lines would be able to throw their *pilum*, severely reducing the possible number of casualties to the enemy.[47]

There could only be one outcome as the armoured cavalry smashed into the Roman line. Many would have been impaled on the long spears. However, once the first impact had been absorbed, the advantage swung towards the Romans. The Parthian cavalrymen were slowed and then stopped. The horse gave the Parthian cavalry a height advantage as blows rained down on the helmets and shoulders of the Roman legionaries, who now had the opportunity to exact vengeance. Swords would have been thrust into the unprotected sides and belly of the horses; blows would have been aimed at the unprotected legs of the riders, and hands would grab any piece of armour or clothing to drag their assailant from his horse. Once dismounted, the armour would weigh down the Parthian, and according to Herodian, they were easily overcome. Many were taken prisoner. These were members of the Parthian nobility, the immense cost of their horse and armour precluding men of lower status becoming *clibanarii* and *cataphracti*. For this type of close-quarter fighting with cavalry, the Romans were gradually replacing the *gladius*, a short stabbing sword ideal for face-to-face combat with barbarian infantry, with the longer-bladed *spatha*. Its greater length allowed the infantryman a greater opportunity to strike at a mounted adversary with either a thrust or slashing action. The longer sword also made the traditional rectangular shield a hindrance, as its corners would impair slashing blows. Consequently, the third century saw the introduction of the oval-shaped shield once favoured by auxiliary units.[48]

The Roman position gradually become untenable due to the sheer weight of enemy numbers. The Roman line retreated, but not before dropping large numbers of caltrops. These devices, still used in modern warfare, were constructed from two or more nails welded together to allow one spike to point upwards, supported by three arms that formed a stable base. These were sown in front of the Roman position as they again turned and faced another cavalry charge. The enemy was completely unaware of the danger buried in the sand. As the horses and camels advanced, the bemused Parthian commanders observed hundreds of the animals collapse onto their knees, the horses' hooves or tender camel pads pierced by the sharp spikes, their riders thrown. Unable to escape, due either to the weight of their armour or the tight-fitting folds of the clothes they wore, the Parthians were struck down by the advancing Roman skirmishers. Night eventually brought an end to the slaughter, before it recommenced on the following day. The heat must have taken a terrible toll on both sides, but in particular on the *clibanarii*, a word literally meaning 'oven men'. This was because their armour resembled an ancient oven. However, encased as they were, the conditions inside their costly protection must have been close to unbearable.[49]

Dio's fragmentary account mentions none of this, but what we have may refer to the events of the final day of the battle. According to Herodian, both sides believed, as they retired to their respective camps at dusk on the second day of fighting, that victory lay within their grasp. As the two armies manoeuvred to face each other on the third day, their view was obscured by the vast numbers of dead men, horses and camels that lay between them. Herodian describes the 'burial ground' that existed between the opponents: 'So heavy was the slaughter of men and animals that the plain was completely choked with them, and the dead bodies were piled high in huge mounds, particularly those of camels that fell over each other.'[50] A frontal assault by either infantry or cavalry was impossible over such ground. The Parthians changed tactics, utilizing their massive advantage in cavalry to sweep around the extremes of the Roman lines to encircle their enemy. Observing this manoeuvre, the Romans extended their line by reducing its depth, sending cohorts to either wing. Herodian suggests this successfully prevented encirclement. However, the account in Dio appears to infer that the Romans failed to prevent the Parthians sweeping past one of the wings. The Roman camp positioned in the rear was attacked and nearly lost. A small number of soldiers would have been left to garrison the camp, but these were supported by large numbers of armour bearers and baggage handlers. The over-confident Parthians were taken completely by surprise as they were charged by what they thought were large numbers of Roman infantry, unaware that in fact these were virtually unarmed civilians. At this point, Dio's account becomes so fragmentary that no real sense can be made of it. What Dio does state is that Macrinus fled the battlefield, and the Roman army, 'overcome by their numbers and by the flight of Macrinus, became dejected and were conquered'.[51]

It is unlikely that an army abandoned by its emperor would be prepared to support him for any length of time, but in Dio's account Macrinus became involved in lengthy negotiations and retired to his winter quarters in Antioch. It would appear Dio's intense dislike of the 'equestrian' emperor may have coloured his interpretation of the outcome of the battle: 'For Macrinus, both because of his natural cowardice (for, being a Moor, he was exceedingly timorous) and because of the soldiers' lack of discipline, did not dare fight the war out.' Here, Dio reveals another of his prejudices, claiming the army lacked discipline. This is a common motif in his account. However, the events of the Battle of Nisibis prove otherwise. For what it is worth, the suspect account in the *Historia Augusta* records that Macrinus fought 'stoutly', and even Dio commends him later for demonstrating 'good generalship'.[52]

The need to remove the bodies from the blood-soaked plain between the two armies necessitated the need for a ceasefire. As the Parthians cremated their dead, Macrinus sent envoys to his adversary, reminding him that it was Caracalla who had broken the peace and desecrated the royal tombs, and he was dead thanks to the actions of Macrinus. Herodian's account suggests peace was concluded on the field of battle, but Dio refers to a series of delegations over the winter months. It is likely the initial ceasefire was extended to allow for negotiations. The Parthian army was suffering from a lack of food, and many of its infantry wished to return to their farms to save the harvests before their crops rotted in the fields. It is also clear that the Parthians had suffered just as grievously as the Romans. Artabanus needed to retain his army for future battles against his brother, who also claimed the throne, and he had to deal with the revolt of the Sassanid, Ardashir. A pyrrhic victory over the Romans would have resulted in his ultimate defeat to his enemies closer to home. All sources agree though that Macrinus had suffered a defeat. The emperor agreed to return all prisoners and pay the massive sum of 200 million sesterces, probably as compensation for Caracalla's devastation of Parthian territory. Significantly, Artabanus appears to have renounced his demand for the return of Roman Mesopotamia. This indicates that the Battle of Nisibis was not a total defeat. The Roman army remained a formidable foe that the Parthians had bloodied, but they had failed to deliver a knockout blow.[53]

The undetermined outcome of the battle allowed Macrinus to claim victory in his letter to the Senate. The facts were clearly massaged, with uncomfortable truths remaining unsaid. Victory was declared, sacrifices made to the gods in gratitude and the emperor voted the title 'Parthicus'. This honour Macrinus politically declined, the numbers of Roman dead left behind in the desert precluding any celebration on the part of the emperor. The army resented and remembered the cost. The coins of AD 218 carry the legend 'vic(toria) Part(hica)', indicating negotiations were not concluded until late AD 217 or early AD 218.[54]

Macrinus is criticized for remaining at Antioch instead of returning to Rome to secure his throne.[55] Yet he could hardly have departed the East with negotiations with the Parthians in full flow. Furthermore, he could not disburse his army back to their permanent stations with the prospect of war still hanging in the balance.

This was to prove his undoing. The soldiers had demanded an end to the war as the price of supporting Macrinus' ascent to the imperial throne. They were now at peace and grew increasingly restive as their expectations of a rapid return to their homes and families did not materialize. They would have been unaware, nor concerned, with the delicate negotiations taking place. Resentment was fanned by the persistent rumour that their emperor had taken a lead role in the murder of their beloved Caracalla.

Macrinus' own actions now ignited the flames of open revolt. The pay rises initiated by Caracalla to win the loyalty of the army had tipped the finances of the empire into crisis. Septimius Severus had increased the pay of a legionary from 450 to 500 denarii, paid in three four-monthly instalments. Caracalla increased this again to 675 and then to 750 denarii. Estimated figures for the sums that the Praetorians received vary widely. Watson suggests their pay rose to 2,250 denarii. However, J.B. Campbell believes their pay rose from 20,000 sesterces or 5,000 denarii, the pay rise awarded by Septimius Severus, to a far higher but unknown amount by Caracalla. As for donatives, Caracalla awarded a number, including one of 10,000 sesterces per man on the murder of Geta, whilst Macrinus awarded the soldiers 3,000 sesterces each on his accession.[56] Long before these pay rises, it is estimated that the financial cost of the army absorbed roughly 50 per cent of all state revenues. Dio provides the figure of 280 million sesterces a year as the cost of the increases made by Caracalla. The financial strain prompted Macrinus to write to the Senate, announcing a reduction of pay for new recruits to the levels introduced by Septimius Severus, as well as the loss of some unspecified privileges. In his account, Dio praises the emperor's motive but criticises its timing. With hindsight, he suggests Macrinus should have waited until the army had been disbursed to their permanent stations throughout the empire, as, concentrated as they were in Syria, rumours and supposition soon became 'facts'. It was increasingly believed by the soldiers that the emperor intended to reduce all their pay on their return home. Veteran soldiers made common cause with new recruits as unrest and anger grew.[57]

Many soldiers had been encamped in temporary accommodation since their arrival in the East in AD 215. They would have experienced the searing heat of the summer months, where temperatures can reach 40° centigrade. These were the months they would have spent on campaign constantly encased in their armour whilst in enemy territory, marching up to 20 miles a day and, with dusk approaching, building a fortified camp to secure their position during the night. At the end of the campaigning season, during the winter months, the army was encamped in Syria, where temperatures can fall to around 1° centigrade. Both Herodian and Dio agree that the living conditions were a primary cause of discontent: 'The long sojourn that they made in practically one and the same spot while wintering in

Syria on account of the war strengthened their purpose.'[58] Added to this was a shortage of food caused by the logistical problems of keeping the vast army supplied: 'They were also angry because, while they were still living in tents in a foreign country, sometimes even on short supplies and not returning to their own countries in spite of apparently peaceful conditions, Macrinus, they noticed, was living in the lap of luxury.'[59] Coins issued at this time carry the legend *fides militum*, the loyalty of the army. Such issues were invariably an indication of the opposite, and were an attempt to appeal to their loyalty using the money the soldiers were paid with.[60] A shortage of food was often the prelude to open revolt, as Maximinus Thrax found to his cost before the gates of Aquileia in AD 238.[61] The imperial prestige had already been tarnished by the huge losses the army had suffered at Nisibis, whilst Macrinus had only partly delivered on his promise to end the war and return the soldiers to their families. In these circumstances, the discontented often found a leader who was willing to satisfy their demands, protect their privileges and address their grievances.[62] Rome and its legions were ripe for insurrection.

Chapter 3

Revolt AD 217–218

'Truly indeed old man, young warriors sorely beset thee,
Spent is thy force, and grievous old age is coming upon thee'
(The reply of the oracle of Zeus Belus at Apamea to the 54-year-old
emperor Macrinus, Dio, 79.40.4)

M acrinus stands accused in the ancient sources of idling away his time in the East in a life of extravagance and leisure when he should have returned to Rome at the earliest opportunity.[1] The war with Artabanus and the drawn-out peace negotiations prevented this. However, peace was concluded by early AD 218 at the latest, and yet the emperor remained rooted at Antioch. The ongoing war with Armenia was also concluded at this time with a compromise: the Parthian nominee, Tiridates, received his crown of Armenia from the Romans, who returned his mother, whom they had been holding as a hostage, as well as captured booty.[2] However, the situation in Rome was deteriorating rapidly. Even the gods appear to have conspired to overthrow the emperor. On 23 August AD 217, on the eve of the Vulcanalia, a lightning bolt hit the Colosseum and started a fire that completely destroyed the wooden upper storey of the arena. The fire was so intense that even a tremendous downpour was unable to extinguish the flames. Instead, the River Tiber broke its banks, causing damage to the buildings built on the flood plain, including the Forum. Ironically, the games were designed to placate the god Vulcan and destructive fire. It was an inauspicious omen which was taken to heart by many, especially as the populace were denied their racing and gladiatorial spectacle.[3]

The poisonous atmosphere in the capital demanded the presence of the emperor, yet still he remained at Antioch. It was clearly in his best interests to disburse his army to its permanent garrisons, and return to the capital with all haste. Something pressing kept him in the East, and this was not his supposed addiction to the lavish lifestyle Syria offered. The sources only provide brief glimpses of the real reason for Macrinus' delay. In the winter of AD 217, he had tried to win over the populace of Antioch with the issue of money and gifts, a *congiaria*. On the official proclamation of his Parthian 'victory', another *congiaria* was distributed, whilst coins issued at this time announce the loyalty of the army, a sure sign of the opposite.[4] Even the city of Pergamum was prepared to publically insult him.[5]

The sands around the Roman fortress of Dura Europas have preserved numerous documents, including one letter from this time demanding the restoration of discipline in the army.[6] The emperor toured the army encampments in an attempt to restore order. However, in an attempt to overawe them with his majesty, he appeared before them bedecked in the ornamentation of imperial power, wearing brooches of gold and jewels. The men's resentment only grew as they compared their own miserable condition to the opulent figure standing before them.[7] Caracalla had worked hard to build an emotional bond with the rank and file, calling them 'fellow soldiers', sharing their food eaten out in the open, sleeping on the cheap, uncomfortable military bed, marching on foot at their side, digging trenches and exposing himself to the dangers they faced. According to the second-century historian Plutarch, it was this, rather than the distributions of cash, that won military respect. The problem for Macrinus was that it was virtually impossible to combine the role of 'fellow soldier' and imperial *Princeps*. Caracalla was despised by the Roman elite for pandering to the soldiers, whilst Macrinus, lacking Caracalla's hereditary legitimacy, courted senatorial support both in Rome and amongst the senior men in his army and in the provinces.[8] He merely succeeded in alienating both.

The suspect life of Macrinus in the *Historia Augusta* is replete with numerous examples of military indiscipline and the increasingly draconian attempts by the emperor to restore order.[9] What this account may reflect is the extent of unrest in the army, although the salacious details may be ignored. This unrest is confirmed in both Dio and Herodian. Macrinus was unable to return to Rome, leaving the opportunity for an ambitious rival in the capital to harness discontent for their own purposes. Nor could he disburse the already mutinous soldiers to their permanent garrisons, where the flames of rebellion would be spread across the whole of the Rhine and Danube frontier. Herodian is right when he wrote: 'It was obviously inevitable that Macrinus would lose the empire, and his life too, whenever chance provided a small trivial excuse for the soldiers to have their way.'[10] Chance, though, played no part, rather the designs and planning of the Machiavellian Maesa and her entourage, who had bided their time patiently at Emesa.

Macrinus had, with hindsight, mistakenly allowed Maesa to retain her immense wealth and landed estates, as well as her life.[11] As the troops in the surrounding areas came to sacrifice at the Temple of Elagabal, she became 'aware of the strong dislike of the soldiers for Macrinus'. Emesa had also received colonial status from Caracalla, with veterans settled in its environs. These men would have despised his successor.[12] Her entourage contained her two daughters: Julia Soamias with her son, the 14-year-old Elagabalus, and Julia Mamaea with her children, the 9-year-old Alexianus (Alexander Severus) and his sister and brother-in-law. Mamaea's husband, Gessius Marcianus, was also in the vicinity, perhaps on his family estates at Arca. Dio records that Gannys had a pivotal role in the plot. He was the lover of Soamias, and foster father and guardian of her son, Elagabalus. This young man had been brought up by Maesa, and at this time is described as having not yet fully reached manhood.[13] Maesa had also been allowed to retain some of Caracalla's imperial freedmen, including Eutychianus, who is described as a man 'who had given people pleasure in amusements and gymnastic exercises'. Festus was another advisor, and both were influential figures.[14] As well as a few freedmen, the conspirators had the services of the council of Emesa and patronal links to a small number of equestrians and clients whom Maesa retained in the army. These officers must have held high-level posts to have gained the patronage of an important member of the Severan imperial family.[15] They would have not only acted as spies and informers, but also helped to undermine the loyalty of other officers and soldiers in the service of Macrinus.

It was obvious that both Elagabalus and Alexianus lacked credible claims to the imperial throne, being merely distantly related to Julia Domna, Septimius Severus' wife. Their claim was even more tenuous than that of Macrinus, hence his decision to let them live. Therefore, a fiction was created that both were the illegitimate children of Caracalla and his cousins, Soamias and Mamaea. In theory, at least, this was possible. The lists of important personages attending the *Ludi Saeculares* held in Rome in AD 204 preserve the names of the elite Roman women present at the time, including those of Julia Soamias and Julia Mamaea, so these liaisons could have happened. So effective were both Elagabalus and Alexander Severus in propagating this fabrication through imperial propaganda and burying the truth, that even the ancient historians are uncertain of their real names: Dio names the future Emperor Elagabalus as Varius Avitus, whilst Herodian calls him Bassianus; Alexander Severus is named Alexianus in Herodian but Bassianus in Dio's account.[16] The name of Caracalla was held dear in the hearts of the soldiers, and any of his offspring , whether legitimate or otherwise, would instantly command the loyalty of many. The soldiers flocked to see Elagabalus officiating at the sacrifices in the temple, assisted by his cousin Alexianus. Regular distributions of food, wine and gifts were part of the religious ceremonies, and these would have helped to draw them in. There may even have been some physical similarity between Elagabalus and Caracalla. This coincidence, in the minds of the impressionable soldiers, added validity to the claim. Maesa also let it be known that she had the wealth to pay for a substantial donative if they supported her. Emesa became a sanctuary for deserters wishing to escape Macrinus' justice. At first this was only a trickle, but later became a steady stream. They came as the pull of future rewards far outweighed the fear of capture and certain death. It took time for the message to be disseminated by word of mouth, but the seeds of rebellion had taken a firm hold.[17]

Here our accounts of these events in Dio and Herodian diverge. Gannys, according to Dio, was the prime mover behind the events of the night of 15 May AD 218. However, according to Herodian, Maesa made the decisive move. A sudden opportunity arose when the conspirators at Emesa were approached by members of the III *Gallica* whose fortress lay 40 miles away at Raphanaea. According to Dio, Gannys secretly brought Elagabalus to them without the knowledge of Maesa and Soamias. The following morning, the legion hailed its new emperor with the name Marcus Aurelius Antoninus, Caracalla's own official name. According to Herodian, Maesa had agreed to the move and, along with her daughters and their children, accompanied the party to the legionary fortress. The young Alexianus and his mother were part of the party that rapidly made their way along the road. They were 'guided by the soldiers who were under her protection'. This suggests many of the deserters Maesa had welcomed came from the III *Gallica*, and it was through their services that the whole legion was suborned, including its probable legate, Verus. The soldiers then moved their families and supplies into the fort to withstand a siege.[18]

Unbeknown to the conspirators, a large force of Praetorians and Moorish auxiliaries were operating in the area under the command of Macrinus' Praetorian Prefect, Ulpius Julianus. He was probably dealing with deserters in the area and rapidly captured Alexianus' sister and brother-in-law, who were immediately executed. A fragmentary section of Dio's account also refers to the capture and execution of Alexianus' father, Marcianus, by Julianus. Why they had failed to seek the protection of the legionary camp is unclear; perhaps they were hoping to secure Emesa, but were caught by the sudden arrival of the Praetorians. The revolt does appear badly planned, with no scouts dispatched to locate forces loyal to Macrinus, nor was the legionary fortress pre-supplied before raising the standard of revolt. It is likely that the officers and soldiers of the III *Gallica* initiated these events, which provided too great an opportunity for Maesa and Gannys to reject, despite the lack of preparations.[19] The cost was dear, especially for the young Alexianus, whose reactions to the death of his sister and father are completely ignored in our sources. The new regime's propaganda stressed Caracalla's illegitimate parentage of Alexianus as the Emperor Alexander Severus, and so our sources ignored the impact of the death of his real father to maintain the illusion of his Severan heritage. There can be little doubt that the young Alexianus was devastated by his loss. He was old enough to grieve but too young to be considered a credible alternative as emperor, unlike his older cousin. After all, it was his cousin who was the main beneficiary of these events; Alexianus was merely an innocent bystander carried along on the tide of imperial politics.

Julianus quickly raised additional men from units stationed nearby and lay siege to the legionary fort. The Moors, fanatically loyal to their fellow countryman Macrinus, launched a ferocious assault on the gates. The gates were forced and the

Moors entered, only to be ordered to retreat by their commander. Dio suggests Julianus was expecting the legion to surrender or that 'he was afraid to rush in'. This would only be an issue if the Moors were left isolated by a lack of support from their comrades. Subsequent events suggest the soldiers at Julianus' disposal were already mutinous and were quite willing to allow the Moors to be surrounded and slaughtered in the fortress. During the night, the gates were blocked up and subsequent attacks failed. Defeat is readily followed by military revolt. The besieged soldiers dressed their 'emperor' in Caracalla's old regalia and brought him up to the ramparts. There he was hailed Marcus Aurelius Antoninus by the besieged legionaries, whilst the boy himself praised his dead 'father'. The pull of Caracalla's name was too great for the soldiers below. Although they had sworn their oath of loyalty to Macrinus, they had previously sworn to protect the person of their imperial patron and his 'divine house'. His 'son' now stood before them. The gods would understand that their oath to Macrinus was now superseded by the one they had made to the Severan dynasty. The legionaries of the III *Gallica* shouted to their besiegers that they were fighting Caracalla's son: 'Why do you do this, fellow soldiers? Why do you fight against your benefactor's son?' Bags of money were waved from the parapet. The centurions and officers below attempted to restrain their men, but their loyalty was finally undermined by the offer of the property and position of each murdered officer. Only Julianus, accompanied by the Moors, survived the resulting bloodletting, hastening to Apamea, where the majority of the army had spent the winter.[20]

The soldiers' loyalty is continually questioned in our senatorial sources, but the facts speak for themselves. They were loyal. Not to the abstract concept of the Roman state, or the idea of the Roman Senate, but to a hereditary monarchy. So the name of the Antonines was retained in imperial nomenclature, even by Macrinus himself. As Dio admits, the last of the true Antonines died with Commodus, but the name still retained lustre in the minds of the soldiers. Caracalla, officially an Antonine through his father's posthumous adoption by Marcus Aurelius, was considered a vicious thug by the senatorial elite, but was loved by the rank and file. This was not only because he led the army to victories across the Rhine and in Parthia, but because he rewarded their loyal service with massive donatives. The early coinage of Elagabalus stressed his descent from Caracalla, carrying the name 'M. Aurelius Antoninus Pius Felix Augustus'. The letters sent to the Senate announcing his victory over Macrinus were signed off 'son of Antoninus Bassianus', and inscriptions refer to him as the 'son of the divine Antoninus the Great, grandson of the divine Severus' (*divi magni Antonini f(ilius) divi Severi nepos*).[21] Even Alexander Severus, despite his attempts to appeal to the senatorial aristocracy, would retain the fiction that he was also the illegitimate son of Caracalla.

Maesa now worked to gather a large enough army around her that was capable of defeating Macrinus' forces, in particular the Praetorian cohorts stationed around the imperial court at Antioch. To reward her present supporters and encourage further desertion, she announced that deserters would have their property and civil status restored and promised a massive donative upon victory. To cement the claim that her grandchildren were the true descendants of Caracalla, she promised to restore the property and status of all those close adherents of the previous emperor who had been exiled by Macrinus.[22]

Macrinus reacted with incredulity when informed of the revolt. This is from one of the few sections of the *Historia Augustus' Life of Macrinus* that can be considered reasonably accurate, based as it is in part on the work of Herodian and the full account of Dio, of which we only have the epitomized summary.[23] The emperor's response reflects the essential weakness of the future regimes of both Elagabalus and Alexander Severus. They were not perceived as legitimate members of the Severan dynasty by many members of the governing classes, both senatorial and equestrian. The rank and file of the soldiery may have been convinced by imperial propaganda and monetary rewards, but essentially, all knew that their claims to the throne were based on a lie. Dio refers to Elagabalus as the 'False Antoninus', yet Alexander Severus' claim to the throne was based on the same assertions.

Just as Julianus had hurried to Apamea, so too did Macrinus. Strategically situated, the city stood halfway between Antioch and Emesa. More importantly, most of the army was encamped in its hinterland. Macrinus knew it was vital to secure the loyalty of these men and the city itself. Tombstones record units drawn from the XIII *Gemina* based at Apulum in Dacia, the XIV *Gemina* based at Carnuntum on the Danube, the IV *Flavia* from Singidunum in Moesia, the *cohors* XIV from the Urban Cohort of Rome and vexillations from the local legions of the III *Gallica* and IV *Scythica* from Zeugma on the Euphrates. The whole of the II *Parthica* was also present. This legion was normally based at Alba outside Rome, and some of these men had also brought their families on campaign with them. A centurion from the legion, Probius Sanctus, erected a memorial for his 'incomparable' 28-year-old wife,[24] a reminder that life for the soldiers and their families was often nasty, brutish and short, yet not necessarily solitary.[25] An invasion of Dacia at this time meant members of the XIII *Gemina* would be agitating for a return home to their loved ones, whilst there would inevitably have been fraternization between the mutinous legionaries of the III *Gallica* at Raphanaea and their comrades posted at Apamea.[26]

Macrinus assembled the legions and announced the promotion of his 9-year-old son, Diadumenianus, to the rank of co-Augustus with the official name of Antoninus. To celebrate this, the emperor announced a donative of 20,000 sesterces per man, 4,000 of which was distributed immediately. No doubt this was to counter the promised donative made by Maesa. He also promised to restore the privileges he had only recently revoked. The emperor took this opportunity to consult the oracle of Zeus Belus, just as his predecessor, Septimius Severus, had. As he ascended the high podium that the temple was built upon, he would have hoped for a favourable reply. He also was sadly disappointed. The god foretold his demise at the hands of 'young warriors', pointedly describing his own efforts as a spent force. The emperor's day was about to get worse. The citizens of Apamea were invited to a banquet costing 600 sesterces per guest. The emperor was approached by a soldier carrying a parcel wrapped in cloth, firmly secured by cords and a signet ring. As Macrinus took his time unravelling the gift, the soldier quietly withdrew. The final folds were finally removed, revealing the severed head of Julianus. The ring was that of his loyal Praetorian Prefect. Macrinus immediately realized the situation was lost and rapidly travelled the 56 miles back to Antioch with his son.

On 30 May, the soldiers stationed around Apamea announced their support for Elagabalus, whilst the town council town dedicated a console on the west portico of the *agora* to Julia Maesa. The local elite were probably clients of Elagabalus' late father, Sextus Varius Marcellus, who was a native of the city. Apamea itself was also a rival to Antioch, which supported Macrinus. Support for the rebellion would, they hoped, be rewarded with honours and privileges that allowed it to supersede its more dominant neighbour. Macrinus secured the loyalty of Antioch itself with a distribution of money to its citizens. However, the defection of the II *Parthica* was recognized as the pivotal moment in the revolt, in recognition of which it was later awarded the title of *Antoniniana*, with the additional epithet of *pia fidelis felix aeterna* (forever faithful, loyal and pious). This, like imperial propaganda professing the loyalty of the army, was an attempt to appeal to the honour of the soldiers rather than a statement of fact.[27]

A key player in these events may have been P. Valerius Comazon. He is described by Dio as a Prefect of the Camp, or *Praefectus Castrorum*, the third-in-command of a legion after the legate and tribune, both posts which were occupied by men of senatorial rank. The Prefect of the Camp tended to be filled by men of low social status who had risen through the ranks. Comazon would have a meteoric career under Elagabalus and then Alexander Severus, becoming Elagabalus' first Praetorian Prefect, followed by *adlection* into the Senate, then awarded a consulship and becoming City Prefect of Rome under both emperors. Clearly a man of immense ability and political acumen, he appears, however, to have earned the hatred of Dio. According to the senatorial historian, he was 'one of the greatest violations of precedent'. Perhaps both the legate and tribune of the II *Parthica* had fled with Macrinus, leaving Comazon in command. Some historians, however, have suggested he was in fact the legate of the II *Parthica*. It was probably through his agency that the legion renounced its allegiance to Macrinus.[28]

On his return to Antioch, Macrinus wrote a letter to the Senate informing them of the revolt, whereupon both Elagabalus and his cousin, Alexianus, were declared *hostes*, enemies of the Roman state, as well as their mothers and grandmother, who had formed an alliance to secure imperial power.[29] The young Alexianus was clearly as much associated with the rebellion as his older cousin. Macrinus also considered the family members led by Maesa as the leaders of the revolt, rather than Gannys. Other letters were sent by both protagonists to governors and army commanders across the empire, each claiming the right to the throne and the more advantageous situation. Legates, governors, procurators and various officials would have faced a difficult choice, that could have serious repercussions for their careers and indeed their lives. Most would have liked to wait upon events, but even that could be seen as an act of treachery by the victor. A choice needed to be made, and many elected to execute messengers from Elagabalus, some those of Macrinus. Those making the wrong choice either lost their lives or incurred 'other penalties'.

Dio uses the situation in Egypt as an example. Its prefect, Basilianus, had been appointed to this illustrious post by Macrinus in an act of *beneficia*. The recipient of imperial gifts, or *beneficia*, which included offices of state, was bound by the rules of *amicitiae* that established the need for a reciprocal show of gratitude. This often took the form of loyalty, or *fides*. Furthermore, the Prefect of Egypt could expect promotion after a number of years to the highest equestrian office, that of Praetorian Prefect. The prefect was based in Alexandria and, although Dio does not mention it as a factor, many of its populace would remember with hatred the massacre perpetrated by Caracalla on their relatives and friends. A usurper bore the name M. Aurelius Antonius and claimed to be Caracalla's son. The messengers from Elagabalus were executed. All now held their breath, both officials and people alike, waiting in suspended animation for the consequences of their choice to become evident. On the news of Macrinus' eventual defeat, a storm broke as soldiers and citizens, supporters of either side, fought each other. Basilianus fled, returning to Italy destitute. He was betrayed by a friend in Rome to whom he had sent requests for food, and sent to Nicomedia, where Elagabalus was spending the winter of AD 218/219. There he was executed. These events would have been repeated numerous times across the empire. Instability and unrest fed ever greater civil strife.[30]

After the loss of the majority of his army, Macrinus would have sent for reinforcements from other legions. However, the nearest, the IV *Scythica*, was 120 miles away at Zeugma, and vexillations of this legion had already joined the rebellion. The XVI *Flavia* was at Samosata, an even greater distance away. Both legions had received letters from Elagabalus. To prevent the arrival of reinforcements, Gannys ordered a rapid advance on Antioch, whilst Macrinus attempted to seize the initiative by besieging the II *Parthica* in its temporary encampment.

The decisive battle took place at Imma on 8 June. A tombstone at Apamea records the death of Atinius Ianuarius at this battle. The village of Imma lay at the foot of the pass through the hills to Coele Syria. All the sources record the effects of months of unrest, indiscipline and widespread desertion on the Roman forces of both sides. The well-oiled fighting machine that met the Parthians at Nisibis had deteriorated into a disordered rabble. Initially, the II *Parthica* and III *Gallica* broke and ran, only to be humiliated into turning to face their pursuers by the actions of Maesa, Soamias and the young Elagabalus, who dismounted and threatened to take on the advancing Praetorians himself. This action saved the day. The actions and whereabouts of Alexianus are not known. It is likely that the historians would have referred to his martial valour if he had been present. It was treachery, however, that undermined Macrinus' hopes. Dio has the emperor losing his nerve and fleeing the battle. It is also clear from Herodian that he fled the battle, but only when he saw his Praetorians start to desert his cause and begin to change sides. He realized the day was lost, despite the fact some units continued to fight. Heralds were dispatched and the remaining Praetorians were won over by the promise that they would be retained as the imperial bodyguard. In despair, Macrinus handed his son over to the care of Epagathus, a trusted imperial official, with instructions to take him to Artabanus. Meanwhile, the emperor, with a number of loyal centurions from the Guard, disguised themselves as *frumentarii*, who were soldiers on special duties who acted as imperial messengers, spies and assassins. The *frumentarii* could pass freely through the provinces, commandeer the resources they needed and expect no questions. Macrinus' plan appears to have been to pass through Asia Minor to the Hellespont, and from there travel to Rome to gather support against the eastern rebels.[31]

Macrinus left behind total anarchy in Antioch. To secure his safe passage, he had told the people and officials in the city that he had won a great victory. However, his departure coincided with the news of his defeat and the advance of the rebel forces on the city.[32] Just as in Alexandria, civil war erupted on the streets of the city, and the roads leading out were littered with dead as scores were settled and many tried to escape the carnage. The citizens could also expect no favours from the army of Elagabalus, as Antioch had been Macrinus' capital. The city could expect to be looted and ravaged by his troops. This scene must have been repeated in numerous cities as the local elite who had found favour under one emperor were now attacked by others, who hoped their actions would win the approval of the new regime. The clients, freedmen and slaves of these local magnates would form private armies to do battle. Even in Rome itself, political crises went hand-in-hand with civil unrest.[33]

Antioch was saved from pillage by the victorious troops by Elagabalus, who promised to distribute 2,000 sesterces per man. Most of the required money was extorted from the surviving populace themselves. Soldiers were dispatched to hunt down Macrinus and his son. Diadumenianus was captured and murdered at Zeugma after being recognized by Claudius Aelius Pollio, a centurion in the IV *Scythica*. The sinister Epagathus played a key role in the boy's betrayal. Both were subsequently rewarded for their actions. Epagathus made the smooth transition from high-ranking imperial official in the court of Macrinus to the entourage of Elagabalus and Maesa. Pollio himself made rapid promotion through the *cursus honorum*, being *adlected* into the Senate with the rank of ex-consul and then made governor of Germania Superior. Another beneficiary was the Emesene senator Aurelius Eubulus, who probably supported the revolt from its earliest stages and was rewarded with the responsibility of the imperial *fiscus*.[34] Comazon also became a key member of the new emperor's advisory council, his *consilium*, probably as Praetorian Prefect. The whereabouts of Macrinus would preoccupy discussions, as he proved far more elusive than his poor son. Until he was caught, the new imperial family felt constrained to remain at Antioch in close proximity to the legions. These clearly remained restive, as Elagabalus' first coinage seems to suggest continued discontent, carrying as it does the legends 'FIDES EXERCITUS' and 'CONCORDIA MILIT(UM)'.[35]

Macrinus was finally captured at Chalcedon in Bithynia, having requested money from a local procurator who recognized him. He was attempting to sail from there to Rome, where both Dio and Herodian state that he would have gained extensive support, as many senators were antagonistic towards the Syrian heritage and youth of the new emperor, as well as the influential positions held by men such as Gannys and Comazon. These were men of low birth and status. Dio even suggests the army was already starting to regret its support for Elagabalus, even while he remained in their midst. Macrinus was probably captured late in AD 218, accounting for Elagabalus' delayed return to Rome, despite increased signs of unrest there. His opponents in Rome would have had months to question the legitimacy of the new emperor. Dio gives the reason for the delay as being that Elagabalus tried to 'establish his authority on all sides'. The time it took to do this suggests many questioned his authority and legitimacy. Fabius Agrippinus, the governor of Syria Coele, was executed, along with Nestor, Macrinus' surviving Praetorian Prefect. An unusual turn of phrase in Dio's account perhaps suggests that some Syrian legionaries attempted to name their governor as emperor. Pica Caesarianus, governor of Arabia, was executed in his province as he had failed to declare fast enough for Elagabalus. Comazon took the opportunity to have the governor of Cyprus, Claudius Attalus, executed in revenge for condemning him to the galleys earlier in his career. The senator Silius Messalla was summoned from Rome, ostensibly to become a member of Elagabalus' *consilium*. Messalla had been speaking openly against the new emperor, possibly on behalf of Macrinus, who was still at large at this time. Once summoned to Antioch, he could not refuse the imperial request. His execution swiftly followed. Other old *amici* and supporters of Macrinus, both in the East and in Rome, were purged. Many lost their lives. Macrinus was escorted back to Antioch, and on the journey he was informed of the death of his son. Heartbroken, he threw himself from the open carriage he was travelling in, only for death to cheat him. He merely fractured his shoulder. Yet he did not have to wait long for the release he welcomed. He was beheaded in Cappadocia, with his head carried to Antioch. His body lay unburied until Elagabalus had the opportunity of viewing it on his journey to Nicomedia at the start of the winter.[36]

Elagabalus, Alexianus and the imperial court had remained in Antioch from June until at least late October AD 218. The imperial palace in the city dated back to the Seleucids and had been the temporary home of numerous emperors and their families. During the second and early third centuries, Antioch had served as the capital city of the empire as Trajan, Lucius Verus and Caracalla had moved their whole court to the city. This continued under Macrinus. The buildings had been badly damaged in the earthquake of AD 115, and much had to be rebuilt. The imperial palace stood on an island in the middle of the River Orontes, next to a stadium in which the Emperor Trajan was forced to take shelter as the city was shaken flat by the earthquake. As the prolonged residence of a series of emperors, the city would have been gradually embellished with the necessary buildings and infrastructure that reflected imperial power. It had only recently been restored to its official status as a *metropolis*, probably by Caracalla, after being demoted to the status of a village by Septimius Severus for the city's support of his rival, Niger. Five miles south of Antioch lay Daphne, famous for its hot springs and waterfalls, sheltered by tall oaks, cypresses and laurels. The rich and affluent had built many villas in the area, and there can be little doubt the young Alexianus would have visited to bathe or indeed remain in this tranquil suburb, away from the heat of the city in the late summer months.[37]

Both Alexianus and Elagabalus would have felt at home in the cultural mix of the city, which contained a population approaching 500,000 people of Greek, Roman, Syrian and Jewish heritage. Neither boy was particularly Romanized, and Elagabalus remained stubbornly dedicated to his role as chief priest to the god Elagabal. Our sources remain suspiciously quiet on his cousin's continued participation in the ceremonies associated with this god, but it is likely he continued to do so, as Alexianus' failure to undertake these duties became a key issue with Elagabalus later in his reign. The black stone had been taken from its home in Emesa and accompanied the emperor on his travels.

On the death of Macrinus, the imperial court felt confident enough to leave Antioch with the army to spend the winter at Nicomedia in Bithynia. The instability of the new regime is exemplified by the series of revolts that broke out in Syria on their departure, and in Bithynia itself, involving the army that had so recently brought them to the throne.

The III *Gallica* and IV *Scythica* rose in revolt with the departure of the emperor, accompanied by the Praetorians and II *Parthica*. The revolt of the III *Gallica* and its legate Verus is particularly surprising given their key support to Elagabalus and Maesa at Emesa when they had few supporters. Verus may have felt he had not received the rewards he had expected for his pivotal role. As a senator, he would have felt he had a greater claim to the throne than a mere child with a slender dynastic link to the Severan house. His resentment must have grown when Comazon, a man of similar status, was promoted to the Praetorian Prefecture. Real power lay with those who had ready access to the emperor, but Verus remained at Raphanaea with his legion whilst the emperor departed to Nicomedia and then Rome. He was joined in his imperial aspirations by Gellius Maximus, a senatorial tribune of the IV *Scythica*. After the capture of Diadumenianus, he may have felt aggrieved that his centurion earned the gratitude of Elagabalus whilst he, the legionary commander, remained at Zeugma. The uprising appears to have been rapidly crushed by the decisive actions of the legate of the XVI *Flavia* stationed at Samosata. We only have a badly damaged inscription that partially preserves this commander's name as '…atus'. However, he appears subsequently to have received a number of prestigious posts in quick succession, becoming prefect of the grain supply, a *comes* of the emperor describing himself as *amicis fidissimus* (most loyal friend) and then Praetorian Prefect in AD 220–222. The disloyal Verus suffered *damnatio memoriae*, with his name removed from several surviving inscriptions, and both legates were executed. Unusually, the whole of the III *Gallica* was disbanded. The soldiers would have received an ignominious discharge and forfeited all their benefits and rights of service. It appears the legion revolted again under the leadership of a son of a centurion, a probable veteran living in the area. A 'worker in wool' also attempted to suborn the IV *Scythia*, yet it was III *Gallica* that was made an example of. Disbanding two legions would have severely weakened the defences in the East.[38]

The city of Tyre also appears to have joined the revolt, suffering imperial punishment as a result. The bronze coinage issued by the city after this time no longer carried the title *metropolis*. It was also deprived of its status as a colony, unlike its rival Sidon, which remained faithful. Sidon received the official title 'Loyal' from the emperor, as well as a guaranteed regular supply of grain. This would ensure it drew migrants to it, not only from the surrounding area but cities like Tyre. Sidon would grow in prosperity at the expense of its competitors.[39]

Revolt also appears to have broken out in Nicomedia and the surrounding province of Bithynia. Castinus, according to Dio, was ' energetic and known to many soldiers in consequence of the commands he had held and of his intimate association with Antoninus'.[40] Not only had he been a close *amicus* of Caracalla, but he had pursued an illustrious career. He had been a tribune of the Pannonian legion I *Adiutrix* in AD 192 and then tribune of the V *Macedonica* in Dacia, legate of I *Minerva*, then placed in command of vexillations from a number of legions on the Rhine in c. AD 207 against *defectores et rebelles* who were the remnants of Albinus' forces that survived his defeat by Septimius Severus. This campaign must have been successfully completed, as he was rewarded with the governorship of Pannonia Inferior, then the consulship of AD 211, becoming a trusted friend of the emperor, and then being appointed to the governorship of Dacia. A large number of the soldiers returning with Elagabalus and his family would have served under him or admired his military record. What Dio significantly fails to mention is his full name, but it is preserved in numerous inscriptions: C. Julius Septimius Castinus. Anthony Birley suggests he was related to C. Septimius Severus, the consul of AD 160, who had been a member of the *concilium* of Marcus Aurelius and Commodus. As such, he was distantly related to the emperors Septimius Severus and Caracalla, but still carried the dynastic name and had a stronger claim to the throne as a member of the imperial family, rather than the fabricated one constructed for Elagabalus and Alexianus. He was clearly a potential threat to Macrinus, who exiled him to his native province.[41]

Despite a recall from Elagabalus, Castinus remained in Bithynia rather than return to Rome. Dio states he 'had been sent on ahead', perhaps to organize the winter quarters around Nicomedia for the army returning with the emperor and the secure provisions. The legionaries were quickly becoming disenchanted with the emperor, whose lack of Romanization and public commitment to the god Elagabal involved his obsessive devotion to oriental ceremonies. The emperor was rarely seen in a toga, and instead wore the 'barbarous' priestly robes associated with his Eastern religion and the Parthians. Dio does not make clear whether Castinus was proactive in raising revolt or whether the soldiers themselves turned to a more 'deserving' claimant. However, the soldiers 'created some little disturbance', which spread to the imperial fleet at Cyzicus that was being collected for transporting the army across the Hellespont in the spring. Dio refers to an unnamed private citizen as the instigator of the revolt amongst the sailors. This must in some way be linked to the revolt of Castinus; perhaps he was one of his supporters or clients.[42] Castinus must have cast doubt on the claim that both Elagabalus and Alexianus were the illegitimate sons of Caracalla, and as a close *amicus* of the murdered emperor, his assertion would have carried a great deal of weight. The revolt also appears to have spread to the province of Bithynia itself, as Pollio, recently promoted from his centurion post, was tasked with suppressing it. His appointment is surprising, as there must have been other more experienced military officers available. This suggests the imperial family lacked a reserve of loyal and trustworthy commanders. Pollio owed everything to his emperor.[43]

The revolt was crushed, but the indiscipline in these legions continued, which the senator Sulla attempted to take advantage of. He had been dismissed from his post of governor of Cappadocia, and upon returning to Rome found orders that he should attend the emperor at Nicomedia. After the recent purges and executions, such a summons would inevitably be treated as a death sentence. Balancing his options, he decided to meet the returning legionaries of the emperor's army as they marched to their permanent garrisons along the Rhine and Danube. He probably hoped to win their support in raising him to the purple, and clearly had every hope of doing so, otherwise he would not have ventured all in such a risky move. However, unlike Castinus, he lacked the necessary imperial link. Failure resulted in his execution.[44]

As if the situation outside the palace in Nicomedia was not bad enough, inside its walls, division and dissent surrounded the young Alexianus. Maesa and Gannys had spent the winter attempting to persuade Elagabalus to become more circumspect in his devotion to his god. The impact of his behaviour was all too evident on the loyalty of the army, both in Syria and Bithynia. Gannys' opinion was valued by Elagabalus, the former being described as his 'associate in government'. The emperor acknowledged his debt to his mother's lover by making him agree to his marriage to Soamias. Furthermore, he was about to make him Caesar, and thus heir apparent. However, Elagabalus vehemently refused to moderate his religious convictions. These divisions came to a head in the private chamber of the emperor. The exchanges between Gannys and Elagabalus became increasingly heated, until Gannys, in a rage, made to unsheathe his sword. This act was a capital offence. Elagabalus demanded his guardsmen dispatch Gannys at once, but they refused. Frustrated, Elagabalus drew a Praetorian's sword and thrust it into Gannys, who died on the spot. Soamias' reaction to the murder of her lover is not recorded, but she remained faithful and loyal to her son until the bitter end. Recognizing it was not just futile, but also dangerous to question Elagabalus' religious devotion, Maesa managed to persuade the emperor to send ahead to Rome a massive picture of the stone obelisk of the god Elagabal. It was placed in the Senate house, high above the statue of Victory, so the senators could become accustomed to a representation of a god that was alien to their Greco Roman heritage. Elagabalus was probably convinced on the grounds that it forced the senators to make offerings to it, as they traditionally made an offering to the gods as they entered the Senate house at the start of meetings; its placement recognized the god Elagabal's supremacy over all other gods.[45]

As the winter snow melted and the thaw made roads passable again for the wagon carrying the huge stone representation of the god Elagabal, the imperial entourage continued their journey towards Rome. However, after passing through Thrace, the party headed north to Moesia and then along the Danube into both of the

Pannonias.[46] This is clearly significant, as their presence in Rome would in normal circumstances have been a priority in order to secure not only his position but the city itself. Only continued military unrest could have demanded the personal presence of the emperor. Aelius Decius Triccianus had commanded the II *Parthica* under Caracalla and was involved in Macrinus' plot. He was rewarded with the post of governor of Pannonia Inferior. Numerous milestones in the province carry his name, as he put the legionaries to work repairing the military roads along the frontier as well as improving discipline and building esprit de corps. He had been commended, as he had previously commanded the II *Parthica* 'with a firm hand'. It is also likely his family originated from the frontier zone, and so he had established links to the families of veterans settled in the area. However, in all surviving inscriptions from Pannonia Inferior, his name has been removed. According to Dio, he suffered '*damnatio memoriae*' and was executed by Elagabalus. This was, according to the historian, 'because of the Alban legion'.[47] The emperor, on his arrival in the province, would have been accompanied by the Praetorians, *equites singularii*, units of the Urban Cohorts and the II *Parthica*, which was based at Alba outside Rome. It can be conjectured that the members of these units held their previous commander in high regard, and the continued attachments of these units provided the opportunity for an attempted revolt by Triccianus. The loyalty of many of the vexillations returning from Syria and Bithynia was questionable, including those accompanying the emperor on his visit to Pannonia. Triccianus' loyalty lay with Macrinus, who had promoted him, rather than with the present incumbent, whom he probably saw as a usurper. He would have known that his career had been dealt a fatal blow with the capture and execution of Macrinus, and his previous role in the murder of Elagabalus' 'father' would, politically, have to be avenged. His decision to strike first was necessitated by previous obligations and service to Macrinus.

Later in the reign of Elagabalus, the distinguished noble Seius Carus was accused of conspiring with some of the soldiers in the II *Parthica* when it had returned to its permanent garrison outside the capital. Seius is described as 'rich, influential and prudent'. His wealth would have made believable promises to provide a donative to the soldiers who supported him, just as Maesa's wealth drew support to her. As the grandson of Fuscianus, a close *amicus* of Marcus Aurelius, he had the necessary '*nobilitas*' to attract support from the senatorial nobility. This must refer to his political conservatism, in contrast to the religious policies of Elagabalus and the emperor's choice of close *amici* whose low birth caused immense resentment amongst Rome's elite. This was more a senatorial conspiracy than a military one. The plot was discovered and Seius Carus was tried in private before the emperor, rather than before his peers in the Senate, and executed.[48]

The continued unrest amongst the legions that had been involved in the rebellion against Macrinus suggests that restoring discipline and loyalty was an extremely difficult task. The revolt of Maesa against Macrinus was one of many insurrections after the murder of what many, and most importantly the army rank and file, considered to be the legitimate emperor. The only difference between the revolt of Maesa and those of Verus, Gellius Maximus, Septimius Castinus, Triccianus and Seius Carus was that hers succeeded. Of them all, Castinus probably held the strongest claim to the throne, being a senator with a distinguished military record and a member of the Severan imperial family, if a distant one. Macrinus was himself a usurper, and had only survived for as long as he did as the soldiers and officers in the East recognized the need for unified leadership in the face of Parthian invasion. Once peace was established, that need was gone. A few months later, Macrinus was a hunted fugitive and declared an enemy of the state by the Senate. Dio repeatedly denounces the spirit of the time where any man in a position of power felt he had a right to the throne. The murders of Commodus, the last of the 'true' Antonines, and Caracalla undermined the dynastic principle of imperial rule.

The situation in AD 218 was essentially a civil war, as a number of men felt qualified to attain the throne, either through the prestige of their aristocratic heritage (such as Seius Carus), by claiming a tentative relationship to the imperial family (Elagabalus, Alexianus and Castinus) or through their control over significant military forces (Verus and Gellius Maximus). Historically, the Roman Empire had been in similar situations. The rule of the founding imperial family, the Julio-Claudians, had been ended with the suicide of Nero. This resulted in a civil war as generals fought for the throne. Vespasian, the ultimate winner of the conflict that erupted in AD 69, had no claim to the throne apart from the right earned at the point of a sword. The Flavian dynasty he founded was ended with the murder of his son, Domitian. Civil war was only averted by the elderly and childless senatorial nominee, Nerva, adopting Trajan, the experienced commander of the legions in Germania Superior. There is a strong possibility that the emperor was forced to do this, as Trajan threatened to revolt.[49] Septimius Severus, the founder of the Severan dynasty, only became emperor after using the legions on the Danube against Didius Julianus, the occupant of the throne in Rome. The army had always made emperors. The founder of the empire, Augustus, was himself the victor of five civil wars.

In many ways, the situation in AD 218 was very similar to these turning points in Roman history, and yet there was one important difference. Vespasian, Trajan and Septimius Severus were senators of undoubted political ability, with a formidable reputation as successful military commanders, who had gained vast experience in a range of offices and posts. These men were established figures. Elagabalus was none of these. He was a teenager who served as a priest in an obscure oriental cult, with no experience in the offices of state. His decisions would aptly demonstrate a complete lack of political acumen. He lacked the flexibility to compromise his all-encompassing religious beliefs with the cultural, political and religious reality of imperial Rome. It is indeed surprising that he survived as long as he did, and a reflection of the desire of the senatorial elite to avoid the bloodshed of another civil war, in which the ranks of the aristocracy would yet again be decimated.[50]

Chapter 4

A Palace Coup AD 218–222

'The False Antoninus [Elagabalus], on being praised once by the senate, remarked: "Yes, you love me, and so, by Jupiter, does the populace, and also the legions abroad; but I do not please the Praetorians, to whom I keep giving so much."' (Dio, 80.18.4)

Elagabalus was first and foremost the chief priest of his god and only secondly emperor of the Roman Empire. His religious devotion dominated his thinking, to the virtual exclusion of all else. The huge black stone representation of the divine, transported across half the empire, was placed in a temple befitting its status as the supreme deity. Medallions and coins portray a vast structure built in an open courtyard surrounded by high enclosing walls. The sacred stone was placed on the Palatine so the emperor could perform his priestly duties and place the imperial house under divine protection. The probable location is now under the church of San Sebastiano. As well as the usual imperial titles conferred on him by the Senate, Elagabalus insisted that these be preceded by the unique title of 'Most High Priest of the God Unconquered Sun Elagabalus'.[1] Another temple was built in the grounds of his suburban palace at Ad Spem Veterem, in the east of the city near the Porta Maggiore.[2] What horrified the Romans was his desire to supplant the supremacy of Jupiter Optimus Maximus, also called Jupiter Capitolinus, with his obscure Eastern god. Jupiter, in his many forms, was perceived as the protector and guardian of the Roman state, and the emperor's actions threatened the very safety of the empire itself. Both Herodian and Dio agree that it was not the emperor's sexual excesses that dominate the salacious *Historia Augusta*, but his religious policy that offended Roman sentiment.[3] The historian Dio, reflecting senatorial opinion, makes this explicit:

'The offence consisted, not in his introducing a foreign god into Rome or in his exalting him in very strange ways, but in his placing him even before Jupiter himself and causing himself to be voted his priest, also in his circumcising himself and abstaining from swine's flesh, on the grounds that his devotion would thereby be purer.'[4]

The cult was associated with orgiastic rites, ritual prostitution and circumcision, with a focus on religious purity. Its origins lay in a synthesis of Semitic, Hellenistic,

Phoenician and Eastern beliefs. However, our sources distort these ceremonies to portray a sex-crazed religious fanatic whose eventual murder was entirely justified in order the save Rome.[5] This propaganda would have been instigated by his successors: his cousin Alexander Severus, along with his mother Mamaea and grandmother Maesa. These rituals were not unusual in ancient religion; however, the supplanting of Jupiter Optimus Maximus was. Instructions were issued that in all public oaths and dedications, the name of the god Elagabal should precede those of the 'lesser' panoply of gods.[6] The traditional morning greeting of the emperor in the formal *salutatio* in the palace was distorted, as eminent senators and officials were instead forced to acknowledge the new supreme deity as well. The great and the good had to observe and often assist their emperor as chief priest in daily ceremonies. At the rising of the sun, the emperor emerged from the palace, probably accompanied by members of the imperial family, to be greeted by his *amici* and state officials gathered before the *Heliogabalium*, where he

'slaughtered a hecatomb of cattle and a large number of sheep which were placed upon the altars and loaded with every variety of spices. In front of the altars many jars of the finest and oldest wines were poured out, so that streams of blood and wine flowed together. Around the altars he and some Phoenician women danced to the sounds of many different instruments, circling the altars with cymbals and drums in their hands. The entire Senate and the equestrian order stood round them in the order they sat in the theatre. The entrails of the sacrificial victims and spices were carried in golden bowls, not on the heads of household servants or lower-class people, but by military prefects and important officials wearing long tunics in the Phoenician style down to their feet, with long sleeves and a single purple stripe in the middle. They also wore linen shoes of the kind used by local oracle priests in Phoenicia. It was considered a great honour had been done to anyone given a part in the sacrifice.'[7]

There are numerous images of the emperor sacrificing to Elagabal on coinage from the first part of the reign. A significant change, though, is evident in late AD 220, with coins carrying the legend *sacerd(os) dei solis Elagab(ali)*, *summus scarerdos Aug(ustus)*, or *Invicts Sacredos Aug(ustus)*, giving emphasis to his priestly rather than political role. Furthermore, the traditional religious imperial title of Pontifex Maximus is referred to second in his official title. The emperor is depicted in the sources as sacrificing in oriental dress rather than the traditional toga, with his head veiled. These religious ceremonies were often associated with grand displays, games, distributions of largesse and banquets to win popular favour for the 'new' god. Elagabalus would climb a large tower and personally throw down gifts upon the crowd below, including gold and silver cups, fine clothes, linen and even animals. In the ensuing crush, many were killed or injured.[8] The future Alexander Severus would have assisted his cousin in his priestly duties as well, but our sources have omitted this unfavourable information in an attempt to disassociate him from a religious policy that inflamed the anger of the elite. Dio is clear that his mother and grandmother took place in rites to Elagabal, so we must assume the whole imperial family did so, especially as both cousins had been brought up as priests in the cult.[9]

The emperor's religious devotion pervaded all aspects of imperial policy. Soamias and Maesa, recognizing his weak claim to the throne, had selected a wife from one of the most aristocratic families in Rome. Julia Cornelia Paula may also have been the daughter of the revered Severan jurist Julius Paulus, although this is open to conjecture. Alexandrian coins dating to August AD 219 carry her image, so their marriage took place soon after Elagabalus' arrival in Rome. Like Maesa and Soamias, she was granted the title of Augusta, but she was rapidly divorced. As chief priest, the emperor felt religious purity was essential and the unfortunate Paula had some blemish on her body which would affect the purity of their children, thus tarnishing their future ability to perform their religious duties to the god Elagabal. Paula was rapidly divorced, deprived of her titles and returned to private life.[10]

Elagabalus further alienated religious sensibilities in his new choice of bride. He chose Aquilia Severa, a Vestal Virgin, who was a priestess dedicated to Vesta, the goddess of the hearth. The college of the Vestal Virgins ensured that the sacred fire that burned in their temple was never extinguished. The Vestal Virgins were carefully selected by the Pontifex Maximus from girls of high birth exhibiting no physical defects. They took a vow of chastity in order to ensure their purity. After thirty years of service, they were freed from their vows and allowed to marry, but before this date, any carnal relations were punished by being sealed inside a room. Elagabalus' desire for pure 'godlike children' worthy to serve as chief priest to his god offended and scandalized Roman religious sensibilities. Dio's outrage is clear in his denouncement of this act 'most flagrantly violating the law' as he 'impiously defiled her'. He goes on to suggest the emperor should have been 'scourged in the Forum, thrown into prison, and then put to death'.[11] The emperor wrote to the Senate attempting to excuse his actions on the grounds that the marriage of a priest and priestess was 'fitting and sacred'. He also asked for their understanding on purely emotional terms: he had simply fallen in love. This was quite possibly the case, as, after a number of further divorces and marriages, he returned to her.[12] The impiety of the emperor was not forgiven, and his subsequent actions only intensified enmity and contempt. In divine symbiosis, the god Elagabal was married to the *Palladium*, which was kept away from public scrutiny in the Temple of

Vesta. The *Palladium* was an ancient statue of Athena and was believed to have been brought to Rome from Troy by the legendary Aeneas. Its safety was said to be linked to the survival of Rome itself, and as such it was considered a crime to move the idol from its secure location. Yet the warlike goddess Athena was not considered an ideal consort for the god, and so the statue of the goddess Urania, or Astarte, was summoned from Carthage, symbolically matching the sun god Elagabal with Astarte, the divine representation of the moon. Worship of this triad of gods had its origins in Syria itself, with Athena represented in her Roman form of Juno. The emperor commanded that the occasion of their marriage was to be celebrated by public and private festivities, and contributions were made towards their dowry.[13]

According to the *Historia Augusta*, probably based on the work of Marius Maximus, the contemporary senator and historian, Elagabalus transferred to the *Heliogabalium* 'the emblem of the Great Mother, the fire of Vesta, the *Palladium*, the shields of the *Salii*, and all that the Romans held sacred, purposing that no god might be worshipped at Rome save only Elagabal'.[14] Although not mentioned in Dio, Herodian describes a religious procession starting at the *Heliogabalium* on the Palatine to another temple, probably in the suburban palace and gardens of 'Ad Spem Veterem'. Dripping with religious symbolism, the black stone was elevated above all, both living and divine, spiritual and temporal:

'In the outlying district of the city he constructed a vast magnificent temple to which he brought the god at each mid-summer. He instituted many different festivals and constructed circuses [for horse-racing] and theatres, imagining that, if he provided chariot races and all kinds of spectacles and entertainments, and if he feasted the people all night long, he would be popular. The god was set up in a chariot studded with gold and precious stones and drawn by a team of six large, pure white horses which had been decorated with lots of gold and ornamented discs. No human person ever sat in the chariot or held the reins, which were fastened to the god as though he were driving himself. Antoninus [Elagabalus] ran along in front of the chariot, but facing backwards as he ran looking at the god and holding the bridles of the horses. He ran the whole way backwards like this looking up at the front of the god. But to stop him tripping and falling while he was not looking where he was going, lots of sand gleaming like gold was put down, and his bodyguard supported him on either side to make sure he was safe as he ran like this. Along both sides of the route the people ran with a great array of torches, showering wreaths and flowers on him. In the procession, in front of the god, went images of all the other gods and valuable or precious temple dedications and all the imperial standards or costly heirlooms. Also the cavalry and all the army joined in.'[15]

The gods of the Roman pantheon were given a secondary role, which would only serve to further alienate the devotees of these cults, as these gods and goddess now had a subsidiary role in serving the emperor's Supreme Being. Some were its servants, some its attendants and others its slaves. Alexandrian coinage celebrating this event dates the ceremony to AD 220/221.

Increasingly, the bemused populace were presented with unfamiliar religious rites with their emperor in his 'Assyrian' robes acting in increasingly 'unRoman' ways.[16] Their emperor was expected to demonstrate certain qualities that exemplified Roman qualities, including *dignitas*, *nobilitas* and *virtus*. *Dignitas* roughly equates to the modern concept of honour and prestige. However, *dignitas* could only be achieved by those held in the highest social esteem, the senatorial class. All ranks of Roman society expected their highest officers of state to hold *dignitas*. When the army which the Emperor Claudius had readied for the invasion of Britain was addressed by the imperial freedman Narcissus, the soldiers prevented him from speaking by loudly chanting over his speech, as they felt their honour was infringed by being addressed by a man lacking the necessary *dignitas*. Additionally, man's authority or *auctoritas* was completely dependent upon his *dignitas*, and indeed in the age of the Roman Republic, wars were waged by powerful politicians in defence of their *dignitas*. However, the emperor's own behaviour undermined his *dignitas* in a number of ways. All the sources criticize his adoption of the Eastern priestly clothes of the cult of Elagabal, although he also wore the traditional Roman toga on non-religious occasions. As part of his religious role, he also epilated himself, according to Dio, in order to appear more like a woman. Herodian elaborates further, describing how the emperor painted his eyes and put rouge on his cheeks, probably derived from the root of *anchusa* on a base of white lead. This was probably linked to his drive for purity rather than to his homosexuality.[17] His sexuality was not in itself an issue for the Romans; second-century emperors Trajan and Hadrian were both in all probability homosexual and also widely admired, especially by the soldiers, for their numerous military victories. What clearly was the issue was his lack of *virtus*. The Latin *virtus* derives from *vir*, meaning man. Originally, this essentially Roman concept did encapsulate masculinity and the strengths of the warrior, from which was derived their ability to rule:

'Now, the soul is divided into two parts, of which one partakes of reason and the other does not. Thus, when we are told to control ourselves, we are really being told to see to it that reason restrains impetuousness. In nearly every soul there is something naturally soft, abject, lowly, in one way or another spineless and listless. If that was all there were, nothing would be more repugnant than humanity; but reason stands ready as sovereign of all reason, which, striving on its own and advancing far, finally becomes perfect virtue [*virtus*].'[18]

Gradually, this concept developed associated qualities, including courage, prudence and self-control, summoned up as moral excellence. All these qualities were an anathema to the teenage emperor granted unlimited power. The emperor appeared to be a slave to self-gratification, rejecting reason, courage and restraint. According to Dio, he married his lover, Hierocles, whom he wished to make his heir, and behaved as his 'wife', contriving to be caught in the act of adultery so he could be reprimanded by his 'husband'. Another advisor, the athlete Zoticus, was supposedly chosen as a close companion in recognition of the size of his private parts. His full name, Aurelius Avitus Zoticus, suggests he was a freedman of Maesa, whilst his father had been a cook.[19] Escorted into the imperial presence along passageways and courts, illuminated by hundreds of torches, he addressed Elagabalus in the traditional manner, 'My Lord Emperor, hail.' The emperor sprang forward in the manner of a courtesan, requesting to be addressed as a 'lady', and was whisked off to the imperial baths. However, the night was only to end in disappointment as Zoticus failed to satisfy the emperor's demands. To those freedmen, imperial officials, senators and soldiers who attended and guarded the court, Elagabalus appeared the quintessential opposite of *virtus*. The Romans measured this ideal against the 'norms' of correct and proper conduct, and Elagabalus was found wanting. The emperor's lack of this quality threatened the very security of the state itself. To the senatorial elite, he would have appeared as totally unfit to govern.[20]

Bound up with the concepts of *dignitas* and *virtus* was that of *nobilitas*. *Nobilitas* was the prestige derived from aristocratic ancestors, based primarily from holding the highest office of state, the consulship. The Roman nobility took immense pride in the deeds of their famous predecessors, whose masks lined the walls of their houses and were carried in procession at their funerals. The ancestry of their present emperor was already questioned, and his claim to be the son of Caracalla, whose own *virtus* was evident to all, was undermined by his apparent addiction to lust and extravagance.[21]

To the Praetorians, mute observers of the emperor's antics, the greater offence was the emperor's choice of *amici*, his friends, who were admitted to the imperial *consilium*, the advisory council. In particular, the Guard were angered by the influence Hierocles held over the emperor. He appears to have been a client of another of the emperor's *amici*, Gordius, himself a chariot driver brought into the imperial inner circle by the emperor and given the post of praefectus vigilum. The Guard would later demand their removal from positions of influence, as their close proximity to the imperial throne, in their eyes, tarnished its prestige and lustre. The *Historia Augusta's Life of Elagabalus*, in contrast to the accounts of Dio and Herodian, emphasizes the sexual excesses of the emperor in order to titillate its audience, and consequently it attempts to link military discontent to Elagabalus' public promiscuity. The Guard would later demand the removal of the imperial advisors as the price of the emperor's life, rather than calling for sexual restraint.[22]

Maesa and Soamias would, as women, have not had an official role in imperial government. However, their unrestricted access to the emperor would have allowed then to regularly and informally influence imperial decisions. Hierocles was despised as an ex-slave and charioteer. He was a partner in the emperor's scandalous behaviour, whom he openly kissed in court. Yet Hierocles held the emperor enthralled, and so became 'exceedingly powerful'. When Zoticus made his appearance and became a serious rival for the emperor's affections, Hierocles engineered his demise and exile. The love-struck and besotted Elagabalus seriously considered making his lover Caesar, despite the objections of Maesa. A nominated successor who possessed even less *dignitas*, *nobilitas* and, most importantly, *virtus* than the present incumbent of the throne was too much for the elite, and especially the soldiers. According to Dio, it was this man's influence and power that the Guard resented above all else.[23]

The senatorial aristocracy would have been as angered as the soldiers at the elevation of lowly born upstarts to the rank of the emperor's friends and advisors, the 'Caesarini amici'. Senatorial opposition coalesced around the figure of Pomponius Bassus, who openly criticized the emperor's lifestyle and censored 'what went on in the palace'.[24] His marriage to Anna Aurelia Faustina, a descendant of the esteemed Emperor Marcus Aurelius, gave him immense prestige. Her two children – Pomponia Ummidia, born in AD 219, and Pomponius Bassus, born AD 220 – had the imperial blood of the 'true' Antonines flowing in their veins.[25] The aristocratic elite needed regular access to the emperor in order to influence imperial decisions on behalf of their clients and add to their own *dignitas* through membership of the imperial *consilium*. The *Historia Augusta* describes how the lowly born Zoticus would use his unrestricted access to the emperor to build up a complex network of obligations centred around the influence he held over Elagabalus. He made extravagant promises here, a threat there, dropped a discreet word on the direction of the emperor's thinking or granted *beneficia*, gifts, in his own name. His first post as a *cubicularius* with responsibility for the imperial bedchamber granted him unrestricted access to the emperor. However, he appears to have been a capable administrator, as he later reappears as a *nomenclator a censibus* under Alexander Severus. Other unpopular appointments included those of Claudius, who became

Prefect of the Annona, and Aurelius Eubulus, who was granted responsibility for state finances as *procurator summarum rerum*.[26] Power rested with those whom the emperor granted the influence to distribute imperial patronage. As the religious duties of the emperor occupied the majority of his time, imperial authority was increasingly delegated to these men of low social status. The senatorial aristocracy saw this position as theirs by right of superior birth, *nobilitas, dignitas* and education. As Elagabalus elevated new men from outside the aristocratic circle, the social cohesion that bound Roman society together came loose. That was the view of the elite, who looked to one of their own to restore their position as brokers of imperial *beneficia* and patronage. Elagabalus' naivety was rapidly producing division and conflict by excluding many members of the aristocracy from imperial favour.[27]

Members of the aristocracy looked to Pomponius Bassus. A descendant of a well-established aristocratic family, he had been governor of Moesia Superior between AD 212–217, which allowed him the opportunity to appeal to the loyalty of a number of legions along the Danube. His father had been a close *amicus* of Septimius Severus. Furthermore, his marriage to Annia Faustina not only gave him a powerful link to the imperial house of the 'true' Antonines through her grandmother, a daughter of Marcus Aurelius, but also to her own prestigious noble family of the Claudii Severi. Faustina's brother, Cn. Claudius Severus, had been granted the *suffect* consul of AD 212. Of lesser status than the 'ordinary' consulship, as the year was named after the two holders of this post, it was still the pinnacle of a senator's career and ennobled the family of the post-holder. A consul could reasonably expect future appointments to illustrious posts as governor of imperial provinces and offices, yet Cn. Claudius Severus was not to be granted another office until AD 223, when he held the prestigious office of Urban Prefect. This was one of the first appointments by Alexander Severus after the murder of Elagabalus. This striking hiatus in this aristocrat's *cursus honorum* can only be due to the emperor's suspicions of his loyalty through his close connections with Pomponius Bassus and links to the Antonines.[28]

Other members of prominent noble families appear, from their *cursus honorum*, to have fallen from favour with the accession of Elagabalus. Q. Anicius Faustinus had been appointed to the proconsular governorship of Asia by Macrinus, but he was understandably replaced in AD 219.[29] The Bruttii had been closely associated with Commodus through his wife, Bruttia Crispina. However, Septimius Severus suspected their allegiance, and it was not until AD 217 that Crispina's nephew, C. Bruttius Praesens, attained the 'ordinary' consulship. There his career appears to have ended, although his brother, C. Bruttius Crispinus, was granted an 'ordinary' consulship in AD 224 by Alexander Severus.[30] The loyal supporter and military commander of Septimius Severus, L. Marius Maximus, had a remarkable career up to the reign of Elagabalus. A Severan general of remarkable ability, he was rewarded with a *suffect* consulship in AD 199/200, and was then appointed to the governorships of Germania Inferior, Syriae Coelis, Africa and Asia by Septimius Severus and Caracalla. Remarkably, Caracalla's nemesis, Macrinus, made him Urban Prefect of Rome in AD 218–219. He then fell from favour under Elagabalus, as did his brother, L. Marius Perpetuus, whose last proconsular post is dated to AD 218–219. Marius Maximus used this as an opportunity to write a series of lost biographies in the style of the salacious historian Suetonius, ending with the life of Elagabalus. The *Historia Augusta* drew upon this work, as well as Herodian and Dio. He was another whose career was saved by Alexander Severus.[31]

Elagabalus was not blind to the consequences of denying all nobles access to the high-status offices that they felt their ancestry and *dignitas* deserved. He appointed as Urban Prefect a Fulvius who was possibly a member of the Antonine noble family, or 'gens', of the Fulvii Aemiliani, or should be identified with the *suffect* consul of AD 210, C. Fulvius Maximus.[32] Elagabalus chose to share the 'ordinary' consulship of AD 219 with the noble and well-connected Q. Tineius Sacredos, himself holding it for a second time. This was an immense honour.[33] Another eminent aristocrat favoured by the emperor was the grandly named M. Nummius Umbrius Primus Senecio Albinus, the 'ordinary' consul of AD 206, who was made proconsul of Asia. He had been adopted into the family of Umbrius Primus, *suffect* consul of AD 185/186. However, his genetic ancestors were even more illustrious, as they were related to the emperor of AD 193, Didius Julianus. A member of the patrician Vetii received the 'ordinary' consulship of AD 221, which he shared with an otherwise unknown Flavius Vitellius Seleucus. His name suggests he was from the Near East, probably Syria. This office was possibly his reward for supporting the revolt against Macrinus.[34]

Despite Elagabalus' attempt to retain the loyalty of the nobility, his close association with men of low birth – men like Gordius, Hierocles and Zoticus – undermined these intentions. Another contentious but powerful figure in the imperial entourage was Aurelius Eubulus, an Emesene who was appointed to the *fiscus*. He was hated and despised for his confiscations and depravity. The two Praetorian Prefects would have been powerful imperial advisors: the mysterious '….atus', whose full name has escaped the historical record, and Comazon. These were the *amici* who controlled access to the emperor, whose hands the aristocracy had to kiss and whose favour they were forced to cultivate. The nobility would feel humiliated having to beg favours from such men. The senator Pliny praised the second-century Emperor Trajan for his accessibility and openness to the flower of the senatorial and equestrian orders.[35] Not so Elagabalus.

The emperor moved to eliminate the senatorial threat to the throne. Pomponius Bassus, the focal point of this opposition, was summoned to the palace, and there was tried in private before the emperor and his *amici*, rather than by his peers in the Senate. He was accused of *majestas* and executed. The Senate was asked to post-humously pass sentence on its deceased leader. Anger and resentment now bubbled to the surface. The Machiavellian Maesa realized that her grandson's actions had not restored the political situation, but endangered the regime's very existence.

The summer of AD 221 saw the beginning of the end for Elagabalus, as Maesa started to formulate an insurance policy in case the Praetorians assassinated the emperor, as their loyalty was becoming increasingly problematic. The idea that Hierocles could be considered heir apparent by the emperor would have been the final straw. A possible revolt in Syria may have been a reflection of unrest in the army. According to the fifth-century historian Polemius Silvius, a Seleucus unsuccessfully revolted against the Emperor Elagabalus. He has tentatively been identified as Julius Antonius Seleucus, recorded as a governor of Moesia Inferior, who was possibly transferred to Syria Coele. Another possibility is the consul of AD 221, M. Flavius Vitellius Seleucus, probably a Syrian, which would place the revolt in early AD 222.[36] Both identifications have their problems. However, Maesa understood that her family's hold on the throne was becoming increasingly precarious. It became necessary for the emperor to appoint a more acceptable Caesar who could ensure the continuation of the 'Antonine' imperial house should her grandson be 'removed'. The difficulty would be in persuading the emperor to follow this course of action.

It is evident from the very beginning that Elagabalus resented any attempt to control his actions. Gannys had paid the price of trying to guide the headstrong teenager to follow the safer course. The emperor was entirely preoccupied with his divine duties as chief priest, to the detriment of his temporal responsibilities. Ingeniously, his grandmother played on these concerns to suggest he needed to share these duties with another who also came from the same priestly house, his cousin.[37] Alexianus, who we shall now call Alexander Severus, had no doubt been serving the god in a more subordinate role, and was clearly too young to take a share of the reins of government. However, the boy had extensive experience of serving as priest, both in Emesa at the great temple of Elagabal and probably in Rome itself. This would account for the unique titles describing the role of Alexander Severus on his adoption by his cousin as Caesar. However, Elagabalus demanded that it should be publically acknowledged that his heir was recognized as receiving his imperial status through the bequest of Elagabalus, the Augustus, who held greater status, power and *dignitas*.

The title borne by Alexander Severus as Caesar can be reconstructed from a number of partial inscriptions and dedications as *Nobilissimus Caesar imperii et sacerdotis*. In the past, this has been mistranslated as 'The most noble Caesar of the state and Elagabal'. However, this is a very clumsy translation, and surviving military diplomas indicate that the Caesar possessed only subsidiary status, carrying lesser *imperium* and lacking tribunician powers. Later inscriptions date Alexander

Severus' first tribunician year as AD 222, long after his adoption. From his title, the new Caesar clearly lacked secondary proconsular or tribunician *imperium*. A better translation would be: 'The most noble Caesar of the priest Emperor.' This title would fit with the political situation, with Elagabalus emphasizing that the Caesar owed his position entirely to him and the favour of the god Elagabal. This interpretation is also supported by coinage issued at the time referring to the *Indulgentia Aug*. A number of inscriptions and military diplomas refer to the Caesar with the title *imperatoris*, the traditional title granted an emperor and so indicating his legal status as heir designate, but Elagabalus saw his cousin's role in government as extremely limited and his status linked purely to his adoption by the Augustus.[38]

Dio provides colourful details of the formal adoption of Alexander Severus. He says Elagabalus

'brought his cousin Bassianus [Alexander Severus] before the Senate, and having caused Maesa and Soaemias [Soamias] to take their places on either side of him, formally adopted him as his son; and he congratulated himself on becoming suddenly the father of so large a boy – though he himself was not much older than the other – and declared that he had no need of any other child to keep his house free from despondency. He said that Elagabal [the god] had ordered him to do this, and further to call his son's name Alexander.'

Normally, when the emperor was present at a sitting of the Senate, he was flanked by the two consuls. The presence of women in a session of the Senate was forbidden and would be seen as an affront to the centuries-old traditions of Rome. Dio records a strange story of the spirit of Alexander the Great rising in the region of the Ister; accompanied by 400 male attendants wearing 'thyrsi and fawn skins', the spirit proceeded unhindered by troops, through Upper Moesia to Thrace. The members of this procession were permitted to use state lodgings and provisions without cost. At Byzantium, they crossed the Hellespont and landed at Chalcedon, where a religious ceremony took place which involved the burying of a wooden horse. The 'apparition' then promptly vanished. Dio is clear this event took place before Alexander Severus' appointment as Caesar and was linked to a premonition made to the emperor 'by someone else' that an Alexander from Emesa would succeed him. These events were clearly linked to the emperor's divine inspiration to adopt his cousin. Such a large procession that was allowed to draw upon state resources and travel unhindered through the provinces must have had some form of official sanction. The hand of Maesa can be seen in this. These 'divinely inspired events' were a vehicle used to convince the emperor of his god's sanctioning of the adoption of his cousin.[39]

The *Feriale Duranum*, a military document preserved in the sands of Dura Europas, dates Alexander Severus' promotion to the status of Caesar to 26 June AD 221.[40] The choice of the official name 'Alexander' for his cousin by Elagabalus was at the command of his god. However, this choice was not in imitation of the great Macedonian general, but the use of a common ancestral name and a logical extension of Alexianus. The first member of this native dynasty who received Roman citizenship from Augustus was also named Alexander. The *nomen* 'Severus' linked him to the founder of the imperial dynasty, Septimius Severus. By adopting this name, Elagabalus and Maesa also emphasized the Roman heritage of their dynasty, masking their Eastern origins. The date for the formal announcement of these new imperial arrangements was also carefully chosen to echo the arrangements of imperial Rome's founding emperor, Augustus, who on 26 June chose to announce the adoption of his wife's son, Tiberius, and in doing so established him as his designated heir. Maesa's purpose was to claim that the roots of the present dynasty could be traced through the Antonines all the way back to Rome's first emperor. It was an open secret that the legitimacy of Elagabalus and Alexander Severus' claim to the throne was based on weak foundations.[41]

Official imperial propaganda continued to disseminate the fiction that Elagabalus was the illegitimate child of Caracalla, but the same claim made on behalf of Alexander Severus now disappears. The name of Marcus Aurelius, that renowned Antonine emperor, was added to his official *nomen*. These names were also adopted by his supposed 'father', Caracalla, whose propaganda linked him to Alexander the Great. Coinage from AD 221 refers to the Caesar as the son of Elagabalus and grandson of Caracalla, not his son. Clearly, Elagabalus was concerned to reduce the status of his cousin. The presence of the emperor's mother and grandmother at his side before a formal meeting of the Senate was highly unusual, a calculated political statement signifying the unity of the imperial house in making this decision. On the same day, Alexander assumed the *toga virilis*, the formal recognition of entry into adulthood, despite the fact he was only a teenager.[42] On 10 July, the new Caesar was co-opted into the priesthood of the *sodales Antoniniani,* possibly to augment his role as emperor priest in the manner of his adopted father. Coinage, dating from AD 221/222, was issued showing M. Aurelius Alexander Caesar as *princeps iuventutis*, the symbolic leader of the equestrian order. Finally, to cement the illusion of a house united, it was agreed that both the senior Augustus and junior Caesar would share the ordinary consulship of AD 222.[43] The year would then carry both of their names and again emphasize the unity of the imperial family.

Letters were despatched to the governors and officials of the empire to announce these arrangements, which were to be circulated to the provincials. A fragmentary inscription has preserved parts of it and the Prefect of Egypt's covering letter. The inscription appears to link the adoption with the divorce of Elagabalus from the Vestal Virgin, Julia Aquilia Severa. In the surviving text, Elagabalus suggests that the removal of Aquilia Severa 'from his bedchamber' was at the insistence of both Maesa and the Praetorian Guard. The Guard were angered by the sacrilegious act of intimate contact with a Vestal Virgin, a crime that carried the death sentence. Maesa, however, was desperate to retain the loyalty of the soldiers. The inscription reads:

'For she, who wished to give you a son of hers [of mine?] ... a fitting prince [or 'future emperor'] and to win favour herself through her honourable character, and through whom, as it behoves me to pass over the rest in silence, my most valiant and most loyal soldiers, including the praetorian guards, ... , [have found?] me [able to refuse nothing that they asked?], shall not remain in my bedchamber.'[44]

The late source Eutropius appears to support this interpretation of events, as he describes how 'Aurelius Alexander ... was designated Caesar by the army.' Furthermore, despite Elagabalus' demand that his Caesar be virtually given honorary status, many appear to have been either ignorant of the subtleties of Alexander Severus' legal position, or deliberately chose to ignore it. A *graffito* from the quarters of the *cohort vigiles*, dated to AD 221, gives the Caesar the same status as Elagabalus. Another refers to Alexander as *Augg*, the double 'g' denoting that he was perceived as a co-Augustus and full partner in government.[45]

Maesa had clearly not lost complete control over Elagabalus. The emperor claimed to love Aquilia Severa, and the fact he later remarried her suggests he actually did. What is remarkable is the threat of Praetorian unrest held in the minds of Maesa, Soamias and the emperor. In a desperate attempt to restore the loyalty of the soldiers, Elagabalus was married to Pomponius Bassus' widow, Annia Aurelia Faustina. Their offspring would be the direct descendants of Marcus Aurelius. After a seemly delay, the couple were married at some point around 29 August AD 221.[46] However, the loveless marriage was soon over and she was divorced early in AD 222. Annia Faustina no doubt hated the man who had executed her first husband. Mercifully, she was allowed to retire to her estates and bring up her two surviving children.

Mamaea, Alexander's mother, appears to have had only a negligible role in these decisions. Unlike her mother and sister, Soamias, she had not been given the status of an 'Augusta', nor did she sit beside the emperor as he addressed the Senate.[47] According to our sources, it was Maesa who was instrumental in the elevation of Alexander Severus.[48] The Caesar's thoughts have been lost to history, but both mother and son were willing to bide their time until the adoption was formalized.

From that moment, Mamaea strove to win over all those alienated by the actions, policies and behaviour of her nephew. She must have known that this division within the imperial family would inevitably lead either to her own death alongside that of her son, or that of her sister and the emperor. She played for high stakes, and appears to have already gained a powerful ally in Maesa.

Alexander Severus was withdrawn by Mamaea from his role as priest to the god Elagabal. Instead, the young Caesar was ostentatiously given a traditional Roman education. The emperor was despised for his oriental, Eastern origins, which he shared with his cousin. Dio says he was given the nickname 'The Assyrian' as a derogatory label, whilst the historian himself calls the emperor 'Sardanapalus', a legendary Assyrian king infamous for dressing in female clothes and living a debauched life of decadence and sexual excess.[49] In contrast, Mamaea was going to 'Romanize' her more malleable offspring:

'After Alexander's appointment as Caesar, Antoninus [as Elagabalus is known in Herodian] wanted him to be trained in his own pursuits of leaping and dancing, and to share in his priesthood by wearing the same dress and following the same practices. But his mother, Mamaea, removed him from contact with such activities which were shameful and unbecoming for emperors. In private she summoned teachers of all the arts, and trained him in the exercise of self-control, introducing him to the wrestling schools and manly exercises, and gave him both a Latin and a Greek education.'[50]

The names of the tutors that appear in the *Historia Augusta's Life of Alexander Severus* are entirely fictional, the author combining real historical figures who had long since died by this period with those whom he has made up.[51] Also fictional is the further claim in the *Historia Augusta* that 'from an early age' Alexander Severus had been nurtured in the arts, literature and military training.[52] This is directly contradicted by Herodian in the above passage, who clearly states that this 'traditional' Roman education only commenced after he had been appointed Caesar. The historian had previously stated the young Alexianus had, along with his cousin, been a priest of Elagabal in Emesa.[53] Our sources are entirely biased in favour of Alexander Severus, and so would omit any mention of his participation in the cult practices of the oriental god once he arrived in Rome, just as his Eastern heritage is ignored. Yet Elagabalus' cultural background is held up for criticism and ridicule. However, the slightly more reliable *Life of Elagabalus*, based partly on the work of the contemporary politician and senator Marius Maximus, does preserve the names of two more probable tutors: a rhetorician named Silvinus and the famous jurist Ulpian.[54] Silvinus is otherwise unknown, but there is evidence that Ulpian was a legal advisor handling petitions (*a libellis*) in the service of the young Caesar at this time. In a later edict, the emperor Alexander Severus refers to Ulpian as *parens meus*, my parent. Herodian describes some of the tutors as 'extremely distinguished', and Ulpian was certainly that.[55]

Along with his own mentor, Papinian, Ulpian is ranked amongst the greatest lawyers in the history of Rome. He had served as a secretary for petitions, *a libellis*, under Septimius Severus, and as a supporter of Caracalla, he survived the purges of Geta's supporters, unlike Papinian. Around AD 213, he was an assessor, or legal advisor, attached to a praetor. The Justinian Codes preserve ninety-five imperial rescripts from these two reigns that bear his name. He remained close to the imperial family, as he knew that Mamaea was permitted to retain the status granted to the wife of a consul despite that fact her second husband, the father of Alexander Severus, had not attained this rank. He appears to have been a part of Julia Domna's intellectual circle, and probably through this, became an *amicus* of her sister, Julia Maesa. Other probable surviving members of this circle were Paul, the historians Marius Maximus and Cassius Dio, the sophist Philostratus and the writer Aelian. Many of these intellectuals would play a significant role in the early years of Alexander Severus' reign, no doubt chosen by Maesa for their previous loyalty and friendship, *amicitia*, to her house. From c. AD 213–217, Ulpian devoted much of his time to writing a significant number of works on Roman law. With the proclamation of the 'Antonine Constitution', virtually all previous non-citizens were now subject to Roman law rather than the laws of their local city or territory. Ulpian was born in Tyre, and would have been well aware that many of his fellow Greeks would need access to legal works that explained the complexities of the Roman legal system. Over 300,000 words survive from this immense catalogue, yet this is probably only an eighth of the total.[56]

The *Historia Augusta* contradicts Herodian in stating that it was Elagabalus who appointed tutors for Alexander Severus.[57] However, the two accounts are not mutually exclusive. Through his adoption of the Caesar, Elagabalus would be expected to ratify the teachers of his 'son', but it appears the choice of teachers was down to Maesa and Mamaea. At this stage, relations between Elagabalus and Maesa remained positive; after all, he had accepted her advice on the appointment of his cousin as Caesar and heir.

The emperor was not adverse to his 'son' being educated along traditional Greco-Roman lines. However, it quickly became evident that this was part of an elaborate presentation of the Caesar as a ready alternative and rival for the throne. The nobility shared a cultural identity that came from an education in the Greek and Roman literary classics, philosophy and the practical skills of rhetoric and oratory. This was termed *padiera*, and defined the elite; those lacking this quality were considered inferior, whatever their 'official' status in the social hierarchy.[58] Wrestling helped to develop the *virtus* of the Caesar, especially as the palace guards would be present in these training sessions. Herodian describes these as 'manly arts'.[59] Yet all this would have been undermined if he continued in his priestly duties. Herodian describes the rites involved in the worship of the god Elagabal as 'leaping and dancing' in a 'frenzy', the priest emperor's 'face made up more elaborately than a modest woman would have done, and effeminately dressed up in golden necklaces and soft clothes, dancing for everyone to see in this state'.[60]

The coinage issued at this time offer a stark contrast in their propaganda. Elagabalus' coins show the priest emperor sacrificing wearing 'Parthian' trousers and long cloak, with the image of the supreme deity on the reverse. Those issued in the name of his Caesar bear no image of Elagabal, and instead carry the legend *pieta augusti*, the piety of the emperor, on the reverse. Instead of depicting the god Elagabal, they show priestly emblems associated with the traditional Roman cults; a *patera* (a libation dish), a *lituus* or curved priest's staff and a *simpulum*, a long-handled ladle. Alexander Severus is, significantly, depicted in the traditional Roman toga.[61] Mamaea clearly had the support of Maesa in this revising of the role of the Caesar. Additionally, Mamaea started to distribute money to the soldiers, clearly to transfer their loyalty to Alexander Severus.[62] Such money must have come from the vast wealth of Maesa. The Praetorians were readily won over. Herodian describes how 'they inclined more favourably towards Alexander, expecting better things of a boy who was receiving such a modest and serious education. And realizing that Antoninus [Elagabalus] was plotting against the boy, they kept a close watch over him.'[63]

The harmony of the divine imperial house collapsed into division, plot and counter-plot. Elagabalus was understandably enraged by this betrayal. Alexander Severus' tutors were removed, some exiled – including Ulpian – while others, including Silvanus, were executed. These men were charged with corrupting the young Caesar. The emperor's own *amici* had also fallen under suspicion of favouring Alexander Severus, Mamaea and Maesa. Both Zoticus and Comazon were also exiled. However, despite Elagabalus bribing the Praetorians himself, the majority remained resolutely loyal to Alexander Severus.[64] The emperor formally forbade his 'son' access to his presence and attempted to annul the adoption. The account of the conspiracies recorded in the *Historia Augusta* are incredibly detailed, and it is quite possible that these were based upon the work of Marius Maximus, who was probably in Rome at this time. He had been held in high regard by Caracalla, being granted the unprecedented distinction of holding the proconsular governorships of both Africa and Asia for a second time, and under Macrinus had been given the prestigious post of Urban Prefect at Rome from AD 218–219. However, his career came to a sudden stop under Elagabalus, but as a member of the aristocratic elite, he probably remained in the capital, watching and waiting, but not, at this stage, writing.[65]

The *Historia Augusta* describes a unique episode in imperial history, with the normally compliant Senate acting as one in resisting an imperial request. Elagabalus 'commanded the Senate to take away from Alexander the name of Caesar. But when this was announced to the Senate, there was a profound silence.' Reading between the lines, the *Historia Augusta* suggests this was due to shock, as Alexander Severus 'was loved by the soldiers and acceptable to the Senate and the equestrian order'.[66] Even in these circumstances, senators risked the charge of *majestas*, or treason, in opposing the emperor's demands, which in themselves had force of law. The *lex de imperio Vespasiani* recognized that the ultimate source of imperial authority derived from the Senate, but once granted, the emperor possessed unlimited power. By the mid-second century, ratification of the emperor's proposals was a mere formality. A series of orations delivered by Marcus Aurelius were not even discussed, but passed in a single vote.[67] Ambitious senators, hoping for imperial favour – a praetorship, consulship, money, estates or access to the imperial *concilium* – could often be found supporting a request. Yet here, none did. The emperor was met with stony silence. The hand of Maesa was surely behind this. Despite holding a catalogue of prestigious titles – *Augusta, mater castrorum et senatus* (mother of the camps and Senate) and *avia Augusta* (grandmother of the emperor) – she held no official or legal position. However, just as the emperor held his position due to her scheming and connections, so too would many of the Senate. Many would also have made a political calculation: who was more likely to emerge victorious from the conflict that divided the court? Maesa, Mamaea and Alexander Severus or the emperor Elagabalus and his mother? It was obvious to all, and a heavy price would be paid for supporting the losing side. A less naïve ruler would now have appreciated the weakness of his position and accepted the status quo whilst slowly consolidating his power. Not so Elagabalus. He now resorted to more underhand methods.

Elagabalus appears to have rejected the advice of his mother and grandmother, and instead sought that of Hierocles and Gordius. The first half of the *Life of Elagabalus* does appear to be based on some reasonably accurate information, unlike the second half, which lapses into flights of fiction that help to add bulk to the author's account. The detailed description of the emperor's attempts to murder his Caesar, which are compressed in both Dio and Herodian, appear stylistically separate from the main body of this work, and were probably incorporated verbatim into the chronological sequence of events leading up to the murder of Elagabalus. This account is probably based upon Marius Maximus' lost work.[68] According to the *Historia Augusta*, the assassination of Alexander Severus was arranged whilst the Caesar was in the imperial palace on the Palatine with Maesa and, no doubt, Mamaea. Elagabalus had attempted to suborn a number of court officials who had access to the boy. They were promised lavish rewards on the successful completion of their task. The emperor sent a letter to the Praetorian Camp that ordered them to 'take away from Alexander the name of Caesar'. By this, he expected the Guard to remove Alexander Severus' name from their standards and, as he would no longer be an official member of the imperial family, he would no longer be entitled to an escort or guard. As a short-term measure, inscriptions carrying the name of Alexander Severus in the Praetorian Camp were smeared with mud. This was in imitation of an official *damnatio memoriae*, where the name of anyone convicted of *majestas* was permanently removed from all public and private inscriptions in order to obliterate their memory from history. To avoid being caught up in the assassination attempt, and perhaps provide a flimsy alibi, the emperor left his mother and the remainder of his family on the Palatine, and retired to his suburban palace in the east of the city, near the modern-day Porta Maggiore. The Gardens of Spes Vetus, translated as the Gardens of Ancient Hope, was the favourite palace of the emperor. It was named after the Temple of Hope, built in 477 BC on the site of the battle where the legendary Horatius had defeated Rome's Etruscan overlords. Septimius Severus had built a massive new residence there, which included a large set of baths and a long colonnaded portico over 350 metres long. A circus had been added by Caracalla, with the starting gates next to the palace. Elagabalus added a tower either side of these gates and had an obelisk transported from Hadrian's villa at Tivoli to stand on the central island. A portico connected the circus with a three-storey amphitheatre was also constructed by Elagabalus. The building could hold 3,500 people and was probably used for private shows provided by the emperor to honoured guests. A massive arcaded audience hall was also added, and a temple to the god Elagabal which housed the black stone when the emperor was in residence, having been transported to its second 'home' from the Palatine with full religious ceremony.[69]

The emperor felt safe and secure in these opulent surroundings, especially as the barracks of the Imperial Horse Guard lay close by. As Soamias was left behind on the Palatine, it would appear she had not been consulted. Furthermore, her absence might have looked suspicious to her mother and sister. The Praetorians, however, were incensed when they saw the statues of Alexander Severus being smeared with mud. Some of the soldiers hurried to the palace on the Palatine to secure the safety of the Caesar, whilst another smaller group rushed to the Gardens of Spes Vetus, with murder in mind. Upon entering the Palatine, the soldiers immediately placed the Caesar, his mother and grandmother under protective guard and proceeded to escort them to the Praetorian Camp. This was a public confirmation of Alexander Severus' status of Caesar. According to Herodian, the plot to murder the Caesar was foiled by Maesa, who 'missed none of Antoninus' [Elagabalus'] machinations, since his behaviour was naturally unsubtle and he was totally indiscreet about his plans in words and actions'. The wily Maesa would have run a network of spies amongst the emperor's *amici*, slaves, freedmen and guards. Significantly, the Praetorians offered no escort to Soamias, who had to trail along behind the imperial litter, walking the whole way on foot. This was not only a deliberate insult – the symbols and accoutrements of her status as an Augusta cast aside – but also indicated that she was considered to be as guilty as her son. The humiliated Soamias can only have feared the worst and despaired of ever seeing her son again.[70]

The *Historia Augusta* provides a vivid description of events at the Gardens of Spes Vetus:

> 'Then the soldiers went to the gardens, where they found Varius [Elagabalus] making preparations for a chariot race and at the same time eagerly awaiting news of his cousin's murder. Alarmed at the sudden clatter of soldiers, he crouched down in a corner and covered himself with a curtain which was at the door of the bed chamber, sending one of the prefects of the Camp [Praetorian Prefects] to quiet the soldiers there and the other to placate those who had just entered the gardens. Then Antiochianus, one of the prefects, reminded the soldiers of their oath of allegiance and finally persuaded them not to kill the Emperor – for, in fact, only a few had come and the majority had remained with the standard.'[71]

The two Praetorian Prefects, Antiochianus and probably the mysterious '…atus',[72] had saved the emperor's life; not, however, by using their authority, as both appear to have been at odds with the general mood of their soldiers, but by an appeal to the soldiers' oath made to the gods to protect the safety of the emperor before all else. The Latin term for the military oath was *sacramentum*, which was derived from the Latin *sacris*, or sacred. Herodian describes the rejection of this oath as an act of impiety, the oath itself possessing some form of religious power and the breaking of such an oath offending the gods and being contrary to divine law.[73] The argument was chosen wisely, as an appeal to the soldiers' loyalty to the imperial house of the Severans, or even to their loyalty to Caracalla – whose son Elagabalus claimed to be – would have had fatal consequences. Dio explicitly states that the soldiers rejected the official propaganda of the emperor, as 'his deeds' showed 'that he was not the son of Antoninus [Caracalla] at all, and was coming to favour Alexander, as really being sprung from him'.[74] Mamaea's money no doubt helped to facilitate this belief. Elagabalus now faced death for a second time as he was brought to the Praetorian barracks.

The situation at the Praetorian Camp had rapidly deteriorated. The Guard had rioted, causing 'a terrible tumult', and demanded the presence of the emperor.

The Praetorian Prefect, probably '...atus', was joined by his colleague and the terrified emperor. Entreaties and 'supplications' gradually extinguished the mutiny. However, the Praetorians made a series of demands that were forced upon the emperor and his Praetorian Prefects. Firstly, his *amici*, who encouraged his licentious lifestyle and undermined the qualities of *virtus*, *nobilitas* and *dignitas* so admired by the rank and file, were to be dismissed, including Gordius and Hierocles. The dismissal of his lover Hierocles was too much for Elagabalus, who 'offered piteous pleas and bewailed him in tears; then pointing to his own throat, he cried: "grant me this one man, whatever you may have been pleased to suspect about him, or else slay me."' The soldiers were unimpressed and he was forced to dismiss them all.[75]

The emperor now had to acquiesce to the remainder of the demands. The Praetorian Prefects, as part of the imperial *consilium*, were charged with ensuring the Augustus chose a more respectable lifestyle. The prefects were also to guard the young Caesar, suggesting Elagabalus had withdrawn the official Praetorian escort when he attempted to reject Alexander Severus' status of Caesar. However, Dio makes clear that the soldiers had continued to protect the safety of the young Caesar 'sedulously'. The restoration of a military escort would publicly demonstrate Alexander Severus' imperial status. None of the emperor's *amici* were allowed access to the boy. The author of the *Historia Augusta* claims that this was in case 'he imitate their baseness'.[76] However, this proviso was more likely due to fears of an assassination attempt, as both Maesa and Mamaea retained control over his education and all other aspects of his life:

> 'Realising that Antoninus [Elagabalus] was plotting against the boy, they kept a close watch over him. Mamaea, his mother, would not allow him to taste any food or drink sent by the emperor. The boy did not make use of cooks and cupbearers who were in the general employment in the palace – only men selected by Mamaea and approved for their complete loyalty.'[77]

The choice of the Praetorian Prefects as censors of the emperor's behaviour is surprising. Soamias was clearly not trusted to fulfil this role, whilst Maesa was now positively identified as siding with Mamaea and Alexander Severus.

Elagabalus was not one to accept a settlement forced upon him, so grew increasingly resentful. Rejecting the agreements with both Maesa and the Praetorians, he divorced Annia Aurelia Faustina, returning to the Vestal Virgin Aquilia Severa. Hierocles also appears to have regained his position at the side of the emperor, as he was to share his lover's fate. Furthermore, Elagabalus refused to acknowledge his Caesar and continued to deny him any opportunity of public recognition.

He was not 'to be seen at public salutations or at the head of processions'.[78] These events probably included the morning salutations in the audience chamber of the palace, religious ceremonies and a seat in the imperial box during the gladiatorial games or chariot races. However, there was one ceremonial occasion where the presence of the Caesar alongside that of the Augustus could not be avoided. Both were to attend the consular procession on 1 January AD 222 as the ordinary consuls for the year. The centuries-old inauguration ceremony started with the two candidates, dressed in purple robes adorned with gold and silk, who proceeded from their residence to the Senate house to greet the senatorial order, who then accompanied them, along with the officers of state, members of all the priestly colleges and the members of the equestrian order, to the Temple of Jupiter Optimus Maximus on the Capitol. Sacrifices, prayers and oaths were made to the god there. The ceremony was one of Rome's most important religious and state occasions.

When the day arrived, the emperor refused to appear in public alongside his cousin. The Praetorians were probably waiting to escort the two to the Senate house and Temple of Jupiter. The ceremony could only take place during daylight hours, and so would probably have begun at dawn. However, Alexander Severus, his mother and grandmother, the guard, senators, equestrians and officers of state were kept waiting. The Praetorians had eventually had enough. It was apparent to all that these soldiers were about to take matters into their own hands. Around midday, Maesa and Soamias entered the private quarters of the emperor to inform him that the soldiers were threatening to kill him 'unless they saw that harmony was established between himself and his cousin'. It was once again the threat of imminent death that brought Elagabalus to his senses. He put on his ceremonial toga and headed the imperial procession alongside Alexander Severus. However, once he had entered the Senate and escorted Maesa to a seat, he refused to continue to the Temple of Jupiter. The city praetor was forced to undertake the religious ceremonies on behalf of the emperor. Although this account only appears in the *Historia Augusta*, it appears to be supported by the coinage issued to commemorate the joint consulship. Coins issued in early AD 222 show the consular procession, but the two consuls appear separately and alone. Herodian also alludes to this episode by stating that the Caesar was not seen 'at the head of processions'.[79]

Shortly after this, a very brave individual, or one exhibiting an astounding lack of emotional intelligence, approached the emperor to congratulate him on holding the consulship with his son. Elagabalus replied cryptically: 'I shall be more fortunate next year; for then I am going to be consul with a real son.' Perhaps his intention was to produce his own offspring with the priestess Aquilia Severa, as had been the original intention of his marriage to her in AD 220.[80]

The *Historia Augusta* also refers to an unusual imperial order commanding the whole Senate to leave the city. The emperor clearly resented its open support for

Alexander Severus. This is placed chronologically after the failure of the emperor to complete the consular ceremonies. However, it does not appear in either Dio or Herodian, and is often dismissed by modern historians.[81] According to the account, many senators were so desperate to leave the city for fear of execution that they commandeered any animal that fell in their path. However, one consular senator, Sabinus, remained in the city. The emperor ordered a centurion to execute him. However, the soldier was partially deaf and misheard the command, thinking he was ordered to 'Drive him out of his house' (*Aede pelle*) instead of the actual order to 'Give him a good slash' (*Caede belle*). Sabinus' life was consequently saved. P. Catius Sabinus could be identified with this individual. He held a 'suffect' consulship in AD 208–210, followed by an 'ordinary' consulship in AD 216. The honour of a second consulship after such a short period suggests he was a close *amicus* of Caracalla. The Catii went on to hold consulships and prestigious positions under Alexander Severus. Ulpian, a stalwart adherent of Maesa, also dedicated a number of his works to this man.[82] Perhaps there is some credence to the story. Could the emperor have exiled some prominent senators from Rome, wrongly interpreted by the author of the *Historia Augusta* as meaning the whole Senate? The leaders of the Senate are often identified as the embodiment of the Senate itself, and it was they who provided the leadership of the senatorial opposition to the emperor.

Inscriptions from AD 222 maintained the fiction of imperial harmony. However, Elagabalus continued to plot his cousin's downfall. Events came to a head on 12 March, when the emperor foolishly decided to test the levels of support that existed for Alexander Severus.[83] He deliberately spread a rumour that the Caesar was seriously ill and on the point of death. The Praetorians naturally assumed he had been poisoned in a conspiracy instigated by the emperor. Refusing to leave their camp or guard the palace, the Praetorians demanded the presence of Alexander Severus in their camp at the shrine dedicated to Mars, the god of war. This was not only a veiled threat but also a deliberate slight against the emperor's promotion of the god Elagabal as supreme deity. The standards and statues of the emperors, including that of the Caesar, were also kept there. The emperor realized he had overreached himself. Symbolically placing his young cousin in the imperial litter beside him, he rushed to the Praetorian Camp. He clearly hoped that as they emerged together, the soldiers would accept that their demand for imperial harmony had finally been attained. The gates to the fortress were opened and the imperial party was escorted to the shrine.[84]

It is likely that at this point the emperor's fate had already been sealed. This was the second time he had been summoned to the Praetorian Camp. On the first occasion, he had been forced to make a number of promises in order to save his life. Those promises had been broken, and all trust in the Augustus and his Praetorian Prefects was now shattered. There would be no second chances. As the two cousins were brought through the barracks, Elagabalus became aware that the Praetorians were greeting Alexander Severus with enthusiastic shouts, which is understandable in the circumstances. However, there were no greetings or salutations directed towards him, as would normally be expected for the emperor. His initial fears were now consumed by fury and rage. Herodian uses the word 'acclaimed' in describing the cheering and adulation the Caesar received. If Alexander Severus was indeed being acclaimed 'Augustus', it would account for Elagabalus' response.[85]

The imperial party remained at the shrine overnight. The accounts of Dio and Herodian diverge at this point, but are not mutually exclusive. Herodian describes the furious emperor issuing orders for the arrest of those Praetorians who had been too enthusiastic in their support of his cousin. He also ordered the arrest of others who were accused of 'sedition and riot'. Surprisingly, these arrests were made, but the consequences were not conducive to the restoration of order. Meanwhile, according to Dio, the two mothers, Soamias and Mamaea, engaged in exchanges of invective, accusation and counter-accusation. The behaviour and actions of all only served to fan the flames of insurrection. The Praetorian Prefects noticeably played no part in calming the passions of their soldiers. Elagabalus and his mother eventually realized their guards had turned into captors, and that they were awaiting execution. In despair, their thoughts turned to escape. The emperor was hidden by his mother in a chest which was to be removed from the Praetorian Camp, and they nearly succeeded in their plan. However, his discovery brought death. Soamias attempted to protect her son by using her body as a shield against the blows that rained down. They died in each other's arms. Elagabalus was 18 years old.[86]

This was not the end of the slaughter. Both Dio and Herodian agree that the Praetorians now attacked all those associated with Elagabalus who were trapped inside the Praetorian Camp. Both Praetorian Prefects died with their emperor, as did Hierocles. It appears the soldiers then went on the rampage, hunting down other *amici* of Elagabalus. Aurelius Eubulus joined his emperor in death; he had made numerous confiscations whilst in charge of the *fiscus*, the imperial finances. These were probably the estates of those charged with *majestas*. The soldiers, who had been joined by a mob of rioters, fell upon him and tore his body apart. The Prefect of Rome, Fulvius, shared the same fate.[87]

The account of these events in the *Historia Augusta* deviates significantly from that in both of our other sources. The attack on the emperor by the Praetorians is described as a pre-planned conspiracy in the *Historia Augusta*, whereas in Dio and Herodian it is presented as a spontaneous response to the news of the supposed illness of the Caesar. The emperor is also described as being murdered in the latrines of the imperial palace after his *amici* had been slain.[88] The late Roman historian Aurelius Victor describes his murder taking place in the Praetorian Camp, whilst the *Epitome de Caesaribus* and Eutropius merely comment on his death in a military insurrection.[89] At this point in its narrative, the *Historia Augusta* is considered reasonably reliable, but the accounts of two contemporary historians, Dio and Herodian, have to be accepted before that of a later author who was drawing upon a now lost work, whether that be Marius Maximus, *Ignotus* or the elusive *Kaisergeschichte*.[90]

However, all our sources agree that the bodies of the emperor and his mother were desecrated, their heads cut off and their corpses handed over to the baying crowds outside the camp. The body of Elagabalus was then dragged by hooks around the city, after which the mob attempted to throw it down a sewer, but the entrance proved to be too small. The body was instead thrown into the River Tiber from the Aemilian Bridge.[91] This was the fate inflicted on the bodies of common criminals. It was an extension of punishment beyond death and was considered an extreme reaction. The corpses of most emperors who were condemned on their fall were treated with respect; only Galba, Vitellius, Macrinus and his son and, later, Maximinus Thrax were defiled in this manner. This is a reflection of the hatred Elagabalus induced amongst many sections of Roman society.[92]

The reign of Elagabalus lasted three years and nine months.[93] His survival for this length of time is in itself remarkable, considering the alienation of the Praetorians, the Senate and significant numbers of the populace. His religious policies were revolutionary in reducing the status of the whole pantheon of Roman gods and raising the position of his god to that of supreme deity. His reign also marked the first time in Roman history that religion was elevated above the secular affairs of state. There had been no official distributions of monies since the emperor's marriage to Julia Cornelia Paula in AD 219, but the discipline of the Praetorians had been undermined by constant bribery and soliciting by Mamaea, supported by Maesa and the emperor himself.[94]

The Praetorians had been instrumental in the preservation or overthrow of all emperors since Septimius Severus. They had been witnesses to the conflict between Caracalla and his brother, Geta. Just as the palace had been physically divided between them, so was the Guard. On the murder of his brother, Caracalla immediately rushed to the Praetorian Camp, and only with difficulty did he win them over. A massive pay rise for the Guard and, to a lesser degree, the rest of the army, helped to secure their loyalty. The soldiers admired the *virtus* of the emperor, who modelled himself on the greatest of all commanders, Alexander the Great. Caracalla described himself as a 'fellow soldier'. Military victories, both real and contrived, secured the soldiers' loyalty. His successor, Macrinus, had to hide his involvement in the assassination of Caracalla from the soldiers, knowing this information would lead to his own death. Macrinus again issued a large donative on his accession, promising another on the elevation of his son. Yet the conditions in the temporary camps and losses at the Battle of Nisibis, combined with persistent rumours of his role in the murder of Caracalla, undermined the loyalty of the army. The emperor's decision to flee the battle against Elagabalus and Maesa was probably precipitated by the sight of the Praetorians changing sides. The majority of these soldiers came from the semi-Romanized Danubian frontier, having gained promotion from the legions stationed on Rome's militarized frontiers. They were loyal to their commanders, not to the concept of a state. As their commander-in-chief, the emperor had to earn their loyalty through displaying those same skills and virtues that win battles.[95] Most Praetorians would have served the emperors through civil wars and palace conflict. Some would have retired and others would have been promoted to senior positions in the army. All, though, would have understood, as did the senator Tacitus, that it was the army that made emperors, especially those that guarded his life.

Herodian, in his description of the Praetorians' decision to murder Elagabalus, tellingly describes how the soldiers felt 'their case was just'.[96] In other words, because of Elagabalus' rejection of his previous promises to share power with Alexander Severus and lead a 'virtuous' life, and his continued attempts to murder their Caesar, their own sacred vow was now invalid. The demotion of the gods before Elagabal would also have served to negate their sacred oath to protect their emperor. On the murder of Elagabalus, the Praetorians would have raised the young Caesar on the tribunal in the centre of their camp. The new emperor would also be expected to address the assembled ranks in the form of an *adlocutio*. He would traditionally have been dressed in armour and the military cloak, or *paludamentum*. The soldiers would stand in serried ranks in full armour, with shields and spears, with the imperial standards, minus the images of Elagabalus, at the front. The centurions and officers would have enforced silence to enable the speech to be heard, although most would have been too far away to hear. The end of the speech was greeted with the roar of the thousands present, with Alexander Severus acclaimed as Augustus.[97] We can only wonder what courage the young boy would have been able to muster, having just witnessed the mutiny of his Guard and perhaps the mutilated bodies of his cousin and aunt. His mother would have been present, although none of our sources mention the whereabouts of his grandmother. After being hailed emperor in the Praetorian Camp, the youngster was escorted by the Guard to the palace on the Palatine.[98]

Maesa had preserved her dynasty, but at the cost of the life of her daughter and grandson. She had tricked Elagabalus into elevating his cousin to the rank of Caesar as insurance against her overthrow. Cold? Calculating? Yes. However, the surprising length of Elagabalus' reign is probably down to her political acumen. Her actions had also probably saved her own life, along with those of both Alexander Severus and Mamaea. Age was rapidly catching up with her, but she now began to build again; this time on firmer foundations.

Chapter 5

Regency AD 222–223

'Domitius Ulpianus, praetorian prefect and my parent'
Taken from an imperial rescript of Alexander Severus, dated 1
December AD 222 (CJ 4.65.4.1)

The *Feriale Duranum* records the official start of the reign of Alexander Severus as sole emperor on 13 March AD 222. This document, preserved in the ruins of the Roman fortress of Dura Europas on the Euphrates, records the religious calendar followed by the garrison throughout the year. It includes the sacrifices due to deified emperors on the day of their accession to the throne. Unfortunately, the section bearing the *dies imperii* for Alexander Severus is badly damaged:

'3 days before the Ides of March: because emperor Caesar Marcus Aurelius Severus Alexander was acclaimed emperor, to Jupiter a male ox, to Juno a female ox, to Minerva a female ox, … to Mars a male ox; and because emperor Caesar Marcus Aurelius Severus Alexander Augustus was first acclaimed emperor by the soldiers …, public prayer.

'1 day before the Ides of March: because Alexander, our Augustus, was acclaimed Augustus, *pater patriae* and *pontifex maximus*, public prayer; to the genius of our lord Alexander Augustus a bull.'

There is a suggestion that he was hailed *imperator* by the soldiers and then recognized as sole emperor by an impromptu session of the Senate, with Alexander Severus safely ensconced in the palace as the mob dragged the mutilated body of his adopted father around the streets of the capital. Once order had been restored, the Senate reconvened to grant the new Augustus additional titles. It is significant that Alexander Severus ordered the army to celebrate both of his acclamations, as his advisors tried to create the impression of the restoration of the traditional Augustan settlement of the imperial government working in harmony with the authority of the Senate. However, no mention is made of the Senate, so as not to offend the army, which, after all, supported him in his conflict with his cousin and played a vital role in his elevation. Herodian does not record any meetings of the

Senate, which granted him the titles of Augustus, then later *pater patriae* (Father of his Country) and *Pontifex Maximus*.[1] Inscriptions also show Alexander Severus' first tribunician year as AD 222 rather than it being granted when he was Caesar. The Senate must have voted him this title at the same time.[2]

Legal authority and titles could not be conferred by the acclamation of the soldiers but the Senate, just as his initial titles associated with his elevation to the status of Caesar were conferred by a vote of the Senate. However, the public support of the army was vital. A month after his elevation to the rank of Augustus, the *legio I Minerva* was honoured with the title *Alexandriana*, probably as it was the first legion to recognize the new emperor. The legalities of his new status could only be confirmed through a vote in the Senate. This presupposes there must have been meetings of the Senate not referred to in either Herodian or Dio. However, there was a clear ideological shift after the death of Elagabalus, which Herodian describes as 'an aristocratic type of government'.[3] The Senate therefore must have conferred these titles in a meeting that is only mentioned in the questionable *Life of Severus Alexander* in the *Historia Augusta*. According to this account, the titles Augustus and Father of his Country, as well as proconsular *imperium* and tribunician power, were granted in the one meeting.[4]

Further offers of honours were turned down by the new emperor, according to the dubious *Life*, including the official name 'Antoninus' and the title of 'Magnus' or 'the Great'. This comes from a passage full of entirely fictional information, including the assertion that Alexander's name derived from the 'fact' he was born in a temple dedicated to the great Macedonian general Alexander the Great. This story is probably the origin of the invention that he was offered the further title in honour of his namesake. Both Caracalla and Elagabalus had taken the official name 'Antoninus', and it was claimed in imperial propaganda that Alexander Severus was the illegitimate son of Caracalla. The memory of Caracalla was despised by the Senate due to his extensive purges of their ranks, and the new regime was keen to dissociate itself from the rule of his predecessor. However, an inscription from the town of Guifi, 50km south-west of Carthage, commemorated Alexander Severus granting the city the status of a *municipium* between December AD 228 and March AD 235, by giving him the grandiose title *Magnus*. As the title does not precede the name of the city but is at the end of a list of official titles, it clearly applies to the emperor. However, this appellation is not found on any other inscriptions throughout the empire, and so is probably more a testament of the gratitude of the councillors towards the honour that was bestowed rather than a reference to an official honour.[5]

Another piece of information recorded only in the *Historia Augusta* has been verified from epigraphic sources. Both the memories of Elagabalus and his mother suffered *damnatio memoriae*. The purpose of this was to expunge the very memory of these individuals from history. Their names were removed from inscriptions and all official documents, images obliterated and wills annulled. The Romans believed that they lived beyond death in the memories and records of their deeds when alive. Coins from Nicaea had the images of Elagabalus removed, whilst the attacks on statues of Soamias were so destructive that none have survived. Just as their corpses were disfigured, so were their statues. The eyes, mouth and nose were the focus for this destruction, whilst numerous inscriptions have had their names chiselled away. His name was removed from the official list of ordinary consuls, and legal edicts issued in his name and that of Alexander Severus only carry the name of his Caesar. Two imperial rescripts from February AD 222 retain the name of Alexander Severus but have had the name of Elagabalus removed.[6] The act of *damnatio memoriae* encouraged widespread criticism of Elagabalus; by doing so, many wished to announce their loyalty to his successor. The sophist Philostratus attacked his contemporary writer Aelian, who denounced Elagabalus 'because by every sort of wanton wickedness he disgraced the Roman Empire'. Yet according to Philostratus, a braver man would have made these criticisms whilst the emperor was still alive.[7] It was now open season on denigrating the memory of the dead emperor. An astrological chart found preserved in Egypt refers to 'Antoninus [Elagabalus] the pervert'.[8] The senatorial historian Dio, who completed his work under Alexander Severus, gave Elagabalus the epithets the 'False Antoninus', the effete 'Sardanapalus' and the criminal 'Tiberinus'.

Cities which had been honoured by Elagabalus also lost their rights and privileges. For example, Sardes and Nicomedia lost the right to a third *neocory*, a right associated with the construction of a temple dedicated to the emperor. Anazarbos lost its right to call itself 'first, biggest and most beautiful' city of Cilicia, which had probably been granted by Elagabalus on a visit to the city. It also had to cancel its *Antoninia*, games to celebrate the previous emperor.[9]

As Elagabalus had now officially never existed, Alexander Severus could dissociate himself from his adoptive father and reassert claims to be the illegitimate son of Caracalla. Inscriptions no longer refer to him as the son of Elagabalus and grandson of Caracalla; instead he becomes the son of Caracalla. In an imperial rescript from AD 225, the emperor, commenting on a work of Ulpian's, refers to Caracalla as 'my divine father Antoninus'. However, inscriptions continue to stress the emperor's maternal line as the 'son of Julia Mamaea, grandson of Julia Maesa'. Both mother and grandmother needed to legitimize their regency through their familial ties to the emperor. In an attempt to reconcile opponents of the previous regime, a general amnesty was issued to all those who had suffered condemnation under his predecessor, just as Macrinus had pardoned those who had been condemned under Caracalla.[10]

In what appears to be a reasonably reliable section of the *Life of Elagabalus*, the author states that the very first act of the Senate after the murder of the emperor was to pass a law making it a capital offence for any woman to enter the Senate, as both Soamias and Maesa had done. These are the only women recorded to have done this. Neither Mamaea nor Maesa attended senatorial sessions in Alexander Severus' reign.[11] The new regime would present itself, in contrast to the previous one, as guardian of tradition and friend of the Senate. To aid the efficiency of senatorial handling of imperial business, emperors had often been granted permission to present at least four pieces of imperial business per session. This right of *ius primae relationis* was first granted to Augustus, then Antoninus Pius, Marcus Aurelius as Caesar, Pertinax and, according to the *Historia Augusta*, Severus Alexander. This is entirely plausible and an indication of the rapprochement between the Senate and the new emperor and his advisors.[12]

It is likely that Mamaea was the titular Augusta at this time. A fragment of Dio preserved by the twelfth-century Byzantine chronicler Zonaras states that upon being granted 'supreme power', Alexander Severus 'immediately proclaimed his mother Augusta'.[13] The *Life of Severus Alexander* appears to agree that a number of measures were passed by the Senate on this day.[14] Most historians agree that she was not Augusta before this date. However, one inscription from the reign of Elagabalus suggests this may be wrong. Although badly damaged, a restored section gives her the title Augusta, as both the names of Soamias and Mamaea are clearly evident, with a gap where their common title would be. But Mamaea's coinage only starts to carry the legend Augusta from AD 222. The author of the article readily admits this conclusion has to be tentative, as it is based on the reconstruction of wording in a badly damaged inscription, and this is also the only inscription that might carry this title for Mamaea before March AD 222. If she was granted the title Augusta before Alexander Severus became emperor, it can only have been after Elagabalus was forced by the Praetorian Guard, under the threat of death, to attend the consular procession alongside his cousin in January AD 222.[15] Julia Soamias had held the title Augusta, *mater Augusti* (mother of the emperor) and also *mater castrorum et senatus et totius domus divinae* (mother of the army camps and the Senate and the whole divine house), whilst Maesa was honoured with *avia Augusti* (grandmother of the emperor) and *mater castrorum* (mother of the camps). Mamaea had also acquired the latter title before the death of Maesa c. AD 224/225, perhaps as old age and increased poor health reduced Maesa's contributions to the decision-making process. Furthermore, it would have appeared appropriate for the new emperor's mother to have been granted the same honours as her deceased sister.[16]

Herodian and Dio agree that Mamaea took over the reins of government. According to the summary of Dio in Zonaras, Mamaea 'took over the direction of affairs and gathered wise men about her son, in order that his habits might be correctly formed by them; she also chose the best men in the Senate as advisors, informing them of all that had to be done'. However, Herodian infers that whilst she retained her health, Maesa kept the primary role in the decision-making process. This was not for long.[17]

This was entirely understandable, given that Alexander Severus was probably only 13 at the time of his accession.[18] Herodian confirms the role of Mamaea, as well as adding Maesa to the regency:

'After Alexander's accession to power he possessed the trappings and name of emperor, but the control of administration and imperial policy was in the hands of his womenfolk, who tried to bring back a complete return to moderate dignified government. The first reform was to choose sixteen senators as councillors and advisors to the emperor, men who presented the appearance of greatest dignity in years and the most moderate way of life. No statement was made or action taken without their considered approval.'[19]

The dominant role of Maesa and Mamaea in these years is supported to some extent by the epigraphical evidence. Inscriptions carrying the name of the emperor refer to him as *Juliae Mamaeae Aug(ustae) filio Juliae Maesae Aug(ustae) nepote* (the son of Julia Mamaea and grandson of Julia Maesa). The young and inexperienced emperor, at this stage of his reign, would clearly acquiesce to the advice of his mother and grandmother. The same wording is found on inscriptions of Julia Domna and her young son, Geta, but no historian claims that once Geta was joint emperor with Caracalla, his actions and thoughts were dominated by his mother.[20] Our sources idealize the character and reign of the pro-senatorial Alexander Severus, whose main fault, according to them, was his 'over-mild' personality, 'being naturally gentle and docile', resulting in him being 'dominated' by his mother as he did 'exactly as he was told'.[21] Herodian blames the eventual fall of Alexander Severus on the influence and power of his mother, an argument followed by subsequent historians. The *Historia Augusta*, although recognizing Mamaea's important role, does not give her the prominence that can be found in Herodian. However, that is to be expected in an account that creates an idealized imagining of his reign. It is far too simplistic, though, to ascribe the mistakes and weakness of the regime to his mother's overbearing authority, and, in all probability, Herodian places far too great an emphasis on her role. The author of the *Historia Augusta* also claimed that Elagabalus was 'under the control' of his mother, which even a cursory examination of events once he reached manhood clearly proves was not the case.[22]

A coin of Julia Mamaea from AD 222 shows her bare-headed with waves through her hair, carrying the legend 'JULIA MAMAEA AUG'. The reverse shows the image of the veiled goddess Juno holding a *patera* in her right hand, which is held towards a peacock, which is stretching its neck to drink the drops falling from the dish, whilst the goddess holds a sceptre in her left hand. The image and legend on the reverse, 'JUNO CONSERVATRIX', can be found on the coinage of both Maesa and Julia Domna. The reverses of Severan coinage have their origins in the reigns of the Antonine emperors. Their use by Maesa and Mamaea was an attempt to emphasize the continuity of the regime. By identifying herself with Juno the Preserver, whose epithet was linked to her role as the protector of the state, Mamaea promoted her role in raising her son to full imperial power.[23] Coinage from April AD 222 celebrates the distribution of largesse to the populace and soldiers to celebrate Alexander Severus' ascent to the throne. A youthful image of the emperor appears, hair cut short in the military fashion and wearing a cuirass. The reverse image has the goddess Liberality holding an abacus used in allotting money, and in her left hand she holds a cornucopia, the symbol of plenty.[24] By presenting Alexander Severus as an adolescent youth, Maesa and Mamaea were advertising the need for a regency.

Other coins from AD 222 show representations of Jupiter holding a thunderbolt in his right hand. In many respects, the new regime stressed continuity with the past. However, it energetically strove to dissociate itself from Elagabalus, especially his religious policy. Jupiter was restored to his rightful position at the head of the Roman pantheon.[25] The god Elagabal was 'banished' from Rome and the statues of other gods were restored to their original temples and shrines. The great temple on the Palatine, which may originally have been dedicated to Sol Invictus, but was then used for the worship of the black stone taken from Emesa, was rededicated to Jupiter Ultor (Jupiter the Avenger). This rededication was celebrated in the coinage of Alexander Severus. Archaeological evidence and a comparison of the images of the three temples depicted on coins from before, during and after the reign of Elagabalus suggest they are one and the same. The images of Sol Invictus and of Jupiter carrying a thunderbolt under the legend 'IOVI PROPVGNATORI' frequently appear, heralding a return to traditional imagery and aimed at the widest possible audience. The image of the sun god Sol on imperial coinage perhaps suggests the emperor was a continued devotee of the more traditional representation of the sun.[26]

Our sources, following imperial propaganda, praise Alexander Severus for removing his predecessor's *amici* and adherents, as 'none of those who had helped him plan his uprising, and had gained great power in consequence, survived, either, save perhaps a single person'.[27] The exception Dio is possibly referring to is Comazon. Having supported Maesa and Elagabalus in their revolt against Macrinus, he was rewarded with the appointment to one of the two Praetorian Prefectures, then a consulship in AD 220, and he was twice made Prefect of Rome.

He then appears to have fallen out of favour with Elagabalus, probably due to his support for Maesa, Mamaea and Alexander Severus. With the need for stability and experience, as well as the political necessity of rewarding loyalty, he was reappointed to the prefecture of the capital. Others were similarly rewarded: Zoticus reappears as *nomenclator a censibus*, a role with less influence and prestige than the probable one he held under Elagabalus as *a cubicularius*, in charge of the imperial bedchamber. This appointment, along with that of Comazon, would, however, have caused immense surprise and has conveniently been airbrushed out by the contemporary historians. Elagabalus' Praetorian Prefect of AD 218, Julius Flavianus, also had his carrier resurrected, being reappointed to the same post alongside Geminius Chrestus, who had held the Prefecture of Egypt in AD 219–220. He was replaced by Domitius Honoratus. The restoration of Ulpian would have won widespread approval. He was placed in charge of the *annona* on the last day in March, a key post in ensuring the steady supply of grain to Rome. Food shortages inevitably led to civil unrest.[28] These were men who had demonstrated loyalty, or *fides*, in their service to Maesa, especially in her struggles on behalf of Alexander Severus. Another beneficiary of the favour of Maesa was M. Antonius Gordian Sempronianus, the future Emperor Gordian I. A probable member of Julia Domna's literary circle and a *comes* to Caracalla, he was given a *suffect* consulship in AD 222. Roman society was based upon a complex network of reciprocal relationships, where the recipient of a gift, favour or support was expected to return it at some point. This system of *amicitiae* was the bedrock of Roman political life. The language used by the Romans in describing its obligations are linked to verbs indicating a relationship between a creditor and debtor. Maesa had to make repayment. Furthermore, imperial rescripts from 3 and 19 February AD 222 during the reign of Elagabalus show remarkable similarities in style to those issued in the reign of his successor, suggesting a continuity of lesser imperial officials as well.[29]

Others who had suffered under Elagabalus were natural supporters of the new imperial government. The senatorial historian Marius Maximus was a vastly experienced general and politician under both Septimius Severus and Caracalla, who had been made Prefect of Rome in AD 218–219, probably by Macrinus, but then appears to have fallen out of favour under Elagabalus. He was appointed to a second consulship to commence in January AD 223. His colleague was to be L. Roscius Aelianus Paculus Salvius Julianus, son of the ordinary consul of AD 187 and related to the powerful senatorial family of the Nummii.[30] The greatest historian of his age, Cassius Dio, after spending most of the reign of Elagabalus in his home province of Bithynia – where he 'fell sick' – returned to Rome and was appointed to the prestigious proconsular province of Africa, and then 'on returning to Italy I was almost immediately sent as governor first to Dalmatia and then Upper Pannonia'. The gap between his *suffect* consulship under Septimius Severus and proconsular governorship was highly unusual, indicating a career placed on hold.[31] Maesa probably knew both men well through her sister Julia Domna's literary acquaintances.[32] Their previous loyalty to her family and influence in the Senate would be important factors in restoring her dynasty's reputation with that body.

Both Maesa and Mamaea fully understood the weakness of their position. The brief reign of Elagabalus had undermined loyalty to the Severans amongst the Praetorians, the army and the Senate. Hence the need to make as clean a break as possible with the previous regime. A general pardon was issued to all those who had been exiled by previous emperors. The distribution of monies on the accession of Alexander Severus would not have been enough to restore discipline in the ranks. The emperor himself was only a young boy, who lacked experience and had, despite claims to be a son of Caracalla, questionable legitimacy. Many would have recognized his tenuous links to the founder of the dynasty, Septimius Severus. To build as wide a foundation of support as possible, a council of senatorial advisors was created, consisting of sixteen of the 'best men of the Senate'.[33] These were 'men who presented the appearance of greatest dignity in years and the most moderate way of life'.[34] This council appears to have existed throughout his reign and joined the emperor on campaign, as Herodian refers to this council in Germany being immediately dismissed by Maximinus Thrax on the murder of Alexander Severus. Herodian is frustratingly vague in his description of these arrangements, but does seem to make a distinction between the emperor's *amici*, who would have been selected by the emperor himself, and the council, which consisted of eminent senators selected by the Senate.[35]

The *Historia Augusta* also refers to this body, but embellishes its account by erroneously adding that it consisted of twenty learned jurists and fifty 'men of wisdom'. In the later empire, a quorate meeting of the Senate had to consist of fifty senators, and this appears to have been mistakenly used by the biographer as a figure in his estimate of the composition for this body.[36]

All emperors had drawn on the skills, advice and experience of a wide range of experts, who were asked to join the *concilium principis*, the emperor's advisory council. Membership was not fixed, but depended upon the matters and issues that were being discussed. This was a purely informal body whose origins lay in the Roman Republic, as magistrates, governors, generals and state officials were expected to consult experts and men of experience as they themselves were often new to the posts they had been allotted to. Invitations to attend as an advisor were purely at the discretion of the emperor. Due to the significant number of legal petitions and requests sent to the emperor by both individuals and imperial officials, the skills and learning of jurists were often required. Lawyers and jurists were often chosen as Praetorian Prefects, which may account for the prominence of Ulpian in the decision-making process, even though his initial post was Prefect of the Annona. An imperial rescript from 31 March AD 222 refers to Ulpian as the emperor's 'Prefect of the Annona, lawyer, and my friend [*amicus*]'. The imperial family clearly had great confidence in him.[37] According to Herodian, legal experts played a prominent role.[38] Paul, a prolific writer of works on jurisprudence and, like Ulpian, a student and legal advisor of the great Severan jurist and Praetorian Prefect, Papinian, was asked to provide advice on the imperial *concilium*. He was recalled from exile, a punishment imposed by Elagabalus. Paul was probably the father of this emperor's first wife, Julia Paula, and so associated with her fall from favour in AD 220. She is described as 'a woman from the most aristocratic family in Rome', so his recall would have also won significant support in the Senate.[39] The assertion in the *Historia Augusta* that Paul was a Praetorian Prefect has to be discounted due to a lack of any supporting evidence. He may have served as an *a libellis* with responsibility for dealing with petitions to the emperor, or as a *cognitionibus*, who was in charge of the emperor's law court and carried out investigations in advance of the hearings. These posts, however, tended to be held by equestrians rather than senators. More likely, he was drafted onto the *consilium* as a legal expert, a *iurisperiti*. This had become regular practice by the Severan period.[40]

Dio, in a fictional speech by Augustus' *amicus* Maecenas, describes the role of these imperial secretaries in his own time: 'Moreover, as regards legal cases, letters and decrees of the cities, petitions of individuals and whatever else concerns the administration of the Empire, you should have helpers and assistants from the equites.'[41] These were the men who held real power through their regular and almost unrestricted access to the emperor.[42] The two Praetorian Prefects were the most prestigious positions in the equestrian career ladder, whose role, after ensuring the safety of the emperor and his family, had expanded to an independent judicial responsibility. Legal cases within 100 miles of Rome were heard by the City Prefect, and those beyond this limit within the boundaries of Italy by the Praetorian Prefects. Many holders of this office were legal experts, and so provided advice on cases heard before the emperor himself or had cases delegated to them by the emperor. Their presence at the side of the emperor meant they were members of the *concilium principis* and controlled access to the imperial presence. In times of war, they not only commanded the elite Praetorian cohorts, but often held independent commands of substantial Roman forces. Their power and proximity to the emperor meant the holders of these posts were trusted for their ability and, most importantly, loyalty.[43]

Other important equestrian posts included that of the secretaries for Greek and Latin letters (*ab epistulis Graecis* and *ab epistulis Latinis*), responsible for drafting imperial replies to either Greek or Latin-speaking cities or individuals. These equestrians were often prominent rhetoricians, orators or literary figures.[44] Their access to the emperor provided them with the opportunity to elicit money, gifts, appointment to posts and favours both for themselves and their clients.[45] The *a rationibus*, who was responsible for state finances, could also be invited to the emperor's *consilium*.[46] An army of imperial freedmen and slaves manned each of these administrative departments. The lowly status of these highly skilled individuals drew contempt from our sources, but these were the professional bureaucrats who enabled the government to function. The aristocratic elite resented approaching these men for favours, but the more prominent freedmen often worked closely with the emperor, thus also allowing them the opportunity to influence imperial decisions. The imperial chamberlain, the *cubicularius*, often spent a great deal of time in the presence of the emperor, as they were responsible for the imperial bedchamber. The emperor Gaius' (Caligula) *cubicularius*, Helicon, a former Egyptian slave, 'played with Gaius, exercised with him, bathed with him, had meals with him and was with him when he went to bed'.[47] According to our senatorial sources, it was the weak or 'bad' emperors who allowed these men of low origins to gain influence and power: Helicon rose to prominence under Gaius; Pallas and Narcissus under Claudius; Parthenius under Domitian; and Cleander under Commodus. 'Good' emperors restrained and restricted the influence of these men, but they were ever present. Vespasian appointed the freedman Hormus to a command over forces in his successful invasion of Italy, and he was raised to equestrian status by the Senate. The literary figure Fronto had to ask Charilas, a freedman of Marcus Aurelius and Lucius Verus, whether it was an opportune time to visit the emperors.[48] Such freedman may have again risen to prominence under Elagabalus, but, on the accession of Alexander Severus, they were 'deprived of their benefices and all instructed to return to their previous status and occupation'.[49] The influence of imperial freedmen again fades into the background, working behind the scenes and kept from public prominence.

The creation of the senatorial council was an astute and clever sop to the aristocracy. Herodian is clear that it could only discuss and offer advice on matters put to it by Alexander Severus, Maesa or Mamaea. In the original 'Augustan settlement', the senators sacrificed real political power for the outward signs of status that maintained their dignity and position in the state. Only the *Historia Augusta* suggests any form of governmental partnership with the Senate, whereas contemporary historians Dio and Herodian merely present the emperor as being respectful of senatorial dignity and privileges.[50] Its advice and recommendations could be accepted or rejected by the emperor or Mamaea. No source records any decision or action initiated by this council. Instead, all our sources record Alexander Severus, Maesa, Mamaea or Ulpian at the heart of the government. Furthermore, no coins support the assertion for an increase in senatorial power or authority in the reign. An issue of bronze coins bearing the title SC (*senatus consulta*) is merely a traditional motif, as the Senate theoretically retained control over the issue of bronze coinage, whilst the emperor controlled issues in gold and silver.[51] For example, upon hearing news of the Sassanid incursions into Roman territory in AD 229, Alexander Severus decided to meet with these 'councillors' before determining upon his response.[52] This body drew the senatorial elite into the decision-making process and so broadened support for the emperor and his family. The young emperor's *amici* would meet informally as part of the *concilium principis*.

A fragment of Dio preserved by Zonoras appears to make a distinction between the senatorial council, made up of illustrious senators and separately his advisors chosen for their experience, skills, abilities and loyalty, and the role of the emperor's *amici*: Mamaea 'gathered wise men about her son' and 'she also chose the best men in the Senate as advisors, informing them all that had to be done'.[53] This appears to contradict Herodian, who explicitly states that the Senate, rather than the Augusta, decided upon membership of this council. Perhaps the empress used her power and influence to ensure the Senate chose her nominees. Alternatively, the differences may be a reflection of how the council evolved over time. Mamaea, at the start of the reign, was understandably keen to ensure the impressionable teenaged emperor was surrounded by men whom she trusted and who would not exploit his youthful inexperience for their own ends. Consequently, on Mamaea's orders 'the palace was put under strict guard and no one with a reputation for loose living was allowed to come near the young lad, for fear his morals would be corrupted if sycophants directed his vigorous enthusiasms towards low desires'.[54] Herodian later describes the situation in AD 235. Aged 27, Alexander Severus had long been capable of identifying and rejecting prejudiced and biased advice. Senatorial support could be strengthened by allowing that prestigious body the right to choose membership of the emperor's council. This illusionary power would help substantiate the regime's propaganda in restoring 'an aristocratic type of government'.[55]

The contemporary senatorial historian Dio composed a fictional speech for Augustus' close *amicus*, Maecenas, which was addressed to his emperor on the role of the *concilium principis*. Fergus Millar believed this was composed by Dio during the middle of Caracalla's reign and was intended to promote the ideals of 'cabinet government' as opposed to that of tyranny. Caracalla was not renowned for his open-minded philosophical approach to constitutional government. In fact, such a publication during his reign was more likely to invite a swift visit from the *frumentarii*, soldiers tasked with the removal of opposition and dissent. As Millar himself recognizes, most historians consider this speech to be composed with Alexander Severus in mind.[56] Dio had received his first consulship c. AD 205/206 and attended Caracalla's *concilium principis*. He describes how the emperor humiliated his senatorial *amici* whilst the court stayed at Nicomedia in the winter of AD 214/215:

'he [Caracalla] would send us word that he was going to hold court or transact some other public business directly after dawn, but he would keep us waiting until noon and often until evening, and would not even admit us to the vestibule, so we had to stand around outside elsewhere; and usually at some late hour he decided that he would not even exchange greetings with us that day. Meanwhile he was engaged in gratifying his curiosity in various ways ... driving chariots, slaying wild beasts, fighting as a gladiator, drinking, nursing the resultant headaches, mixing great bowls of wine – in addition to all their other food – for the soldiers that guarded him inside the palace, and passing it round in cups, in our presence and before our eyes; and after this he would now and again hold court.'[57]

Dio's outrage and humiliation resonate in every word. The Praetorians were treated with greater reverence and consideration than the 'best men' of the Senate. It would be quite remarkable if Dio directed Maecenas' speech on the advantages of ruling in partnership with the leading aristocrats of the Senate to an emperor so intent on following his father's advice: 'enrich the soldiers, and scorn all other men.' Towards the end of the reign of Macrinus, Dio was appointed to the post of curator of Pergamum and Smyrna, and was still in post to witness the revolt of Castinus whilst Elagabalus wintered in Nicomedia in AD 218/219. Then he fell ill and probably recuperated on his estates around his native city of Nicaea in Bithynia. His career until that point seemed to have come to a disappointing end. However, his star was to dramatically rise with the accession of Alexander Severus. He was appointed to the prestigious proconsular province of Africa c. AD 223, then returned to Rome, only to be sent to govern Dalmatia, probably in AD 224–226, and was made governor of Upper Pannonia around AD 226–228. This province was only given to loyal supporters of the regime, as it controlled two legions within easy reach of Italy. Furthermore, many soldiers of the Praetorian Guard were from the legions of Pannonia and Moesia. His reward for his unswerving loyalty was the greatest honour of a second consulship in AD 229, with the emperor as his colleague.[58]

Placed into historical context, it would make greater sense for Maecenas's speech on the benefits of 'aristocratic government' to be made to honour the policies of his greatest benefactors, Mamaea and Alexander Severus. Imperial propaganda heralded the rejection of tyranny as encapsulated by the reign of Elagabalus for a return to the 'Augustan settlement'. What better way to demonstrate this than in a speech to Augustus by his one of his closest *amici*? Of course the speech is a highly idealized presentation of the role of Alexander Severus' senatorial councillors and *amici*, but it does reflect the gratitude of these senatorial aristocrats, as they now had the opportunity to influence imperial decisions:

'you [Augustus] should yourself, in consultation with the best men, enact all the appropriate laws, without the possibility of any opposition or remonstrance to these laws on the part of any one from the masses; that you and your councillors should conduct wars according to your own wishes, all other citizens rendering instant obedience to your commands; that the choice of the officials should rest with you and your advisors.'[59]

Interestingly, Dio again makes a distinction between councillors and advisors, perhaps referring to the situation in AD 222, with a senatorial council of sixteen members called by the emperor to discuss significant and strategic events, and the emperor's own advisors, his *amici*, who helped the emperor manage the day-to-day concerns of imperial administration. Dio also clearly states that including the aristocracy in the government reduced opposition to the emperor by drawing support from the disaffected. This would have been a primary concern in AD 222, with both Maesa and Mamaea attempting to build as much support as possible for their fragile hold on the throne.

One of the advantages that Maecenas identifies for this type of government is that those 'good' men appointed to the important offices of state 'would be honoured without arousing jealousy and the bad punished without causing rebellion'.[60] There is again concern over pre-empting rebellion and building support; the situation at the start of Alexander Severus' reign. These 'bad' men are those who failed to gain the offices, posts or 'gifts' that they felt was their due based upon their perceived *fides*, *dignitas* or *nobilitas*.

There were only about 100 senatorial and equestrian appointments available each year, which dramatically limited the ability of the emperor to satisfy the expectations of these classes.[61] However, quaestorships, tribunates, aedileships and praetorships would not be appropriate for senators who had previously been awarded a consulship. The opportunity to grant an aristocrat a second consulship had been extended with the creation of *suffect* consulships that could be held during the year, but these were far less prestigious than the two 'ordinary' consulships. Furthermore, of the senatorial governorships, there were only two which were considered commensurate for the aristocracy, these 'best men': Asia and Africa. For every man gratified by appointment to one of these posts, another would be offended by being overlooked. However, the creation of a senatorial council cemented the loyalty of sixteen of the most eminent men in the Senate to the new regime. Each of these would have their own *amici* in the senatorial and equestrian classes, as well as a large network of clients. Emperors secured loyalty through distributing *beneficia* in the form of gifts, offices, money, estates and favours to their *amici*, establishing bonds of patronage extending from themselves. These resources then allowed the *amici Caesaris* to extend their own network of patronage and build up their own *clientelia*, whose loyalty to the emperor was indirectly secured. Appointments were made through patronal influences, and so access to the emperor, as the ultimate patron, was essential. Consequently, Mamaea and Alexander Severus were making themselves as accessible as possible to these senatorial power-brokers. The second-century senator Pliny praised the Emperor Trajan for his openness to the 'flower of the senatorial and equestrian orders'.[62]

The emperor would have used the morning salutations to allow petitioners to pass on their requests for themselves or on behalf of their own clients. These would take place in the vast atrium of the imperial palace. A crowd would await the arrival of the emperor, and appear to have been divided into three categories. The first, high-status group were allowed to approach the emperor individually, and so had the greatest chance to have their petition granted. This honour was granted to the most illustrious senators and equestrians. The next category presented their petitions in small groups, whilst those in the final group were admitted en masse. Invitations to imperial banquets were used for the same purpose, with guests of honour placed closest to the emperor, where they could engage him in private conversation. The future Emperor Vespasian publically thanked the Emperor Gaius (Caligula) for such an invitation. A funerary monument from the reign of Antonius Pius records the pride of the praetor L. Plotius Sabinus, who attended the 'second *salutio*' of the emperor. Alexander Severus would not have repeated the mistake of Elagabalus, who caused great offence by receiving the *salutio* of these eminent figures whilst reclining on his couch.[63] The greatest prestige was to be counted amongst the *amici Caesaris*. These men had regular access to the imperial presence and were often invited to the *concilium principis*.

A unique inscription from Bansa in Africa, dated to AD 177, preserves membership of an imperial *consilium*. There were twelve members summoned to the side of the emperors Marcus Aurelius and Commodus. They included six members of the senatorial aristocracy, all ex-consuls. One, C. Septimius Severus, was the cousin of the future Emperor L. Septimius Severus, and his early career probably benefited from the patronage of his relative. Also present were eminent members of the equestrian order; both Praetorian Prefects, the Prefect of the Annona and the Prefect of the Vigiles. One of the Praetorian Prefects, Paternus, and the Prefect of the Vigiles were legal experts. One of the senators, T. Varius Clemens, had been an *ab epistulis Latinis* before being promoted to the Senate and a *suffect* consulship for his services. The remaining two equestrians were clearly well-respected and skilled individuals, as one was later promoted to the Senate and rose to the consulship under Commodus, whilst the other is later recorded as a Prefect of Egypt, a post only eclipsed by the Praetorian Prefecture in the equestrian career ladder.[64]

The composition of the emperor's *concilium* varied according to the issues to be addressed.[65] However, a number of eminent senators and equestrians can be identified who were probably called to Alexander Severus' initial *concilium principis*. As a private forum, Maesa and Mamaea were probably present, although no source mentions this. Ulpian certainly was, at first as Prefect of the Annona. Another legal expert and eminent senator, Paul, was called upon to offer advice.[66] The two Praetorian Prefects, Chrestus and Flavianus, were certainly present, along with the *suffect* consul, Gordian. Also present were the two nominated consuls for AD 223, Marius Maximus – the old Severan general and loyal adherent – and the aristocrat, L. Roscius Aelianus Salvius Julianus. As Prefect of Rome and a supporter of Mamaea in opposition to Elagabalus, we would expect Comazon to be a member. Senatorial aristocrats would also be honoured with an imperial summons, and representatives of the great houses of the noble families: the Acilii, whose ancestors dated from the Republican period; the Anicii; the Brutii, who had close marriage connections with Commodus; the Caesonii; the Claudii Pompeiani, whose members were descended from Commodus' sister Lucilla; the Egnatii; and the Claudii Severii, who were descended from another of Commodus' sisters, Annia Faustina. Antonine blood flowed in the veins of these men, and their ancestors had been the advisors and *amici* of a long line of occupants of the throne. More importantly, they represented potential rivals. It was vital to draw these in as stakeholders in the fragile imperial regime.

On the accession of a new emperor, all cities and communities were expected to send a gold crown (*aurum coronarium*) to the imperial fiscus. Ambassadors from around the empire would present these to the emperor, using the opportunity to remind him of their previous loyalty and service to the dynasty, as well as making additional requests for further honours and privileges. An Egyptian papyrus preserves Alexander Severus' remission of this tax, due on his promotion to the senior office of Augustus, but he regrets that he is unable to cancel those gold crowns that were still outstanding from his appointment as Caesar. He regrets that the shortage of funds prohibits the cancellation of these debts,

> 'in order that communities not be compelled to make contributions greater than they can afford through their desire to express joy at my entering into rule. Hence arises this plan of mine, in designing which I did not lack for precedents, among whom I will be imitating especially Trajan and Marcus, my ancestors, emperors most worthy of admiration, whose practice in other respects, too, I plan to emulate.
>
> 'If the state of public finances did not interfere, I would make a clearer display of magnanimity and would not hesitate to cancel whatever contributions [of] this type [i.e. gold crowns] were still coming in, being owed from the past, and to cancel as well any monies for crowns that were voted in connection with my elevation as Caesar, or were yet to be voted upon

... But because of what I mentioned just now, I do not think this will be possible. For neither my own welfare nor anything else will be a concern for me except to increase the empire through love of human kind and doing good, in order that my own conduct might stand as an example of the greatest moderation for the governors of the provinces and the procurators sent out by me, whom I dispatch after a most rigorous examination. Let the governors of the provinces learn more and more with how great zeal they should look after the provinces over which they are appointed, when it is possible for them all to see the emperor conducting the duties of kingship with so much orderliness and wisdom and self-control.'[67]

The empire had struggled from the reign of Marcus Aurelius to match income and expenditure. A plague brought back from the East by Lucius Verus' victorious soldiers had decimated the population. This had not only affected state revenues, but also reduced agricultural production as land fell fallow and the cost of labour rapidly increased. This sudden reduction in income was made worse by the need to raise additional forces, as Rome faced barbarian invasions and then civil war.[68] A series of emperors, from Marcus Aurelius to Caracalla, had repeatedly debased the coinage, but a massive increase in soldiers' pay by Septimius Severus and Caracalla had left imperial finances in a perilous state. Macrinus' brave but naïve attempt to reduce expenditure by reducing the pay of new recruits to that set by Septimius Severus had greatly contributed to the revolt that led to his death. Alexander Severus and his advisors had learnt from his predecessors' mistakes and never attempted to reduce pay, yet neither did they increase it. Donatives were distributed on his accession to the throne, but the army had come to expect regular pay rises. Our pro-senatorial sources direct their ire at his mother, Mamaea, accusing her of avarice and greed. She stands accused of having an 'absolute obsession with money'.[69] Yet the monetary crisis gnawed at the entrails of military support throughout his reign, as it would appear that units were retained below strength in order to save money, and this would contribute to his eventual demise.

The remission of taxes at a time of financial strain was born from a desire to cement support in the provinces. Such an act, when the government faced a financial crisis and the need to distribute a donative to the army and *liberalitas* to the people, demonstrates just how desperate Maesa and Mamaea were to establish firm foundations for their regime. Promises of good government laced with stock phrases would only be believed with responsible administration.[70] The remission of taxes was to serve as a practical first step as the central government recognized the problems faced by provincials, especially the wealthy members of the city councils, across the empire. The edict recognizes a decline of empire, with responsibility placed at the feet of depraved rulers, a clear reference to Elagabalus.

By inference, reform and revival could be secured through placing their faith in Alexander Severus. The restoration of a golden age is promised by reference to the reigns of Trajan and Marcus Aurelius.[71]

It was probably during an audience with the embassy from Alexandria congratulating the new emperor on becoming the Augustus that Alexander Severus decided to honour the city with an imperial visit. Egypt was the bread basket of Rome and Alexandria the naval base of the grain fleet. However, the city would still remember the 'purge' of Caracalla in AD 215, when he unleashed the soldiers on the population in revenge for demonstrating against him. Thousands died and many were expelled from the city.[72] Alexander Severus, as Elagabalus had done, claimed to be the son of this man. The honour of a visit by the emperor, who shared the name of the city's founder, would help to assure the loyalty of this key province and provide further opportunities to provide gifts and privileges. The letter appears to retain the youthful enthusiasm of the teenager; perhaps he dictated it to one of his officials after consultation with his *amici*:

> 'Alexander [Caesar Augustus to those] in [authority greeting?]. [Having heard from others of your] good will [towards] me ... [and how] you still [?] preserve in keeping in your breasts this good disposition, [I am?] coming to you, having with fortune's blessing been elected Emperor by the most noble soldiery, and being about to make my auspicious entry upon office [with a visit to you?] and having made a beginning with you, especially of my opportunities for benefaction, as much as will be just to grant to the maternal[?] city [of the Alexandrians?] I will bestow. Farewell[?] year 1 Pharmouthi the [?]. address to Apolinarius, senior [?] senator.'

The tone of the letter appears to contrast with its official formality. It is suggested that this papyrus preserves the words of the 13-year-old emperor, perhaps written under the guidance of his mother or Ulpian. Surprisingly for a regime propagating the message of imperial rule in close co-operation, the unabashed truth of his election 'by the most noble soldiery', without reference to the legal and formal recognition of his right to rule by the Senate, is striking. There is no evidence that the proposed visit ever took place. Events were to overtake these wishful intentions. Another city that was the beneficiary of Alexander Severus' *beneficia* was Caesarea, which had been named in honour of Caesar Augustus. Coins of the city carry the title *metropolis* from the very beginning of Alexander Severus' reign, suggesting this was awarded when its ambassadors went to Rome to congratulate the new emperor. This, clearly, is an attempt to establish the image of an Augustan façade and a return to the founding principles of the Principate. Another city, founded by the admired conqueror Trajan, Ulpia Traiana Sarmizegetusa in Dacia, was also elevated from a *colonia* to a *metropolis*.[73]

By 1 December AD 222, Ulpian had been promoted to senior Praetorian Prefect. Promotion to this prefecture was not unusual from the prefectures of Egypt, the Annona or that of the Vigiles. What is almost unique is his position as supervisor of the two recently appointed Praetorian Prefects, Chrestus and Flavianus. Commodus had appointed the freedman Cleander to a similar role, but this had led to widespread unrest amongst the Guard, the death of Cleander and the execution of the two original Praetorian Prefects.[74] History was about to repeat itself. An imperial receipt from the emperor dated to 1 December tells the owner of a warehouse which had been broken into and looted that the case should heard before the provincial governor, who, if severe punishment was to be imposed of the guilty party, was to refer the perpetrator of the crime to 'Domitius Ulpianus, Praetorian Prefect and my parent'. Parent, *parens* in Latin, was used to refer in imperial rescripts to actual parents of the emperor, as Alexander Severus does in a rescript issued two days later. This term confers immense honour upon Ulpian and reflects the close relationship that now existed between the two.[75]

The *dignitas* and prestige from holding the office of Praetorian Prefect was immense, and its holders ensured they were given due public acknowledgement as they journeyed though the city. Dio describes the arrogance of a predecessor in this post who 'was terrifying in his progress: so no one addressed him; but those whom he came across turned aside, and his advance men announced that no-one was to stand by nor stare at him. They should step aside and cast down their eyes.' All our sources confirm the power and influence held by Ulpian, who, in conjunction with Mamaea, formed a regency. Dio records that the emperor 'entrusted to one Domitius Ulpian the command of the Praetorians and the other business of the empire'. Although Herodian does not, strangely, mention Ulpian by name, his account supports Dio's in stating: 'All civil and legal business and administration was put in the charge of the men with the highest rhetorical reputation and legal skill.'[76] The twelfth-century Byzantine historian Zonoras, whose history at this point is based upon Dio, echoes this: 'In addition, Domitius Ulpianus was entrusted with command of the Praetorian Guard and the administration of public affairs.'[77] Ulpian is also given a prominent role in the *Historia Augusta*, where he is described as being a member of the imperial *consilium* alongside Paul. The '*Life*' appears to reflect these reports, describing how the emperor refused to give a private audience to anyone apart from Ulpian.[78]

This unusual administrative arrangement appears, from Zosimus, to be the idea of Mamaea. According to this late Roman historian, the emperor was responsible for the original appointment of Flavianus and Chrestus, as they were 'not only acquainted with military affairs, but excelling in the management of civil business'. This was indeed the case. Flavianus had been a Praetorian Prefect under Elagabalus, and Chrestus a Prefect of Egypt in AD 219–222. Clearly, these men must have been recommended to the young emperor for their ability and loyalty; but by whom? Maesa appears to be the only likely candidate, as it was Mamaea who appointed Ulpian over them. The elderly grandmother fades from the historical records at this point, and it is likely that she was gradually succumbing to old age and illness. She was to die shortly after these events. As she receded into the background of the imperial government, her daughter increasingly took the reins. Zosimus elaborates further on Ulpian's appointment: 'But Mamaea, the emperor's mother, placed over them Ulpianus, as an inspector of their conduct, and indeed a partner in their office, he being an excellent lawyer, and knowing not only how to regulate present affairs, but to provide prudently for the future.'[79] Both Chrestus and Flavianus would have had extensive legal experience in their previous roles, although they did not possess the same renown as the great jurist. What is remarkable is Ulpian's responsibility to 'inspect the conduct' of his juniors. Perhaps Mamaea wished to use Ulpian's experience and skills to help educate her son in a key role of imperial governance. This would have been difficult for Ulpian as Prefect of the Annona, but the job of Praetorian Prefect would be ideal.[80] Chrestus and Flavianus would not have been appointed to their posts if their loyalty had ever been doubted by Maesa and Mamaea, and it is difficult to see how they could have fallen under suspicion from March to November, a mere nine months. If they had, they would have been removed from their posts by promotion to the Senate or execution. More likely, the empress was dissatisfied with their ability to control the Praetorians, whose discipline continued to be problematic.[81]

R. Syme suggested that Ulpian's appointment was due to the influence of Comazon. However, Appius Claudius Julianus appears from a rescript to have replaced Comazon in the post of Urban Prefect of Rome at some point in AD 223. Comazon was then honoured with a second consulship in AD 224. An imperial letter is addressed to an Urban Prefect called Julianus; surely the same man. Appius Claudius came from a prestigious aristocratic family and had held a *suffect* consulship c. AD 200 and was proconsular governor of Africa under Caracalla. He would have been an important member of the recently established senatorial council. The other nomination for the ordinary consulship was C. Bruttius Crispinus. This high-status Antonine family had immaculate aristocratic connections. His aunt had been the wife of the Emperor Commodus, whilst his grandfather, father and more recently his brother had been consuls. The Bruttii were no doubt also represented on this council. However, Comazon's star was in the descent and he disappears from our historical records after AD 224. He was rewarded by Maesa with the Prefecture of Rome in AD 222 for his loyalty during the internecine struggle with Elagabalus, but now Mamaea was constructing her own network. Another surprising change was the appointment of M. Aedinius Julianus as Egyptian Prefect in AD 223. He had served as temporary governor of Lugdunensis Gaul in the absence of its usual senatorial occupant. However, Domitius Honoartus had only recently been appointed to the Egyptian Prefecture in AD 222. This equestrian post was normally held for two or three years before the occupant was moved on. Both Aedinius Julianus and Honoratus would become Praetorian Prefects. In his short tenure of the Egyptian prefecture, Honoratus had clearly not raised the ire of Mamaea and Ulpian. It is likely the rapid turnover was the desire to reward powerful men with these posts at the apex of the equestrian *cursus honorum*.[82] Ulpian's probable replacement at the Annona was the shadowy Aurelius Epagathus. He would later replace M. Aedinius Julianus as Prefect of Egypt in AD 224, the Prefecture of the Annona often being the precursor to such a move. Already a powerful imperial official under Macrinus, the defeated and desperate emperor entrusted this man with the life and safety of his young son, Diadumenianus. He was to escort the boy to the Parthian king, but he had betrayed him at Zeugma. The youth was executed, whilst Epagathus made the smooth transition from the court of Macrinus to that of Elagabalus.[83]

The regency of Ulpian is commended in the ancient sources, but they overestimate its importance. He was probably dead within a year, so his impact upon the education of his young imperial student and the administration of the empire was understandably limited. In order to raise Ulpian's status and prestige above his fellow Praetorian Prefects, he appears to have been given the honorary status of a senator. In the second century, the Antonine emperors awarded *ornamenta consularia*, the status of an ex-consul, to some Praetorian Prefects whilst they were still in office. Sex. Cornelius Repentinus, the Praetorian Prefect to Antoninus Pius and Marcus Aurelius, was awarded this senatorial *ornementa* in AD 163, as was Caracalla's prefect, Macrinus, the future emperor. Another man honoured in this way was the great Severan prefect, C. Fulvius Plautianus, who was awarded *ornamenta consularia* then made ordinary consul in AD 203. Valerius Comazon, Elagabalus' first Praetorian Prefect, was also awarded the rank of *ornamenta consularia* and later *adlectus consulares*, before becoming Urban Prefect. The granting of this status strengthened the position of these equestrian officials in their daily encounters with the senatorial elite, especially when presiding in court. An honorary inscription from Ulpian's native city of Tyre confirms his tenure of the prefecture of the Annona and that of Praetorian Prefect, as well as confirming that he never became a senator.[84] The author of the *Historia Augusta*, writing in the later empire, confuses this honorary status with the actual appointment of the equestrian Praetorian Prefects to that of a consular senator. Nor is there any evidence that these appointments and those to the office of Urban Prefect were made, as asserted in this work, by the Senate. More likely, the emperor submitted their names to the Senate as a gesture towards its ancient dignity, in the confident expectation that all the names would be approved.[85] However, it is likely and understandable that Mamaea would have been concerned at the close bond Ulpian rapidly established with Alexander Severus, perhaps fearing for her own influence over her son, but she soon came to realize his influence and experience complimented her own position.[86]

Ulpian used his new authority to reward his own clients. As a prominent citizen of Tyre, and patron of this great city, he secured the restoration of its title of *metropolis* with its associated privileges after the reduction of its status by Elagabalus for supporting the revolt of the III *Gallica*. His clients and *amici* also benefited from his access to the emperor. Analysis of imperial rescripts demonstrates a continuity of style from October AD 222 until around October of the following year. Tony Honoré suggests these dates correspond to Ulpian's tenure of the Praetorian Prefecture. He proposes the secretary of petitions, the *a libellus*, was given to Paul's student, Licinius Rufinus. This jurist started his career under Septimius Severus as a legal advisor to the emperor, then was promoted to the post of *ab epistulis Graecis*, followed by *a studiis*, who was attached to the emperor's judicial court. This post led to appointment to *a rationibus* and then *a libellis*. A massive number of rescripts were issued in this year; ninety-six in total. Rufinus appears to have been rewarded with *adlection* into the Senate by Alexander Severus in late AD 223, oddly at the rank of ex-aedile rather than that of an ex-praetor. He then became a praetor, a governor of Noricum and was finally awarded a consulship, either *suffect* or granted the rank of a consul, *adlectio inter consulares*. His remarkable career reached its zenith when he was chosen by his peers as one of the twenty senators tasked with organizing opposition to Maximinus Thrax in AD 238.[87]

The death of Ulpian probably coincides with the promotion of Rufinus to senatorial status. Honoré identifies his replacement as Herennius Modestinus, Ulpian's student. It is probable that Modestinus served on Ulpian's own *concilium* during this period.[88] Roman jurists were, according to Ulpian's testimony recorded in the preface of the *Digest*, dedicated to a philosophy that was not simulated but genuine. He saw the application of the legal process as a close study of the legislative texts, careful evaluation of the meaning of words and considered analysis of their implications. He believed the jurist pursued a higher form of philosophy based on reason, rather than lofty ideals, that could be transformed into practical outcomes. This dogmatic, even pedantic approach may have been interpreted by friends and enemies alike as arrogance.[89] Even Dio, an admirer of his aims, skills and intellect, refers to him with a degree of contempt.[90]

The contemporary writer Athenaeus includes the figure of Oulpianos in his work *Sophists at Dinner*. The writer places a number of famous intellectuals as guests at a dinner provided by the real-life figure of Publius Livius Larensis, who held the body of Commodus after his murder in AD 192. Each of the guests, as was probably typical of these symposiums, hold forth, trying to outdo each other in their skills, knowledge and learning. Oulpianos emerges as an unpleasant pedant who painstakingly and painfully dissects the meaning of words. Scholars have argued over whether Oulpianos is to be identified with Ulpian. Both were natives of Tyre, both specialists in the terminology of words, and the fictional dinner does appear to have been hosted by a historical figure with 'real' guests, including the famous Greek physician Galen. However, Oulpianos dies in the work, unlike Galen. The real Galen probably died c. AD 216/217, whilst Ulpian died later in c. AD 223. However, Tony Honoré appears to undermine his carefully constructed argument, rejecting the supposed link between the two figures by making the tenuous suggestion that the figure of Oulpianos was based on an otherwise unknown family of intellectuals from Tyre. In contrast, Michael Trapp compares the *Sophists at Dinner* with the contemporary work of the sophist Philostratus, the author of the *Lives of the Sophists*. The *Lives* attempts to record the teachings and experiences of famous philosophers and rhetors over a period of 600 years down to his own time. Athenaeus and Philostratus both present their works as a celebration of contemporary learning. The guests at the dining table of Larensis include eight grammarians and men of literature, four philosophers, three doctors, an expert in music and our jurist Oulpianos. Both writers revel in the late flowering of classical Greek culture, this Second Sophistic Movement, which was in their eyes a continuation of the quality of learning exemplified by their illustrious predecessors.[91]

Dio grudgingly admits that Ulpian 'corrected many of the irregularities introduced by Sardanapalus [Elagabalus]'.[92] Unfortunately, his brief summary of the reign fails to elucidate on what these were. He is probably alluding to the removal of the surviving protégés of Elagabalus. Comazon disappears from imperial politics, and we hear no more of Zoticus. Perhaps Herodian is referring to this when he says: 'Those who had been advanced to positions of honour and power without justification, or had been promoted for their notoriety in crimes, were deprived of their benefices and all instructed to return to their previous status and occupation.'[93] The *Historia Augusta* echoes Herodian, not surprisingly, as the author used this work as one of his primary sources. However, this account goes much further, alleging that the Senate, equestrian order and whole citizenship body were purged of the adherents and appointments of Alexander Severus' predecessor.[94] If this was the case, both the Praetorian Prefect, Flavianus, and Epagathus, Prefect of the Annona, would have felt their position threatened.

These men, dismissed from their positions of influence, were now vulnerable to charges of *majestas* that were often brought by *delatores* who were entitled to half of the property and assets of the condemned. The remainder went to the imperial *fiscus*. Substantial wealth and vast estates could be accumulated by emperors who allowed *delatores* unrestricted licence to make accusations of treason. However, as the majority of those condemned were leading members of the senatorial and equestrian orders, the loyalty of the elite to the emperor was often fatally undermined. For this reason, Ulpian issued a rescript dated to 11 April AD 223 announcing that accusations and prosecutions for *majestas* were to be dramatically restricted.[95] It was probably at this time that the emperor promised never to put a senator to death.[96] All this was music to the ears of the elite.

By the early third century, the Praetorian Prefects had acquired a range of military, judicial and administrative responsibilities. This is reflected in a number of new offices that appear in the Praetorian Guard associated with the extended civil responsibilities of their prefect. However, their chief responsibility remained the safety of the emperor and his family. They were joint commanders of the Praetorian cohorts and in times of war had command of armies. Yet their power lay in their almost unrestricted access to the emperor. They were members of his *concilium* and were in constant attendance at his side. Many of these men were appointed for their legal expertise and advised the emperor on the cases he heard. These skilled and experienced officials had reached the very summit of the equestrian career ladder and were powerful patrons in their own right. They also controlled access to the emperor, deciding what business needed to be dealt with by the emperor rather than themselves or delegated to another official. Emperors also delegated imperial business to them. At some point in the late second or early third century, they acquired an independent judicial court of their own. Legal cases within 100 miles of Rome were heard by the Urban Prefect, whilst those cases beyond that up to the borders of Italy were referred to the Praetorian Prefects. We increasingly find provincial governors being asked to refer cases from the provinces to the Praetorian Prefects, as Alexander Severus advised a provincial governor to do. Around AD 220/221, the Praetorian Prefects found the sophist Heliodorus innocent of the charge of murder and recalled him from his island exile. Praetorian Prefects formed their own *concilium* of advisors who were supposed to be chosen by the emperor. However, it is doubtful Alexander Severus or Mamaea utilized this right during Ulpian's prefecture. As the Praetorian Prefect was acting as the representative of the emperor (*vice princips*), their decisions were final. Ulpian was chosen for his loyalty, but primarily because he was an outstanding jurist.[97]

The rescripts of Ulpian and Alexander Severus continue to propagate the official line heralding a restoration of the Augustan settlement with a return to an 'aristocratic' form of government. Imperial letters and replies proclaim 'the purity of my times' and 'the demise of treason charges in my era'. A rescript from 11 April AD 223 announces a policy of restricting prosecution for treason, in particular rejecting a judge's refusal to follow an imperial ruling as a treasonous act. In a letter to the city of Aphrodisias, the emperor idealistically states that 'to take away anything from the rights belonging to the city is foreign to the guardianship [extended to all in my] reign.' However, the reality remained, and was confirmed in an imperial reply from Ulpian, that despite these lofty platitudes, the emperor remained above the law. An imperial rescript proclaims 'that it is particularly appropriate in the exercise of power to abide by the laws' yet 'the law conferring imperial power exempts the emperor from the formalities of the law'. Another of his pronouncements puts this matter more succinctly: 'Whatever the emperor has decided has force of law.' Another rescript defines the ways this can be done: 'Therefore whatever the emperor has laid down by *epistula* [letter] and *subscriptio* [the addition of a reply below the original petition], or has determined in giving justice or has given extra judicially as a provisional judgement or has ordered by *edictum* [imperial edict], is agreed to be a law.' Ulpian is merely restating the centuries-old practice established by Vespasian. The *lex de imperio Vespasiani* from AD 69 added a legal veneer to the political reality of imperial Rome in that the Senate reserved its right to confer ultimate imperial power upon the emperor. This legitimized the right of the emperor to pass laws without consulting the Senate. Imperial rescripts, decrees and edicts passed directly into the statute books without the need for senatorial ratification. The emperor's very words were law. For all the fine ideals expressed in his imperial edicts, Alexander Severus was not at any stage advocating a reduction of his autocratic powers or allowing the Senate any increase in its own powers.[98]

The promotion of Ulpian effectively led to a demotion for Flavianus and Chrestus. Although retaining command over the Praetorians, Ulpian would not have allowed them the same opportunity as himself to attend the imperial *consilium* or preside over legal cases, nor permitted them unrestricted access to the emperor. Their power and influence curtailed, their ability to grant the requests and petitions of their own clients would have been greatly reduced. The appointment of an 'inspector of their conduct' inferred that their leadership, ability or even their loyalty was called into question. This was an affront to their dignity and honour. These were men who are described by Zosimus as not only 'well acquainted with military affairs' but 'excelling in the management of civil business'. This must refer to their skills and experience in jurisprudence. Understandably, Zosimus describes them as being greatly offended. Flavianus, as a previous Praetorian Prefect of Elagabalus, may also have found his loyalty being questioned by Ulpian. Their grievances may have become public knowledge. They were both executed. According to Dio and Zonoras, Ulpian had them put to death so 'that he might succeed them'. According to Zosimus, however, they conspired to murder Ulpian, but Mamaea discovered the plot and had them 'put aside'.[99] Any conspiracy by the Praetorian Prefects would have involved the Guard. This would have served to further undermine the soldiers' discipline and loyalty. Mamaea retained Ulpian as sole prefect.

Shortly after these events, rioting broke out in the city. Zonoras, probably drawing on the full account of Dio, describes how Ulpian's murder took place shortly after his appointment as sole Praetorian Prefect. As sole prefect, Ulpian would have to take responsibility for the re-imposition of discipline on the Praetorian cohorts. In all likelihood, Flavianus and Chrestus had allowed this to lapse in order to curry favour with the soldiers. Unlike Ulpian, both these men had military experience. The soldiers were probably less than impressed by their aged prefect hailing from the Greek east. The Praetorians were battled-hardened veterans, mainly drawn from the semi-civilized provinces along the Rhine and Danube, especially the Pannonias. They are described by Dio as 'savage in appearance … terrifying in speech, and most boorish in conversation'. Their perceptions of the cultivated, status-driven, punctilious and elitist senators is unfortunately unrecorded. There was, however, no love lost between them and the Senate. The populace of Rome also hated these half-Romanized soldiers in their midst, who often used their privileged position to rob, steal and intimidate without fear. Until now, Ulpian had little to recommend him to the Guard, lacking any military renown, and, if Oulpianus is to be identified with Ulpian, being pedantic and yet rigorous in a desire to restore order. Zosimus appears to suggest the personality of the Praetorian Prefect was an issue, 'there being many different reports as to his inclination'. The Praetorians' guiding principle was the defence of their privileges and benefits. Ulpian was clearly a threat to these. Zosimus again describes their new commander as being 'suspected by the army'.[100]

The duplicitous Epagathus played a key role in these and subsequent events. The probable Prefect of the Annona 'was believed to have been chiefly responsible for the death of Ulpian'.[101] It is difficult to understand why he would work to undermine Ulpian unless he too felt threatened by him. As with the executed Flavianus, he had been a highly placed official in the court of Elagabalus and had also been a trusted member of the entourage of Caracalla's murderer, Macrinus. Ulpian's desire to purge Roman political life of all associates of the deposed emperor may have resulted in Epagathus deciding that it was better to strike first, rather than waiting for the axe to fall. A Prefect of the Annona had no real opportunity to influence the actions of the Praetorians. However, this position was instrumental in keeping order in the city by ensuring that those members of the populace entitled to the free corn dole were fed on time and that there was a surplus of grain so the price remained low for the rest. It is estimated 200,000 households in Rome were entitled to the free grain dole out of an urban population of a million. In AD 190, Papyrius Dionysuis had engineered the death of Commodus' chief advisor, Cleander, through creating a shortage of grain which precipitated riots and a virtual civil war in the capital. Delaying the grain fleet in Carthage or Alexandria would have required the co-operation of the senatorial governor of Africa or the Prefect of Egypt. This is unlikely, especially as the Prefect of Egypt was promoted to the Praetorian Prefecture upon the death of Ulpian. More likely, Epagathus hoarded the grain in the massive warehouses in Ostia and Portus, delaying its distribution and forcing up the price of food for the majority of the urban poor. This, of course, is purely supposition, but the ensuing riots would have to have been crushed by the Vigiles and Praetorians. The mutinous Praetorians could be expected to use the resultant chaos to settle some scores of their own.[102]

There is some admittedly tentative evidence to suggest there was a famine in Rome at this time. We know of a number of occasions of rioting caused by food shortages: one in AD 190 caused by Papirius Dionysius, another in the reign of Septimius Severus due to the unrest in the countryside caused by the bandit Bulla Felix, who used an army of runaway slaves and former imperial freedmen to rob his way across southern Italy. The notoriously unreliable *Historia Augusta* twice suggests civil unrest caused by food shortages at some point in the reign of Alexander Severus before AD 226. The populace of Rome petitioned the emperor for a reduction in the price of beef and pork. It is difficult to see many of the urban poor being able to afford any type of meat. Archaeological analysis of faeces in Pompeii suggest the staple diet in this port city was grain, olives and fish. Meat, even here, was the preserve of the rich. Perhaps the *Historia Augusta* does preserve a record of grain shortages, but the account was adapted to present the emperor as refusing to pander to the urban poor as he refused to issue a decree reducing prices, which would have affected the profits of the rich landowners, and instead prohibited the slaughter of cattle and pigs to allow breeding to increase supply. This resulted in a reduction of meat prices, but a year later. The starving clearly would have spent the intervening time, if this element of the story was accurate, either rioting or dying.[103]

Byzantine historian Cedrenus also mentions a famine during the reign of Alexander Severus.[104] This is partly supported by the *Historia Augusta*, which states that the emperor on another occasion 'greatly improved the provisioning of the populace of Rome ... by purchasing grain at his own expense'.[105] Archaeological evidence points to the emperor either extending or restoring *horrea*, or grain warehouses, used to store the grain that was distributed for the grain dole. A bronze medallion issued at some point in the reign proclaims 'ABUNDANTIA AUG', suggesting that a shortage had previously existed.[106] A healthy interest in securing the unhindered distribution of grain was a primary concern of all emperors. However, the building work of the *horrea* by Alexander Severus suggests that the network of warehouses was extended due to a need to increase the volume of grain kept near Rome, as mentioned in the *Historia Augusta*,[107] or they were badly damaged by fire. This may have been an accidental conflagration, which was common, or as a consequence of the fires caused by the fighting that broke out in the capital.

What is for certain is that the streets of Rome became a battleground for three days and nights as the Praetorians fought with the populace. This bloodshed is described in Dio as emanating 'from some small cause' which he unfortunately fails to explain. Many lives were lost, but it was the untrained mob that gradually gained the upper hand and the Praetorians retreated to their fortress. Similar fighting between the mob and the Praetorians in AD 238 resulted in the same outcome, with the Praetorian Camp besieged and assaulted. There must be parallels in the nature of the fighting and the reasons for the soldiers' defeat. The Praetorians were drawn from legionaries recommended for service in the Guard. They were not a ceremonial, pampered unit, but men who had fought with distinction in the East and in the civil wars. This surprising defeat was due to the nature of urban fighting, where the soldiers were vulnerable to attack from above as they advanced through the streets. The populace looted the gladiatorial barracks and temples for their weapons, and their ranks were perhaps supplemented by gladiators and members of the Vigiles.[108]

The account of the fighting as described by Herodian in AD 238 would be similar to the conflict in AD 223. At first the populace engaged in close hand-to-hand combat, but they were no match for the seasoned soldiers. They broke and fled, finding refuge in the high tenement blocks that dominated the capital. The tide then turned as the people

'swarmed up into the upper rooms of the houses and caused casualties among the soldiers by showering them with tiles and a hail of stones and broken pots. The soldiers did not dare climb up after the people because of their unfamiliarity with the houses, and the doors of the houses and shops were closed. So they set fire to the wooden balconies of such houses that possessed them (of which there were a lot in the city). Because the buildings adjoined each other very closely, and a great number of them in a row were made of wood, the fire very easily burned down most of the city.'[109]

Similar tactics are described by Herodian in his account of the rioting engineered by the Prefect of the Annona, Papirius Dionysius, in AD 190. For this reason some scholars have doubted the accuracy of these passages, believing they are stock descriptions in imitation of Thucydides. The similarities exist because this is exactly what tended to happen when poorly armed civilians were faced with heavily armed soldiers in street fighting. Doors were locked and barricaded and the inhabitants climbed on the roofs, hurtling down tiles and stones. The soldiers retreated with heavy casualties.[110]

The situation in AD 223 was now completely out of control. Anarchy ruled in Rome. It was probably in these riots that the Pope, Callistus, was killed, perhaps the victim of a vengeful pagan mob using this opportunity to sate their prejudices and bigotry. The emperor and his family must have feared for their lives.

The Praetorians, as they did in AD 238, set fire to the buildings. Barred from entry, they would have used the overhanging wooden balconies to start the fires, burning their tormentors alive in their fortress tenements. Ulpian was probably desperately trying to restore order, but was now exposed and vulnerable. Zosimus describes how he lost his life in a 'tumult'. Dio provides a little more detail. A group of Praetorians decided to put an end to the life of their prefect. As the flames of the city illuminated the scenes of chaos and destruction, they hunted him down. Ulpian managed to flee to the palace, seeking the protection of the emperor and his mother, but to no avail. He was struck down before their eyes. The young emperor must have been traumatized, standing impotent as the man he considered his friend and parent was butchered before him.[111]

Epagathus was held to be primarily responsible for these events, yet he could not be punished whilst he remained in Rome. According to Dio, his execution in the capital would have resulted in a 'disturbance'. Would this be from the Praetorians or the mob? His Prefecture of the Annona would have given him some control over the populace. If there was a famine in Rome, he may have presented himself as the sole guarantor of ending the shortages. The *horrea* may have been opened flooding the capital with cheap grain and so presenting himself as the champion of the starving poor. Perhaps he had connections with the leaders of the circus factions or the shipping guild. In order to remove him from his power base, he was promoted to the Prefecture of Egypt. Epagathus must have felt his position was still secure in this distant province. Perhaps he believed his control over the Egyptian grain fleet would ensure his safety. It didn't. He was arrested and taken to Crete, where he was executed. His transfer to Crete suggests he had considerable connections in Egypt or Alexandria. However, our sources fail us on this matter. Yet a chance find securely placed Epagathus in Egypt in AD 224. A fragment of papyrus preserved in the sands of the Egyptian desert records the presence of Epagathus in May/June of that year. As Dio places Ulpian's murder not long after he was appointed sole prefect, and factoring in Epagathus' appointment and journey time to Egypt, it is likely Ulpian was murdered around October AD 223.[112]

This date is supported, although not conclusively, by the Album of Canusium. The council of this important Italian city set up a commemorative inscription in October AD 223 upon being given imperial permission to extend its membership, so reducing the individual costs of sitting on the city council. The inscription lists the city's important patrons. The name of Ulpian fails to appear, which may be due to the fact he was not a patron of the city, but it is a surprising omission considering the powerful and influential figures that are on it. The list is headed by two new Praetorian Prefects. These must have been appointed after the death of Ulpian, who is consistently described as sole prefect.[113]

As Ulpian's death can be securely dated to late AD 223, a statement by Dio complaining about the indiscipline of the soldiers in general, and in particular those under his command as governor of Pannonia Superior in AD 226–228, appears puzzling. The senatorial historian describes how 'the Praetorians complained of me to Ulpianus, because I ruled the soldiers in Pannonia with a strong hand'.[114] However, this reading of the ancient Greek is clearly wrong as Ulpian was long dead when Dio was governor of Pannonia. Tony Honoré reinterprets the Greek to mean that the Pannonian legions warned Dio not to impose the severe disciplinary measures that were introduced by Ulpian in his failed attempt to reassert some semblance of control over the imperial Guard.[115]

Despite riots and the virtual revolt of the Praetorian Guard, Alexander Severus survived. The soldiers clearly did not associate Ulpian's attempt to break their power with the young emperor. Perhaps his youth counted in his favour. Mamaea's bribery of the soldiers during her conflict with Soamias and Elagabalus a year earlier probably saved her, as well as a desire not to orphan the child. The soldiers would also have sworn their oath to protect the Augusta as a member of the 'divine house'. This was an additional reason for her survival. Not so Ulpian. As he was slain in front of them, mother and child must have expected to be next to be butchered. If the soldiers had suspected that they would have been punished for what they had done, the remainder of the imperial family would have shared Ulpian's fate, despite their oath. This clearly illustrates the weakness of the regime. The Praetorians would remain unruly and seditious throughout the reign of Alexander Severus. Coins issued in AD 224 hopefully proclaim 'Fides Militum', with the divine embodiment of loyalty holding two standards. Such legends on coins invariably suggest the reality was very different. Other coins issued in this year show the young emperor standing in military dress holding a globe and spear.[116] No further attempt was made to reimpose authority on the Praetorians. In these circumstances, it is quite remarkable that Alexander Severus survived for a further twelve years.

The absence of Maesa from these events suggests either a sudden collapse in her influence or, more likely, that she had been incapacitated by illness, old age or a combination of both. Ulpian fled to the presence of Mamaea and Alexander Severus rather than Maesa. Herodian describes her as an 'old lady' in AD 218.[117] She was born around AD 165, a date based on the birth of her first daughter in AD 180. Roman women usually married young, so it is possible Maesa was married by the age of 15. Although possibly in her late fifties in AD 223, Roman life expectancy was much lower in comparison to modern times. Ulpian's promotion to the Praetorian Prefecture over the two original appointees was Mamaea's decision, his original appointment to the Annona probably Maesa's. It was this appointment to the Praetorian Prefecture that precipitated the fateful events that lead to virtual civil war in the capital.

Chapter 6

Restoring the 'Golden Age' AD 224–228

'for thirteen years Alexander ruled without cause for complaint as far as
he himself was concerned.'

(Herodian, 6.2.1)

Mamaea had learnt well from her mother. She waited patiently for the
right moment to move against Epagathus and then struck with consummate skill. His appointment to the prefecture of Egypt blinded
him to the real reason for this appointment. His execution in AD 224 had to be
delayed until he had been separated from his *amici* and clients.[1]

The murder of Ulpian necessitated the appointment of new Praetorian Prefects.
The experiment in having one prefect was abandoned. A sole prefect possessed a
massive amount of power and influence without the check of a colleague. Ulpian
was a supremely skilled individual and trusted not to abuse this position to further
his own interests. Although men of similar ability continued to serve the regime –
such as Modestinus and Paul – the experiment was abandoned. Historically, the
employment of a sole Praetorian Prefect had ended disastrously. Commodus elevated the freedman Cleander over two equestrian prefects, leading to rioting, revolt
and the execution of all three. Laetus, another sole prefect under Commodus, conspired against his master. Septimius Severus advanced his trusted *amicus* Fulvius
Plautianus to the role. However, rivalries and jealousies increased as his power
and influence grew. His position was eventually undermined through a whispering
campaign led by Caracalla. The emperor, increasingly suspicious of Plautianus'
loyalty, ordered his execution. The sole prefecture was a poisoned chalice.

L. Domitius Honoratus and M. Aedinius Julianus were promoted to the post by
Mamaea and Alexander Severus. Honoratus had been Prefect of Egypt in AD 222
and had been replaced in his old post by his new colleague, Aedinius Julianus. The
logic of replacing Aedinius Julianus with Epagathus lulled the unsuspecting court-
ier into a false sense of security, especially as he could reasonably expect appointment to the Praetorian Prefecture at some point in the future. A copy of a letter,
written by Aedinius Julianus in AD 223 as Praetorian Prefect, has been preserved
on the base of a statue of Titus Sennius Sollemnis at Thorigny in western France.
The letter was inscribed on his statue to illustrate the services Sollemnis provided
on behalf of Aedinius Julianus. Whilst serving as acting governor of Lugdunensis

Gaul, Aedinius Julianus had become well acquainted with Sollemnis, who was the priest of the Imperial cult in the province and, with it, chairman of the Gallic Assembly. Certain members of the Gallic Assembly had felt aggrieved by the actions and conduct of the previous governor of the province, Claudius Paulinus, and had indicted him on trumped-up charges. Sollemnis blocked the legal challenge at the Gallic Assembly in August AD 220, claiming he had never been asked to present a legal case against Paulinus, and went on to praise the governor and his administration of the province. The case was subsequently dropped. What the inscription fails to add, but can be deduced from his actions, is that Sollemnis was a client of both Paulinus and Aedinius Julianus. After Aedinius Julianus had returned to Rome on his appointment as Praetorian Prefect, Sollemnis went to the capital to pay his respects to his patron and congratulate him. Upon his departure, Sollemnis requested a letter of recommendation from Aedinius Julianus addressed to Badius Comnianus, the new governor of his native province of Lugdunensis. Such was the complexity of the bonds that underscored political and social relationships in Rome.

Another inscription from Sollemnis' statue preserves a letter from Paulinus, now an ex-consul and governor of Lower Britain, testifying to the services Sollemnis offered him. Paulinus was now indebted to his client, and in payment employed him on his staff in York. The inscription lists the gifts Paulinus gave his client on appointment to the governorship: a woollen cloak from Canusium, a Dalmatian tunic from Laodiceia, a gold brooch set with jewels, two cloaks, a British tunic and a sealskin. Part of this *beneficia* included the promise to send him a letter of appointment to a six-month tenure of a tribunate when a vacancy arose. The vacancy apparently did not arise, so he was made a judicial assessor to the governor instead. He was also sent his salary in advance: 25,000 sesterces in gold.[2] These inscriptions typify how the Roman Empire functioned. The nexus of reciprocal favours bound patron and client, and was the foundation of public life. Patrons used their influence to protect and assist their clients through a reciprocal exchange of goods, gifts and services between two or more parties of unequal status. Links between social equals was clothed in the language of friendship (*amicitaea*), but their obligations to return a favour were the same.[3]

Another important inscription from AD 223 is the Album of Canusium from Apulia. This bronze tablet lists the names of the patrons of the city in order of precedence. Although only containing the names of those eminent persons associated with the city, it does still provide a snapshot of those aristocrats and senior equestrians who played a significant role in the imperial government in the opinion of the leaders of this city. Heading the list is Appius Claudius Julianus. He held a particular prominence in the circle around Mamaea and Alexander Severus, being appointed Prefect of Rome and having the honour of a second consulship in

AD 224. He may have been descended from the Appii Claudii who played a significant role in the history of the Roman Republic.[4]

Next on the list is the otherwise unknown T. Lorenius Celsus. His position
on the album suggests he was a Praetorian Prefect at some point in AD 223 with
Aedinius Julianus. Nothing else is known about him. This may have been a temporary appointment after the sudden death of Ulpian and the delay in the arrival
of Aedinius Julianus from Egypt. After the failure of Ulpian's sole prefecture, the
idea of Honoratus continuing in this role on his own, if only for a few months, was
deemed to be too risky. Another suggestion is that T. Lorenius Celsus held the
Praetorian Prefecture until AD 226, with Honoratus being Prefect of the Vigiles
in AD 223 and later being awarded the Praetorian Prefecture in AD 226. However,
this is a very unusual career structure, with the Prefect of Egypt often promoted
to the Praetorian Prefecture and the Prefecture of the Vigiles being a lesser post. A
L. Lorenius Crispinus was a senator in AD 231 and *suffect* consul before AD 244. He
must be a relative of the Praetorian Prefect; perhaps his son. We might conjecture
that the temporary nature of his appointment was compensated by *adlection* to the
Senate, with his son receiving favourable and rapid promotion in return for his
father's loyal service.[5]

Below T. Lorenius Cesus on the list we find the Praetorian Prefect, Aedinius
Julianus. The appearance of his name and the absence of Ulpian's, as already discussed, suggests that the sole prefect had been murdered by the time the list was
drawn up by the councillors of the city. His presence in a list of eminent senators has been used to suggest Alexander Severus elevated Praetorian Prefects to
full senatorial rank, with the rank of ex-consuls. However, it is clear that they
had merely been awarded honorary consular status. This title entitled them to be
counted amongst those with senatorial status. These prefects had almost unrestricted access to the emperor, which suggests that Appius Claudius, who appears
above him, had equal if not greater access. Praetorian Prefects also held judicial
powers over the whole of Italy, including Canusium. The wealthy decurions of the
city would have wanted these men as their patrons.

The next name is that of L. Didius Marinus. Six inscriptions from around the
empire testify to his very successful equestrian career. He is probably to be identified with the husband of Annia Cornificia, the sister of Commodus. Their names
appear on water pipes from Ostia, suggesting they had joint ownership of the
water supply to the city. He survived the forced suicide of his wife on the orders
of Caracalla to reappear as an important patron of Canusium in AD 223. His name
appears under the list of Praetorian Prefects, leading to the suggestion he was one
too. If so, it would have to be c. AD 223. His tenure of office could only have been
for a matter of weeks if this were the case. B. Salway suggests he was Prefect of
the Annona, perhaps replacing Epagathus, who had been moved to the prefecture

of Egypt. His position on the list suggests that whatever office he held, he was an important figure on the *concilium principis*.[6]

The final equestrian in this part of the album is L. Domitius Honoratus. A papyrus securely dates Honoratus as Prefect of Egypt on 6 January AD 222. A statue base found near the legionary base outside Alexandria records him as Praetorian Prefect, but unfortunately gives no date. His predecessor, Chrestus, is attested by papyrus as Egyptian Prefect from 19 August AD 219 to c. AD 220, and his successor was Aedinius Julianus, whose presence in the province is recorded on 3 November, presumably in AD 222.[7] Historians continue to argue over the reasons why Honoratus appears below the more obscure figures of Lorenius Celsus and L. Didius Marinus. However, the function of a patron was to use their access to power and superior position to further the interests of their client, in this case the councillors of Canusium. The positioning of these holders of the prestigious equestrian posts above members of the senatorial aristocracy demonstrates where real power lay, despite the imperial propaganda heralding a partnership with the Senate. Power and influence was dependent upon regular personal contact with the emperor and his mother. These equestrian officials were perceived as possessing greater influence than the prominent senators who appear below them.[8]

The next group on the list consists of senators who were of consular rank. Three M. Antonii are prominent magistrates in Canusium and probably held large estates around the city. M. Antonius Balbus, L. Pontius Verus and C. Gavivius Maximus are otherwise unknown, but most likely held the consulship before AD 217. An M. Antonius Balbus who appears lower down the list (number twenty-two) was probably the son of his namesake (sixth on the list). Pontius Bassus and Pontius Mauricus (numbers twenty and twenty-one) were probably the sons of Pontius Verus (number eight). M. Statius Longinus was governor of Moesia Inferior in AD 217–218 and probably the father of M. Statius Longinus and M. Statius Patruinus, who appear further down the list (numbers twenty-nine and thirty). B. Furius Octavianus was a consul before AD 217 and a *pontifex*. His family held large estates in Moesia. The family of A. Betitius Pius held magistracies in the cities of Aeclanum, Nola and Venusia.[9]

The career of L. Lucilius Priscilianus (nineteenth on the list) was considered both scandalous and disreputable. He had crossed the bounds of social decency by appearing in the arena, but his actions appear to have won the admiration of the Emperor Caracalla, who was fascinated with gladiatorial combat. Priscilianus then became a *delator*, acting as an informer on his peers. Caracalla rewarded him by *adlecting* him into the Senate with the rank of ex-praetor. A man of proven usefulness and loyalty, he was made governor of Achaea in AD 217. Dio, probably typical of the majority of senators, hated this 'traitor' within their ranks. His comments on the man and his career are full of bitterness and enmity. The fall of Caracalla resulted in Priscilianus' fall from grace. He was condemned, exiled and his wealth confiscated. However, in AD 223, he must have been recalled in order to appear on the album. The policy of the emperor and his mother of building their new regime on as wide a foundation as possible even encompassed embracing men hated by their senatorial contemporaries.[10]

In contrast to Priscilianus, the next two names were members of one of the noblest families in Rome. C. Bruttius Praesens, the consul of AD 217, and his brother, C. Bruttius Crispinus, the nominated consul of AD 224, appear at numbers thirteen and fourteen. The family had been granted patrician status by Antoninus Pius, whilst their aunt, Bruttia Crispina, had married Commodus. The family had held no consulships under Caracalla as they were too closely associated with Commodus. Historians have suggested that Appius Claudius Julianus headed the list on the album due to his position as consul elect, yet his colleague of the year appears thirteen places below. Appius Claudius clearly heads the list for the closeness of his relationship with the emperor and his mother.[11]

Surprisingly placed one below the Bruttii is C. Petronius Magnus. He held a praetorship under Caracalla, a year after Bruttius Crispinus, so he was probably consul in AD 225/226. His name has been erased on the album, probably as he suffered *damnatio memoriae*. He can consequently be identified with the 'Magnus' in Herodian who is described as a 'patrician consul'. In AD 235, Petronius Magnus became the leader of a senatorial revolt against Alexander Severus' successor, Maximinus Thrax. He must have had considerable status and influence in the reign of Alexander Severus to be recognized by his fellow aristocrats as a potential emperor whom they were willing to serve.[12]

There are over 100 decurions (councillors) listed on the album. Many of those are clearly sons or close relatives of the leading councillors. Included towards the bottom of the list are twenty-five *praetextati*, young men who still wore the *toga praetexta*, a toga with a purple hem worn by children before reaching manhood. Adults wore an all-white toga. The names of these children also indicate that they are the offspring of current councillors. By this period, membership of a town council had become hereditary, and these *praetexti*, although having no vote, were waiting for a vacancy to arise. However, the fact that there were an ample number of candidates to fill places on the town council, and the clear evidence that the councillors took immense pride in the large number of prestigious patrons they were attached to, counters the prevalent view that these councils were in decline in this period. However, the situation should not be generalized, as Canusium, through its location on the route to the important port of Brundisium, was in a favourable geographical position. Yet many towns across the empire, though not all, still showed clear evidence of prosperity and financial investment by the local nobility.

Alexander Severus also invested in an extensive building programme in the capital. The *Historia Augusta* appears for once to be remarkably accurate in its description of the buildings erected. Archaeological evidence seems to support its assertions. Perhaps the author of the work was based in Rome and knew from exterior inscriptions work carried out by the emperor:

'He restored the public works of former emperors and built many new ones himself, among them the bath which was called by his own name adjacent to what had been the Neronian and also the aqueduct which still has the name Alexandriana. Next to this bath he planted a grove of trees and the site of some private dwellings which he purchased and then tore down. One bath tub he called 'the Ocean' ... The Baths of Antoninus Caracalla he completed and beautified by the addition of a portico. Moreover, he was the first to use the so-called Alexandrian marble-work, which is made of two kinds of stone, porphyry and Lacedaemonian marble, and he employed this kind of material in the ornamentation of the open places in the Palace. He set up in the city many statues of colossal size, calling together sculptors from all places.'[13]

The Baths of Caracalla were built on a vast scale, employing up to 9,000 workmen per day for five years between AD 211–216. However, it is clear from brick stamps that the outer precinct was added later, under Alexander Severus. A precinct was surrounded by a multifunctional array of buildings, with the exterior walls covered in statues. The remains of one such statue, probably a Doryphoros, was held to the wall by a dowel, the hole still discernible. Doryphoros statues depict a muscular athlete holding a spear over his left shoulder. The enclosed area held a stadium-shaped structure with tiered seating, which archaeologists suggest was used for foot races and athletics events. A large eagle was discovered in this area, which probably came from a statue of the emperor depicted as Jupiter. The remains of a marble altar to Diana, Silvanus and Bono Dea was also associated with the stadium. Temples to all three stood in the surrounding area of the baths and were meant to add to the rustic charm of the gardens and park, which was planted with trees in and around the buildings. Another rectangular building with a series of niches built into the walls may have served as a library. The largest niche traditionally held a statue of Athena, the goddess of wisdom. Archaeologists discovered a number of bearded herms, which were the standard ornamentation of libraries and gymnasia as they were associated with Apollo and Hercules. A large staircase and grand entrance built at this time provided access to the baths from the Aventine. A massive central hall was also constructed on the south-eastern side which held a huge statue, probably another of the emperor himself. A large underground *mithraeum* was constructed beneath these structures, linked to the vast network of tunnels used by the army of slaves that serviced the baths. Nearby, a water mill was constructed that made use of the large volume of water that was used in the baths on a daily basis.[14]

The Baths of Nero were rebuilt by Alexander Severus on a gigantic scale, measuring 200x120 metres. On completion, the building was known as the Baths of Alexander. A number of buildings along the Via della Dogana Vecchia still make use of the bath's considerable superstructure, including the church of S. Luigi dei Francesi, the Palazzo Giustiniana and Palazzo Madama. The walls still stand over four storeys high in places around the Piazza Rondanini. Columns of grey and pink granite quarried from Aswan in Egypt have emerged from the area for centuries, two being reused in the restoration of the porch of the Pantheon in 1666. Another two can be seen as part of the decoration of the church of S. Eustachio, whilst many more form part of the cellars of the surrounding buildings. A great basin on the Via dei Staderari was originally located in the hot room of the baths. Work must have started early in the reign, but it was completed by AD 227. A number of coins dated from AD 224–226 show the exterior of a large building, the arcaded lower storey shown surmounted by what appears to be a triple triumphal arch decorated with trophies and statues.[15]

The baths were served by the completion of a new aqueduct, the Alexandrina. It ran for 22km along the Via Praenestina to meet the outskirts of Rome at the Porta Maggiore, and then ran underground to the Field of Mars, the location of the Baths of Alexander.[16]

A massive public fountain, the Nymphaeum of Alexander Severus, was completed at the same time as the aqueduct in AD 226. A series of coins were issued to celebrate its construction. A gold aureus shows the reclining figure of Oceanus. The reclining figure of this god traditionally adorned *nymphaea* across the empire. A third or fourth-century hymn to Oceanus refers to him as, 'Lord of the waves, Father of the sea, Arbiter of the globe.' The emperor clearly associated himself with this god's divine and temporal power. Today, all that is left is an 18 metre mound made of concrete and brick. It would have originally been covered in marble, beautified with numerous sculptures. Water arrived at the rear from an extension of the Aqua Claudia or Anio Novus, where it divided into two 'rivers' that cascaded down the front and sides in three 'streams' at the front and one on each side. The water was collected in an upper basin, where pipes fed fountains at floor level which filled a large basin at the base. The people would have collected fresh water here under the gaze of the massive statue of Oceanus. The whole structure resonated with triumphal imagery. Two massive trophies that can now be found at the top of the stairs on the Piazza del Campidoglio originally stood on the nymphaeum. Statues from the Trajanic era were deliberately reused to associate the present reign with Rome's glorious military past. The nymphaeum took the form of an honorary arch, with coins showing three large arches above the structure. The emperor was clearly asserting his military ambitions. Its prominent position near the Esquiline Gate and function as an important supply of water ensured the message was seen by as wide an audience as possible. The nymphaeum also appears to have incorporated an earlier structure which has been subsumed within it. The *Historia Augusta* does remark that he 'restored the public works of former emperors'.[17]

Another monumental Severan construction was probably augmented by Alexander Severus. The Septizodium, constructed by Septimius Severus, stood on the Via Appia, the major thoroughfare from the Colosseum and the Circus Maximus at the foot of the Palatine. Ninety to ninety-five feet in length, this free-standing structure was covered in statues of the seven prominent gods, surrounded by statues of the emperor and the imperial family.[18] Statues of Alexander Severus and Mamaea would have been moved to the most eminent locations, advertising their dynastic claims, tenuous as they were, and proclaiming their association with the divine. Alexander Severus appears to have built similar structures in the provinces to propagate his claims. A Septizodium was built at Lambaesis in North Africa in AD 226, with its associated aqueduct that was built by the *III Augusta* legion. This was another freestanding construction, consisting of a single exedra flanked by two wings. A water basin ran along its whole length, drawing a regular crowd who could gaze at the array of statues of the gods, the emperor and his mother. Another similar structure has been discovered at Cincari in Tunisia, built in association with a bathing complex and water fountain. According to the *Historia Augusta*, the emperor restored many bridges built by Trajan as well as constructing new ones, provided the temples of Isis and Serapis in the Campus Martius with statues and other paraphernalia linked to their rites, as well as starting construction of a Basilica Alexandrina, but his death curtailed its completion. There is as yet no archaeological evidence to support this, as the basilica has never been located.[19]

A gold aureus of AD 223 shows the four stories of the Colosseum, with statues prominent in its niches and supports for the roof awning. A sesterces from the same year shows two gladiators fighting in the Colosseum, with the Meta Sudans standing to the right.[20] The top wooden tiers of the amphitheatre had been hit by lightning in AD 217, resulting in a severe fire. The fires had been so intense that not only had the upper tiers needed to be replaced, but also the wooden floor of the arena and the whole of the north-western sector's brick vaults and external marble façade. Repairs would take until AD 240, but by AD 223 the arena could again be used for gladiatorial contests, with some areas remaining closed. However, the new Augustus understandably wished to associate his reign with the restoration of the gladiatorial contests in their 'home'. The appearance of the Meta Sudans on the coinage issued at this time suggests it too was damaged in the fire and restored by the emperor. An inscription relating to the restoration of an important structure was found nearby. This large conical fountain, standing 17 metres high, 'sweated' water ('*sudans*' is Latin for 'sweating' or 'dripping'), with the water being collected in a large pool at the base, 16 metres in diameter and 1.4 metres deep.[21]

Archaeology only hints at the extensive restoration and building programme initiated by the emperor. Along with the work on the Baths of Nero, the Baths of Caracalla, the Colosseum and the Alexandrian nymphaeum, fragmentary inscriptions point to restorations to the Temple of Serapis on the Quirinal Hill, and another inscription from AD 225 was found in the Circus Maximus, referring to another restoration. According to the *Historia Augusta*, he also intended to repair the Theatre of Marcellus, but this was never carried out. However, in a political move, Alexander Severus appears to have virtually abandoned the imperial villa and gardens of 'Old Hope', so beloved by his predecessor. It was here that Elagabalus had awaited news on what he hoped would be the successful assassination of his Caesar. These associations led to it being rarely used, and the baths might have been opened up to the public. Alexander Severus appears to have regularly used the Gardens of Sallust that partially covered the Pincio and Quirinal Hills. Much of the structural remains have been lost, but many famous statues and art works have been recovered, including the beautiful 'Ludovisi throne', a range of statues depicting mythological subjects, defeated and vanquished barbarians and an unusual red hippopotamus now in Copenhagen.[22]

The gigantism and monumentalism of the Alexandrian building programme was extended to the larger-than-life presentation of him in statuary. All emperors had done this, typified by the 'Colossus' of Nero that stood over 35 metres high outside the Colosseum. Fragments of huge statues of Alexander Severus have been found in Rome and across the empire. The torso from such a statue has been discovered at the Villa of Alexander Severus on the Via Ostiensis. The torso was covered with a corset on the back and Nereids on sea horses on the front. Military imagery appears, with a shield and a greave partly covered by the *paludamentum*, the cloak worn by commanders, and the arms of Achilles. All are stock imperial decorative themes. Another massive statue depicting either Elagabalus or Alexander Severus has been discovered in Naples, whilst in Alexandria a colossal marble statue that started life representing Ptolemy IV, VI or Mark Antony was transformed with the addition of a stucco beard into Alexander Severus as the god Serapis. However, much of the emperor's construction programme was centred on establishing a link between his reign and that of his illustrious predecessors in order to establish a firmer foundation for his rule.[23]

The rioting of AD 224 had a profound effect upon the emperor and his mother. Coinage of this year shows a distribution of *congiaria*, usually provided in the form of money. The image of the young emperor is shown draped in a toga, facing right, with *Liberalitas*, standing on the left, who is holding an abacus and *cornucopiae*, signifying abundance. The coin carries the legend '*Liberalitas Augusti II*'.[24] This distribution of largesse may have helped to calm the situation in the short term, but it was not enough for people to buy food and pay rent over the long term. Even the free grain dole, which only about a quarter of Rome's population was entitled to, amounted to 5 *modii* a month and was only enough to feed a single man but not his family. It is estimated that Rome's population stood at around a million, with only about 200,000-250,000 eligible for the grain dole. Yet even those who received this had to hand a percentage of it over to the mill owners as payment for grinding it into flour, and then more was given to the baker for using his ovens. On top of this, money was required for oil for lighting, cooking and cleaning at the baths. Shortages of grain rapidly resulted in a steep rise in prices, leading to urban unrest. The great aristocratic houses would support their clients and freedmen, but it is doubtful that the vast majority of the urban poor benefitted from the patron–client network.[25]

The primary function of Alexander Severus' massive construction programme was to provide paid work for the urban poor. A lack of sanitation was also a concern, caused by overcrowding and a lack of space. The focus on increasing access to fresh water and bathing attempted to cater for some of the people's needs, with imperial handouts of money used to pay for the exorbitant rents charged in the capital. There appears to have been a reduction in private construction at this time, leading to increased reliance on imperial resources. From the reign of Hadrian onwards, there was increasing use of *coloni* for simple construction on imperial lands. This appears to have increased significantly under Alexander Severus. A decrease in construction would have led to a reduction in skilled labour, in particular architects and engineers. For this reason, Ramsey MacMullen suggests that the emperor was forced to pay regular salaries to these craftsman, as well as providing lecture rooms and rations, paid for out of the public purse, for students in these areas. Rhetors, philosophers and grammarians had for a considerable period of time benefitted from imperial appointments to salaried posts. The simple economics of supply and demand rendered the extension of this policy inevitable.[26]

According to the *Historia Augusta*, public storehouses (*horrea*) were built in each of the fourteen regions of Rome so that merchants without access to their own might store their goods and property. These vast warehouses stored not only grain, but everything from clothing and olive oil to marble. Some were massive, even by today's standards. The *Horrea Galbae*, built in the first century, had 140 rooms on the ground floor alone and covered 21,000 square metres.[27] There is very tentative archaeological evidence to support this assertion in the suspect *Life of Severus Alexander*. Excavations on the Via Sacra at the base of the Palatine have identified a series of *horrea* built around this time. It would make sense to increase the state's control of the supply of grain. When shortages were caused by famine, political crisis or a delay in the Carthaginian or Alexandrian grain fleets, the price could be forced up even higher by private hoarding by profiteers. Imperial control of an increased number of these warehouses made this more difficult. As mentioned, the twelfth-century Byzantine historian Cedrenus does refer to a significant famine in the reign of Alexander Severus, which was so severe that some were forced to resort to cannibalism. This may account for the reorganization of the capital's stockpile of grain, but it is surprising such an event was not recorded in the account of Herodian. However, the historian does appear to be more concerned with the emperor's military campaigns than domestic events.[28]

The possible construction of these warehouses could also be linked to the state's collection of customs duties. All goods entering the city were taxed at customs stations based around the main roads entering the capital. At one station on the Flaminian Way, the name of Commodus has been erased and replaced by that of Alexander Severus. As Commodus suffered *damnatio memoriae*, it is not surprising that his name was removed.[29] However, this occurred thirty-one years before the accession of Alexander Severus. The imperial regime appears to have taken an interest in the efficient imposition of taxes, with Mamaea being accused in all the sources of greed and avarice. The reform of the *horrea* might be linked to this, as merchants could be encouraged to transport their goods into the city when they were struggling to find adequate warehousing elsewhere on the outskirts of the city, so avoiding the custom stations. The *Historia Augusta*, as usual frustratingly vague, comments that 'in order to bring merchants to Rome of their own accord he bestowed the greatest privileges on them'.[30] This might suggest the use of the public warehouses was either free or at low cost.

In order to further ingratiate himself with the populace of Rome, a series of watermills were constructed at this time. One was built as part of the extension to the Baths of Caracalla, using the abundant supply of water to and from the baths themselves.[31] A pottery shard from the construction trench of a watermill complex on the Janiculum Hill suggests it was built in the first half of the third century. The *Aqua Trajana* descends the steep slope of the hill, and its fast-flowing water was used to power a series of waterwheels. There is enough room for four mills, with three or four wheels on the northern mill race and a single larger wheel on the southern race driving a large mill or two smaller ones. The sixth-century writer Procopius records that these mills were important for converting grain into flour for the grain dole during the reign of Aurelian from AD 270–275. At some point between the late second century and the late third, bread was distributed instead of grain. As the mills drew water from the state-owned aqueduct, these were clearly not privately owned. The inadequate nature of our sources renders a definitive date for this change tentative at the least. However, according to the *Historia Augusta*, Alexander Severus 'erected in Rome very many great engineering works', which may refer to these mills.[32] The construction of a mill associated with the building of the precinct attached to the Baths of Caracalla and the pottery shard in the construction trench points to the change being part of the Alexandrian reform of the grain dole. Contextually, along with his reforms to the production and distribution of olive oil, this appears the best fit.[33] After AD 235, Roman emperors would be more concerned with barbarian invasions or military revolts, and very rarely visited the capital. Their concern for placating the urban poor of Rome would not have been a priority.

Archaeology also appears to support the assertion in the *Historia Augusta* that Alexander Severus 'established anew the largess of oil which Severus had given to the populace'.[34] Stamps or painted inscriptions written on each amphora record weight, origin and names of the persons making the record, the name of the merchant and the producer of the amphora. This information provides a unique record of the Roman economy. Analysis of amphorae *testae* on the massive artificial mountain of broken and discarded amphorae that is Monte Testaccio shows trade peaking under Antoninus Pius before entering into a steady decline, until recovering at the start of the reign of Alexander Severus. The amphorae originally contained olive oil, wine and fish sauce imported from Africa and Baetica in Spain. The analysis of shipwrecks mirrors this evaluation, with numbers declining after Antoninus Pius before recovering temporarily under Alexander Severus. The earlier wrecks generally carried a mixed cargo of olive oil, sauce and wine. However, under Alexander Severus there is a significant increase of wrecks with a single cargo: olive oil. This change was probably the result of increased demand stimulated by the increased distribution of oil by the state.[35]

The amphorae stamps also record another significant change in the production of olive oil in Baetica. Under Septimius Severus, a large number of estates which were originally held in private ownership became part of the imperial estates. Many landowners who had supported Niger or Clodius Albinus in the civil war were condemned and their land confiscated. The export of these products was also taken over by the state. However, stamps show that Alexander Severus restored this export trade to the private sphere, probably due to the financial costs to the treasury of maintaining the merchant fleet as well as the continuing costs of the army and extensive construction programme. No private names appear on amphorae stamps from Monte Testaccio from AD 198–230. The restoration of the involvement of merchants in the *annona* is probably one of the measures referred to in the *Historia Augusta*, along with the possible construction of public *horrea* that were free to use, that 'bestowed the greatest privileges on' the merchants.[36]

The character and personality of the teenage emperor must have been shaped in some form by the events of AD 222 and 223. The two men he had called his 'father' had been brutally murdered, at least one of them before his eyes. He is described in the *Life of Severus Alexander* as 'a most righteous man'.[37] However, the utopian picture painted in the *Historia Augusta* has to be discounted and ignored. The *Life*, written in the late fourth century, is a political homily on the nature of good government. To pursue this aim, the author distorts and adjusts the figure of Alexander Severus to fit his theme.[38] Herodian also presents an idealized portrait of the emperor, whose one fatal flaw was his submissive compliance to his mother's wishes, and in particular her avarice. He is described as being full of 'youthful vigour', his character being 'naturally gentle and docile, always inclined to show sympathy' and 'humane and benevolent behaviour. This he demonstrated as he grew older.' However, Herodian criticizes the emperor, as he was 'completely dominated by his mother' and 'obeyed his mother in matters of which he disapproved because he was over-mild and showed greater respect to her than he ought to have done'. Furthermore, she ' may have restrained him because of her womanly timidity and excessive love of her son. She used to blunt Alexander's efforts to behave bravely by convincing him that it was other people's job to take risks for him.' He was predisposed towards peace and only turned to war after all else had failed; the antithesis of the Roman concept of *virtus*. At the moment of death, he is described as hysterically clinging to his mother, blaming her for his untimely end.[39]

Herodian, a contemporary historian, clearly disliked Mamaea. His account is based upon female stereotypes. She is too caught up in her motherly affections for her son to see and understand the 'big picture', especially when faced with decisions that men should take, notably involving war and violence. She is surprisingly described as 'timid'. Yet this is a woman who successfully plotted the overthrow and murder of her own sister and nephew. She had stood before the Praetorians in a verbal duel with Soamias, the loser facing certain death. Timid, no; a loving mother, without doubt. Yet Herodian's own account betrays contradictions which undermine his presentation of the dynamics between mother and son. He uses the word 'may' when describing Mamaea's attempts to persuade her son not to take risks. He clearly had no factual evidence to support his assertion. Furthermore, after AD 224, Herodian presents Alexander Severus as taking sole responsibility for most of the key decisions. The account of the emperor's murder is based on 'reports'. As all of Alexander Severus' councillors and advisors were murdered along with the emperor, we have to wonder where these reports came from. The assassins sent by Maximinus Thrax would not make the most reliable of sources.

The tone of the letter sent by the newly acclaimed emperor to Alexandria is indeed resonant with youthful enthusiasm and informality,[40] but other sources contradict Herodian's description of him as 'docile' and 'gentle'. Perhaps our sources confuse supposed 'feminine' qualities of gentility with simple human compassion. This is evident in a legal ruling of the emperor promoting the freeing of slave girls on the death of their master, even if this manumission was not included in the will. Even Herodian admits Alexander Severus 'found fault with his mother',[41] whilst Dio commends him for standing up to the hostility of the Praetorians towards him for the reimposition of discipline on the Pannonian legions, and indeed deliberately granting Dio considerable honours in opposition to the guards' resistance, including a second consulship he shared with the emperor himself. This only served to enrage the soldiers further, so, fearing that Dio would be murdered by his Guard, the emperor suggested Dio spend his consulship away from Rome. This illuminates the stubborn and determined streak in the emperor, but also the weakness of the regime.[42]

This is not to say that Mamaea was not greatly influential. She clearly remained the single most important advisor to the emperor. Her prominence allowed Herodian and the author of the *Historia Augusta* to blame the ultimate failure of the regime on her, rather than on the idealized emperor himself. However, we should discount the pliable nonentity that Herodian invites his readers to believe. An inscription from Djemila, often cited as an example of her supposed dominance, refers to the emperor as the 'son of Julia Mamaea Augusta, grandson of Julia Maesa Augusta'. Maesa was probably dead by late AD 225 or early AD 226. The emperor would have been around 17 years old at the time, and yet similar inscriptions can be found in relation to the adolescent Geta and his mother, Julia Domna.[43]

In comparison to Julia Maesa and Julia Domna, inscriptions dedicated to Mamaea are nowhere near as prevalent. The honours and titles that appear in the epigraphical record are not unique to her, but had been previously awarded to Julia Domna and her own mother. The precedent having been set, Mamaea was free to use them herself. Like Maesa and Julia Domna, she was 'Mother of the Camps', to which, like Julia Domna, she added in AD 227 'of the Senate and her Native Land'. Her name appears on milestones alongside that of Alexander Severus, another precedent set by Julia Domna. An inscription from the Balkans refers to her as 'Mistress of the inhabited World'. Both Augusta and Augustus are also referred to as 'My Lords'.[44] Most inscriptions were made by members of the lower strata of society. M. Aurelius Heraclitus, a centurion in the *Statores Praetoriani*, a special unit of the Praetorians, made a dedication to Jupiter Optimus Maximus for the safety of Alexander Severus and Mamaea. A legionary of the VII *Gemina* legion in Spain made a dedication 'to her divine spirit and majesty'. At Aquincum, most recovered dedications are to Alexander Severus and his mother. Many appear to have been made by veterans of an Emesene cohort stationed there. The spread of inscriptions dedicated to Mamaea is interesting, with over a third from Moesia and Thrace, whilst they are a rarity in Africa and her native land of Syria.[45]

Julia Domna, Maesa and Mamaea appear to have also been closely associated with the Syrian manifestation of Jupiter, Jupiter Dolichenus. Aurelius Sabinus, a wine merchant and priest of this god from Augusta Trajana, makes a dedication on her behalf, as does a Prefect of the First Cohort of Treverans, along with Primitivius, a freedman in Dacia Apulensis. Dedications have also been found in Rome made by Praetorians and from sailors based at the naval base on the Tiber Island, suggesting the presence of a *Dolicheneum*.[46] This sun god originated in the Syrian Doliche during the time of Hadrian, and was spread around the empire by Eastern soldiers and merchants. The god is represented as a bearded figure standing in front of a bull, with the disc of the sun above his head. He wears a bonnet, tunic and sword, whilst brandishing an axe in one hand and a thunderbolt in the other. His warlike characteristics appealed to the soldiers, particularly men stationed along the Rhine and Danube. The god is sometimes represented as an eagle standing over a stag's head, as found at Alishar Huyuk in Turkey along with a coin of Alexander Severus. Over fifty such temples, shrines, inscriptions and votive offerings have been discovered near forts in these provinces. Temples to the god were built, with assembly rooms complete with hypocaust for communal meals, with worshippers organized into a hierarchy, led by a scribe. It appears to have been popular with the lower ranks of the army, and for a time rivalled the worship of Mithras. In Rome, a temple has been discovered on the Aventine, and one on the Esquiline that was used by worshippers from the *Cohors II Vigilum*.[47]

After the murder of Alexander Severus, these temples in the German and Danubian provinces were systematically looted and demolished from AD 235. The sanctuary at Vetus Salina (modern Adony) must have been one of the last to suffer this fate. Around AD 238, it was demolished and then deliberately set on fire. This desecration of religious sites can only have been at the command of Maximinus Thrax. This was in part an attempt to pay for the massive military expenditure that resulted from the barbarian invasions from AD 234 onwards and his increase in army pay. However, temples to other gods were not treated in this manner. Jupiter Dolichenus was clearly closely associated with the Severans and threatened Maximinus' hold over the army. Analysis of the derivation of priests of the cult shows that many were of Eastern or Greaco-Eastern origin, another reason for the Thracian Maximinus to destroy this probable bedrock of support for the Syrian emperor and his mother.[48]

We are left wondering what part Maesa played in these events. She was not present when Ulpian ran to the palace to unsuccessfully gain protection from the vengeful Praetorians. The paucity of coinage carrying her name and that of her grandson suggests she died early in the reign. Coinage of Alexander Severus from Marcianopolis in Lower Moesia carries the name of Maesa under three governors: Firmius Philopappus (c. AD 223), Ummidius Tereventinus (c. AD 226) and Tiberius Julius Festus (c. AD 226). We can assume Philopappus was an appointment of Elagabalus, and as such was rapidly replaced by his successor. This might put the death of Maesa to c. AD 225/226.[49] In the *Feriale Duranum*, the list of religious observances of the *Cohors XX Palmyrenorum*, dating to c. AD 227, Maesa is listed as deified. Coins commemorating this deification show her borne aloft on the back of a peacock. Unfortunately they are undated.[50] However, she does not appear as deified on the *Acta Fratrum Arvalium* of 7 November AD 224, which lists the number of gods and goddesses the *Arval Brethren* sacrificed to on that date; the same number is recorded on a list from AD 218. Herodian, however, appears to place the death of Maesa before the marriage of Alexander Severus to Orbiana, which was arranged solely by Mamaea. Coins issued to celebrate the marriage are dated between August AD 225 and August AD 226.[51]

All we can say with any certainty is that Maesa died between November AD 224 and AD 227, when she appears deified on the *Feriale Duranum*. Herodian appears to exaggerate the length of time Maesa ruled in conjunction with her daughter and grandson, stating that: 'After a long period of this type of government ['aristocratic'] in the empire, Maesa, already an old woman, died and received imperial honours and deification, according to Roman practice.'[52] The weight of the evidence does suggest that she died in late AD 225 to early AD 226 after a prolonged period of illness, and probably before the marriage of her grandson.

A much restored fragmentary inscription refers to Seia Herrenia Orbianna as Augusta, along with Mamaea and Maesa. Herodian makes clear that the death of the elderly matriarch resulted in a change in the relationship between mother and son. Mamaea became increasingly aware that he was demonstrating independence, and so she 'urged him to occupy himself continually with judicial work for most of the day, hoping that while he was busy on extremely important business, essential to imperial rule, he would have no chance to turn his attention to any vice'. The emperor would hear cases submitted to him through petitions, surrounded by a team of legal advisors whose expertise would be called upon at the emperor's discretion. Once the emperor had come to his decision, the *a libellis* would draw up the legal rescript, which would then be checked by the emperor who added his *subscriptio* underneath. This may have been a detailed addition to the imperial reply or, as in one subscription of Commodus, merely a brief statement: 'I have written it, I have checked it.' After his military responsibilities, this was one of the most important tasks of all emperors and a vital point of contact between ruler and ruled.[53]

The volume of work the emperor had to deal with was immense. Many imperial edicts are in response to disputes over legal status or inheritances and wealth. Wealth and status were often interlinked, wealth being a reflection of status. The emperor wrote to a Severiana on the question of her status: '[I]f as you state, you had a grandfather of consular and a father of praetorian rank and have been married to men not of private station but *clarissimi*, you retain your *claritas* of birth.' Furthermore, imperial officials referred contentious cases to the emperor, as in that of a grandmother whose case had been heard by Ulpian's successor as Praetorian Prefect, who then passed it on to the emperor for clarification: 'If it is clear to you, dearest Julianus, that the grandmother, in order to forestall a claim that the will was improper, has exhausted her property by making gifts to her grandson, reason demands that half of such gifts should be recalled.' Ulpian had attempted to reduce the numerous petitions and referrals to the emperor by instructing the *legati* of proconsuls that they should consult their superior and not seek the advice of the emperor. An almost unique rescript is perhaps a reflection of this workload, with Alexander Severus delegating the case presented by a certain Socrates who appealed on behalf of a slave girl whose purchaser was illegally using her as a prostitute. Instead of dealing with the case himself, the emperor directed the Prefect of Rome to have it heard by one of the praetors. Almost all the imperial rescripts recorded in the Theodosian Code, and a significant number in the Digest and Justinian Code, are imperial replies to enquiries made by governors or imperial officials. However, unscrupulous and corrupt governors who had passed unfair judgements were known to prevent provincials from appealing directly to the emperor. An inscription from Bithynia records the anger of Alexander Severus in finding the right of appeal to the imperial person being frustrated by such an abuse of power:

'How anyone could be prevented by those exercising jurisdiction from appealing I do not see, since it is possible to achieve the same result by taking a different course, and to come to me instead. I forbid procurators and provincial governors to treat with insolence and violence those who make appeals, to put a guard of soldiers on them and literally to bar their road hither. They will obey this pronouncement of mine knowing that the freedom of my subjects is of as much concern to me as is their loyalty and obedience. Those however who have been condemned or have appealed against capital charges ...'

Added to the everyday business brought to the emperor's attention would have been the many appeals against real or perceived injustice.[54]

At 15 or 16 years of age, he would certainly have become more strong-willed and capable of making his own decisions based on the advice available to him. From October AD 222 to sometime after October AD 223, ninety-six rescripts are recorded. These probably correspond to Ulpian's sole prefecture and the promotion of Licinius Rufinus as *a libellis* and *amicus* of the emperor. After the murder of Ulpian and the *adlection* of Rufinus to the Senate in late AD 223, the emperor probably relied on Paul and Herennius Modestinus, Ulpian's former pupil who held the post of *a libellis* until AD 226. From March AD 226 to August AD 229, a total of fifty-seven rescripts have survived, written in the same style by the unknown successor of Modestinus, still a significant number considering many more would have been issued but have been lost. The *Historia Augusta* describes how the emperor spent much of his afternoon devoted to correspondence and petitions, yet this is a generic description typifying the work of most emperors:

> 'He always gave up the afternoon hours to subscribing and reading letters with the *ab epistulis*, *a libellis*, and *a memoria* always in attendance … the *librarii* and those in charge of the *scrinium* reading everything back, so that Alexander could add anything that was necessary in his own hand, but always on the basis of the opinion of whoever was regarded as more learned.'[55]

At some point between AD 226 and AD 244, Modestinus was rewarded for his work with the Prefecture of the Vigiles. Aelius Marcianus, another jurist and student of Ulpian's, appears as part of the emperor's advisors. He is cited by both Ulpian and Paul, and one rescript of Alexander Severus appears to be addressed to him. To Paul, the application of justice had always to be for the greater good and be equitable, a purpose he defined as 'Natural Law'. Ulpian, however, took this concept a step further, believing all people were born free and equal and had the right to live according to nature in a community bound together by reason. Marcianus, continuing his mentor's humanist beliefs, understood the law to be sovereign over all things, both human and divine. The works of Modestinus closely follow the style and wording of his teacher and mentor. It is likely that it was Modestinus who received Ulpian's papers on his death.[56]

An intriguing law issued by Paul provides some credence to the *Historia Augusta's* statement that the emperor issued a concubine to any of his unmarried provincial governors who required female companionship. A law in the Digest allowed for provincial governors to take concubines with them, but they were forbidden to marry them.[57] Paul also records that on two occasions, whilst part of the imperial *consilium*, he gave legal advice that was rejected by the emperor. Here we again see a different side to the emperor than that portrayed by Herodian.

Historians have suggested the marriage of Alexander Severus to Orbiana was to cement the loyalty of the Senate to the regime. Orbiana's full name comes from Alexandrian coins of AD 225/226, issued to celebrate the imperial marriage: Gneia Seia Herennia Sullustia Barbia. Coinage issued in all denominations at Rome refer to her as Sallustia Barbia Orbiana, with images of the emperor and his new wife facing each other. The reverse carries the image of Mamaea. Another coin shows husband and wife shaking hands under the legend 'CONCORDIA

AUGUSTORUM', stressing the harmony within the imperial house. Her name suggests familial connections to Herennii Orbiani. An M. Herennius Secundus is recorded as a *suffect* consul in AD 94, and another senator of the same name a *suffect* consul in AD 183. Other elements of her cognomen suggest a link to Seius Fuscianus, an *amicus* of Marcus Aurelius who had been an Urban Prefect and been granted a second consulship in AD 188 by Commodus. His grandson, Seius Carus, had been executed by Elagabalus. The Barbii appear rarely in the historical record, but an M. Barbius Aemilianus was a *suffect* consul in AD 140. They are otherwise unknown in the time of Alexander Severus. However, the Sallustii are well recorded throughout Rome's imperial past. A T. Flavius Sallustius Paelignianus was an ordinary consul in AD 231, probably a distant relation. Inscriptions also record a Q. Sallustius Macrinianus as governor of Mauretania Caesariensis between AD 198–209. Another inscription describes his son, also of the same name, as a *clarissimus puer*, indicating a youth of the highest rank of senator. He may have been a closer relation. Herodian simply describes Orbiana as coming from a noble patrician family, yet it is clear she was well connected.[58]

Coins issued to celebrate the marriage carry the legend 'LIBERALITAS III', showing the emperor distributing money from a raised platform with the images of *Liberalitas* holding a coin counter and *cornucopiae*, with a citizen standing to the lower left of the image. Another coin issued shows Orbiana, a *cornucopiae*, some children and the goddess Fecundity, symbolizing fertility and the ability to produce numerous healthy offspring.[59] The clear reference is to some form of *alimentia* (charity), specifically for the welfare of children. According to the *Historia Augusta*, which erroneously states it was created to commemorate his 'victory' over the Sassanids in AD 233, the emperor founded a charity for this purpose called the 'Mamaenae and Mamaeni', as his predecessor Antoninus Pius had done.[60] Coinage from this time does indicate a similar distribution was made then, but the earlier coinage indicating a similar distribution does, according to Hazel Ramsey, appear to have been ignored by most historians. The emperor appears to have recreated a system of government support, or *alimentia*, for orphans in the manner of his illustrious predecessors, Trajan and Antoninus Pius. Alexander Severus' propaganda continually looked back to this supposed golden age under the 'good' emperors in order to create an image of its restoration under his aegis. This was later renamed solely in honour of his mother after the embarrassing end of his marriage.[61]

Dio does not mention the marriage in his brief account of the reign. This was probably to save the emperor further ignominy. Herodian does, however, contain a reasonably detailed account and can be used to some degree, and with care, with that in the *Historia Augusta*. However, the biographer names Orbiana 'Memmia, the daughter of Sulpicius, a man of consular rank, and the grand-daughter of Catullus', and then later, citing the Athenian historian Dexippus as a source, states the emperor married 'the daughter of a certain Macrinus and he gave this man the name of Caesar'.[62] Coinage and inscriptions confirm the name of Orbiana, whilst there is no evidence of any Augusta named Memmia. This passage has to be rejected as complete fiction. Furthermore, if the father's name included the cognomen Macrinus, you would expect this to appear in his daughter's name. Again, it is another fiction. However, Herodian, and epigraphic evidence, does support the assertion that the emperor's new father-in-law was made a Caesar, the heir to the throne. An inscription from Thugga in North Africa, dated c. AD 225, refers to a Caesar during his reign, but the name has been lost.[63] However, the *Feriale Duranum* does appear to preserve it. A Seius Caesar appears on the list, which, if he is Orbiana's father, could allow for a reconstruction of his full name as L. or Cn. Seius Herennius Sallustius Barbius.[64]

A lack of commemorative coinage, inscriptions and supplementary honours suggest the Caesar's position was to be mainly honorary, with only a minor and subsidiary role envisaged for him. The very least he perhaps expected was nomination to an ordinary consulship. However, the two consuls of AD 225 were Ti. Manilius Fuscus, who had previously held a consulship in AD 196 – his sister or daughter was probably married to Caesonius Macer Rufinianus, who had held an illustrious career under a series of emperors, ending as a *comes* to Alexander Severus and accompanying the emperor on his campaign against the Sassanids in the East – and Ser. Calpurnius Domitius Dexter. The latter was probably a close relation of the Severan general and consul of AD 196, Domitius Dexter. In AD 226, the emperor singularly honoured C. Aufidius Marcellus by sharing the consulship with him. The Aufidii were ennobled during the Republic but remained a powerful aristocratic family, with C. Aufidius Victorinus the consul of AD 183, an *amicus* of both Marcus Aurelius and Commodus, whilst his two sons were ordinary consuls in AD 199 and 200 respectively.[65] We can assume a familial link to the consul of AD 226, yet he too had previously held a consulship. So why appoint Orbiana's father Caesar in the first place? The marriage was expected to produce a son of noble lineage, much as when Elagabalus was married to Annia Faustina, a descendant of Marcus Aurelius. The emperor's weak dynastic claims, despite repeated claims to be the illegitimate child of Caracalla, would be enhanced by links to families of great nobility. It is likely that Sallustius' role was seen in terms of an insurance policy. Should Alexander Severus die during the minority of his prospective offspring, his father-in-law could act as the male figurehead of the regime, working in co-operation with Mamaea until the son of his daughter and son-in-law came of age. This plan of course relied upon the birth of a male heir and the understanding that the Caesar, a man of distinguished lineage, was willing to take a minor role. However, as Caesar and designated heir, he would have regular access to the emperor and advise him on the *concilium principis*. This was an opportunity that Sallustius could have been expected to seize with both hands.

In contrast to these happy nuptials taking place in Rome, the situation in Pannonia appears to have caused increasing concern. Cassius Dio's career was transformed under Alexander Severus, from gradual decline with the expectation of leisurely retirement on his family estates in Bithynia, to appointment to the prestigious proconsular governorship of Africa in AD 223, then governorship of Dalmatia from AD 224–226, then immediately being allocated the governorship of Pannonia Superior from AD 226–228. Pannonia was normally given to senators with extensive military experience, yet Dio appears to have had little of that in his career.[66] Pannonia Superior was garrisoned by 13,800 infantry and 3,500 cavalry, including the X and XIV *Gemina*. Perhaps deliberately, this province and its sister, Pannonia Inferior, had large numbers of Syrian auxiliary regiments. One, the *Cohors I Nova Severiana Surorum Milliaria Sagittaria*, had certainly been transferred to Pannonia Superior by Alexander Severus. Other Syrian units were possibly transferred to the province at the same time, but there is no evidence to support this. The redeployment of at least one Syrian unit who would be naturally well-disposed towards their Syrian emperor, and the rapid arrival of Dio, certainly suggests there were concerns over the discipline and loyalty of the locally recruited Pannonian soldiers.[67]

Dio rapidly imposed a level of discipline not formerly experienced by the Pannonian troops, who complained to their comrades in the Praetorian Guard, who in turn agitated for Dio's removal.[68] Inscriptions confirm a strong relationship between the legions along the Danube and the elite units in Rome. Ever since the reign of Septimius Severus, legionaries from these provinces were promoted to the Praetorian Guard in large numbers. Recent discoveries from Monte Sacro on the outskirts of Rome list the full names, tribes and city of origin of fifteen men serving in the Praetorians from AD 215–225. Twelve of these guardsmen came from Pannonia, Dacia or Thracia. The remaining three came from Carthage, Tarsus and Caesarea Germanica. Promotion from the Praetorians often involved a posting as a centurion back to the legions around the empire. From this post, many continued through the hierarchy of ranks on the centurion career ladder or were promoted to the office of procurator in the imperial bureaucracy. In the third century, we increasingly find veterans serving in administrative posts. These northern semi-Romanized soldiers often wore the long-sleeved tunics and trousers of their homeland when off-duty, arousing the discerning disapproval of the supposedly more civilized population of the capital. These guardsmen had recently murdered their own Praetorian Prefect and fought with the Roman mob, without suffering any censure.[69]

There were a number of laws passed at this time attempting to deal with military indiscipline. The emperor was asked to clarify the legal status of soldiers dishonourably discharged from the army. His reply seeks a compromise between the implementation of the rule of law and the need to act benevolently towards the armed forces:

> 'Since soldiers who have been dishonourably discharged are designated with a mark of bad repute, they may not have the benefit of the privileges normally given to men of unstained character. They do however have the right of living wherever they wish, provided that is not in one of those places from which they were specifically excluded.'[70]

A rescript of Paul also shows that, in the case of soldiers, the strictest imposition of the law was often modified. Soldiers had long been granted special privileges in the creation and implementation of wills, as qualified lawyers were a rare commodity in a war zone. A civilian's will had to fulfil stringent legal requirements unlike their military counterpart. However, an official referred the case of the legal status of a soldier's will to the emperor, as the man in question had made his will whilst serving in the army, left, and then a year later rejoined another unit. The question put to the emperor was whether the original will was still valid, as on discharge his will failed to meet the legalities of a civilian's will. It was decided that, as a veteran, the law could be applied with greater latitude and charity.[71]

The emperor's legal experts, Paul and Modestinus, made numerous rulings on the imposition of military punishments. These would have been in response to queries sent to the emperor from commanders and governors. Both make a distinction between 'abuse' and 'minor complaints', which were sanctioned with demotion, and those who disturbed the peace or showed insubordination, including striking a superior. Such an act resulted in execution. Modestinus refers specifically to a soldier who led a serious disturbance amongst the troops. Desertion also appears to have been a significant issue since the Marcomannic wars. The problem was ignored until the reign of Commodus, when an army of deserters, criminals and freed slaves led by Maternus, probably a deserter himself, was sufficiently strong to loot towns and cities, and even lay siege to an entire legion in its camp. The uprising was crushed, yet desertion appears to have remained a serious problem.[72] Desertion in the face of the enemy was punishable by death, whilst deserters who intended to join the enemy were tortured before capital punishment was inflicted. Loss of weapons was also deemed a capital crime, but a more lenient punishment could be enforced, such as demotion to another less prestigious unit. Modestinus also makes a distinction between deserters who were captured and forcibly returned to their unit and those who returned voluntarily. A soldier who failed to rejoin the ranks due to illness or difficulties in returning to his unit, caused by the activities of robbers and bandits, was to be pardoned.[73]

An inscription from Thrace records a petition presented to the Emperor Gordian III in AD 238 by a soldier from the tenth Praetorian cohort on behalf of his native village of Scaptopara, which had suffered from the exactions of officials and soldiers visiting their market and demanding by right hospitality and services from the villagers. They had complained to the local governor, but he had ignored them. As a consequence, the villagers threatened to leave their homes, which would result in a reduction of tax revenues. The unsympathetic emperor merely told them to refer the matter to his governor. However, this situation does appear to have originated in the reign of Alexander Severus and reflects the injustices many provincials must have endured, with the emperor and his Praetorian Prefects their only hope of remedy.[74]

The state of the imperial finances had at the best of times been precarious, but the increases of army pay by Septimius Severus and Caracalla had made the task of balancing income and expenditure almost impossible. Macrinus had made the mistake of attempting to reduce the pay of new recruits, but this had contributed to the revolt that overthrew him. Alexander Severus and his mother knew not to repeat this mistake. However, the previous pay rises had heightened the soldiers' expectations, which were not to be fulfilled. Expenditure on the army is estimated to have been between 286–370 million denarii a year, excluding monies spent on the fleet, pensions, donatives and the purchasing of resources and food for the upkeep of the troops. Herodian accuses Mamaea of greed in her insatiable desire to raise revenue. The emperor supposedly criticized his mother for this, but he must have been as concerned as her about the financial situation. The late Roman historian Zosimus, probably basing his account on a lost source, explicitly states that the emperor himself was responsible for the careful husbanding of limited resources; beset as he was by 'so many difficulties', he 'was infected with an insatiable avarice, amassing riches with the utmost solicitude, which he confided to the care of his mother'.[75] The 'bad' emperors such as Commodus, Caracalla and Maximinus Thrax are routinely accused of avarice as they looked to impose additional taxes on the rich. 'Good' emperors found the necessary money from cutbacks in imperial spending on ostentatious displays of wealth, characterized in our sources as 'moderate dignified government'.[76] Consequently, Mamaea was blamed for the financial measures introduced; otherwise, the idealized image of Alexander Severus would have been tarnished.

Herodian refers to the 'confiscation of some people's inherited property'.[77] The historian also alludes to a significant number of treason trials for *majestas* which resulted in the guilty being spared the death penalty. However, conviction would have led to exile and the confiscation of their estates, which were added to the imperial *fiscus*.[78] Dio's fictional account of the speech of Maecenas to Augustus is the part of his history which reveals the most about the senatorial attitudes of his time.[79] Dio attempts here to offer solutions to the problems facing the empire in the time of Alexander Severus. He recognizes the importance of achieving a sustainable and secure revenue in order to provide the resources for the army, who secured the safety of the empire. However, this should be done without drawing on the assets of the elite. Instead, the senatorial historian, himself the owner of vast estates in Italy and in his native Bithynia, urges the emperor to rely purely on the resources of the state itself, through income raised from state owned mines and imperial estates. He also advocates the sale of all properties acquired by the state during the civil wars to be sold, with the profits used to provide cheap loans to encourage the cultivation of deserted land, thus increasing revenue. He suggests that any shortfall between income and expenditure could be met through indirect taxation on produce.[80] Wealth was primarily based on land, yet the elite resented any attempt by the state to draw upon their assets in supporting the costs of empire. Emperors that threatened their privileges and wealth are characterized as greedy and avaricious, labels now applied to Mamaea, while Alexander Severus was held up as a paragon of imperial virtue and good government.

The supply of gold and silver was finite. Supply did not match demand, especially silver, which was used to pay the soldiers, and this had led to a steady debasement of the silver coinage. Caracalla had introduced the *antoninianus*, which was meant to be equivalent to two *denarii* but contained only 50 per cent silver, the same precious metal content as a single *denarius*. The gold content of the *aureus* had also been reduced slightly by Septimius Severus, with fifty being struck to a pound of gold rather than forty-five. An increasing lack of confidence in the intrinsic value of the coinage is reflected in the jurist Paul's definition of coins as a 'price' (*petrium*) rather than a 'commodity' (*merx*). Severe penalties were imposed on those who failed to accept the theoretical value of the coin. A probable lack of confidence in the *antoninianus* had led to it being discontinued by Elagabalus. Alexander Severus appears to have attempted to halt this decline in confidence by refusing to debase the coinage any further, retaining an exchange rate of one *aureus* to twenty-five *denarii* despite the need to balance imperial income and expenditure. It is perhaps for this reason that a series of coins were issued carrying the legend 'IMP.SEV.ALEXANDER. AUG. RESTITVTOR. MONETAE' and 'IMP. SEV.ALEXANDER.AUG.RESTITVTA.MONITA' ('restorer of the coinage'). However, the purity of the coins was not restored to levels seen before Septimius Severus, suggesting this assertion was merely an attempt to restore trust in the precious metal content.[81]

Silver coinage was used to pay the troops, whilst gold was used by the elite. Silver coinage was also used by the emperor when distributing donatives to the legions and *congiaria* to the populace. Such distributions were made on the emperor's accession to the throne, his marriage to Orbiana, and would be needed to commemorate the tenth anniversary of the commencement of his reign, as well as to pay for the massive building works in the capital. The costs of construction were huge, even on a small scale. An aqueduct built at Alexander Troas cost a staggering seven million *denarii*, equivalent to the pay of 27,000 legionaries. In the second century, Pliny mentions a theatre at Nicaea which lay unfinished due to a lack of money, having already cost two-and-a-half million *denarii*.[82] The urgent necessity to raise bullion is reflected in the sale of imperial estates. Amphora stamps indicate imperial property acquired in Baetica, Spain, by Septimius Severus during the civil wars were sold to private owners at this time. Excavations on the massive mountain of discarded amphorae at Monte Testaccio in Rome show no private names from AD 198–230, when they reappear. Alexander Severus appears to have relinquished state control of the trade in oil to the capital and returned it to private ownership, so reducing costs and raising revenue. Furthermore, spending on the upkeep of fortifications was reduced to a minimum and units not kept at full strength. This would lead to accusations of 'rapacity and miserliness' by the soldiers.[83]

Incremental evidence indicates the emperor, like all of his predecessors, took a healthy interest in improving the efficiency and effectiveness of tax collection. The previous century had seen increased numbers of *curatores*, who were appointed by the central authority to oversee the efficient running of individual cities, especially in their financial administration. Dio himself had been appointed to such a post overseeing the administrations of Pergamum and Smyrna by Macrinus. Statue bases from Ulia in Baetica record the appointment of *curatores* by Alexander Severus to review the finances of the city. Curators could also be appointed at the request of a city. A rescript of Alexander Severus refers to a financial dispute between a city and a wealthy citizen over debts. Both sides requested an independent curator to investigate the case and pass judgement. Curators were regularly appointed to cities in Italy itself, which was gradually losing its privileged status and was increasingly treated as a province of the empire. From the time of Marcus Aurelius, the majority of these posts were filled by senators rather than equites, probably as military posts were increasingly filled by equestrians, who were also required to fill the rapidly increasing number of procuratorships which were needed after the bringing of vast estates into imperial administration in the civil wars. These senators who were appointed to the post of *curatores* were often from the locality, and so well-acquainted with the issues and in an advantageous position to use their network of patronage and clients to facilitate a successful conclusion. From the reign of Caracalla, *correctores*, whose role was similar to those of *curatores* but with responsibility for a number of cities, are increasingly found honoured in a large number of Italian communities. By the third century, imperial procurators appear to have usurped the powers of criminal jurisdiction, despite the efforts of both Caracalla and Alexander Severus, who both issued edicts attempting to counter their attempt to extend their legal jurisdiction from fiscal to criminal matters, to the detriment of the powers and status of the provincial governors. An edict of AD 228 stipulated procurators did not have the right of deportation, and a letter issued to the *Koinon* of Bithynia by Alexander Severus ordered both governors and procurators not to block appeals to the emperor. By the third century, there effectively existed two parallel systems of government, one centred on the governors appointed by the emperor and the Senate, the other on the ever-increasing power of the imperial procurators.[84]

The Romans had allowed provincial cities to continue to raise revenue according to their own traditional procedures, but the central government gradually took greater control over the collection of revenue and food surpluses. It was perhaps in response to the increased interference of the state in their affairs that the city of Aphrodisias created an inscribed wall recording their historic freedom and independence in the reign of Alexander Severus. However, increased centralization was probably a response to the inefficient and often corrupt system administered by the local elite and a reflection of the stresses created by a reduction in resources available. Communities and individuals regularly appealed to the emperor to have their financial obligations reduced to a 'fairer' rate, using the overly complex local measures as the basis of their appeal. The jurist Licinius Rufinus, who was a *comes* of the emperor, successfully presented a case before Alexander Severus on behalf of the 'Macedonian Confederation', who disputed their contribution to the revenues due from Thessaly. The success of his presentation can be inferred from the statue erected in his honour.[85]

There is a large body of evidence from this period for tax avoidance. This may be a reflection of an increased tax burden or the preservation of a large number of imperial rescripts from the reign of Alexander Severus in the late Roman legal compendiums. One law relates how the emperor constantly forbade a taxpayer to force another person to pay their taxes. The provincial elite, as members of the city council, were also expected to provide *munera*; that is, the municipal and religious duties to provide festivals, religious games and contests and other forms of public works. These obligations came with a significant financial cost. Towns and cities increasingly attempted to make the inhabitants of their rural hinterland shoulder some or all of the burden. Both Ulpian and Modestinus exempted people living in the countryside from being forced to contribute to these, on the grounds that they did not share in the facilities and benefits of urban life, its baths, forum, theatres and games. This conflict between the wealthy urban elite and the rural poor appears to have existed across the empire and remained an issue. Despite the rulings of Ulpian and Modestinus, an Egyptian papyrus from c. AD 250 preserves an appeal to the Prefect of Egypt by villagers who were being forced to provide resources to the local city for festivals, despite the fact Septimius Severus had issued a rescript specifically stating that they were exempt.[86]

An inscription from the AD 240s to the Emperor Philip records a long-standing dispute between villagers on an imperial estate at Aragua in the Upper Trembris Valley and 'powerful and influential men in the city' who had, over a number of years, made repeated illegal exactions. A previous petition to an emperor, probably Alexander Severus, had led to the governor ensuring these actions ceased, but was then subsequently ignored. These were imperial tenants with access to procurators and the emperor himself, so we must assume that tenants and labourers on private land suffered grievously as they had little access to any form of redress.[87]

Understandably, individuals also attempted to reduce the amount of tax they had to pay, both to the central and local authorities. Emperors had regularly removed financial obligations from wealthy individuals or institutions as a policy initiative, a gift or in order to gratify a request made by an *amicus* on behalf of one of their clients. Alexander Severus was not adverse to this. A commemorative arch at Thugga in Africa is dedicated to the emperor as *conservator libertatis* for restoring or preserving its tax privileges. Despite this, the financial concerns of the state made such generosity on an individual basis an exception rather than the rule. Septimius Severus had removed the burden of holding local offices and priesthoods, with their associated duty to provide *munera*, from local landowners who had five or more children. Alexander Severus rescinded this law.[88] Other laws prohibited teachers, doctors and sophists from claiming exemptions granted in one city in another. Another law forbade individuals from joining guilds and 'collegia', which had previously been granted financial privileges for their members, when they did not practice in the trade or profession.[89] Despite the dire financial straits of the administration, veterans were again granted a certain degree of latitude not provided to ordinary civilians. A previous law had obligated veterans who enrolled in a town council as a decurion to provide *munera*. However, the emperor, replying to a petition by the veteran Felicianus, granted a provisional dispensation:

'Veterans, who when they could have protected themselves from the immunity granted to them [as veterans], have preferred to be made decurions in their home towns, cannot return to the exemption which they have abandoned, unless by a formal rule and agreement for the preservation of their immunity they have accepted [only] a part of the burden.'[90]

Modestinus confirmed that veterans were granted immunity from local taxes and office for life. However, as landowners, they were obliged to repair roads that crossed their land. This was a military necessity to facilitate the rapid movement of troops and supplies.[91] Despite the pay rises afforded the soldiers by Septimius Severus and Caracalla, deductions made for clothing, food, boots, equipment, burial club and the yearly Saturnalia festival greatly reduced the amount of actual pay each soldier received. Consequently, soldiers relied heavily on regular donatives, paid in coins, made by the emperor.[92] However, financial constraints precluded this distribution on a regular basis, and soldiers were increasingly paid in kind through the *annona militaris*. It is not known when this was introduced, but the state appears to have increasingly relied upon this form of payment to the soldiers from the early third century. It is difficult to see any emperor after Alexander Severus having the logistical capacity or time to introduce the required structural network to create such a system. Soldiers were tasked with the collection and transportation of foodstuffs to army depots. The *frumentarii*, soldiers who acted in a range of capacities – from scouts and messengers to spies and imperial executioners – are attested in inscriptions from across the empire, working in association with the Prefecture of the Annona.[93] *Stationarii*, soldiers placed in villages and hamlets on police duties, are also recorded as involved in the collection of food surpluses, as were *collectiones*, who were originally tax collectors. The Roman mindset was not to innovate but to respond to problems, utilizing existing offices and structures. In areas where resources were limited, these armed men would have taken what they had been ordered to collect without concern for the needs of the locals or legal niceties. This is reflected in numerous petitions made by oppressed villagers to the governor or emperor seeking redress. A significant number of inscriptions from Lydia give an insight into the situation facing many of the rural poor across the empire. Villagers on an imperial estate in the territory of the city of Philadelphia complain of oppression by *collectiones* and other officials, whilst the villagers of Mendechora complain of illegal seizures by *frumentarii*, *collectiones* and 'similar agents'. The village near Ekiskuru, in the same vicinity, also complains of 'unbearable burdens', whilst villagers near Demirci make similar complaints, as does a village near Satala. A further inscription from AD 247/248 from Kavacik compares the actions of these imperial agents and soldiers to the ravages inflicted by barbarian raiding parties.[94]

Another inscription, already mentioned, from Thrace records a petition from the villagers of Skaptopara to the Emperor Gordian III in AD 238. The villagers had for many years been forced by soldiers to hand over provisions without payment, and, as the village lay near a main road, local market and therapeutic hot water springs, they had to regularly provide accommodation to the governor and other officials. This situation had temporarily been rectified by petitions to imperial authority. However, the situation had again deteriorated to such an extent that many of the villagers had left rather than suffer violence and starvation. This probably occurred in the political uncertainty and barbarian incursions following the murder of Alexander Severus.[95] This was not a unique situation. Another inscription from Ağa Bey Köyü in Asia Minor either predates or postdates our period by a few years. Like Skaptopara, the villagers had the misfortune to live close to a main road used regularly by soldiers. A party of *frumentarii* entered the village, located on an imperial estate, and seized nine men, placing them in chains. They then ransomed them for 1,000 Attic *drachma*, which the village managed to pay. However, only one of the prisoners was released. Clearly unable to meet any further demands, the villagers must have petitioned the imperial procurator. Like the villagers of Skaptopara, they threatened to leave the land, so reducing imperial revenue, unless their persecutors were punished and they were allowed to devote themselves 'to working the land' unmolested.[96] It would be reassuring to think that the erection of this inscription resulted from a successful conclusion to this unsavoury exploitation of the weak by the strong.

The rich always had the power to exploit the poor. However, under Caracalla and Alexander Severus, the legal distinctions became formalized, with the legal status of the free poor equated to that of the slaves. This was a direct consequence of the Antonine Constitution, which granted Roman citizenship to virtually all free citizens of the empire. Roman citizenship was previously often a privilege of the wealthy and the elite. Senators also came into ever-increasing contact with powerful equestrians in the administration. During the Hadrianic period, there were 104 procurators. These had risen to 182 by the mid-third century. Many equestrian procurators managed extensive imperial estates extending across a number of senatorial and imperial provinces. Senators, ever conscious to preserve their elite status, looked to reinforce their prestige. Edicts now carried adjectives meant to make these distinctions, with the poor labelled as *humiliores* (lowly), *tenuiores* (thinner) or *sordidiores* (filthier), whilst the elite were *vir clarissimus* (most respected man), *vir egregius* (excellent man), *vir perfectissimus* (more prefect man) and *honestiores* (more honourable man). These epithets gained legal distinction. Roman law increasingly differentiated how a man was to be treated according to rank, especially when imposing punishment. The lesser a person's status, the more violent the punishment. Paul, citing an earlier ruling, decreed that:

> 'In the case of free offenders, you will have them beaten with clubs and relegate them for three years, or if they are *sordidiores*, persons with lower status (i.e. more filthy), condemn them to public works for the same period. Slaves you will flog with the lash and condemn to the mines.'

As the third century progressed, these distinctions were solidified. Ulpian considered an insult made by a person of 'lower status' against a 'superior' had to be dealt with severely. Furthermore, Aemilius Macer, a jurist who produced a number of works under Alexander Severus, including *On Criminal Proceedings*, illustrates how the status of the free poor by this time had fallen to the position of slaves. Addressing the question of how slaves should be punished, he suggests: 'They should be punished following the example of more humble persons.'[97] The early third century saw the rapid undermining of the legal protections of the poor at the same time as the reduction of state income led to an increased pressure to meet the demands of the army.

The increased use of soldiers in the collection of resources coincides with the greater use of government officials, in the form of *curatores* and *correctores*, in the administrative affairs of provincial cities. A number of inscriptions from the Greek East also record a reduction in the number of inscriptions made in honour of the local elite and an increase in those to governors and other members of imperial administration. At Miletus, Tralles, Priene, Side, Termessos and Nysa, new podia were constructed in the theatres for the provincial governor, suggesting regular visits. Excavations at Aphrodisias have revealed an inscription on a statue base incorporated into the elaborate new podium built in honour of the local governor:

> 'The people of the most splendid city of the Aphrodisians [set up a statue of] Sulpicius Priscus, perfectissimus vir, proconsul, according to [the instructions] of our greatest and most revered lord Imperator Severus [Alexander].'

A second inscription records the reply from the governor, Sulpicius Priscus:

> 'I will gladly come to you and make a stay in your most splendid city and sacrifice to your native goddess for the safety and eternal continuance of our lord Imperator [Alexander] and our lady Augusta [Mamaea].'

Inscriptions also indicate a gradual reduction in public building by private individuals, whilst those honouring the benefactions of government officials rose. Laws passed by Septimius Severus also increased central control over the provinces. The management of monies bequeathed to the *alimentia* for the support of the children of poor citizens was removed from the administration of town councils and transferred to the control of provincial governors, whilst towns were no longer able to raise new taxes from local market duties without the permission of the governor. Reduction in taxation and revenues at a time when the costs of the army had risen massively under Septimius Severus and Caracalla necessitated greater efficiency in their collection.[98]

The empire was still suffering from the effects of the Antonine Plague, which had been spread by the returning soldiers of Lucius Verus who had defeated the Parthians in AD 166. Symptoms described by the Roman physician Galen suggest this was probably a virulent form of smallpox. By AD 189, Dio records that 2,000 people were dying each day in the unsanitary conditions of the capital. The population of the empire had been growing up to this cataclysmic event, which some historians estimate killed between 7–33 per cent of the population. The preservation of papyri in the arid conditions of the Egyptian desert provides a snapshot of the economic impact of this plague. In one village, the total land under production fell dramatically from AD 158–216. A shortage of workers lead to a significant rise in wages, whilst documentation recording the collection of wheat tax shows a fall in revenue from AD 184/5.[99] Excavations in the catacombs of Saints Peter and Marcellinus in Rome were found to contain a mass grave from the late second and early third centuries, buried in three underground galleries. The skeletons lacked any indication of trauma to the bones, suggesting they died from an epidemic, such as typhus, dysentery or a continuation of the Antonine Plague.[100] Another devastating outbreak of plague occurred in AD 250, hitting an empire already reeling from civil war and barbarian invasions across virtually all its frontiers. Pontius of Carthage describes its horror:

'Afterwards there broke out a dreadful plague, and excessive destruction of a hateful disease invaded every house in succession of the trembling populace, carrying off day by day with abrupt attack numberless people, everyone from his own house. All were shuddering, fleeing, shunning the contagion, impiously exposing their own friends, as if with the exclusion of the person who was sure to die of the plague, one could exclude death itself also. There lay about the meanwhile, over the whole city [Carthage], no longer bodies, but the carcasses of many, and, by the contemplation of a lot which in their turn would be theirs, demanded the pity of the passers-by for themselves. No one regarded anything besides his cruel gains. No one trembled at the remembrance of a similar event. No one did to another what he himself wished to experience.'[101]

Some historians consider this a continuation of the Antonine Plague, others a new disease. However, there is a growing consensus that both were outbreaks of smallpox.[102] The demographic decline of the third century is clearly linked to these epidemics. The costs of labour increased, leading to a decrease in the farming of marginal land, although the cities were still expected to raise the same amount of taxes as these were based on the acreage of land attached to each city. Difficulty in meeting these demands led to an increase in the appointment of *curatores* and increased demands on the rural poor by landowners. Added to this, climatologists have noted that Europe was getting cooler and wetter from the second century, further reducing yields. The economic effects would have further destabilized state finances.[103]

However, in AD 227, political complications took precedent over economic ones. The last honorary inscription dedicated to Orbiana is dated to this year, whilst her coinage disappears partway through. The marriage had been arranged with the daughter of a noble senatorial family to add *nobilitas* to the emperor's claim to the throne and provide an heir whose ancestry could rival that of the senatorial aristocracy, but her position had been weakened by the failure to produce a child. In typical fashion, Herodian blames Orbiana's fall on the personality of Mamaea, who was jealous of her use of the title 'Augusta'. This can be easily discounted, as all wives of the emperor were awarded the title 'Augusta' and Mamaea would have known this. The historian also accuses Mamaea of abusing and insulting the girl and Seius Sallustius Caesar to such a degree that her father went to the Praetorian Camp to raise a revolt. There, the Caesar railed against Mamaea whilst at the same time praising the emperor. Perhaps he naively hoped the Guard would remove the empress whilst retaining Alexander Severus as emperor and also promote him to joint Augustus.[104] This account seems far too simplistic. Herodian appears to generalize and summarize a complex situation. The conflict between Mamaea and her daughter and father-in-law was more likely to revolve around influence with the emperor, prestige and symbols of status. Seius Sallustius had not been granted the status symbols normally given to the heir to the throne. He had not been appointed to a consulship, no coins were issued in his name, nor does he appear to have even held the minimal titles awarded to Alexander Severus in AD 222 when he was appointed Caesar by Elagabalus. This tardy treatment of the father presupposes a similar treatment of his daughter. Other such symbols of status included a prominent seat in the imperial box during the 'games', the right to have the imperial fire carried before them when moving around the capital, including the imperial *vexilla* or flag, and have twelve *fasces laureati* carried by the *lictors*. An escort of Praetorians would also be expected to accompany all members of the imperial house.

Symbols of status still dominate the modern psyche, but to the Roman aristocratic elite, such issues of precedence completely dominated their mindset. The Emperor Commodus' sister attempted to murder her own brother in AD 182 for this very reason, feeling slighted and insulted as 'the emperor [Commodus] with his own marriage to Crispina, precedence was bound to be assigned to the wife of the emperor. Lucilla was angered by this honour paid to Crispina, which she considered to be an insult to herself.'[105] Perhaps Seius Sallustius Caesar felt similarly insulted. Mamaea may also have felt her position threatened. After her conflicts with Elagabalus and her own sister, she was a master of courtly intrigue, whilst Seius Sallustius Caesar and Orbiana were mere novices.

The author of the *Historia Augusta*, citing the mid-third-century Athenian historian P. Herennius Dexippus as a source, records the execution of a Caesar he names as Macrinus, charged with plotting to murder the emperor. His daughter, whom the work names as Memmia, who was married to the emperor, was also divorced.[106] There are no other references to these names, either in coinage or inscriptions. Alexander Severus was clearly only married once, and the author of the *Historia Augusta* is mixing fact and fiction.[107] The principal source of the *Historia Augusta* for the reign, Herodian, fails to mention the name of the emperor's wife, and so the biographer appeared to have inserted a suitably aristocratic name, that of the first-century Emperor Galba's wife from Suetonius.[108]

The information taken from Dexippus probably reflects, albeit in garbled form, the official proclamation of the reasons for the execution of the emperor's Caesar and the divorce of his wife. In AD 227, Mamaea extended her official title, exalting her status from 'Mother of the Camps' to 'and the Senate and Native Land'. These were all held by her sister, Julia Domna, and, as the precedent had been set, were now available to Julia Mamaea. However, the timing must be more than coincidental. The imperial family was advertising the real and substantial threat the 'revolt' of Seius Sallustius Caesar caused to the safety of the empire and the role of all members of the imperial house in conserving peace and prosperity. Herodian records the reality of the power struggle between Mamaea and her in-laws, with Alexander Severus attempting to mediate between the rival parties. Our sources all agree that the emperor loved his wife but was caught between the bitter rivalries that divided his family. She is depicted on coins as a young attractive woman, roughly the same age as her husband. Herodian is clear that Orbiana's divorce and exile from the imperial palace led to Seius Sallustius Caesar's attempt to sojourn the Praetorians. He would not have attempted this unless he had previously ventured to win their support or they were already in seditious mood. We can imagine these rough and ready soldiers, many retaining links to their Pannonian comrades on the Danube, who had already complained of Dio's imposition of severe disciplinary measures, debating whether to abandon their oath of loyalty or honour their divine pledge made to protect the emperor and his family, one of whom stood before them. But the soldiers had little in common with the aristocratic, senatorial elite and, although nothing is known of Seius Sallustius' military career, he perhaps lacked the necessary *virtus* that could command their respect. The Guard remained loyal, the Caesar was executed and his daughter exiled to Libya.[109]

Herodian, attempting to compare the reign of Alexander Severus to that of the supposedly ideal emperor, Marcus Aurelius, states that like his illustrious predecessor,

> 'he ruled without bloodshed (and one could not name anyone executed by him). Even though some people were guilty of very serious crimes, Alexander spared them from execution, an ideal which no other emperor of our time has found easy to practise or preserve since Marcus' reign.'

Yet the historian then qualifies this statement a few sentences later with 'it would be impossible to recall the name of a person executed without trial'.[110] It would firstly appear that Herodian had merely senators in mind when making this assertion, as he fails to consider the fates of Epagathus, Chrestus and Flavianus. It would also appear senators were executed, as Seius Sallustius Caesar was himself from this class. By blaming the execution of Seius Sallustius on the orders of Mamaea, the historian avoided contradicting his earlier statement. Some, however, do appear to have had their property confiscated and were no doubt exiled. In a preceding passage, before Herodian describes the plot itself, the historian, in one of his regular criticisms of Mamaea's greed, accuses her of 'making a private hoard. This cast a certain cloud upon the reign, though Alexander opposed and deplored her forcible confiscation of some peoples' inherited property.' This statement is not placed in any kind of historical context, yet this was a punishment, along with exile or execution, for those sentenced under the laws governing *majestas*. The coup attempt by Seius Sallustius is presented by Herodian as a spontaneous bid to overthrow Mamaea in response to her constant barbed comments directed at himself and his daughter. However, digging deeper, we start to find hints of a well-prepared plot involving a number a wealthy individuals, probably *amici* and clients of the Caesar and his family. The Praetorians, however, remained loyal, but only after listening to what he had to offer. This noble senator lacked the qualities the soldiers so admired: military experience and proven bravery forged in battle. He was not a 'fellow soldier' but a representative of the aristocratic nobility, described by Herodian as a scion of a patrician family. A noble senator as emperor was unlikely to defend and preserve the vested interests and privileges of the army. The soldiers decided in favour of the status quo.[111]

These events had done nothing to restore discipline in the ranks of the Praetorians. The situation had not been restored by AD 229, when Alexander Severus attempted to reward the efforts and loyalty of Dio in Pannonia Superior with the ordinary consulship. As a further honour, the imperial *fiscus* paid for all of the expenses he had incurred whilst governor. Dio's experiences on the Danube led to a deep contempt of the native provincials:

'The Pannonians ... lead the most miserable existence of all mankind. For they are not well off as regards either soil or climate; they cultivate no olives and produce no wine except to a very slight extent and a wretched quality at that, since the winter is very rigorous and occupies the greater part of their year, but drink as well as eat both barley and millet. For all that they are considered the bravest of all men of whom we have knowledge; for they are very high-spirited and bloodthirsty, as men who possess nothing that makes an honourable life worthwhile ... This I know, not from hearsay, or reading only, but I have learned it from actual experience as once their governor.'

This passage appears to have been a later addition to his work, inserted after AD 228.[112] Although he considered the Pannonians to be excellent soldiers, they were volatile and lacked the attributes that Roman 'civilization' developed in the more urbane Greek East from which Dio hailed. The feeling was clearly mutual. The Praetorians, dominated by soldiers from this region, threatened to murder the consul-elect if he should set foot in the capital. The emperor's control over his Guard was minimal and he was forced to advise the man he had so recently honoured to spend his consulship elsewhere in Italy. Later in the year, the situation had calmed and so Dio 'came both to Rome and to Campania to visit him, and spent a few days in his company, during which the soldiers saw me without offering to do me any harm'.[113] The consul was probably invited to the emperor's villas on the outskirts of Rome on the Via Ostiensis and on the Bay of Naples, where the more reliable units of the guard could be employed.

The imperial villa at Baiae commanded spectacular views towards Puteoli and Vesuvius from its position on the cliff top now covered by Castello de Baia. The palace had been gradually extended down the slope by successive emperors to finally level out at extensive fish ponds. The so-called 'Temple of Diana' is in fact part of the vast bathing complex extended by Alexander Severus. Archaeology has further revealed a large complex of vaulted chambers, terraces, colonnades, cisterns and baths built near or over hot springs, including domed halls, a nymphaeum and fountains. It is unclear whether these belonged to the imperial complex or were the property of other members of the aristocracy. Much of these structures now lie underwater. Dio could enjoy bathing in the hot springs, walk in the shaded parks or take a stroll along pristine beaches. The aristocratic resort of Baiae was renowned for its boat parties, debauchery, drinking and feasting. The elderly Dio though would probably have taken greatest pleasure in the public recognition of his status as an *amicus* of the emperor. Yet this was not enough to compensate for the previous indignities he had suffered. Dio announced his retirement, on the grounds that he was suffering from an ailment in his feet; an ignominious end to a career of loyal service. He returned to his native Bithynia to complete his great historical work.[114]

Chapter 7

The Empire of Alexander Severus AD 222–235

'How much of the world has been changed in this period? How many towns have been produced or enlarged or refounded by the triple virtue of the current government? Now that God favours so many Augusti [Alexander Severus, Julia Maesa and Julia Mamaea] at the same time, how many census lists have been transcribed, how many peoples cleaned up, how many orders given their former splendour, how many barbarians excluded? Really, the earth is now the well-cultivated estate of this government. All aconites of enmity have been eradicated, the cactus and bramble of treacherous friendship have been torn out: the world is lovely, surpassing the orchard of Alcinous and the rosary of Midas. If you praise this world in change, how can you disparage man?'

(Tertullian, *De Pallio*, 2.7)

By c. AD 250, the world had changed. Cyprian, the Bishop of Carthage, wrote a response to the proconsular governor of Asia, refuting his claim that the misfortunes facing the empire were manifestations of divine anger at the failure of the Christians to worship the pagan gods:

'[T]he world has now grown old, and does not abide in that strength in which it formerly stood; nor has it that vigour and force which it formerly possessed. This, even were we silent, and if we alleged no proofs from the sacred Scriptures and from the divine declarations, the world itself is now announcing, and, bearing witness to its decline by the testimony of its failing estate. In the winter there is not such an abundance of showers for nourishing the seeds; in the summer the sun has not so much heat for cherishing the harvest; nor in the spring season are the grain-fields so joyous; nor are the autumnal seasons so fruitful in their leafy products. The layers of marble are dug out in less quantity from the disembowelled and wearied mountains; the diminished quantities of gold and silver suggest the early exhaustion of the metals, and the impoverished veins are straitened and decreased day by day; the husbandman is failing in the fields, the sailor at sea, the soldier in the camp, innocence in the market, justice in the tribunal, concord in friendships, skilfulness in the arts, discipline in morals.'[1]

Contemporary literature only starts to recognize the empire was in crisis around the mid-third century, nearly twenty years after the murder of Alexander Severus. Political and cultural thought at any time in history frequently looks to a restoration of a previous golden age. Perhaps this is a reflection of human nature that rejects the perceived vicissitudes of the present for an imagined past time of plenty. So Alexander Severus claimed to restore the Roman state to its military, political and social apotheosis during the supposed golden ages of Augustus, Trajan and Marcus Aurelius. The rejection of the supreme deity Elagabal for the reassertion of the traditional Roman pantheon worshipped by their ancestors, and headed by Jupiter Optimus Maximus, was a reflection of this. The security and safety of the empire depended upon the 'correct' worship of these traditional gods. Tiberius Manilius Fuscus, who had been awarded a second consulship in AD 225, reflected the attitude of many when addressing the Senate in AD 203: 'For the security and eternity of the empire you should frequent, with all due worship and veneration of the immortal gods, the most sacred shrines for the rendering and giving of thanks, so that the immortal gods may pass on to future generations what our ancestors have built up.'[2]

Yet people's trust and confidence in these traditional gods was increasingly questioned. New religions offered a new relationship with the divine, where spiritual progress was rewarded in the afterlife. Many were drawn to the mystery cults. Initiates of Mithras saw him as the mediator between Heaven and Earth, whilst followers of Orpheus attempted to purify their minds and bodies by abstaining from meat and other contaminants, including contact with birth and death. Maintenance of the purity of the soul was essential in reaching the afterlife. A number of tomb mosaics from Syria dated to AD 227/228 show Orpheus surrounded by animals, and were perhaps created to honour Alexander Severus, himself a Syrian and, according to the *Historia Augusta*, a devotee. However, the foremost of these religions promising the immortality of the soul was Christianity. At the turn of the third century, there were probably only 200,000 Christians across the whole empire, or about 0.5 per cent of the population. But the religion spread rapidly over the course of the following 100 years.[3] At first its appeal drew in the poor, as the early Church's emphasis on the importance of the body after death and the promise of resurrection meant they could use cemeteries when most could not afford a sepulchre or the payments necessary for membership of a burial club. Conversion also did not involve long and elaborate ceremonies, but a public assertion of a belief in one benevolent god to the exclusion of all others.[4]

The third century saw the belief in an afterlife increasingly influence classical carvings on the sarcophagi of the wealthy. From the AD 220s, the deceased are given realistic portrait features and form part of a central sculptured group. The Pelops sarcophagus, from a decade or so after the reign of Alexander Severus, depicts

Pelops as a charioteer with his right hand held aloft in victory in the manner of a successful general. The face of the mythical king is carved in portrait rather than in a heroic manner, so associating the deceased with victory. But victory in death or over death?[5] Early Christian sarcophagi also tend to use pagan motifs, but combined these with Christian beliefs. The Adonis sarcophagus, now in the Vatican Museum, depicts the deity sat upright with an old man ministering to his leg wound, when traditionally he is shown dying in the arms of the goddess Venus. Here, death is overcome, instead of the classical focus on grief at his passing. The Persephone sarcophagus in the Capitoline Museum from the end of the reign of Alexander Severus does not use the traditional pose showing her abduction and rape, but instead she is borne aloft in a chariot, the arm of Hades placed reassuringly round her waist. Her face, which portrays the features of the deceased, is calm and full of expectation. In ferocious contrast, the Ludovisi Battle Sarcophagus shows in one continuous panel the full brutality of war. The beautiful, deeply chiselled carvings show bearded barbarians succumbing under the collective weight of heavily armed Roman soldiers. The faces of the vanquished embody the full emotions of their defeat and loss. Hovering above the carnage rides the general, marked with an X on his forehead. His right arm is raised, outstretched, denoting victory; victory in life and, more importantly, victory over death.[6]

Under the tolerant regime of Alexander Severus, Christianity flourished. According to the Church historian Eusebius:

> 'When Alexander the emperor of the Romans had brought his principate to an end after thirteen years, he was succeeded by Maximin Caesar. He, through ill-will towards the house of Alexander, since it consisted for the most part of believers, raised a persecution, ordering the leaders of the church alone to be put to death, as being responsible for the teaching of the gospel.'[7]

It is difficult to believe Eusebius' assertion that the 'house of Alexander', whether that be a reference to the imperial family or the imperial administration itself, consisted of a majority of Christians, but we do have evidence that Christians formed part of the courtly circle. The Christian historian and philosopher, Julius Africanus, created a library for the emperor in the Pantheon. He wrote a number of works, including the *Chronographies*, written in five books, which attempted to synchronize Christian and pagan histories from the Creation to AD 221. The compendious work *Kestoi*, or 'Magical Embrioderies', has also been ascribed to Africanus and is said to have been dedicated to Alexander Severus. The book covered natural history, military science and agriculture, as well as ascribing magic to the discipline of science rather than religion. It described appeals and incantations to a range of pagan gods, including Anubis, Ra, Ptah, the demons Ablanatho and Abraxas found on Egyptian papyri, as well as Yahweh.[8] This and other religious works influenced his contemporary, Origen.

The mixed culture heritage of many early Christian theologians is reflected in the upbringing of Origen. Born in Alexandria in Egypt c. AD 184/185, he was given the traditional Greek education by his Christian father, Leonides, along with study of the scriptures. He lost his father in a persecution during the reign of Septimius Severus, but he was taken in by a wealthy woman. However, as part of her household she supported a Christian teacher who held heretical views:

> 'But when his father had been perfected by martyrdom, he was left desti-
> tute with his mother and six smaller brothers, when he was not quite sev-
> enteen. His father's property was confiscated for the imperial treasury,
> and he found himself, along with his relatives, in want of the necessaries
> of life. Yet he was deemed worthy of divine aid, and met with both wel-
> come and refreshment from a certain lady, very rich in this world's goods,
> and otherwise distinguished, who nevertheless was treating with honour
> a well-known person, one of the heretics at Alexandria at that time. He
> was an Antiochene by race, but the lady we have mentioned kept him
> at her house as her adopted son, and treated him with especial honour.
> But although Origen of necessity had to consort with him, he used to
> give clear proofs of his orthodoxy, at that age, in the faith. For though
> very great numbers, not only of heretics but also of our own people, were
> gathered together with Paul (for that was the man's name), attracted by
> his apparent skilfulness in speech, Origen could never be persuaded to
> associate with him in prayer, keeping the rule of the church, even from
> boyhood, and "loathing" – the very word he himself uses somewhere –
> the teachings of the heresies.'[9]

Alexandria was a melting pot of both Christian and pagan beliefs. Origen joined, or perhaps set up, an orthodox school of Christian learning, whose reputation rap-idly spread, attracting students from far and wide. True to his cultural heritage, Origen pursued a path of open theological enquiry; amongst his copious works is the *Hexapla*. This is a word-for-word comparison and commentary on six dif-ferent versions of the Hebrew Scriptures. His commentaries on Christian writ-ings were influential in the formulation of the agreed texts that later formed the *New Testament*. However, a long-running conflict with Demetrius, the bishop of Alexandria, eventually led to him moving permanently to Caesarea in Palestine around AD 231, where he continued his work under the protection of the local bishop and long-term friend, Theoctistus.[10]

Arguments over a definition of heretical and orthodox Christian belief dominated the works of Origen's contemporary, Hippolytus (c. AD 170–236), the possible writer of the *Refutation of All Heresies*. The persecutions under Septimius Severus are reflected in the apocalyptical focus of his early works announcing the return of Christ and the 'End of Days'. However, later works reflect the peaceful security offered by the reign of Alexander Severus. His *Chronicle* attempts to trace the 5,738 days of human history from Creation to the thirteenth year of Alexander Severus, whilst the work *On the Resurrection* was dedicated to Julia Mamaea. Focusing his ire upon rivalries within the Christian community, and claiming to champion orthodoxy, he was elected as a rival pope to Urban I (AD 222–230). Upon Urban's death, he then opposed Pope Pontian (AD 230–235). Divided in life, both were united in death. The accession of Maximus Thrax led to the resumption of religious persecution. Hippolytus and Pontius were exiled to the imperial mines on Sardinia, where they both appear to have died.[11]

Another great Christian writer from the Severan period was Tertullian of Carthage. With Christianity flourishing in North Africa, he proudly asserts that 'Such are our numbers, amounting to almost a majority in every city', adding, in typically fulsome language, 'the earth groans with our numbers'. In the AD 220s, seventy African bishops met at a synod convened by Agrippinus, the Bishop of Carthage. By the early 240s, their numbers had grown to ninety, who met at a meeting called by Bishop Donatus. These figures probably suggest that a twentieth of the population in the provinces of North Africa were Christian. There are similar figures for the Christian population of Rome c. AD 250, based on the numbers of support and clerical staff supporting 1,500 widows.[12]

The brilliance of Tertullian's literary style, and that of his student Cyprian, reflect the high culture and education of the Graeco-Roman elite, brought up on the literary classics of ancient Greece and Rome. His works can be divided into two categories: the first consists of practical guides on Christianity and religious discipline; the second group are attacks and refutations on heresies and Judaism, such as *Apologeticus* and *De praescriptione hereticorum*. Recent converts had been brought up worshipping the pagan gods and looked for guidance and knowledge. Furthermore, many 'heretical' texts circulated amongst the literary elite, adding to a whirlpool of ideas and beliefs that permeated early Christian thought. *De praescriptione hereticorum* and *Scorpiace* were written to counter Gnostic beliefs. Gnosticism, or the search for 'spiritual knowledge or enlightenment', was born within a Christian theological framework, merged with Platonic beliefs, where devotees rejected the material world of the flesh for a spiritual one of the soul, represented by God himself. Many of these non-canonical texts were destroyed by the early Church and thought to be lost. However, in 1945, two brothers looking for fertilizer at Nag Hammadi in Upper Egypt broke open a jar containing fragments of dried papyri. After their mother burnt some of the fragments, worried about their 'dangerous effects', her sons attempted to sell them piecemeal on the black market. These priceless texts gradually came to the attention of the Egyptian authorities, and can now be found in the Coptic Museum in Cairo. The papyri date from the third and fourth centuries, but many are copies of original documents from the first to third centuries. These books or codices include a modified copy of *The Republic* by Plato, which had been adapted to reflect Gnostic beliefs, along with *The Prayer of the Apostle Paul* and *Gospel of Philip* of late second or third century date. Other works include *The Secret Book of James*, *The Gospel of Truth* and *The Gospel of Thomas*, where the reader is invited on a spiritual journey to find the 'true' meaning of Jesus' message: 'These are the hidden words that the living Jesus spoke, and that Didymos Judas Thomas wrote down. And He said: "Whoever finds the meaning of these words will not taste death."'[13]

Ironically, Tertullian, the champion of orthodoxy, was drawn towards the ideas and beliefs of the 'New Prophecy'. Converted to Christianity in the mid-second century, Montanus declared himself a prophet. He asserted that the 'Holy Spirit' could reveal new revelations to him. His followers became known as the 'New Prophecy'. Although essentially adhering to the central tenets of Christianity, the Bishop of Rome rejected Montanus' revelations and declared his beliefs heretical. Montanus proclaimed the towns of Pepuza and Tymion in Phrygia to be the site of a 'New Jerusalem'. His ideas spread rapidly to the cities of the empire, including those in North Africa and Rome. Tertullian clearly admired some of the movement's ideas, especially its discipline and religious fervour. Montanists, unlike their more orthodox contemporaries, raised the status of women to the same level as men. Two female prophetesses, Priscilla and Maximilla, were held in the same regard as Montanus himself. The church historian Eusebius accuses them of being possessed by devils rather than the 'Holy Spirit'.[14]

The *hypogaeum* or house tomb of the Aurelii on viale Manzoni in Rome belonged to members of a Gnostic or Montanist sect. Built between AD 220–240, the brick building is raised on a podium accessed from a courtyard, but the upper stories are now lost. A stairwell descends to three interconnecting rooms above two underground tombs, with burials placed in the floor. An inscription in the mosaic floor records that Aurelius Felicissimus constructed the *hypogaeum* for Aurelius Onesimus, Aurelius Papirius and Aurelius Prima, who were his 'brothers' and fellow 'freedmen'. Also included in the inscription is a girl named Aurelia Prima. It is doubtful they were freed at the same time, but some of the group were clearly related. It is suggested they might have been imperial freedmen, but all were members of the same religious community. Preserved on the walls are outstanding murals depicting the religious beliefs of the deceased. Scenes illustrate life after death in a heavenly Jerusalem. Some form of initiation ceremony is depicted, with a man pointing a wand in the direction of another man and woman. A group of twelve men and twelve women look on, surrounded by animals. Another room shows a Christ-like figure symbolized as a shepherd holding a book, perhaps a reference to the 'good shepherd'. In another scene, a man on horseback is followed by a large group, who approach a city gate with a figure awaiting his arrival. This could be Jesus entering the 'Kingdom of Heaven' or the Gnostic Epiphanes entering the great temple of Samē located on Cephalonia. In a further mural, a crowd gathers around a religious figure in a walled garden guarded by figures in white robes. This is mirrored with a picture of an empty city, perhaps indicating the Montanist belief in the arrival of the heavenly Jerusalem on earth. In the final room, a figure, probably Odysseus, enters a palace in disguise, to confront his wife's unsolicited suitors, symbolizing the imminent arrival of a new religious order. The juxtapositioning of both Christian and classical pagan imagery is typical of the dissemination of the rich fusion of ideas, beliefs and cultural identities that embodies the era of Alexander Severus.[15]

Since the early Principate, the state itself had supported education in the traditional disciplines of learning by financially supporting chairs of Greek and Latin rhetoric and philosophy in major centres of learning around the empire. According to the *Historia Augusta*, this was a practice continued by the emperor, who also paid the salaries of soothsayers, astrologers, engineers and architects. However, there is no other evidence that soothsayers or astrologers were retained on state bursaries. The extensive building programme in Rome would necessitate the employment of those specialists involved in construction. Aelian, a Roman who specialized in Greek works, held the prestigious chair of Rhetoric in Rome under Alexander Severus. According to the Sophist Philostratus, he 'was feted at Rome because of his privilege of their way of life', though he himself supposedly renounced the court, money, honours and power for the pursuit of knowledge. This is probably a reference to his predecessor in the chair, Aspasius of Ravenna, who was promoted to the post of *ab epistulis graecis* by either Caracalla or Alexander Severus, and who is criticized by Philostratus for employing an inappropriate style for imperial correspondence.[16] His two main works, *De Natura Animalium* and the *Varia Historia* (*On Human Life* and *History*), are encyclopaedic collections of information.[17] Ammonius Saccas probably held a chair in the intellectual melting pot of Alexandria. He pioneered the revival of Platonism and his lectures inspired his many students, but most importantly his tutee Plotinus. Instead of focusing on differences between Plato and Aristotle, a pursuit in vogue with the intellectual elite of the time, Ammonius Saccas worked to reconcile the ideas of the two. Plotinus arrived at his provincial capital in AD 232 and, on the death of his tutor and mentor in AD 244, moved to Rome, as it was the centre of intellectual life and patronage. Following the spirit of his times, Plotinus' ideas combined Aristolean logic, Stoic cosmology and Platonic metaphysics. He started writing soon after his arrival in the Alexandrian school. His works promoted the study and pursuit of virtue in order to elevate the divine core of our being. He summarized his principles as 'the One, the intellect and the Soul', and urged the rejection of the world of materialism. These ideas find echoes in pagan, Gnostic and Christian beliefs. His dying words were: 'I am trying to give back the Divine in myself to the Divine in the All.'[18]

Hand in hand with the revival of Neoplatonism went a renaissance in the ideas of Pythagoras. Plato was heavily influenced by the mathematician's works, which focused the mind of the philosophers on the immaterial and unsubstantial world. The Pythagoreans extolled the concept of *philia* (friendship) between the Greek and 'barbarian' ideas, just as Pythagoras himself had utilized ideas already espoused by the Chaldaeans, Egyptians and Greek religion. His followers acknowledged that these ideas not only influenced their own works, but their way of life. Ammonius Saccas wished to blend differing ideas 'into one and the same spirit'. Plotinus' works were collected by his own student, Porphyry, in the *Enneads*, and he also wrote a *Life* on his teacher, as well as another on Pythagoras.[19]

These ideas resonated within the imperial household. A neo-Platonist school had been founded at Apamea in the late second century, close to Emesa. It is highly likely both Julia Domna and Julia Mamaea attended intellectual debates in their youth. Numenius, the school's founder, was a neo-Pythagorean who devoted his life to trace the development of the ideas of Pythagoras and Plato in the religious beliefs of the Egyptians, the mystery cults and Judaism. Both imperial sisters continued in their interest in these ideas. In later life, Julia Domna asked Philostratus to write an account of the first-century mystic and neo-Pythagorean philosopher Apollonius of Tyana. All of the works of Apollonius are now lost, but he is also said to have been a miracle worker, having the power to raise the dead and heal the sick. Later pagans drew comparisons with Christ in order to undermine the basic tenants of Christianity. The work was probably commissioned late in Domna's life, as it was not completed by her death, so was not dedicated to her. At this time, the empress was accompanied by Julia Mamaea, who no doubt belonged to her sister's literary and intellectual circle. Philostratus completed the work before AD 238, probably around AD 222.[20] Both Julia Mamaea and Alexander Severus shared this intellectual curiosity and openness to ideas. Philostratus' later work, *Heroicus*, tells the tale of a Phoenician seafarer who recounts the stories of the Trojan War from the perspective of Protesilaus, the first Greek to be killed in the conflict. The work has been interpreted as a discussion on the nature of religion or, at a deeper level, a homage to Alexander Severus' defence of Hellenism in the face of 'Eastern' aggression from Sassanid Persia.[21]

Philostratus' *Lives of the Sophists*, completed between AD 231–237, recounts the lives of a number of Sophists, from ancient times to the contemporary.

It is dedicated to Antonius Gordianus, perhaps the *suffect* consul of AD 223 and future Emperor Gordian I or his son, the future Gordian II. In the work, Philostratus recalls a discussion on sophists with a Gordianus whilst staying with the imperial court at Daphne, outside Antioch, in AD 215/216. The elder Gordian would have been present as a governor of Coele Syria, and his son was either commander of the IV Scythian legion or in the entourage of his father.[22] Both remained prominent figures in the regime of Alexander Severus. The discussion does appear to have inspired Philostratus to write his *Lives*, even though many years had subsequently passed. Philostratus was concerned with a restoration of the golden age of Greek cultural traditions. This 'Second Sophistic Movement' originated in the late first century and ended with the barbarian invasions and civil wars that brought the empire to the edge of destruction after AD 235. Proponents focused on a restoration of purity in oratorical techniques, the correct use of language and reproduction of rhetorical styles that prevailed in Athens around 400 BC.[23] Highly educated, their services were sought after in all levels of government by philhellene emperors and provincial cities which employed them to deliver petitions to the emperor. An inscription from Sebastplois in Caria dedicated to Alexander Severus refers to a P A Antiochus, who is described as a *logistes*, equivalent to a *curatores*, and also a sophist. Philostratus also refers to Valerius Apsines of Gadara, who was awarded a consulship in AD 238 by Maximinus Thrax, suggesting a steady rise through the *cursus honorum* under his predecessor.[24]

Other contemporary Sophists mentioned by Philostratus include Nicagoras of Athens, whose works, including the thirteen-book *On Issues*, are now lost. His great rival was Hippodromus, who held the chair of rhetoric in Athens from c. AD 213. Others include the aforementioned Apsines of Gadara and Philostratus of Lemnos, whilst Heraclides of Lycia and Philiscus of Thessaly held chairs of rhetoric. The schools at Rome and Athens were considered equal, closely followed in prestige by the Alexandrian. Schools also existed at Ephesus and Smyrna, with a legal school at Beirut which had been attended by Ulpian. According to the Suda, Aspasius of Tyre wrote the *Art of Rhetoric* at this time, while Diogenes Laetius is believed to have completed his *Lives and Opinions of Eminent Philosophers in Ten Books* in the reign of Alexander Severus. This work was written in similar vein to the *Lives of the Sophists* and provides an overview of the eminent philosophers from Thales to Epicurus. However, it was criticized for its generally superficial nature, and the author's impassioned defence of Epicurus has led historians to believe he, himself was an Epicurian. Philostratus claims the early third-century philosophers were the equals of their more illustrious predecessors.[25] The Syrian Alexander Severus, keen to advertise his love of learning and patronage of Hellenistic culture, accepted the offer of Athenian citizenship in the tribe *Hadrianus*, which had been named after the second-century philhellene emperor. Significantly, Elagabalus had held Athenian citizenship in a different tribe, that of *Attalis*.[26]

The reign of Alexander Severus was the aesthetic and intellectual dénouement of classical Roman culture. Longinus' work *On the End*, composed slightly after our period of study and dedicated to Plotinus, lists nine recent Platonists and eight Stoics, but he laments that there were far fewer philosophers at his time of writing than in his youth in the 220s.[27] Public orations and debate were clearly still popular in the third-century empire. The works of the biographers and historians of the reign would have been read by the literary elite of the empire. Marius Maximus probably started composing his biographies of emperors from Nero to Elagabalus after his second consulship in AD 223, whilst Cassius Dio retired to his estates in Bithynia to put the final touches to his mammoth history of Rome after completing his consulship.[28] Another more ephemeral figure is the elusive historian labelled 'Ignotus' by Ronald Syme and Timothy Barnes. Based on their study of the *Historia Augusta*, they identified material which they reasoned did not originate with the biographies of Marius Maximus, and so suggested the existence of a now lost historian who wrote at this time and was also used by the biographer of the problematic source.[29]

To this wealth of learning can be added the many legal treatises, including the *Responsa* (or 'expert opinions') in nineteen books, composed by Modestinus, whilst the great jurist Paul produced 320 books, with book nineteen of his *Responsa* composed under Alexander Severus. Aelius Marcianus also wrote many commentaries, with his *Institutiones* frequently quoted in the *Digest of Justinian*. Marcianus and Modestinus, both students of Ulpian, continued his work in disseminating Roman law as far as possible in attempting to establish the sovereignty of the law over all things, both human and divine. To Aelius Marcianus, law was an invention and gift from the gods to all mankind, irrespective of birth. Licinius Rufinus, like Ulpian a product of the law school at Beirut, wrote the *libri regularum*, of which only fragments are preserved from quotes in the *Digest*. After his career in the court of Alexander Severus as an *a libellis* from AD 223–225, he was adlected into the Senate to rise to the consulship. He remained a powerful figure even after the fall of Alexander Severus. Another late Severan jurist was Aemilius Macer. His book on the duties of provincial governors, entitled *de officio praesidis*, may have been written under Caracalla or Alexander Severus. His *de appellationibus* was certainly written under the latter. Significantly, Macer makes no distinction between governors appointed by the Senate and those appointed directly by the emperor, nor between *procuratores* and *praefecti*.[30]

The reign of Alexander Severus saw an openness and acceptance of religions, cultures, traditions and beliefs that reflected the mood of the times. Influenced by their own multicultural heritage in Emesa, and perhaps Neo-Pythagorian ideas prevalent in the local school at Apamea and discussed in Julia Domna's intellectual circle, Julia Mamaea and her son fostered the prevailing intellectual current mood of acceptance and open debate. Many people were increasingly questioning traditional customs, beliefs and thought, and the underlying assumption that these were automatically correct because of their age or they had been held true by their ancestors. People looked to religion, philosophy and politics to provide a more rational, universal answer to existence and the problems that beset them as individuals and beleaguered society as whole. Religions that offered a new relationship with god and the reward of an afterlife grew rapidly, often abandoning the traditional divine pantheon for monotheism, such as the worship of the sun represented as Sol Invictus or Elagabal, or in the belief in one benevolent god as embodied in Christianity. Ancient Christian literature contrasts the fear and dread that existed in the times of religious persecution with the psychological, political and intellectual freedom that prevailed during the reign of Alexander Severus.[31]

Another group that appear to have perceived the rule of their emperor in a favourable light were the Jews. The use of the name Severus by Jewish families is very common in this period and found on inscriptions in synagogues across the empire. The name *swryb(s)*, Hebrew for (S)everus, was found during excavations of a synagogue in Sardis, *srbs* at another near Hebron and another in Greek script at Hammath-Tiberias. Another inscription dedicated to Alexander Severus and his mother from Spondilla near Intercisa, a frontier fortress on the Danube, was made by Cosimus, the head of a customs station. The inscription describes Cosimus as '*archisynagogus* of the Jews'. There was clearly a significant Jewish community at Intercisa led by this Cosimus. Interestingly, the *Historia Augusta* alleges that Antiochenes and Alexandrians, wishing to insult the emperor, referred to him as '*Syrus archisynagogus et archierum*' (Syrian synagogue head and priest). The reference to the priesthood was clearly alluding to his role as priest to Elagabal in his youth. Perhaps there is some credence to the statement in the *Historia Augusta* with the mob attempting to personalize his favourable treatment of Jews. This tradition of positive treatment of the Jewish community by the emperor can also be found in rabbinic sources. Since AD 176, Intercisa had been garrisoned by the *Cohors I milliaria Hemesorum*, who could be expected to be particularly loyal to their 'Syrian' emperor. Many of these soldiers would have been Jewish, and, upon retirement, settled on farms in the area or in the town attached to the fort.[32]

Pannonia had long since recovered from the devastation caused by invading tribes in the Marcomannic Wars. Vacant lands in both Pannonias, Moesia and Dacia had been forcibly settled by large numbers of Marcomanni, Quadi, Cotini and Naristae. These were supplemented by people from the Eastern provinces who were encouraged to move to the fortified towns. Many of the inscriptions from the late second century and first half of the third are made by people of Eastern origin, as denoted by their names. Names of native Illyrians with Romanized names also continue. Tombstones of interpreters refer to *interprex Dacorum* and *interprex Sarmatarum*, denoting not only a continued interaction across the frontier but also a lack of Romanization in the countryside where members of the defeated tribes were settled. The provinces along the Danube were dominated by the army. The garrisons required food and fodder for their animals, especially millet and barley. There were opportunities for carpenters, blacksmiths and potters, whilst other entrepreneurs provided services for the off-duty soldiers in the military settlements associated with the fortresses. The number of villas and farms increase in both Pannonian provinces in the third century, with the villa at Tác in Hungary reaching the zenith of its prosperity. Upon retirement, veterans received land totalling 100 acres in the local area. These ex-soldiers would turn to farming and interact with the serving soldiers from their unit, as well as other veterans settled in the area. Furthermore, two-thirds of inscriptions relating to the manumission of slaves refer to women, with many becoming the soldiers' wives. A further twenty-three tombstones from Dunaopentele show many veterans married local women. A lot of land in the hinterland of the fortress was also owned by the legion as '*territorium legionis*'. Soldiers were also able to rent some of this land by the third century, as inscriptions refer to legionaries acting as tenants, selling produce for fodder whilst retaining the profits made. Other inscriptions record soldiers described as *miles pequarius*, who were in charge of cattle and the supply of meat to the legion.[33]

Apart from Carnuntum, the towns along the Danube flourished. Excavations in and around the forum of Aquincum (Budapest) have found many terracotta workshops producing large quantities of *terra sigillata* pottery and terracotta statues between AD 200–240. An inscription of AD 223 describes the town as 'a most glorious colony'. Like all Pannonian towns, there are many inscriptions made by *collegia* or trade guilds, especially those related to carpentry, timber and construction. The wealth of these *collegia* is reflected in an unusual find from excavations in the headquarters of the textile dealers in the town. Archaeologists were surprised to discover a well-preserved water organ, dated from a bronze plaque to AD 228. This intricate piece of musical machinery is powered in a similar fashion to a pipe organ, but with air being forced through the pipes by a manual water pump rather than employing bellows. An inscription made by the textile dealers in the small town of Solva in Noricum lists over 100 members, so membership of Aquinum's *collegia* must have been considerably larger. Inscriptions were also made by a *collegium* of veterans and soldiers, who dedicated an altar to Mars and Minerva. The vast majority of inscriptions from the town were made to Alexander Severus and his mother. This is perhaps not surprising, as the fortress was garrisoned by a cohort from Emesa whose soldiers were also drawn from Oshroene, Samosata and Apamea. The other two major towns of Lower Pannonia also prospered. Bregetio was probably granted colonial status by Alexander Severus, its military town (*canabae*) growing to four times the civilian settlement. The buildings in the military section were much grander than those in the civilian counterpart, with corresponding grave goods in its cemetery far richer. Many of the names again suggest its inhabitants were of Eastern origin, but there is a decrease in native names. Brieto also prospered, as did Intercisa, with its large Jewish community. Syrian troops were used to strengthen the frontier north of Aquincum at Ulcisia Castra, with the stationing of an auxiliary unit from Antiochia, the *Cohors I milliaria nova severiana Surorum sagittariorum Antiochensium*. There appears to have been a deliberate policy of increasing the numbers of Eastern units along the Danube, who would be inherently loyal to their Syrian emperor, perhaps to counter the increased indiscipline of the Pannonian legions who were recruited locally.[34]

In comparison, Upper Pannonia appears not to have recovered from the Marcomannic War as well as Lower Pannonia. Carnuntum had been utterly destroyed in the war. We still find inscriptions of a range of *collegia* linked to construction, agriculture and trade, as well as a soldiers' *collegium* and references to the slaves and freedmen of soldiers and veterans. Initially the town prospered under Septimius Severus, but its growth lacked momentum. This is reflected in its brickworks, which increased production but the quality of its products declined. Its civil and military settlement did not reach the size of those in its sister province. Prosperity and the spread of Romanization appears to have been limited to the fortress towns and their hinterland. Only one inscription has been found in the interior of both of these provinces. The veterans were the social superiors who settled on farms in and around their old garrison fortress, often retaining links with their former comrades through the *collegium* and selling their produce to the army. Even serving soldiers had vested roots in the locality through marriage, family, property, land and economic links to the agricultural land owned by the legion. However, neither wealth nor Romanization appears to have reached the interior, settled by defeated 'barbarian' tribesmen and their families who were increasingly tied to the land as *coloni*, with few rights and treated as little better than slaves. These, and the settlements surrounding the forts, were the recruiting grounds of the Pannonian legions, whose soldiers were often promoted to serve in the Praetorian Guard.[35]

Like the Danubian provinces, the wealth of the two provinces in Britain were based on manufacture, commerce and, most importantly, agriculture. There is clear archaeological evidence for the rapid growth of civil settlements associated with forts along Hadrian's Wall in the third century. Fortifications along the wall appear at this time to have adapted their defences to the local terrain rather than rigidly adhering to the uniform playing card shape of earlier Roman fortifications.

Cast of a bust of Emperor
Caracalla in the Pushkin Museum.
The original is part of the Farnese
Collection in the National
Archaeological Museum in Naples.
(*Shakko, Wikimedia Commons*)

Marble bust of Emperor
Septimius Severus in the
Altes Museum, Berlin.
(*Angoria, Wikimedia
Commons*)

Statue of Julia Domna in the Römisch-Germanisches Museum, Cologne. She was the wife of Septimius Severus and sister of Julia Mamaea. (*Wikimedia Commons*)

Bust of Emperor Elagabalus in the Capitoline Museum, Rome. (*Wikimedia Commons*)

Denarius showing Empress Julia Maesa. (*Heinz-Joachim Krenzer, Wikimedia Commons*)

Cast of a statue of Julia Mamaea; the original is in the British Museum. (*Shakko, Wikimedia Commons*)

Gold aureus of Emperor Macrinus (AD 217–218), struck in 218 to celebrate the elevation of his son Diadumenianus to the rank of Augustus. The image shows the emperor sat on a curule chair alongside his son. Macrinus extends his hand towards a small figure ascending the platform holding out their toga to receive their token. Liberalitas stands to the left, holding an abacus and cornucopia symbolising plenty. A lictor stands behind the imperial chair holding fasces (RIC IV 79; Clay Issue 3; BMCRE 71; Calicó 2947; Cohen 43). (*CNG, Wikimedia Commons*)

Denarius of Julia Mamaea struck in AD 228. The obverse shows a bust of the empress with diadem and carries the legend IVLIA MA-MAEA AVG. The reverse shows Felicitas (good fortune) holding a caduceus in her right hand and her left elbow resting on a column. The legend *FELICI-TAS PVBLICA* means 'public happiness' (RIC IV 335 (Severus Alexander); Pink III, p.19; BMCRE 483 (Severus Alexander); RSC 17). (*CNG, Wikimedia Commons*)

A gold aureus of Emperor Elagabalus struck c. AD 218–219 in Antioch. It show the emperor draped, laureate and wearing a cuirass with the legend *IMP C M AVR ANTONINVS P F AVG*. The reverse shows a triumphal chariot, a quadriga, carrying the god Elagabalus alongside an eagle and four parasols. The legend above is *SANCT DEO SOLI, ELAGABAL*. (*CNG, Wikimedia Commons*)

DEO PATRO

SOL ELAGABAL O

G IVL AVITVS

ALEXIANVS

SO D AL FLA

TITIALIS

LEG AVG P P

PRO V RAET

Altar dedicated to the god Elagabalus by Gaius Julius Avitus Alexianus c.AD 196–200, housed in the Römisches Museum, Augsburg. (*Philippus Arabs, Wikimedia Commons*)

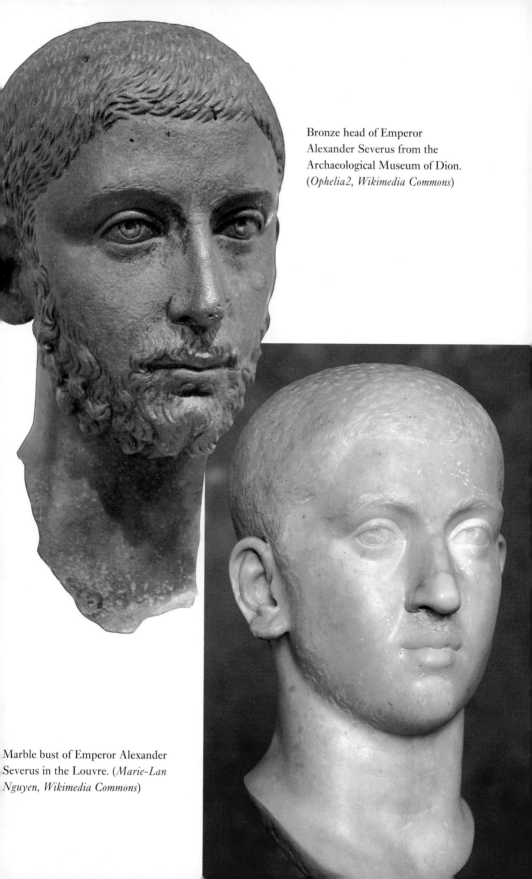

Bronze head of Emperor Alexander Severus from the Archaeological Museum of Dion. (*Ophelia2, Wikimedia Commons*)

Marble bust of Emperor Alexander Severus in the Louvre. (*Marie–Lan Nguyen, Wikimedia Commons*)

Colossal head of Alexander Severus in The Hermitage, St Petersburg. (*George Shuklin, Wikimedia Commons*)

Shattered bust of Alexander Severus, which was probably destroyed during the *damnatio memoriae* of Maximinus Thrax. Now at the Glyptothek, Munich. (*Bibi Saint-Pol, Wikimedia Commons*)

Gold multiple of a cuirassed Alexander Severus struck c. AD 230 from the Treasury of Tarsus. (*Jastrow, Wikimedia Commons*)

Bust of Emperor Maximinus Thrax in the Capitoline Museum, Rome. (*Jastrow, Wikimedia Commons*)

Bronze sesterces of Alexander Severus minted to celebrate the profectio of the emperor as he embarked from Rome to the East. The obverse carries the legend *IMP SEV ALEXANDER AVG*, whilst the reverse reads *PROFECTIO AVGVSTI* (RIC 596, Cohen 492). (*CNG, Wikimedia Commons*)

A sesterces of Alexander Severus minted in Rome in AD 229. The reverse shows the emperor driving a triumphal chariot, holding an eagle-tipped sceptre and reins (RIC IV 495; BMCRE 575; Banti 93). (*CNG, Wikimedia Commons*)

Medallion of Alexander Severus from AD 224. The obverse shows a bust of the emperor draped with laurels carrying the legend *IMP CAES M AVREL SEV ALEXANDER AVG*. The reverse shows the restored facade of the Colosseum. On the first storey are a series of arches, the second shows arches with statues, the

third flat pediment niches containing statues and the fourth square windows. The interior can be seen, with two tiers of spectators. The emperor stands outside to the left, sacrificing over an altar. Behind the emperor can be seen the Meta Sudans and a large statue of Sol. To the right is a two-storied building with two pediments, one above the other, and a statue, possibly of Jupiter. The legend around the image of the Colosseum

is *PONTIF MAX TR P III COS P P* (apparently unpublished, but see Gnecchi II, p.80, 9 (obverse) and Gnecchi III, p.42 = Toynbee pl. 29, 7 (the reverse). See also BMC 156–57 and Cohen 468 for sestertii with the same types but dating to 223). (*CNG, Wikimedia Commons*)

Sesterces of Alexander Severus struck in AD 231. The obverse shows the emperor laureate, draped, and cuirassed, with the legend *IMP ALEXANDER PIVS AVG*. The reverse shows Jupiter holding a thunderbolt and the legend *IOVI PRO PVGNATORI, S C* (RIC IV 628; BMCRE 794; Cohen 79). (*CNG, Wikimedia Commons*)

Tetradrachum from Alexandria, Egypt. Struck in AD 234/235, the obverse shows Alexander Severus with laurels, draped and wearing a cuirass. The reverse shows a trophy with two bound captives at the base. (*CNG, Wikimedia Commons*)

The fountain made of Aswan granite in the via degli Staderari, Rome, was originally in the caldarium (hot room) of the Baths of Alexander. (*Lalupa, Wikimedia Commons*)

The monumental Nymphaeum of Alexander Severus, whose construction was celebrated on a special issue of coins in AD 226, stands in the Piazza Victtorio Emanuele in Rome. The brick-faced concrete structure would have been covered in marble and a large number of statues. (*Lalupa, Wikimedia Commons*)

SIXTI·V·PONT·MAX·AVCTORITATE
TROPHAEA·C·MARII·VII·COS·DE·TEVTONIS
ET·CIMBRIS·EX·COLLE·ESQVILINO·ET·RVINOSO

One of two marble statues that stood on the Nymphaeum of Alexander Severus until the late sixteenth century, when they were moved to the Capitoline Hill. (*TcfkaPanairjdde, Wikimedia Commons*)

Relief showing the Praetorian Guard in full battle panoply in the Louvre-Lens. (*Jérémy-Günther-Heinz Jähnick, Wikimedia Commons*)

(*Top right*) Relief from the Grand
Ludovisi Battle Sarcophagus depicting
Romans conquering barbarians, from
the mid-third century AD. It is in the
Palazzo Altemps, the venue of
the National Museum of Rome.
(*Mary Harrsch, Wikimedia Commons*)

(*Top left*) Marble relief of a Praetorian
at the Antikensammlung, Berlin.
(*Wikimedia Commons*)

Relief from the Grand Ludovisi Battle
Sarcophagus depicting a Roman soldier
with a captive barbarian from the mid-
third century AD. (*Marie-Lan Nguyen,
Wikimedia Commons*)

Ruins of a temple from Hatra. (*Wikimedia Commons*)

The temple at Cuicul (Djemila), viewed from the forum, dedicated to gens Septimianca 'for the health, eternity and victory of Alexander Severus'. The forum was completed in AD 229. (*Michel-georges bernard, Wikimedia Commons*)

Aqueduct Alexandrina, Rome. Built c. AD 226 AD, it ran for 22km along the Via Praenestina to enter the city at the Porta Maggiore, where it ran underground to the Field of Mars. Its waters were used to supply the Baths of Alexander Severus. (*Nicholas Gemini, Wikimedia Commons*)

The theatre of Lepcis Magna, dedicated by the 'Septimian people of Lepcis' to Alexander Severus. (Daviegunn, Wikimedia Commons)

Arches surrounding the Forum Severiarum at Lepcis Magna decorated with Gorgons' heads. The Forum Severiarum and Forum Vetis were dedicated to Julia Mamaea. (SashaCoachman, Wikimedia Commons)

Remains of a private house converted into a Christian Church at Dura Europas. A poorly executed fresco dated to AD 232/233 depicts the 'Good Sheppard' along with Adam and Eve above a pool, which acted as the font. Other paintings around the walls are divided into an upper and lower register. The lower shows a procession of women holding torches approaching a sarcophagus, which has been interpreted as the 'Holy Women at the Sepulchre'. The upper paintings are badly damaged but appear to show Christ walking on water and the healing of the lame. Other images show the Sarmatian woman at the well and David slaying Goliath. Next to this building stand two pagan temples and a nearby synagogue. (*Heretiq, Wikimedia Commons*)

View of the caldarium of the Baths of Caracalla, Rome, from the gardens and precinct area constructed by Alexander Severus. This open expanse would have been filled with statues and tiered seating around an athletics track. The buildings around the perimeter would possibly have housed a library, a colossal central hall perhaps containing a massive statue of the emperor and steps leading to an underground mithraeum. (*Massimo Baldi, Wikimedia Commons*)

Statue of Jupiter Dolichenus from Carnuntum, now in the Museum Carnuntinum (CIL III, 11134). (*Matthias Kabel, Wikimedia Commons*)

A coin of the usurper Uranius, showing the conical stone representation of the god Elagabal housed in its temple in Emesa. An eagle is perched on top of the stone, shaded by two umbrellas. The pediment to the temple is ornamented with a crest. (BMC Galatia etc. p.241, 24; Delbrück, 'Uranius of Emesa', NumChron (1948), p.12, 2d; Baldus 38–42 (pl. IV, dies I/5)). (*CNG, Wikimedia Commons*)

Relief of Ardashir from Naqsh-e-Rostam (Iran). It shows the god Ahura Mazda, right, handing the ring of kingship to Ardashir I on the left. The body of the evil god Ahriman lies trampled beneath the horse of Ahura Mazda, whilst that of the last Arsacid king, Artabanus, lies beneath that of Ardashir. The fact Ardashir is represented on horseback, like Ahura Mazda, suggests he believed he not only had a divine mandate but equal divine status. (*Hara1603, Wikimedia Commons*)

Reconstruction of the Roman palisade and ditch of the Upper German limes near Saalburg, Germany. (*Wikimedia Commons*)

The remains of a Zoroastrian fire temple from Isfahan, Iran. (*Ivan Mlinaric, Wikimedia Commons*)

Perhaps this was a consequence of more officers pursuing a career in the army. Wall turrets with no practical use were abandoned, whilst a significant number of double archways in mile castles were reduced to single points of entry. This does not appear to have been a defensive measure, as forts both behind and in front of the wall were strengthened and some, abandoned in the barbarian incursions of AD 180, were reoccupied, including Risingham, High Rochester and Newstaed Neterby. Furthermore, Lanchester, south of the wall, was reoccupied, suggesting it was used as a patrol base. The construction of new baths and a basilica have been dated to the reign of Alexander Severus. The fact that the civil settlements grew at the same time suggests a period of peace and stability. The garrison was also supplemented by new units of *cunei* and *numeri*, units of native or semi-barbarian troops who retained their traditional equipment. They lived in the local settlement or in the fort if the garrison was under-strength. Inscriptions record the building of a new fort at Vindolanda in the AD 220s, whilst building work at Birdoswald appears to have continued throughout the third century.

There does appear to have been an increase in raids across the North Sea threatening the southern coast of England at the start of the century. In response, the fort at Branchester on the Wash was built to defend the densely populated areas in the interior, which included large imperial estates. It also appears to have been used as a base for coastal patrols, as the local grain was exported to soldiers based along the Rhine. The fort retains the traditional second-century design. Another fort was constructed at Reculver to defend access to London from the Thames. Its *principa* was built during the governorship of Rufinus, c. AD 225–230. This fort was too large to hold just its garrison of *Cohors I Baetasiorum*, which had been transferred from Maryport as it was experienced in coastal protection. The size of the fort suggests it was also a base for the fleet used to defend the island, which may have been transferred from Dover. This fort and settlement went into decline until the AD 270s. The fort at Caister-by-Yarmouth was probably constructed at the same time, positioned to defend the entrance to two rivers and the Nene Valley, which saw a rapid increase in industrial and agricultural production in the first half of the third century. London's earthen walls were also replaced with stone, a development seen in many British towns. However, the walls encircled the entire circumference of the town, suggesting a large population that would be able to defend them. There is no indication of civic decline in the province, although some villas did fall into disrepair. This many reflect the widespread confiscation of the estates of supporters of Clodius Albinus and his failed attempt to wrest the throne from Septimius Severus.[36]

Across the channel in Gaul, many cities allowed their defences to fall into disrepair or simply retained their ditch and earth bank. It was not until AD 258 and the barbarian invasions that penetrated deep into Spain that stone defences were rapidly constructed, as is evident from excavations at Le Mans, Dax, Senlis, Bordeaux, Tours, Arlon, Poitiers and Noyon.[37] A study of the villas of Brittany shows a period of growth and prosperity from the reign of Marcus Aurelius up to c. AD 235. However, an analysis of amphora excavated at Ostia found that imports of wine, olive oil, fruit and sauces from the Gallic provinces and Spain had gradually decreased over a period of 100 years up to AD 235, whilst imports from Africa and the Aegean had increased. This was perhaps due to competition rather than indicative of economic decline. The area between the Seine and the Rhine, including Boulogne and Strasbourg, only started to suffer from population loss in the second half of the century. It was at this time that the provincials moved from the widely scattered rural settlements to nearby nucleated settlements, where added numbers offered greater protection from raiders. Iron Age hill forts only appear to be reoccupied long after the fall of Alexander Severus.[38]

Excavations and analysis of the vast mountain of discarded amphora deposited on the outskirts of ancient Rome at Monte Testaccio show that trade in olive oil, wine and fish sauce peak with the reign of Antoninus Pius, then fall into a gradual decline until the reign of Alexander Severus, where they rise rapidly until c. AD 235, when there is a gradual decline followed by a rapid fall in the AD 260s. This pattern can also be seen with the number of shipwrecks found in the Mediterranean. Statue bases from the reigns of Caracalla and Alexander Severus record the appointment of *curatores* to the regional town of Ulia.[39] Olive oil was an imported constituent of the ancient Roman's daily requirements, as it was used for light, cooking and cleaning themselves at the baths. The cities of the Spanish peninsula, like their counterparts in Britain, gradually acquired stone circuit walls. A wall was constructed around the hill of Asturica Augusta, the principle city of north-west Spain. However, this seems to have been a gradual process. The wall at Barcino (Barcelona) dates to the second and third centuries, that of Castra Legiois Septimae Geminae (Leon) to the second, Salduba Caesarea Augusta (Zaragoza) to the third, and that of Lucus Augusti (Lugo) was built between AD 250–325.[40]

The construction of walls required the permission of the emperor and were very expensive. In the mid to late third century, barbarian invasions deep into the heartlands of the empire necessitated this expense. There had been no serious incursions since the Marcomannic Wars, yet towns and cities slowly replaced earthen ramparts with stone. This may be a direct consequence of an increase in brigandage over the late second and third centuries. The 'Deserters War' from AD 184–185 had resulted in the sack of major towns and cities, with a whole legion being besieged in its winter quarters in Strasbourg. According to Herodian, the unrest extended from the Rhine, through Gaul and into Spain.[41] During the reign of Septimius Severus, Bulla Felix led a force of runaway slaves, freedmen and deserters which, for a while at least, defied central authority to terrorize central and southern Italy. It is likely that Bulla Felix and Maternus, the leader of the brigands in the 'Deserters War', were both ex-legionaries. Their forces were both heavily reliant on former soldiers and, in the case of Bulla Felix, were mainly Praetorians who had been dismissed en masse by Septimius Severus when he first occupied Rome.[42]

Legal rescripts also reflect the threat of brigandage in the provinces. Ulpian reminds governors that they can only keep order in their provinces if they repress brigands and punish those who give them shelter. This is reiterated by Paul, who reminds local authorities that 'those who give shelter to brigands and assassins suffer the same punishment as these criminals'. Significant numbers of rural poor clearly felt either compelled to give assistance to the local brigands or that they could gain more from sheltering them than in supporting the representatives of central authority. After all, these *humiliores* were increasingly equated to slaves in the Roman legal system and they also felt the full demands of taxation and other obligations to the state, which were often extracted at sword-point by the soldiers. This discontent is evident in another rescript of Paul, who urges severe punishment for those who 'initiate rebellion and revolt or who rouse the people'. A new post was created in the reign of Caracalla, that of *latrunculator*, who was a judge appointed to try cases of robbery. At the same time there is widespread evidence for an ever-increasing network of military stations, particularly in border provinces.[43] The social and economic gap between the Romanized elite, based principally in the urban centres and rural villas, and the poor, who predominantly provided the agricultural wealth and manpower of the legions, grew ever wider. By the second half of the century, hostile peasants would form armed groups, the *bagaudae*, who would present a considerable military threat to emperors who, at the same time, were attempting to restore Rome's borders in the face of devastating barbarian invasions and repeated military revolts.

Rome's ever-increasing demand for grain, wine and olive oil benefited North Africa as well as southern Spain. This prosperity lasted until AD 238, as evidenced by a building boom that lasted from the Antonines to the end of the Severan era. The production of olive oil appears to have been centred on Sullechtum, Leptis Minor, Acholla and other port cities. The oil was processed, packaged and exported from these commercial hubs to satisfy the demand of the immense population of the capital. Archaeological excavations reveal the urban elite enjoying a high standard of living throughout the third century and into the fourth, with a corresponding expansion of rural sites. This is reflected in the work of the Carthaginian Christian luminary Tertullian, who takes considerable pride in the affluence of his province, with 'everywhere dwellings, everywhere people, everywhere cities, everywhere life'. He describes the wives of the wealthy discussing new styles copied from their more illustrious counterparts in Rome, whilst even prostitutes wore silk. Numerous inscriptions recorded costly building projects, paid for by the cities themselves or wealthy individuals. At Bulla Regia, a huge bathing complex constructed by a private individual was dedicated to Julia Mamaea around AD 230. However, the vast majority of new constructions were dedicated to the emperor himself or his 'divine house'. In AD 229, the colony of Cuicul (Djemila) augmented its newly completed forum with a temple. This incorporated an imposing rectangular colonnaded precinct, with the temple itself constructed on a raised podium reached by a triangular staircase. It dominated the centre of the town. The building bore remarkable similarity to the temple at Lepcis dedicated to the *gens Septimianca* for the health, eternity and victory of Alexander Severus.[44]

The immense cost of both stand testament not only to the continuing wealth of North Africa, but the loyalty of these provinces to the Severii and the African founder of the dynasty, Septimius Severus. A theatre was also dedicated by the 'Septimian people of Lepcis' to Alexander Severus, and the Forum Severiarum and Forum Vetis to Julia Mamaea. Less ostentatious building projects were enacted by other African cities. Riscade raised an honorific arch to either Elagabalus or Alexander Severus, and, at the same time, a *flamen*, or priest, of the divine Caracalla erected a statue of the goddess Victoria. Mastar spent 100,000 sesterces on baths, which inscriptions proudly record took seventeen-and-a-half months to complete. Two *aediles* from the small town of Guifi dedicated a fountain in AD 233, commemorated by a handout to the people and a feast for the decurions at their expense. Legionaries from the Third Augustan legion based at Lambaesis built several aqueducts in Africa and Numidia named *Aqua Alexandriane* around AD 226, and a *septizonium* and nymphaeum made up of a single exedra set between two wings with a large basin to the catch water that cascaded down the structure. However, as a foretaste of things to come, there is some epigraphic evidence of either some kind of civil unrest or small-scale tribal raiding. Altars were raised at the remote fortresses of Cadmus and Wadi Zemzem, garrisoned with vexillations from the *III Augusta*, as well as Volubilis in Mauretania, for the successful return of commanders from some form of armed conflict. T. Licinius Claudius Hierocles records on another inscription that, as governor of Mauretania Caesariensis, he had to deal with '*desperatissimam turbam et factionem*', a desperate crowd and faction, whilst his bodyguard raised a dedication to Alexander Severus. Another inscription from Mauretania Caesariensis records the creation of an elite unit of Moors to deal with barbarian incursions, whilst the construction of ramparts in the province may indicate unrest. Lixus in the neighbouring province of Mauretania Tingitana was razed to the ground in the mid-AD 250s. The *Historia Augusta* refers to a victory won in Mauretania Tingitana by an otherwise unknown Furius Celsus. The name of the successful general is probably spurious, but an issue of '*victoria*' type coins in AD 225 may be linked to this event. Much further to the east, in Tripolitania, a small fort, or *burgum*, was built twenty miles to the south of Lepcis Magna as part of the 'Limes Tripolitanus' between AD 230–235 in order to monitor the border crossing and combat local raids. However, these minor concerns do not appear to have had any lasting effect on the prosperity of the region in the reign.[45]

Further along the coast, in Cyrenaica, there is no evidence of decline until the mid-third century, when large and opulent town houses with sumptuous mosaics in Bernice (Benghazi) were demolished to make way for a massive defensive wall with projecting defensive towers. The wall was a rapid, makeshift affair making use of demolished blocks, enclosing only a small proportion of the city. The principal city, Cyrene, only made sudden and significant repairs to its walls in the latter half of the century. This was probably in response to raids by the Marmaric tribes, which were eventually crushed in AD 268. Before this, there appears to have been no concerns regarding security, with the evidence pointing to a period of wealth, peace and stability.[46]

Alongside the province of Africa, Egypt remained the principal bread basket of Rome. Its main city, Alexandria, had recovered from the brutal massacre exacted on the orders of Caracalla. Dio records 20,000 males were summarily put to death in revenge for some cutting satires made at his expense. The stock of the Severan dynasty appears to have recovered. A colossal marble statue of Ptolemy IV, VI or Mark Anthony was reused to represent Alexander Severus in the guise of Serapis, an Egyptian-Greek god who combined a number of characteristics, including healing, the underworld and fertility.[47] Egypt, alongside its African neighbours, appears to have prospered throughout the majority of the third century, but it did see the continued migration of rural poor to the major cities, especially Alexandria. Many moved for a better standard of living and employment, but they were to be badly disappointed. At first they replaced those massacred in AD 215, but many rapidly found themselves unemployed, adding to the volatility of the mob and the increasing siege mentality of the wealthy elite.[48]

The unique climatic conditions around the city of Oxyrhynchus have preserved a valuable insight into the minutiae of everyday life in Egypt in the form of a treasure trove of fragmentary papyri. One document from AD 223 records how a Julia Dionysia was questioned before the highest official of the town, Aurelius Ammonius, who had the responsibility of appointing men to public office. This was increasingly a demanding and onerous task, the elite gradually beginning to shun appointment to the town council as decurions, as administrative and especially religious posts were extremely expensive because they had to provide games, festivals and performances out of their own funds. This was seen as an honour by most, who took pride in contributing to their city, but these offices were increasingly seen as a burden. Eligibility for public office was based on property, and refusal to serve was punishable with its confiscation. The extension of Roman citizenship by Caracalla had greatly increased the numbers of those qualified to serve. Julia Dionysia appears to have held considerable property, but women were barred from serving as decurions. Ammonius questioned whether this wealth was hers or in reality owned by her husband, who was attempting to avoid his commitments. An oath sworn before the gods settled the matter. However, numerous papyri demonstrate that these types of disputes were common. Two fragments dated to AD 222 and 227 refer to the application of Aurelius Claudianus to share in the privileges of the town's *Gerusia*, which took over some of the responsibilities for organizing religious festivals. Claudianus wished to have his status acknowledged by sitting in a prominent seat in the theatre alongside his fellow members, but sought dispensation from the associated administrative and financial obligations on account of his age. Cities increasingly drew upon the resources of their hinterland to satisfy the growing demands of the state, whilst the elite were increasingly reluctant to contribute to supporting municipal liabilities.[49]

Other fragments from Oxyrhynchus preserve the prices of everyday commodities bought and sold on a daily basis: wheat, oil, wine, slaves, donkeys. These demonstrate considerable price stability from the AD 190s to c. AD 270, despite the reduced precious metal content of third-century coinage.[50] The preservation of official documentation has given historians an insight into the administration of this vital province. The execution of M. Aurelius Epagathus in AD 224 helped to reconstruct the chronology of the fleeting regency of Ulpian. Documents record that a *juridicus*, Ti. Claudius Herennianus, was promoted to acting prefect on the removal of Epagathus, an office he retained until May/June AD 225. The short tenure of many of these office-holders indicates the potential threat that existed to the stability of Rome with its control of food supply. An exception to this appears to be Maevius Honoratianus, who remained prefect from AD 231/232 (December/January) until AD 236, a date beyond the reign of Alexander Severus. He must have been a trusted and experienced equestrian, as the province at this time served as a vital storehouse of food for the Roman army campaigning against the Sassanids. Another official, M. Aurelius Zeno Ianuarius, held the military office of 'dux' rather than prefect. As he had previously been a governor of Mauretania Caesariensis, this appointment must have been of a high status, but he served under a Prefect of Egypt. This suggests that the prefect lacked the necessary military experience, which is difficult to imagine with the rapidly expanding military posts available under the Severans. More likely, the appointment was made in response to unrest in the province, which would partly explain the extended tenure of Honoratianus. The Prefect of Egypt's responsibility probably remained the administration of this vital province and ensuring the efficient delivery of supplies to the army, whilst the 'dux' ensured no internal disorders threatened the production and transportation of grain. This was important, as Egyptian soldiers mutinied in Syria, delaying

Alexander Severus' campaign against the Sassanids. It was probably at this time that Alexander Severus transferred the *IV Scythica* from Zeugma to Alexandria.[51]

Roman's eastern provinces of Arabia, Syria Palestina, Syria Phoenice, Syria Coele, Osrhoene and Mesopotamia were sandwiched between the Mediterranean and the desert. Septimius Severus' invasion of Parthia had destabilized this ancient kingdom, resulting in the rise of the expansionist Sassanids. The annexation of the province of Mesopotamia had also sown the seeds of future conflict with their eastern neigbours for control over the fertile land between the upper reaches of the Euphrates and Tigris. Roman Mesopotamia served as a barrier to invasions of Syria, with the *I* and *III Parthica* placed at Nisibis and Resaina under the command of an equestrian governor who inevitably had extensive military experience. This is exemplified by the career of L. Valerius Valerianus, who was appointed as Prefect of Mesopotamia and Osrhoene in the early AD 220s. He had served his initial *tres militia* in Pannonia and Dacia before promotion to a procuratorship in Cyprus, and had then accompanied Septimius Severus on his march on Rome as a commander of a vexillation. His loyalty and ability were rewarded with commands in the war against Niger, followed by command of a *peregrine* cohort in the war against the Parthians. He was then appointed to a special post of *praepositus summae* (*rationis* or *rationis privatae*) in the newly created province of Mesopotamia, followed by another administrative post as procurator in an unknown province, before being appointed as procurator of Syria Palestina by either Caracalla or Elagabalus. He was clearly trusted, loyal and possessed extensive military and administrative experience, making him an obvious choice to take responsibility for this crucial province of Mesopotamia at the start of the reign of Alexander Severus. As a patron of Caesarea, he probably used his influence to persuade the emperor to raise its status to that of a *metropolis* in the first half of the AD 220s. The regions surrounding the city are described in the Talmud as 'the land of life'.[52]

The Syrian provinces remained amongst the richest in the empire, with Antioch rivalling Alexandria as the principal city of the Near East. Archaeology has discovered that the city's hinterland was occupied by many affluent villas surrounded by fertile farmland producing olives, grain, grapes and supporting livestock. This is typified by the third-century villa at Yakto. A colonnaded courtyard was enclosed by a suite of rooms and two *exhedras* (large rectangular meeting rooms). An ornamental pool occupied a considerable portion of the courtyard, and was probably used as a fish pond. The owners also built a private bath house, and the sumptuous mosaics attested to their status and culture. This wealth is reflected in the increasing number of senators from the East. The names of 471 senators are known from the reigns of Elagabalus and Alexander Severus, of whom we know the origins of 238. Of these, 113 were Italians – a decrease of 75 per cent from the reign of Domitian – seventeen were from Western provinces and thirty-three from Africa, whilst seventy-two were of Eastern origin. This was a gradual but significant change in the composition of the Senate. The emperor built on the inherent loyalty of his fellow Syrians by raising his birth city of Arca and Damascus to colonial status. Other cities show no outward signs of decline. Construction programmes initiated after the devastating earthquake of AD 115 continued without break into the third century in the cities of Antioch, Apamea and Palmyra. Third-century mosaics from Emesa mostly draw upon their local cultural heritage, although many display representations of Orpheus or the phoenix, looking towards a belief in the resurrection of the soul. They are shown as frontal portraits rather than in profile, and use Syraic script rather than Greek. Further to the south, the *odeum* at Gerasa was enlarged, doubling its seating capacity, indicating continued growth and confidence.[53]

Civic construction was mirrored by monumentalizing seen in temple building, which only ended in the middle of the third century. The rural districts around Syrian towns and cities also appear to have shared in this prosperity. The superbly preserved Roman highland villages to the east of Antioch continued to expand up to AD 250, their wealth indicated by the increased number of olive oil presses and helpfully evidenced by the local custom of inscribing the year of construction on each building. Even the war with the Sassanids in the AD 230s appears to have had no effect on the confidence of the local population, who continued to invest in planting olive trees, which take a considerable amount of time to mature before they bear fruit. The majority of the rural areas were settled by a free peasantry and veterans concentrated around the various towns designated as colonies. This is seen in the coinage of cities such as Hierapolis and Carrhae, which carry representations of temples housing their local gods alongside military standards, as these veterans would worship the local deities in temples decorated with the military banners they had served under.[54]

The city of Dura Europas on the Euphrates has produced a wealth of artefacts preserved by the arid conditions and its abandonment after its sacking by the Sassanids in AD 257. A pagan temple dedicated to Zeus Theos is sited close to a Jewish synagogue and a private house that appears to have been converted into a Christian church. A *graffito* dates a poorly executed fresco to AD 232/233, depicting the 'Good Shepard' along with Adam and Eve above a pool which acted as the font. Other paintings around the walls are divided into an upper and lower register. The lower shows a procession of women holding torches approaching a sarcophagus, which has been interpreted as the 'Holy Women at the Sepulchre'. As the members of the congregation followed the representation of the procession, their eyes would have been drawn towards the font. The upper paintings are badly damaged, but appear to show Christ walking on water and the healing of the lame. Other images show the Sarmatian woman at the well and David slaying Goliath.

The close juxtaposition of Christian, pagan and Jewish places of worship in one location represents a physical confirmation of the open and enlightened policies of the imperial house.[55] Christianity had set firm foundations in other areas of the Graeco-Roman East. Caesarea, the provincial capital of Syria Palestina, grew under Origen into a great centre of Christian scholarship that rivalled Jerusalem. Passing references in the works of a number of Christian writers suggest there existed numerous Christian communities in the vicinity of Caesarea and Jerusalem.[56]

A similar socio-economic position appears at first glance to have existed in Roman Asia Minor. The number of Attic inscriptions discovered in Lydia from c. AD 220–230 show only a small reduction from the peak under the Antonines.[57] However, other studies clearly demonstrate that the local elites, as in Egypt, were increasingly reluctant to hold municipal offices. This is reflected in the steep decline of benefactions of inscriptions after AD 220. Some cities such as Aphrodisias appear to have continued to suffer from depopulation caused by the Antonine Plague, with the resultant impact on finances and income. The rural poor in Lydian villages complain of unbearable burdens placed on them by *frumentarii, colletiones* and *stationes*. The state's attempts to ensure it secured its share of increasingly scarce resources resulted in a rapid deterioration in the position of the poor.[58] Disputes over tax liabilities were common. Inscriptions record a prolonged legal dispute between two villages, Anossa and Antimacheia, from AD 213 to at least AD 237. Both sought to reduce their obligations to provide the state with animals for use on the road that ran through their territories; the *cursus publicus*. Each village's liability was based upon the length of the road that ran through its territory, and its overall tax burden probably paid in grain and other resources rather than cash. As both villages were part of a large imperial estate, the case was heard by a series of procurators. However, once a verdict was delivered, the loser then appealed to the procurator's successor. The case was heard by three different procurators, who wrote a series of letters to the village councils attempting to enforce their decisions. At one point, a soldier was appointed to enforce the verdict and protect Anossa from revenge attacks by its rival. There are many inscriptions across Asia Minor recording the appointment of these soldiers (*stationarius*) to keep order, suppress banditry or enforce governmental decisions. The powers of central authority were clearly severely curtailed by legal prevarication or refusal to obey unless accompanied by the point of a sword.[59]

Across the Aegean, the region of Thessaly appears to have experienced imperial disfavour due to some form of illegality in the production of purple dye. This industry was carefully controlled by emperors, this colour being used to indicate the imperial status of an Augustus or Caesar. However, Philostratus records that the area had as a consequence suffered economically, to the extent that the inhabitants had been forced to sell their family tombs. An inscription from Corinth also records the existence of a procurator of the 'purple-account' for Thessaly. The *Historia Augusta* records that Alexander Severus took a special interest in the 'use' of this colour.[60]

Italy continued to be dominated by the political, social and economic position of Rome. A study of the Liris Valley in Campania shows small rural sites disappearing in the third century, indicating a concentration of land-holding by the emperor and the wealthy elite in the form of vast estates.[61] Marcus Aurelius had stipulated that all senators had to invest a quarter of their capital in Italy, which was a reduction from the third demanded by Trajan. Although these restrictions may have lapsed by the third century, it is clear from Paul that senators were expected to have at least two homes, or *domicilium*, one in Rome and the other their native land. The jurist also states that if a senator was demoted from the order he could only be allowed to live in his native province at the special permission of the emperor. Cassius Dio clearly possessed a sumptuous villa in Rome, but he also refers to property he held in Capua, whilst at the end of his career he retired to his estates in his native Bithynia.[62]

However, although extremely wealthy, the resources of these provincial senators were eclipsed by that of the aristocracy. Inge Mennon has identified eighteen of these elite families between AD 193–284 whose ancestry included at least three consuls with careers stretching back over two decades. Many members of these families benefitted from honours, offices and gifts from Alexander Severus, and no doubt sat on the senatorial *concilium*. These families dominated the highest offices of the *cursus honorum*, holding between 34–39 per cent of the ordinary consulships in the third century, 25–27 per cent of the city prefectures and 17–20 per cent of the proconsulships of Asia and Africa.[63] At least eight of the eighteen families were of Italian origin, whilst most of the others were fully integrated into the economic and social fabric of Rome and Italy. These included the Claudii Pompeiani from Antioch and the Pontian Greek Claudii Severi, who had familial ties to the Antonine emperors.[64]

The nobility would have known each other and, it appears, acted to the exclusion of other more recent senatorial families through intermarriage and adoption amongst members of their aristocratic circle. This was done to secure their privileged position in society and retain their name and *gens* as it passed through their children and on down the generations. In order to gain their support, the emperor rewarded their loyalty with access to his person and granted them the highest magistracies, which carried the status they craved; the trappings of power without its reality. However, plague and civil war had decimated the old Antonine aristocracy. It was in the interests of the remaining nobles – their numbers supplemented by a small number of loyal and successful Severan generals and politicians – to work for peace and stability. The persons of Mamaea and Alexander Severus offered their best chances of long-term survival.[65] The name of the ordinary consul of AD 233 and 256, Lucius Valerius Claudius Acilius Priscilianus Maximus, denotes the degree to which his family had solidified their fortunes with other aristocratic families. The family claimed descent from the Republican '*gens* Valerii'. He was the grandson of L. Valerius Messalla Thrasea Priscus, the ordinary consul of AD 196 executed by Caracalla, possibly for his support for Geta. Dio describes this noble senator as 'a man second to none either in birth or intelligence'. His probable father, Lucius Valerius Messalla Apollinaris, was the ordinary consul of AD 214. His son's name denotes marriage into the greatest of aristocratic families, the Acilii, perhaps to a daughter of M. Acilius Glabrio, the consul of AD 186 who refused the throne when offered it by Pertinax. The fact that Lucius Valerius Claudius Acilius Priscilianus Maximus shared his second consulship in AD 256 with a M. Acilius Glabrio suggests there existed a close link between these two families. Lucius Valerius Claudius Acilius Priscilianus Maximus was an influential player in the politics of the empire after the death of Alexander Severus. He was selected by the Senate along with nineteen other eminent senators to lead the revolt against Maximinus Thrax, and was described as an *amicus* of the co-emperor Pupienus and helped to raise Gordian III to the throne. This emperor shared his consulship in AD 239 with another Acilli, M. Acilius Avola.[66] The significance of his role after the murder of Alexander Severus suggests he was a prominent politician before AD 235.

Other noble families strengthened their ties with each other in the first half of the third century. Ti. Claudius Severus Proculus, whose own mother was a daughter of the Emperor Marcus Aurelius, married his daughter Annia Faustina to Pomponius Bassus, scion of the Pomponii, who was executed by Elagabalus.[67] L. Egnatius Victor married into the Hedii, probably a daughter of Quintus Hedius Rufus Lollianus Gentianus, who had been a patron of Pertinax before he became emperor. His children, like the offspring of many of these aristocratic unions, were amply rewarded and honoured by Alexander Severus. L. Egnatius Victor Lollianus was appointed *suffect* consul (c. AD 225–230), then made governor of Bithynia and Pontus (AD 230/235), followed by Pannonia Inferior (AD 222/235). His brother, Egnatius Victor Marianus, was *suffect* consul in AD 230 and governor of Moesia Superior c. AD 230. Their sister, Egnatia Mariniana, married the leading senator and future Emperor Valerian, himself a member of a noble family.[68] The aristocratic Nummii are represented by M. Nummius Senecio Albinus, the ordinary consul of AD 227, whose step-brother held the consulship of AD 223. His father had been adopted by Umbrius Primus, the *suffect* consul of AD 185, but his genetic father was related to the noble Didius Julianus, the emperor in AD 193.[69] The brother of the salacious historian and aristocratic senator, L. Marius Maximus, probably married his son to an Egnatia.[70] The Claudii Pompeiani and Claudii Severii also appear to have been granted the honour of sharing the ordinary consulships of AD 235 in the figures of Cn. Claudius Severus and Lucius Tiberius Claudius Aurelius Quintianus, both being descended from daughters of Marcus Aurelius. A number of these families also seem to have been given patrician status by Alexander Severus, probably including the Virii by AD 232 and perhaps the Vetii.[71]

The wealth of these great families was primarily based on the ownership of land, a significant proportion of which would have been held in Italy. As the network of familial bonds drew these aristocratic families together, so land ownership would have coalesced. The greatest landowner of all was the emperor, especially after the confiscation by Septimius Severus of the senatorial supporters of Niger and his aristocratic rival Clodius Albinus.[72] So much property now fell under imperial control in the form of the *res private* or *ratio private* that regional offices had to be created to administer these estates.[73] Few of these imperial estates have been excavated, but excavations at Vagnari in Apulia have revealed the extensive use of slave labour, supplemented by free labourers and tenants used to produce wine for the emperor's table until the early fourth century.[74] However, other areas of the Italian peninsula appear to have suffered economic decline and depopulation. The area around Verona had been suffering from clear signs of diminishing wealth from the first century, and around Luni from the second, although this was offset by the mass production of terracotta lamps, which continued until the second half of the third century. On the periphery of Italy, Istria and Cisalpine Gaul suffered from reduced demand for their main exports of marble and in particular, wine.[75] If the imperial estate and winery at Vagnari were replicated across Italy, the decline in demand for wine imports from the provinces would not be a surprise, yet nor should it be taken as indicative of a general economic decline.

The empire of Alexander Severus was a world in a state of flux. In his propaganda, the emperor looked to the past, promising a restoration of a golden age that existed in the time of the 'best' emperors, embodied in the reigns of Augustus, Trajan, Hadrian and Marcus Aurelius. The aristocratic elite supported the emperor and his fiction of a continuance of the Severan dynasty, as the alternative was the renewal of the civil war that had decimated their numbers and diminished their wealth. The economy of the empire appeared to have gradually recovered from warfare and the devastations of the Antonine Plague. Confidence seems to have been restored, with public and private munificence evident across the provinces of the empire. However, scratch the surface and the misery of the rural poor becomes increasingly clear. The voices of this near-silent majority only appear fleetingly in the historical and epigraphical record. Yet even these ephemeral glimpses show a class of peasantry, the future *coloni*, increasingly at the mercy of the demands of the wealthy in the cities and the state at a time when resources were increasingly limited due to the political, social, economic and natural turmoil of the preceding thirty years. Some turned to banditry. The army was the primary escape route from poverty and exploitation, and yet, ironically, the soldiers were often the instrument of their injury. Plague, war, revolt and death had led many to question their relationship with the divine and seek answers to their suffering. Both paganism and Christianity in its various forms promised a life after death. The imperial family, themselves the heirs of a mixed Graeco-Roman, Semitic and 'Syrian' heritage, not only allowed open discourse but took an active role in questioning, debating and investigating the world around them. This fertile intellectual and religious climate allowed a late flowering of philosophical, theological and creative thought that found its expression in art, literature and learning. However, this 'age of enlightenment' was soon to be brought to a sudden close by a storm gathering in the East.

Chapter 8

War in the East AD 228–233

'And then the kings of Persia shall rise, and Roman Mars [will smite] the
Roman king and pastoral Phrygia shall with earthquakes groan. Woe, woe
Laodicea, woe to thee sad Hierapolis, for you the first the yawning earth
shall receive ... of Rome ... vast Aus[onia?]. All things as many ... shall
wail ... [the] men destroyed by the hands of Mars.'

(Sibylline Oracle: Book X (XII), 344–354)

A lexander Severus had unwittingly been the short-term beneficiary of a
protracted period of peace, a consequence of the aggressive campaigns of
Septimius Severus and Caracalla against the Caledonians beyond Hadrian's
Wall, the Parthians in the East and the Alamanni on the Rhine. This was, however,
a mixed blessing. On the one hand it allowed the new regime the opportunity to
build secure foundations to his rule, but it also deprived the emperor of the opportunity to display the martial virtues considered essential by the soldiers. These men
were willing to risk their lives serving an emperor, who was their ultimate commander-in-chief, if they felt confident in his *virtus* and military abilities. Caracalla
had pursued an aggressive war against a weakened Parthian Empire in order to
establish this reputation. He was loved by his men. Even Elagabalus had led men
in war, rallying fleeing soldiers to turn the tide of battle. Alexander Severus failed
to use the peaceful interlude from his accession in AD 222 to AD 228 by building up
these martial credentials. Rome had never been averse to launching an unprovoked
military campaign against some weak and surprised foe. The wars of Alexander
Severus would, however, be entirely reactive, with the army led by an emperor
lacking any military experience. By AD 224, a war in the East could have been fore-
seen, with the rise of Ardashir and his defeat of his Parthian opponent. Septimius
Severus' and Caracalla's invasions of Mesopotamia had served to entirely destabilize the Parthian regime, leading to a bloody civil war between Artabanus V (also
known as Ardavan V) and his brother, Vologases VI. Caracalla had written to the
Senate in AD 216 that this was a situation entirely to Rome's advantage.[1] Neither
he nor his successors, Macrinus and Elagabalus, had any inkling that the Parthian
Empire was about to collapse, its place taken by a highly centralized and far more
aggressive Sassanid Empire. However, by AD 224, the situation had become clearer,
with evidence that a new and far more aggressive power had risen in the East.

The bloody and indecisive Battle of Nisibis in AD 217 and the resultant peace treaty had allowed Artabanus V to focus his energies on defeating Vologases VI, whose territory had been reduced to Babylonia. Artabanus managed to defeat his brother at a battle near Susa by 5 September AD 221, but he was immediately faced with a far greater threat.[2] The lack of stable government had allowed a power vacuum to develop, and Ardashir (also called Artaxerxes in our sources), a minor king in Pars (a territory in southern Iran running along the Arabian Gulf), to expand his territory at the expense of other minor rulers in the area. These actions appear to have been tolerated by Artabanus, as Ardashir had recognized Artabanus' claim to the Parthian throne and was preoccupied in establishing his own authority. However, Aradashir then appears to have threatened royal authority by either founding a new city of Ardashir-Khurra (also called Gor, now the modern Furuzabad) or establishing this city as the provincial capital in opposition to the established capital at Istakhr. This action was undertaken without the permission of Artabanus. Ardashir later established a citadel at his city and built a fire temple there, the city being renamed Shahr I Gor.[3] Ardashir and his Sassanid successors asserted their divine right to rule through their fervent support of Zoroastrianism. The Greek sixth-century poet and historian Agathias, who used Sassanid court records in his works, writes:

'This man [Ardashir] was bound by the rights of the Magi and a practitioner of secrets. So it was that the tribe of the Magi also grew powerful and lordly as a result of him ... It had never been so honoured or enjoyed so much freedom ... and public affairs are conducted at their wish and instigation.'[4]

In the massive carved reliefs at Naqsh-e Rustam which celebrate his final victory over Artabanus, Ardashir is shown receiving his crown, and so his right to rule, from the god Ahura Mazda. What is striking is the depiction of the earthly ruler and the ruler of all things divine on an equal level. They face each other on horseback in figures of equal size. Each tramples underfoot smaller figures of their defeated enemies; Artabanus V is crushed under the horse of Ardashir, and Ahura Mazda's horse does the same to Ahriman, the Zoroastrian religion's demon of demons. Order is restored both in heaven and on earth. Underneath, Ardashir's son and successor, Shapor, added the text: 'This is the visage of the Mazda worshipping lord Ardashir, the King of kings of Iran, who is of the radiant image of gods, son of the lord Papag, the king.'[5]

Artabanus' forces were defeated and destroyed in a series of three battles. The last and decisive Battle of Hormizdjan was fought, according to Persian tradition, in April AD 224 in the vicinity of Isphahan and Ray, near the palace of Artabanus.

This date is based upon contemporary sources and is supported by other literary and numismatic evidence. Furthermore, the eleventh-century Persian poet Firdausi dates the death of Artabanus to AD 224, as does the ninth-century Arabic historian Al-Tabari. Ardashir's coinage from AD 222–224 carries the legend 'King of Pars', but from AD 224–227/228, the title 'King of Iran' appears.[6]

The defeat and death of the Arsacid Artabanus led to other members of the Parthian royal house claiming the throne. Ardashir's main concern throughout his reign was not the complete conquest of Rome's eastern provinces but the establishment of his rule in the face of numerous revolts and invasions. Roman control over the northern Mesopotamian plain, however, threatened his position in Babylonia and Assyria, especially as these remained centres of Arsacid opposition to his rule. After the Battle of Hormizdjan, many Parthian nobles accompanied some of the sons of Artabanus to Armenia, where they were welcomed by Armenian King Tiridates II (also known as Khosrov the Great in Armenian sources), who continued to encourage other Parthian nobles who had accepted Sassanid rule to revolt. Other sons of the deposed king may also have gone to Bactria, which was ruled by their relatives. Coins carrying the name Artavasdes, another son of Artabanus, have been found in some parts of the empire, including Khurramabad, a town between the Zagros Mountains and Babylonia, Nihavand, situated in the Zagros Mountains themselves, and Adharbaijan to the north-east of Armenia. The geographical location of these areas of resistance suggests he was supported by the king of Armenia. These coins end around AD 227. Meanwhile, other surviving sons of Vologases VI led a revolt in Babylonia, and the great desert city of Hatra, ruled by a family related to the Arsacids, rejected Sassanid suzerainty.[7]

According to the later account of Firdausi, Ardashir stayed for a short time in Ray, probably consolidating his control over the vital satrapy of Media before returning to his homeland of Pars. Although the chronology and accuracy of Fardausi's account cannot be relied upon, it does provide an insight into the depth of resistance to the Sassanids. According to the *Book of Kings*, Ardashir led a campaign against the Kurds before returning to Pars, having sent another expedition to Kirman. One of Ardashir's sons probably led the army to Kirman, located in the south-west of modern Iran. The city, whose ancient name was Veh-Ardashir, was founded as a strongpoint in the vast open plain and is famous for the remains of its numerous Zoroastrian fire temples. Ardashir then marched on Shahrazur in Assyria. From there he moved to the old Parthian capital at Ctesiphon, where he was crowned *Shahanshah*, or 'King of Kings'. This can be dated from his coinage to AD 227. An expedition against the Kurds might suggest a campaign in the Zagros Mountains, which would make sense in light of the resistance led by Artavasdes. However, the fourteenth-century Egyptian historian Nihayat al-arab provides an alternative chronology between the defeat of Artabanus in AD 224 and Ardashir's coronation in AD 227/228. According to this account, Ardashir marched to Khorasan, which can be assumed to be Bactria, and stayed in Merv for a year. Numismatic evidence supports Ardashir's conquest of the city, but the date of this is open to interpretation. He then returned to Ray before launching an attack on Adharbaijan and Armenia. Again, this makes contextual sense. Mosel was then conquered and he marched over the Tigris into what would become the Sassanid province of Assyria, where he defeated a confederation of Mesopotamian kings before being crowned in Ctesiphon. Whilst Al Tabari confirms the date of the Battle of Hormidjan as 28 April AD 224, he goes on to provide yet another alternative list of conquests up to AD 227. According to his *History of the Prophets and Kings*, Ardashir conquered Hamadan (located 258 miles to the north of Khurramabad), then Media, Adharbaijan and Armenia, and then captured Mosul before following the Tigris to Ctesiphon. These accounts should not be dismissed out of hand. They do preserve a sometimes surprisingly accurate oral tradition, as well as drawing upon contemporary accounts, although the chronology of events was not preserved.[8]

Roman accounts can also be used to add to our picture. The late Roman *Acta Martyrum*, a compendium of the martyrdom of Christians predominantly in the reign of Decius, written in Syriac, records that:

> 'The war began in the spring, the Parthian ruler [Artabanus] was forever annihilated, they [the Sassanids] thereupon attacked Mesopotamia, then Babylonia, and later Zabdicene [modern Colemerik in south-east Turkey, located on the route from Armenia to Mosul] and Arzanene [a province in the ancient kingdom of Armenia], and in one year they conquered those countries ... and finally all the Parthians fled to the high mountains and abandoned all their countries and cities to the Persians.'[9]

Added to this is the *History of St Gregory and the Conversion of Armenia*, written by Agathangelos in classical Armenian in the fifth century. According to this account, the Armenian King Tiridates II, himself an Arsacid, not satisfied with merely harbouring Parthian nobles who had rejected the overtures of Ardashir, launched an aggressive campaign to assert his own claims to the Parthian throne. He appears to have allowed an army of Huns to cross the Caucasian passes at Dariel so they could raid Sassanian Mesopotamia to Ctesiphon, whilst he gathered together a large army of Armenians, Parthians and soldiers from the territory of Georgia and Albania. Tiridates II used Armenia as a base for repeated incursions into surrounding territories that had previously accepted Ardashir's authority, hoping to incite revolt. Although he appears to have been able to ravage the land almost at will, those Parthians who had pledged their allegiance to Ardashir refused to join him. There is a tradition that he sacked Ctesiphon itself, but this is probably patriotic exaggeration or reference to the pillaging of the Huns. This campaign naturally provoked a response from Ardashir, who invaded Armenia but had to retreat without establishing his control over the kingdom.[10]

Dio's brief, truncated account written around AD 229 is probably based on contemporary reports from the East, which as consul he would have been privy to:

> 'For Artaxerxes [Ardashir], a Persian, after conquering the Parthians in three battles and killing their king, Artabanus, made a campaign against Hatra, in an endeavour to capture it as a base for attacking the Romans. He actually did make a breach in the wall, but when he lost a good many soldiers through an ambuscade, he moved against Media. Of this country, as also of Parthia, he acquired no small portion, partly by force and partly by intimidation, and then marched against Armenia. Here he suffered a reverse at the hands of the natives, some Medes, and the sons of Artabanus, and either fled as some say, or as others assert, retired to prepare a larger expedition. He accordingly became a source of great fear to us; for he was encamped with a large army so as to threaten not only Mesopotamia but also Syria, and he boasted that he would win back everything that the ancient Persians had once held as far as the Grecian Sea, claiming it as his rightful inheritance from his forefathers.'[11]

Herodian repeats Ardashir's claim as the true successor to the Persian Achaemenid Empire that had been destroyed by Alexander the Great. Ardashir claimed as his right all the territories that had been theirs. Iranian and Sassanid sources are, however, far more ambiguous on whether Ardashir's demands were more substantive than dynastic propaganda. However, northern Mesopotamia would have been regarded as legitimate Sassanian territory which could be used by Rome as a base for invasions down the Euphrates and Tigris into the vulnerable plain between the two rivers. In the short term, his main concern remained consolidating control over all the territory ruled by his Parthian predecessors and crushing Arsacid opposition to his rule. Hence his campaigns against Hatra, Media and Armenia. He was in no position to reclaim Egypt, Palestine, Syria, Asia Minor and Thrace, all satrapies of the ancient Persian Empire. The Byzantine chronicler Zonoras, supported by Syncellus, states that Ardashir advanced into Cappadocia and captured Nisibis and Carrhae in Roman-held Mesopotamia:

> '..Artaxerxes [Ardashir] defeated him [Artabanus] in three main battles finally capturing and killing him. Then he marched on Armenia and was

defeated by the Armenians and the Medians who attacked him with the sons of Artabanus. Recovering from the previous defeat, he then laid siege to Mesopotamia and Syria with a greater force threatening to recover all that had belonged to the Persians his ancestors. Then Artaxerxes overran Cappadocia with his Persians and laid siege to Nisibis.'

Herodian is frustratingly vague in recounting these events, merely describing how Ardashir's actions caused unrest as he crossed the Tigris, overran Roman Mesopotamia and threatened Syria. However, he does suggest that there were two attacks upon the Roman province of Mesopotamia, resulting in an embassy being sent to Ardashir, which was rejected and followed by a more sustained attack upon Mesopotamia and Syria that involved carrying off extensive plunder and laying siege to Roman garrisons 'on the river banks'.[12]

Numismatic evidence can be used to make some sense of the chronology of these events. Ardashir's coinage can be divided into three phases: the first placed during his conflict with Artabanus up to AD 224, the second from his defeat of the Parthian king and his coronation at Ctesiphon in AD 227 and the final phase after this date. This third phase is associated with the mint established at Ctesiphon, which carried the legend *Shahanshah*. The old Parthian capital is likely to have been captured in AD 226/227. The coinage of Artavasdes ends at this time. Around AD 233/234, Indo/Parthian rule in Sakastan came to an end, at the same time as Sassanid coinage can be found in Merv. It makes complete strategic sense that Ardashir's immediate concern would be the complete submission of other Arsacids who could claim the throne after the death of Artabanus. Furthermore, Mesopotamia and Babylonia, with the Parthian capital, was held by one of the sons of Vologases, whilst sons of Artabanus had found safe refuge in Armenia. These threats would have had to be dealt with before he moved hundreds of miles east to establish his rule in the peripheries of the old Parthian Empire around Bactria and Merv.[13]

The coinage of Alexander Severus also shows a distinct change in the second half of AD 228. Coins of this year carry the legend '*Romae Aeternae*', which had been regularly used since the time of Septimius Severus. This was clearly an attempt to reassure the populace in the face of the rise of an aggressive power in the East. Coins also carry the title '*Fides Militum*' (loyalty of the army), normally an indication that the loyalty of the soldiers was questionable. These coins appear in vast numbers from AD 228 until the end of his reign. A number of *denarii*, the coinage denomination used predominantly by the army, shows '*Fides*' carrying a *vexillum* and standard. Fifty-one per cent of imperial coinage from AD 228–231 has a military theme, with Alexander Severus portrayed as a soldier emperor, in stark contrast to those issues that preceded it. The Senate is rarely mentioned.

From AD 229, Alexander Severus adopted the title *Invictus* to give himself a more martial image in light of the deteriorating situation in the East.[14]

The fixed points in our chronology are the defeat of Artabanus in April AD 224, the capture of Ctesiphon by Ardashir in AD 227 and at the same time the end of the revolt of Artavasdes, followed later by the capture of Merv in the east in c. AD 233. It would make sense that Ardashir spent AD 224–227 campaigning in Mesopotamia against an alliance of kings who remained loyal to the Arsacids and attempting to capture the great fortress city of Hatra. He had certainly gained control of Spasinu Charax on Satt al-Arab in the Tigris and Euphrates delta at this time, so gaining control of the vital trade routes and threatening the economic prosperity of the trading centre of Palmyra. This timeframe gives some indication of the intensity of the opposition he faced. The chronology would also fit into the sequence of events described by Dio and the *Acta Martyrum*. Dio also mentions a campaign in Media and Parthia, which may have been in response to the Armenian King Tiridates II's attempts to stir up revolt amongst those Parthians who had previously pledged their loyalty to Ardashir after the defeat of Artabanus. This precipitated a response from the Sassanid king, who perhaps invaded Armenia and Adharbaijan from Media in AD 228, descending through the Armenian province of Arzanene and raiding the Roman province of Cappadocia, and then to Zabdicene, which from the *Acta Martyrum* appears to have been attacked as part of the same campaign. The city of Bezabde is the main town in the district of Zabdicene. It appears to have been a significant Roman strongpoint, situated 13km north of Cizne at Eski Hendek on the west bank of the headwaters of the Tigris.[15] The attack on Armenia failed to destroy the power of Tiridates II, and so attacks on the Roman province of Cappadocia would help sustain Ardashir's military standing. From there, the Sassanid army could follow either the Euphrates or the Tigris down into Roman-held Mesopotamia, approaching the Roman defences from the rear. This must have caused panic amongst the population and garrisons in the heavyily defended province. This act resonated across the empire, its echoes seen in the Roman coinage of the second half of AD 228. Ardashir's primary objective must have been to deliver a telling blow to the state of Armenia and its Arsacid ruler. In this he failed. His raids on Cappadocia and descent on Roman-held Mesopotamia were secondary in their purpose in sustaining his military repute, surrounded as he was by opposition and resistance to his rule, as well as asserting his claim to these territories.

The focus of the campaign of AD 229, however, was the conquest of Roman-held Mesopotamia. Ardashir's strategic aim was to control the fortified transportation routes along the Euphrates from Palmyra to Characene and the strongholds of Middle and Northern Mesopotamia, including Hatra, Nisibis and Edessa. Hatra's position threatened the security of Ctesiphon.[16] Further raiding parties also penetrated deep into Cappadocia. This was the second of Herodian's two invasions of the province. According to Zonoras and Syncellus, Carrhae was captured and Nisibis fell. They were certainly held by Ardashir by AD 236, but there is uncertainty as to the exact time of their capture. It is, however, likely they fell in the immediate aftermath of the murder of Alexander Severus, when the Sassanids attempted to take advantage of the disruption caused by the demise of their previous adversary. They were probably unsuccessfully besieged in AD 229 and again in AD 230, as no contemporary source records their fall and it is doubtful Alexander Severus would have launched his offensive deep into Sassanid territory if these two fortress cities were held by the enemy. Herodian describes a number of Roman fortifications being besieged, but none captured.[17] Roman forces in the East concentrated on preventing an advance across the Roman province of Mesopotamia into Syria or Cappadocia. The *I* and *III Parthica* were stationed at Singara and Resaina respectively, with some vexillations garrisoning Nisibis. Resaina commanded the route between Edessa and Nisibis. These were supported by extensive numbers of auxiliary units, including the *Cohors XX Palmyrenorum* at Dura Europas and *Cohors XII Palaestinorum Severiana Alexandriana* in Lower Khabur. All told, Mesopotamia was defended by 8,000 infantry and 1,500 cavalry. In Syria, the *XVI Flavia Firma* garrisoned Samosata, whilst the *IV Scythia* was at Zeugma. Cappadocia was defended by the *XV Apollonaris* at Satala and *XII Fulminata* at Melitene. These were supplemented by numerous auxiliary units, bringing the numbers defending the province to 19,000 infantry and 2,800 cavalry. The *III Gallica* may had been restored at this time, after being disbanded by Elagabalus, but had been moved to Danaba near Damascus. These forces were supplemented by legions in surrounding provinces. Syria Coele had a standing force of 20,000 infantry, with 10,000 in Syria Phoenice. The *VI Ferrata* and *X Fretensis* were located at Bostra and Jerusalem (Aelia Capitolina) in Palestine, with the *III Cyrenaica* in Arabia and *II Traiana* from Nicopolis near Alexandria in Egypt. In total, there were twelve legions and over eighty auxiliary units guarding Rome's frontier from Cappadocia to Egypt.[18]

These forces should have been adequate to defend the provinces from the Sassanid attacks. Yet revolt and indiscipline undermined resistance. Dio, writing in c. AD 229, despairs at the rapid collapse of the Roman forces. He writes: 'Many uprisings were begun by many persons, some of which caused great alarm, but they were all put down.' He describes some troops joining the Sassanids whilst others were 'refusing to defend themselves'. Some elements of the garrison in Mesopotamia killed their commander, Flavius Heracleo. There are no surviving inscriptions preserving his name as a governor of the province, so it is likely he was one of the commanders of the two legions stationed in the province. Indiscipline does appear to have been a major problem, as inscriptions from Lambaesis in

North Africa record the temporary transfer of two veterans from the *III Augusta* to the *III Parthica* and the posting of a certain Virilis to this legion to restore discipline.[19] The *III Parthica* at Resaina would have been caught in the eye of the storm, sandwiched between the Sassanid forces besieging Nisibis and the revolt that appears to have been centred on Edessa.

The murder of their commander would have necessitated the mutinous soldiers choosing a replacement and, in order to avoid severe punishment for their actions, electing him emperor. At this point, the sequence of events becomes increasingly problematic, but all sources appear to fit into the historical context that existed in Syria and Roman Mesopotamia during the Sassanid invasions from AD 228 to late summer AD 232, when Alexander Severus arrived with a huge army at Antioch. According to the *Epitome De Caesaribus*: 'Under his rule [that of Alexander Severus], Taurinius, who had been made Augustus, on account of fear, threw himself into the Euphrates.'[20] There are no other epigraphic or literary references to this Taurinus, but the fact that he ended his life by throwing himself into the Euphrates suggests he led a revolt in Mesopotamia and may have killed himself whilst attempting to escape to Sassanid territory, perhaps with the arrival of the forces of the legitimate emperor in the area. Dio does state that all the revolts were put down.

Zosimus refers to a separate revolt:

'The soldiers after this event [the murder of Ulpian], forgetting by degrees their former regard for Alexander, appeared unwilling to put his commands in execution, and in order to avoid being punished for their negligence, excited public commotions, in which they promoted a person, named Antoninus, to the empire. But he, being incapable of sustaining so weighty a charge, declined, it. They chose in his stead Uranius, a man of low and servile condition, whom they immediately placed before Alexander, dressed in purple, by which they intended to express more strongly their contempt for the emperor.'[21]

Uranius appears to have been connected to Edessa. In AD 252/253, an Uranius Antoninus defended Edessa and parts of Syria after the total defeat of Roman forces at the Battle of Barbalissos and the capture of all legionary bases in the area by Ardashir's son and successor, Shapor I. Some historians suggest he was a claimant to the throne of Oshroene, which had been absorbed by Caracalla into the empire in AD 214, and the two were close relatives, perhaps father and son.[22] Some coins issued by Emesa around AD 252 AD carry the name of L. or C. Julius Aurelius Sulpicius Uranius Antoninus. On the reverse, some issues depict the star of Emesa, symbolizing the sun god Elagabal, whilst others show the image of the black stone in the temple. The usurper clearly wished to associate himself with Caracalla, and may have been a distant relative of Julia Maesa and Julia Domna. The usurper Iotapianus, who rebelled late in the reign of Philip (AD 244–249), claimed kinship with Alexander Severus. The assertion of a familial link to the imperial house made it easier for soldiers to switch loyalty having previously made a solemn oath to protect the emperor and his family. Uranius may also have been a priest of Elagabal, as the reverse side of the coins show the image of the god.[23] Zosimus describes Uranius as 'a man of low and servile condition', which appears to exclude a connection to the Severans. However, Dio himself called Julia Domna 'plebeian'.[24] The fact Uranius appears to have been brought before the emperor by Roman soldiers clad in the imperial purple suggests his revolt only ended in the late summer of AD 232 when Alexander Severus arrived at Antioch. The usurper may have presented himself as a relative of the legitimate emperor defending the empire in the face of Sassanid aggression, hence his decision not to engage Alexander Severus in battle but attempt to persuade him of his honourable intentions in an imperial audience. This was a mistake, as any attempt to assume military or political powers without having them conferred by the legitimate authorities would have to be punished severely in order to pre-empt further insurrections. His dénouement is describe by Syncellus: 'A certain Uranius was named emperor at Edessa in Osrhoene, and, in taking power in opposition to Alexander, he was killed by him when Alexander drove out the Persians who were raiding Cappadocia and besieging Nisibis.'[25]

The fifth-century writer Polemius Silvius, in his calendar that chronicles festivals, the birthdays of emperors, consular years and key events, refers to Uranius with additional nomenclature, as well as an otherwise unknown usurper: 'Elagabalus Antoninus was slain. After which Marcellus and Sallust Uranius Seleucus and Taurinius, the tyrant were made Caesars.' Seleucus I Nicator had founded Edessa after the death of Alexander the Great, and this may have been an attempt by Uranius to strengthen his link with the city. Ronald Syme suggests this enigmatic figure may be Julius Antonius Seleucus, a legate of Moesia Inferior under Elagabalus, or the consul for AD 221, M. Flavius Vitellius Seleucus. An inscription from AD 231 records Julius Antoninus Seleucus as the governor of Syria Coele. However, neither of these figures have the name Sallust or Uranius in their nomenclature. Should Uranius, Antoninus and Seleucus be considered separate figures? A lack of reliable evidence precludes the formation of any firm conclusions. All that can be said with any certainty is that upon his arrival in Syria, the emperor had to handle a chaotic situation before attempting to deal with Ardashir.[26]

The absence of the emperor for such a protracted period of time is striking. The war on the borders of the empire in Mesopotamia had been waged between the rival claimants for the throne of the *Shahanshah* since c. AD 224. The warning signs were long in evidence before the actual attacks on Roman territory in late AD 228. Yet Alexander Severus did not arrive in the East until the late summer of AD 232. This was clearly an error of judgement on the part of Alexander Severus, Julia Mamaea and their advisors. By the reign of Alexander Severus, the emperor was virtually obliged to lead the army in person, especially during periods of crisis. The emperor was titled *imperator* and 'fellow soldier'. Septimius Severus, Caracalla and Elagabalus had all led armies into battle. Furthermore, Alexander Severus had increased his personal identification with the army by adding his name to all the legions, as had Commodus and Caracalla. For example, the *I Minervia Antoniniana* became the *I Minervia Severiana Alexandriana* at the start of his reign. However, in times of stress an absent emperor became an increasingly abstract concept in the minds of the soldiers faced with a daily struggle for survival.[27] The emperor claimed to be the son of the soldier's hero, Antoninus or Caracalla. It is striking that the rebellious soldiers in the East turned first to an Antoninus, who sensibly rejected their dubious advances, and in turn they chose Uranius Antoninus.

When news of the Sassanid aggression reached him in Rome, the emperor assembled his *concilium* and listened to their advice. Caution prevailed and an embassy was sent to Ardashir demanding he cease his aggression and remain within the established territories of the Parthian Empire. He was also reminded of previous successful Roman campaigns in the East, led by Augustus, Trajan, Lucius Verus and Septimius Severus. Ardashir simply ignored the letter and launched another campaign into Roman Mesopotamia. The governors of Rome's eastern provinces demanded the presence of the emperor, beset as they were by external invasion and internal insurrection. Alexander Severus was not, as Herodian would have us believe, simply 'lingering' in Rome.[28] From AD 230 onwards, there is clear evidence of extensive preparations for war. One problem the emperor faced was that it appears many units in the army had been maintained well below strength, probably due to the already stretched nature of imperial finances. Time was needed to recruit and train troops to meet the challenge of an aggressive and experienced enemy. Herodian describes how recruits were gathered:

> 'From Italy and all the provinces special levies were recruited for the army, all men passed as physically fit and of the right age for battle. The whole Roman empire was in a state of complete upheaval, gathering together a force to match the reported size of the barbarian invasion.'

A badly damaged inscription appears to record the appointment of L. Fulvius Gavius Numisius Petronius Aemilianus, who was tasked with the raising of soldiers in Transpadanum.[29] In the suspect account of Maximinus Thrax in the *Historia Augusta*, Maximinus is appointed to a tribunate in 'the Fourth Legion, which he himself had formed out of recruits'.[30] This has led some historians to suggest that Alexander Severus raised a new legion for his campaign in the East. However, evidence to support this is tenuous at best. An inscription recording road repairs from Aquilaea under the Emperor Maximinus Thrax refers to it being completed by '(legio) nova Italica sua'.[31] The early fifth-century AD Roman Notitia Dignitatum, a list of offices across the empire, does include a IV Italica under the command of the Magister Militum per Orientem. Yet it is surprising that a legion raised under Alexander Severus would be referred to by his successor as 'his' legion. David Magie even suggests that the author of the Historia Augusta was in fact referring to the IV Flavia stationed in Upper Moesia, and had confused a tribunate held by the future emperor with the later post which had responsibility for raising recruits for the campaign on the Rhine.[32]

Troops were raised across the empire to fill the gaps in the under-strength legions and auxiliary cohorts. Analysis of the names on the tombstones of the II Parthica show most of the soldiers were from the Balkans and probably joined the legion as it marched through the region in AD 232 on its way to the East. The prominent fifth-century Armenian historian Agathangelos records troops being raised from Egypt to the Black Sea and even the desert. This is supported by archaeological and epigraphic evidence recording levies raised in Mauretania, Palmyra and Osrhoene. A regiment of cataphracts from Bostra was probably also created at this time; the Arabia Ala Nova Firma Milliaria Cataphractaria. This would see service in the East and then return with the emperor to the Rhine. The Roman fort at Ain Sinu in northern Iraq provides further evidence of Alexander Severus' extensive recruitment. The fort itself commands the pass at Gaulet, controlling the road to Nisibis from Hatra across the strategic Jebel Sinjar mountain range that rises above the vast plain of northern Mesopotamia. The fort itself held detachments from the III Parthica, but next to the fort an extensive castellum was constructed without the usual administrative buildings, covering 11½ hectares. In comparison, the legionary fortress of the II Parthica outside Rome at Alba covers 10½ hectares. Some coins excavated from the castellum are from the reign of Caracalla, but the majority are from that of Alexander Severus. The castellum appears to have then been dismantled after a short period of use, whilst the adjacent fort has a destruction layer dated to the reign of Maximinus Thrax as no coins have been found from the reign of his successor, Gordian III. The open area inside the castellum suggests it was used as a cavalry training area. Contextually, this probably corresponds to the re-establishment of Roman control over the area between AD 232 and the emperor's return to the West in AD 234. These auxiliary forces, probably light cavalry, would be drawn from the area between the Tigris and Euphrates, the old Parthian province of Arabaya which was now controlled by Ardashir's enemy and Rome's new ally, Hatra. Pottery shards found in the castellum and fort are remarkably similar to those discovered in the mid-third century destruction levels at Hatra. Further training camps probably existed at Tell Brak and Tell Brati, but these await excavation.[33]

Alexander Severus' preparations appear to have been understandably concerned with countering the Sassanid cavalry advantage. The massive frieze of Ardashir at Firuzabad shows the Sassanid *clibanarii* in detail. These heavy armoured cavalry wear a heavy mail shirt of chain links, equipped with a long lance. Ardashir himself carries a quiver of arrows. A contemporary amulet also shows a *clibanarii* armed with a mace, similar to those carried by Parsi priests.[34] Heliodorus, in his *Aethiopica*, written in the mid-third century, gives a more detailed description of these cavalrymen, the ancient world's equivalent to the modern-day tank. He describes how the head is covered by a one-piece helmet that leaves an opening for the eyes and extends down to protect his neck. In his right hand he holds a long pike, whilst holding the reins with his left. A metal corselet covering his whole body is composed of square interlocking plates of bronze or iron. This allowed for a certain degree of movement. His legs are covered by greaves from the foot to the knee. The horse is also covered in armour. A sabre is hung under his arm for use in close-quarter fighting. Attacks were launched en masse, with the pike held against the horse's neck and fastened by a rope, with the rear end tied to the horse's thigh to aid balance and ensure it was not lost upon impact. On contact, the pike often transfixed two enemy soldiers. Archers would have been used to wear down the opposing ranks before the frontal attack, with lighter cavalry used to move round the enemy's flanks. The *clibanarii*, composed of the nobility, were supported by a levy of poorly armed infantry and archers. These archers could be devastatingly effective, as Macrinus found at the Battle of Nisibis where his army suffered grievously from the rain of arrows that fell upon his men. This was no standing professional army like the Roman forces, but would be dismissed at the end of the campaigning season as the nobles returned to their estates and the infantry and archers to their farms.[35]

The Romans had long used heavy cavalry called *cataphracts*, but these were not as well protected as the *clibanarii*, having no helmets and generally their horses were unprotected. Two inscriptions dated to the Persian campaigns of Caracalla or Alexander Severus record the names of two cavalrymen attached to two units raised in Mesopotamia: Barsemis Abbei '*ex numero Hosroruorum*' and Biribam Absei of a cataphract ala.[36] The Romans had gradually adapted tactics and equipment to match their enemies' use of cavalry, especially the Sarmatians on the Danube and the Parthians. By the third century, the *gladius*, a short stabbing sword, was replaced by the longer *spatha*, which allowed for a greater reach, essential against a mounted opponent. The old rectangular shields inhibited the slashing strokes that were used with the *spatha*, so these were slowly replaced with oval shields. Helmet design also responded to the blows inflicted by a cavalryman that would fall across the top of the helmet. The *Niedermormter* helmet was increasingly adopted, with its cross piece across the top of the helmet for added strength and an extended neck and face guard. A protecting bar across the brow provided a defence against a blow cutting downwards across the face. However, this came at a cost. The heavy cavalry were now unable to look upwards, as the neck piece came into contact with the shoulder armour, requiring soldiers to crouch behind their shields rather than stand and fight over the top of them. This also made it more difficult for a mounted cavalryman to make bodily contact with their sword.[37]

The spear remained the primary weapon of the Roman soldier in close-quarter fighting, with the *pilum* continuing to be used. This was thrown before contact with the enemy, its pyramidal point piercing armour, whilst its spine was designed to twist and bend, making it impossible to throw back. However, in the late second and early third centuries, some units consisting of around 500 men were armed with a shorter throwing spear called the *lancea*. Tombstones at Apamea from Caracalla's campaign show these troops carrying bundles of such weapons, whilst they were used by Macrinus at the Battle of Nisibis to fill in the gaps between the Roman lines and launch rapid attacks on enemy formations. Apamea was regularly used as a winter base for Roman armies. The city was ideally located at an important crossroads, three to five days' march from the ports of Seleucia and Aegeae. The encamped army could be easily supplied and the imperial headquarters at Antioch was within easy reach, only 56 miles away. Other tombstones clearly show *phalangiarii* armed with extra-long spears, reminiscent of the phalanx used by Alexander the Great and the Hellenistic armies. These men probably formed the front three ranks of a line to counter the cavalry charge of the *clibanarii*. The ranks behind would likely throw their *pilum* to break the charge.[38] The account in the *Historia Augusta* of Alexander Severus equipping soldiers to form a phalanx has been dismissed as pure fiction. The biographer does, true to form, add his own dramatic details, but in this instance epigraphic evidence appears to support it. This, however, was not a separate army numbering 30,000 men, composing six legions, as described in the *Historia Augusta*, but an understandable tactical response using small elite units employed to counter Sassanid tactics, probably originally utilized by Caracalla. The tombstone of a Spartan auxiliary named Alexys appears to refer to this contingent. It depicts a light-armed Peloponnesian soldier wearing a close-fitting cap resembling the traditional Laconian *pilos* and carrying a wooden club. It was probably these men that Caracalla armed with the extended pikes reminiscent of the Macedonian phalanx. Many of the officers serving with Alexander Severus would have also marched with Caracalla. It is then not surprising that the idea was resurrected.[39]

The reign of Alexander Severus saw the increased use of units of soldiers who were retained in their ethnic group and appear to have not been incorporated into the traditional organization of the *auxilia*. These *numeri* were composed of units of 200–300 men who employed their native weapons and tactics. Trajan had used such units of Moors in his campaigns in Dacia and Parthia. Many were elite units, especially the cavalry associated with units recruited from Mauretania, Palmyra and Osrhoene who used the highly effective composite bow. Britain also appears to have been a prime recruiting ground for these types of soldiers. The Romans recognized the flexibility offered by these specialist troops, as mounted javelin men and archers helped to harass enemy formations and offered a degree of manoeuvrability that was denied the heavily armed infantry.[40] Septimius Severus had included about 2,000 Moors in the *equites singulares*, the guard cavalry, which formed part of his strategic reserve in Rome. Another force of cavalry, provided by the King of Osrhoene, was stationed in the *Castra Peregrine* in the capital. Alexander Severus appears to have increased their numbers. Alongside these were the elite Praetorians, totalling 10,000 men, six urban cohorts of 1,500 men each and 5,000 legionaries of the *II Parthica* at Alba. In all, Alexander Severus had 21,000 elite soldiers in and around Rome which would form the core of his expeditionary force.[41] The vast majority of this reserve was taken to the East, with only a minimal garrison left to ensure order in the capital. Only those Praetorians who were nearing the end of their sixteen years of service and awaiting discharge remained behind.[42] However, the discipline and loyalty of the Praetorians remained an issue, having only recently threatened the life of the consul Cassius Dio, angered by his severe imposition of discipline on the Pannonian legions.

Vexillations of the Pannonian legions and others on the Rhine and Danube were used to supplement this force. They were collected as the emperor moved through these provinces in AD 232 on his march to Antioch. The tombstones at Apamea record soldiers from *II Parthica*, *XIII Gemina* from Apulum in Dacia, *IV Flavia* from Moesia Superior, *XIV Gemina* from Carnuntum in Pannonia Superior as well as the aforementioned *XIV cohors urbana*. Units would have been withdrawn from many more garrisons and legions along the Rhine and Danube. The Eastern legions also contributed, with cohorts from the *XV Apollinaris*, *XII Fulminata*, *XVI Flavia*, *IV Scythia*, *III Gallica* and *VI Ferrata*, the *III Cyrenaica* from Bostra and *II Traiana* from Nicopolis near Alexandria. The presence of this Egyptian legion was confirmed by the discovery of the log book of the *strategos* of the *nome* of Ombos and Elephantine. According to Herodian, Alexander Severus drew from the garrisons of the 'Illyrian provinces'. Inscriptions record the presence of the Ala *I Flavia Gaetulorum* from Moesia Inferior in the East, under its commander Sedatius Apollonius. An epitaph from Ephesus commemorates a centurion of *Legio XXX Ulpia Victrix* from Xanten in Germania Inferior. Dated to c. AD 232–235, he must have died on the march. Soldiers of the *Legio VII Claudia* of Moesia Inferior took part in the campaign through Armenia, as a soldier from this legion is recorded on an inscription as '*interfectus* (dying) *in expeditione Partica et Ar(meniaca)*'. The names of many of the deceased from these legions indicate they were natives of Thrace and the Balkans. Across the Balkans, tombs and epitaphs carry the names of these soldiers who died far from home: Boscila, Bitius, Caelepor and Dissa, also Mucatra, Mucianus, Nomipor and Seutes, and another monument to a Lubius Ianuarius which records that he died '*in barbarico*'. Another epitaph to Aurelius Mucapor records that he was a centurion in the Praetorians who previously served in the *II Parthica*. He probably died of natural causes. Another inscription refers to Ignotus, a centurion in the *II Parthica* who originated in Illyria. Many of these men would have resented leaving behind their families for a campaign that many could expect never to return from. A number of these legions lost their honorary epithets of 'Alexandriana', 'Severiana' or 'Severiana Alexandriana'; three from Upper Germany, and one each from Upper and Lower Pannonia. The *VIII Augusta* from Upper Germany lost its title in AD 231, as did *XXII Primigenia* based at Moguntiacum, which had not been restored by AD 232. The *II Adiutrix* in Pannonia Inferior, based at Aquincum, suffered a similar fate in AD 230, whilst *X Gemina* from Pannonia Superior had it removed in AD 232 but restored in AD 234. This can only have been in response to unrest caused by the resentment of men who were to march far from home to fight against the Sassanids.[43]

The cavalry arm of the Roman army appears to have gone through an extended period of innovation and development in the late second and early third centuries. A new unit called a *cuneus* is first found during the reign of Marcus Aurelius on an inscription from Ribchester associated with a unit of Sarmatian cavalry. They are not described as *ala* or *dediticii*, which suggests they were a different and distinctive type of cavalry regiment. These types of regiments were increasingly employed under the Severans. The prominence given to the cavalry is reflected in the creation of a new post that first appears in his reign. A *magister campi* is preserved on an inscription related to the *III Augusta* and the *Cohors XX Palmyrenorum*. It is suggested that this office was in some way linked to the use of increased numbers of cavalry in the war against Ardashir.[44]

Careful consideration had also to be made for the provisioning of this immense force of men and animals. Each soldier required 1.5kg of grain a day, whilst horses required 4.5kg of grain and the equivalent amount of forage. One legion therefore needed 7,500kg of grain and 450kg of forage daily, or 225 tonnes of grain and 13.5 tonnes of forage. Added to this was an equivalent amount for auxiliary units. The army would take five months to reach its destination, and its daily needs would have to be provided for along its line of march. Already in the East were 60,000 soldiers that garrisoned the forts and cities, who consumed at least 22,000 tonnes of grain a year. Hunger invariably led to indiscipline and unrest amongst the troops.

The concentration of such a large number of men could place an intolerable burden on the local population, who faced famine or starvation unless provisions were brought in from the resources of other provinces of the empire.[45] In times of war, the *a rationibus* was responsible for ensuring that the necessary finances were available to oil the wheels of war, whilst the Prefect of the Annona planned, organized and supervised the collection, transportation and storage of grain. The *a vehiculis*, or *praefecti vehiculorum*, was tasked with its transport along the roads. Demands for supplies and resources were sent out by the *a epistulis* to the provinces. These officials would use their influence to recommend experienced officers for special posts. Inscriptions record the populace of Cilicia and Pamphylia having to provide resources for the campaign.[46]

In order to facilitate the movement of grain and soldiers across the empire, a huge road repair programme was initiated, focused on Pannonia, the Balkan provinces, Asia Minor, Syria and Mesopotamia. Grain was to be collected and stockpiled in huge depots called *mansiones* along the planned route. In times of crisis, villages and towns were expected to contribute additional grain in the form of the *annona militaris* and oxen or donkeys, the *angareia* proportional to their tax liability. Modestinus refers to regular tax burdens, as opposed to 'temporary contributions', which must refer to levies in times of war. Those communities that were situated along the main transport routes suffered the most. The requisitioned oxen used to pull the grain carts rarely returned in any fit condition to plough the fields, if indeed the soldiers ever returned them. The grain taken was probably the reserve retained by the peasants for years of shortage or for the following year's seed. Many could expect ruin, shortages and starvation. Until the reign of Caracalla, soldiers had to pay for their rations and equipment out of their own pay. However, as part of his attempts to curry favour with his troops after the murder of Geta, Caracalla had removed this obligation. Provincials were increasingly expected to provide this in kind in time of emergency, which after AD 230 became the normal state of affairs. The payment of soldiers through the *annona militaris* was not introduced by Alexander Severus, but became established practice through the necessity of adapting to the crisis caused by repeated barbarian incursions.[47]

Road construction also necessitated the requisitioning of resources from the local populace in the form of materials, labour and animals. Soldiers themselves were involved in the construction, and this was seen as a useful means of imposing discipline and building an esprit de corps. A significant number of road repairs in Pannonia Inferior may attest to this. The main roads emanating from Aquincum to Sirmium and Brigetio were understandably improved, but also a large number of lesser roads.[48] However, much effort was focused on the roads of Asia Minor. The governorship of L. Julius Apronius Maenius Pius Salamallianus in Pontus has been dated to late in the reign of Alexander Severus, and a number of milestones are testimony to maintenance work in Pontus and in the neighbouring province of Galatia. Road repairs near Zela bear the name of the governor of Cappadocia of AD 231, Q. Julius Proculianus. Another milestone at Ordek records repairs to the Caesarea Melitene road under the same governor 11 miles from the Cilician Gates, and more construction work 2 miles from the Gates. Another inscription from Ponzanti is dated to AD 230/231, whilst road improvements in Cilicia itself are evidenced by a milestone from Adana dated to AD 231. Roads around Sebastopolis were also improved. Two milestones bear the name of Q. Julius Proculianus, whilst a third on the same road that of Aradius Paternus. We can assume Paternus was Proculianus' predecessor, as milestones indicate he was governor in AD 231. This indicates the hurried nature of the road reconstruction or the death of Paternus in Sassanid raids. This strategic route to the Cilician Gates gave access to Cilicia, Syria and Antioch through the Taurus Mountains, and was the artery upon which the army would rely for its supplies, reinforcements and communications with the rest of the empire.[49]

The construction work on another two roads shows clear evidence of the hurried nature of these repairs. Both were vital communication routes. The first ran across Cappadocia to the Euphrates from Melitene, and the second ran east-west across the Cilician plain. From the numbering of the milestones, it is evident the repair work started at both ends simultaneously, rather than following the usual method of starting at one end and working progressively along it. It is unlikely that work would have begun with Sassanid forces in the area. Work was therefore delayed until the arrival of sufficient Roman troops to secure the province, which led to the hurried nature of the repairs. Bridges would also have been repaired as part of this programme. According to the *Historia Augusta*, the bridges retained the name of the emperor who reigned when they were originally constructed, despite the fact some bridges were virtually rebuilt. The more established practice was to either remove the predecessor's name or add that of the present ruler. However, many of these constructions were built by Alexander Severus' more illustrious predecessors, such as Trajan, emperors he wished to associate himself with. This can be found at Dyrrachium, where an aqueduct built in the reign of Hadrian was reconstructed under Alexander Severus, with Hadrian's name retained. Dyrrachium was a vital port on the *Via Egnatia* where men and provisions from Brundisium in Italy were offloaded before continuing their journey through Macedonia and Thrace to the Hellespont, and across to Asia Minor. Securing the supply of water was just as important as food for the army on its journey east.[50]

Supplies and reinforcements by sea were guaranteed by the appointment of P. Sallustius Sempronius Victor, with responsibility for initially ridding the seas around Sardinia of pirates. The island must have been used as a base for their raids along the coast of Italy and Gaul. Once this had been achieved, his ships were to patrol the sea lanes, ensuring the provisions sent to the army in the East reached their destination. He must have carried out his instructions well, as he was later appointed to the post of Procurator of Bithynia and Pontus, and at the end of the reign was made Procurator of Mauretania Caesariensis.[51]

Herodian remarks that the 'whole Roman empire was in a state of complete upheaval, gathering together a force to match the reported size of the barbarian invasion'. This is echoed in the *Historia Augusta*: 'During his campaigns he made such careful provision for the soldiers that they were furnished with supplies at each halting place, and were never compelled to carry food for the usual period of seventeen days, except when in the enemy's country. And even then he lightened their burdens by using mules and camels.' The biographer further illustrates the thoroughness of the preparations by detailing how the emperor 'listed in order all the halting places, next the camping stations, and next the places where provisions were to be found, for the whole length of the march as far as the boundaries of the barbarians' country'. Archaeological evidence does appear to give some substance to these claims.[52]

Alexander Severus and his advisors would also have given serious consideration to appointments to commands and provinces. The emperor was to be absent from the capital for a prolonged period of time. *Legates* and officers in command of the legions along Rome's frontiers had to be carefully selected. These men would have to be experienced but, most importantly, considered absolutely loyal. Furthermore, in the war zones, they required proven military ability. This would be particularly important in view of the disciplinary record of the Pannonian legions. Rome was probably left in the capable hands of M. Clodius Pupienus Maximus, who was appointed to the urban prefecture. He had served the Severii loyally and been rewarded with a smooth career progression through the *cursus honorum*. He was held in such high regard by his fellow senators that they elected him emperor, alongside the patrician Balbinus, in AD 238.[53] The elderly C. Caesonius Macer Rufinianus, described as a *comes* of the emperor, probably remained in Rome to act as an advisor. Born around AD 160 to an Italian family of unknown origins, his career was at first unspectacular but productive enough to reach the *suffect* consulship c. AD 197, an office that ennobled his family. Around AD 200, he became governor of Germania Superior, and was then appointed to the prestigious governorship of Africa, perhaps by Alexander Severus. At some point between AD 225–230, his son was also made a *suffect* consul. This may have been due to his father's influence with the emperor or, perhaps a little cynically, a result of a political calculation to ensure the loyalty of the father in the absence of the emperor from Rome. Aged at least 70, the journey to the East would have been beyond him.[54] His son would be selected by the Senate as a member of the council of twenty senators to organize resistance to Maximinus Thrax in AD 238. The prestige of these two men could command the loyalty and obedience of the Senate, and in particular the members of the aristocratic families. It is also likely that one of the two Praetorian Prefects remained to supervise the members of the Guard who were not taken on campaign.

The governorships of the two key German provinces were given to men of proven loyalty. The garrisons were once more under-strength due to the withdrawal of vexillations for the war against Ardashir. These men would have felt resentful at both the absence of their comrades and their continued vulnerability to attacks from across the Rhine. The families of absent loved ones would add to this unruly atmosphere. The senators in charge of these two provinces would have a difficult job to fulfil. Sextus Catius Clementinus Priscillianus was appointed to Germania Superior in AD 231. He had just completed his year as ordinary consul. He held the post of governor until AD 234. He was then surprisingly appointed to the governorship of Cappadocia by Maximinus Thrax, an office he held in the presence of Maximinus' son. Perhaps he was in some way blamed for a less than effective response to the Alemannic invasion in AD 234, but he appears to have supported the senatorial revolt of AD 238.[55] Flavius Julius Latronianus was appointed to the governorship of Germania Inferior, also in AD 231. He had been a *suffect* consul at some point before this date, suggesting a clear pattern to these vital appointments. He was also a senator on the rise, having married into the aristocratic family of the Pollieni and later becoming the Prefect of Rome under Gordian III in c. AD 243.[56]

The governors of the two Pannonias faced similar problems, but with the added difficulty that the discipline of these legions had long been an issue, Cassius Dio's attempts to rectify this resulting in complaints sent to their comrades in the Praetorian Guard in Rome. Cassius Dio ended his governorship of Pannonia Superior in AD 228, but the names of his immediate successors remain elusive. Flavius Marcianus was made governor of Pannonia Inferior in c. AD 231, a post he held until AD 233. He was replaced by a member of the aristocratic Egnatii, possibly L. Egnatius Victor Lollianus, a *suffect* consul between AD 225–230 who had been governor of Galatia. This family had clearly profited during the reign of the emperor and remained leading members of the Senate long after his demise. The fact that none of the Egnatii are associated with military provinces after AD 235 suggests they were too closely associated with Alexander Severus by Maximinus Thrax. The daughter of Egnatius Lollianus had married Licinius Valerianus, the future Emperor Valerian.[57]

Further along the Danube, Moesia Inferior was governed by Anicius Faustus Paulinus. His father was a 'new man' who had benefited from the rule of the Severii, being the first of his family to receive a consulship in AD 198. His son was awarded a *suffect* consulship at some point in the reign of Alexander Severus. He had previously been governor of Numidia, erecting an honorary inscription to the emperor and Orbiana. He was replaced in AD 234 by Caius Decius Valerianus, the future Emperor Decius.[58] Moesia Superior was probably given to Egnatius (Victor) Marinianus, possibly the brother of the governor of Pannonia Inferior. He had just held a *suffect* consulship and a governorship of Arabia. These appointments are a remarkable testimony to the trust the emperor placed in this powerful aristocratic family considering the number of troops they commanded. Conversely, it also provides an insight into the lack of suitable senatorial candidates for these posts.[59]

Crossing the Hellespont to Asia Minor, the governor of Galatia, Q. Servaeus Fuscus Cornelianus, appears to have been a safe pair of hands. He had been legate of the *I Italica*, and was then appointed to the governorship of Moesia Inferior before that of Galatia around AD 229/230. He appears to have been replaced by M. Domitius Valerianus, who in AD 238 would become governor of Arabia.[60] The governor of Pontus was probably L. Julius Apronius Maenius Pius Salamallianus, whose name is found on two milestones. He had previously been a governor of Numidia, so his appointment to Pontus must have been late in the reign of Alexander Severus. His *cursus honorum* has been discovered on an inscription from Lambaesis in North Africa, which makes no reference to such a governorship. However, the inscription is fragmentary and a reading of a damaged line could refer to 'P', which may be the province. An alternative candidate for this post is Q. Faltonius Restitutianus, who was clearly a very able administrator as he later became the procurator of Mauretania Caesariensis in AD 239, Prefect of Vigiles in AD 244 and Prefect of Egypt in AD 250. The province of Pontus-Bithynia appears to have been split by Alexander Severus, perhaps to allow more opportunity to promote able equestrians or enable the governors of both to micro-manage its administration at a time of increased demands on resources.[61]

As already noted, the vital province of Cappadocia appears to have been administered by Q. Julius Proculeianus. He was replaced in the last year of Alexander Severus' reign by Licinnius Serenianus, whose name, like that of Sextus Catius Clementinus Priscillianus, was erased from many milestones in his province as a result of a *damnatio memoriae*. There was no doubt that this condemnation was due to his support of the senatorial revolt against Maximinus Thrax. The presence of a milestone from Adana naming Asinius Lepidus, dated to AD 231, suggests he was the governor at Cilicia at this time.[62] The identity of the governor of the vital province of Syria Coele is problematic. From a damaged inscription, (? Claudius Sollem)nius Pacatianus has been tentatively identified as a governor of the province late in the reign of Alexander Severus, or perhaps shortly after. He was certainly a governor of Arabia before this, and previously the commander of *III Legio Cyrenaica Severiana Alexandriana* as well as holding a *suffect* consulship.[63]

Rutilius Pudens Crispinus has been suggested as the governor of Syria Phoenice from AD 231–234. His *cursus honorum* has been preserved from an inscription, but unfortunately it does not record the dates of his tenure of each office. He was not a member of the nobility, nor, as far as we know, had any member of his family held the consulship. His first post was command of an auxiliary unit in Egypt, the *'cohors I Lusitanorum equitata quingenaria'*, followed by appointment to the *praefectura urbi feriarum Latinarum*, which was usually awarded to young members of aristocratic senatorial families. A number of administrative posts followed, but his career really benefited from the patronage of Caracalla, who rewarded his support during his conflict with Geta. Quickly rising to a praetorship, his progress came to a shuddering halt with the accession of Macrinus, probably because he was too closely associated with his predecessor. Elagabalus appointed him to a series of minor offices, but it was Alexander Severus who returned him to favour. He was made commander of the *XV Apollinaris*, followed by the governorships of Lusitaniae, Thrace and Syria Phoenice, and then proconsular governor of Achaiae. At some point between AD 234–238, he was granted the honour of a consulship. We catch a glimpse of him in AD 232, accompanying the emperor and his army, in an honorary inscription on a column along the main avenue at Palmyra:

> 'The Senate and people have placed this in honour of Julius Aurelius Zenobius and Zabdilas, the son of Dichmalchus, the son of Nassumus, leader of the army on the arrival of the divine Alexander, perpetual deputy of Rutilius Crispinus, the leader of the cavalry bands; overseer also of the distribution of the corn, a liberal man, not sparing even his own private property, most creditably, administering the affairs of state, and on that account approved of by the divine Jaribolus and Julius [Philippus], the most illustrious prefect and sacred praetor, and also a great lover of his country, in the year 554 [Palmyrene dating].'

Rutilius Crispinus was clearly a close *amicus* of the emperor, especially as he was specifically identified by name on the inscription alongside the emperor himself. Rutilius Crispinus must have been an important commander of the imperial forces. Zenobius himself would have led the Palmyrene cohorts, which would have included both light and heavy cavalry during the campaign. After the murder of Alexander Severus, Rutilius Crispinus is described by Herodian in AD 238 as a probable member of the elected senatorial council of twenty who appointed him to lead the resistance of Aquileia to Maximinus Thrax. He was clearly a man of great skill and ability, organizing the provisioning of the city in the face of a prolonged siege. His actions at Aquileia show him to be a born leader, 'a man that won respect naturally, was a fluent Latin orator, and a fair commander'. He was a man chosen for his ability, not nobility.[64]

Another man of undoubted ability was the equestrian C. Furius Sabinius Aquila Timesitheus. His career would culminate in the Praetorian Prefecture under Gordian III, acting as virtual regent for the child emperor. It was under his auspices that the Roman army crushed a Sassanid force at the Battle of Resaina in AD 242 that enabled Rome to retake Nisibis and Singara. However, his death led to a catastrophic Roman defeat and the temporary collapse of Roman power in the East. His career started with the typical appointment to command of an auxiliary unit, in this case to the *cohortis I Gallicae* in Spain. His abilities were soon brought to the attention of Caracalla, who made him Procurator *Rationis Privata*, with responsibility for imperial estates in Belgica and the two German provinces. Promotions continued under Elagabalus made him Procurator *provinciae Arabiae*, with oversight of the finances of the province. His career went from strength to strength, being made an acting governor, *vice praeses*, in AD 218 and again in AD 222. This second appointment was probably in response to the chaos resulting from the death of Macrinus and revolt of Elagabalus, as supporters of the old regime were executed or removed. This practice of equestrians serving as a substitute governor in a senatorial post was to become increasingly common, especially from the reign of Alexander Severus onwards. A number of administrative offices followed, including *Magister XX heredatium*, an important financial office. These may at first appear as low-ranking offices of state, but in fact they gave him access to the inner court circle. Here, his abilities clearly drew admiration, as he was made *Procurator provinciae Syriae Palaestinae ibi Exactor Reliquorum Annonae Sacrae Expeditionis*. This over-arching commission gave him responsibility for collecting the *annona* and resources necessary for the logistical requirements of the campaign against the Sassanids. In times of crisis, the emperor and his advisors were prepared to abandon tradition and appoint reliable men of proven loyalty, ability and experience to offices and posts of vital importance, even if senatorial status and prestige was compromised.[65]

Since Septimius Severus had created the province of Mesopotamia, all governors had been of equestrian rank rather than senatorial. This continued under his successors. The province acted as a bulwark to Syria. Geographically, it consisted of a wide open plain with its defence focused on the fortress cities rather than geographical barriers such as mountains or rivers. A small mountain range, the Jebel Sinjar, was an important strategic point and held by a series of Roman forts centred on the fortress city of Singara. Before the acquisition of Roman Mesopotamia, the River Euphrates had acted as the frontier of the Roman Empire, but the control of its crossing points still acted as a line of defence to Syria. Past Roman invasions of Parthian territory had also followed the river down to Ctesiphon, as the river provided a ready supply of water for the troops and animals and acted as an easy supply line that provisions could be brought down. Of course the return journey was more problematic. A new military office appears to have been created at this time, the *Dux Ripae*, with its headquarters at Dura Europas. The purpose of this new post was to control the upper and middle reaches of the Euphrates down to Khabur on the bend of the river. The *Dux Ripae* is first mentioned in AD 245, but it was clearly created before this date. The papyrus from AD 245 refers to three previous holders of the post, suggesting the reign of Alexander Severus as the likeliest date for its creation. This was a territorial command rather than over a specific unit, probably encompassing the garrisons along the river and the river fleet. Similar later commands along the Danube were over both land and river forces. The *dux*'s command was subordinate to the governor of Syria Coele.[66]

Unfortunately, the identity of the equestrian governor of Mesopotamia remains elusive. The likeliest candidate is Maximinus Thrax. In a speech in Herodian, the historian makes the general remind his soldiers that: 'Keeping them [the Sassanids] in check is your reputation for bravery in fighting and their knowledge and experience of my activities when I was a commander of legions on the frontier banks of the river.' In describing his career, Herodian writes how 'he progressed through all the ranks in the army and was given charge of legions and provinces'.[67] He cannot be referring to the office of *Dux Ripae*, as the legionary legates in the province were subordinate to the governor. Nor was he the commander of a single legion. The likeliest explanation is that he was *Praeses Mesopotamiae*, the acting governor of Mesopotamia, despite the late Roman historian Zosimus stating he was in charge of a cavalry regiment in AD 235. What is clear is that he was an experienced and talented military officer; exactly the sort of person the situation in Mesopotamia required.[68]

The importance of Egypt is indicated by the appointment of an equestrian governor, like in Mesopotamia. Senators were barred from entering the province without the permission of the emperor. Egypt remained the bread basket of Rome, but in AD 232, its fertile abundance would also support the needs of the army in the East. The office of Prefect of Egypt was one step away from the Praetorian Prefecture, its holders being men of proven administrative ability and implicitly trusted. This prefecture was normally held for only two to three years to allow opportunity to reward able equestrian officials, but also to minimize the risk of revolt. In AD 231, Claudius Masculinus was replaced by M. Aurelius Zeno Ianurius. He is likely to have gained administrative experience as Procurator of Mauretania Caesariensis, and could have acted as the acting governor of Mauretania. There, he may have successfully dealt with the conflict mentioned on a number of inscriptions, including one at Volubilis. It is now clear that he operated under the title of *dux* rather than as a prefect of the province, suggesting a military function to his role in response to some form of unrest. His colleague in the administration of the province was Maevius Honoratianus, who had been the commander of the fleet at Ravenna and was appointed to the prefecture in late AD 231. There had been disciplinary issues affecting the vexillations of the *II Traiana* at Antioch.

The emperor was clearly concerned that the remaining units and veterans of the legions around Alexandria might cause unrest in support of their comrades, many of whom had been severely punished. Two men with military experience would be an advantage in this dangerous situation.[69]

The emperor would have taken his close *amici* and court officials with him. Modestinus and Paul in all likelihood accompanied the emperor, as indicated by the flurry of legal edicts on military discipline. The whole imperial bureaucracy would have moved to Antioch, including the heads of the four main administrative departments of *a rationibus* with responsibility for finance, the two *ab epistulis* for imperial letters in Greek and Latin, the *a libellis* for petitions and the *a cognitionibus* for enquiries. They would have taken with them their experienced imperial freedmen and slaves. Mamaea also accompanied the emperor. A silver denarius of AD 230 shows the empress with her hair partly covered by a drape, a centre parting dividing waves of hair that flow down either side of her head. Her face depicts an energetic and intelligent woman. Alexander Severus looked to his mother for advice, and she knew the area well. The emperor had spent most of his life in Rome, and his memories of Syria would have been ephemeral. His mother knew the people and the land, the language, customs, religion and its mixed culture of Hellenistic Greek, Roman and Syrian. She was no doubt fluent in the Aramaic and Syraic languages used by the provincials, Greek and Latin being mainly the preserve of the elite and soldiers. It was not unusual for an emperor to take his mother or wife on campaign. Marcus Aurelius had taken his wife Faustina, who had died at Halala in Asia Minor. Septimus Severus took Julia Domna, and when Caracalla in turn campaigned against the Parthians, she also went with him, managing the government and administration from Antioch as her son focused on his military preparations. Mamaea's name and titles appear on milestones from Hadrianopolis in Thrace and Anazarbus in Cilicia, along with the name of her son. What is unique is another milestone from Thrace that just carries her name. This is the only example of a milestone that solely carries the name of an empress. Perhaps it indicates her presence as the work was being completed on the road.[70]

The financial implications of these extensive preparations for war must have been immense. This would have been made worse by the decision to celebrate the emperor's ten years of rule, the *Decennalia*, at this time. The tradition had been initiated by Augustus and was now an expectation. Alexander Severus would have taken his accession to the office of Caesar in AD 222 as the start of his rule. However, he expected to be in the East in the summer of AD 232 and so would have to celebrate the stability and longevity of his reign in the spring of that year. This would afford him the opportunity to provide games and festivities to the people, who would make a vow to the emperor for the success and perpetuity of his empire. The fear of unrest in the capital during his prolonged absence would have been a primary concern, as well as the need to appease the gods and solicit their support. A medallion of AD 231 shows Salus, the goddess of safety and welfare, in her traditional representation of feeding a serpent rising from an altar using a sacrificial dish, the emperor in military dress, flanked by a soldier. Coins increasingly depict the emperor in armour, with the short-cut hair typically employed by soldiers. The divine embodiment of *Virtus* appears carrying a spear and trophy. The legend proclaims '*Virtus Augusti*', with 'victory' placing a crown upon his head. Coins issued both before and after the campaign proclaim '*Victoria Augusti*'. Those coins produced preceding his departure would have attempted to reassure the populace of the expectation of victory. Romulus also appears on issues of coins from this time. As the son of the god of war, Mars, the emperor was extolling his courage and military ability. This propaganda indicates that the people and army were only too aware that he had little or no military experience, unlike all of his predecessors, including his cousin Elagabalus. The emperor drops the title 'Severus' at this time whilst retaining 'Alexander'. This was clearly an allusion to his namesake, the conqueror of the Persian Empire. From AD 229, he had also added 'Invictus' to his titles. All this smacks of an acute awareness of his vulnerabilities and criticisms that were no doubt spreading round the garrisons of the empire. Other issues continue to hopefully declare '*Fides Militum*'. This was an attempt to counteract the rumours of the situation in Mesopotamia and Syria and remind the soldiers of where their true loyalties should lie.[71]

A series of coins announce the *adlocutio* of the emperor. The *adlocutio* was a formal address given to the assembled troops by the emperor on the eve of a campaign. His speech, delivered from a high platform, was expected to be uplifting, raising the spirits of those listening. Many would not be able to hear, but the spectacle itself – the emperor standing before them in his armour and military cloak, surrounded by his *amici* and military advisors – was meant to inspire. The assembled soldiers in battle dress would stand with their standards in complete and respectful silence until the end of their commander-in-chief's speech. At the given signal, the massed ranks would roar their approval. Coins show the emperor on a tribunal with his Praetorian Prefect and other officers, addressing three soldiers. An image of the emperor in his military apparel is on the reverse. Another again shows Alexander Severus on a platform alongside two officers, with three soldiers carrying a standard, shield and spear. The name of Mamaea appears on the other side. Even more surprisingly, another issue of *adlocutio* coins have both mother and son facing one another. The association of Mamaea with such a formal, militaristic occasion can only have detracted from the emperor's desired aim of presenting his credentials for *virtus*, courage and military competence.[72]

Herodian, in his history, uses the speech of Alexander Severus to the assembled Praetorians and legionaries to demonstrate his own rhetorical skills. Needless to say, the emperor would have given a speech, probably in the open ground next to the Praetorians' fortress. The historian may have been present; he describes the ritual vocal response from the serried ranks. A large donative was then distributed to fix the loyalty of the soldiers. The money would have been distributed in front of the images of the emperor and his mother. An inscription records some kind of special ceremony at this time, perhaps after his *adlocutio*, in which the army made dedications to their emperor and Mamaea, linking the imperial family to Jupiter Optimus Maximus, the god of thunder and guarantor of victory. This may have included a public prayer for the safe return of the emperor and his army, as preserved in the *Acta Fratrum Arvalium*. The emperor then gave a speech before the Senate, announcing the date of his departure. This was probably in the late spring of AD 232. The journey would take about five months and cover 2,000 miles, suggesting he arrived at Antioch in the late summer, perhaps September, of that year. This was at the very end of the campaigning season. Herodian is frustratingly vague on the exact route of the emperor and his vast army, merely stating that it 'was completed with all speed, first to the garrisons of the Illyrian provinces, where he collected a large force; then on to Antioch'. The emperor's thorough preparations and planning would have decreased the journey time and allowed the soldiers to arrive at their destination in the best condition ready to fight.[73]

As vexillations were gradually withdrawn from the garrisons along the Rhine and sent on to Rome or posted on the route of the emperor's planned journey, formal and private offerings would have been made for the safe return of the army and loved ones. One such dedication is preserved from Bonna in Germania Inferior on 26 June AD 231. An altar was erected to Alexander, Julia Mamaea, his army and the whole divine house by the legionaries of the *I Minerva* and its associated auxiliary units by their commanders.[74]

We are provided with brief glimpses of the army's march. One such clue came from the discovery of a group of gold medallions celebrating both Caracalla and Alexander the Great. They show Alexander the Great holding a spear and Athena throwing a rock onto his breast plate, an image symbolic of victory over a barbarian foe. Their cost indicates that they were probably awarded as prizes by the emperor himself. Unfortunately, they are difficult to date. They may have been produced by Caracalla as he passed through Macedonia, an emperor who projected himself as Alexander the Great incarnate, or by Gordian III on his journey east during the Olympiad of AD 242/243. A final suggestion is they could have been struck by Alexander Severus on his confirmation of the ancient privileges of Macedonia in AD 232, wishing to associate himself with illustrious predecessors who had engaged similar foes and won significant victories.[75] It would also appear the emperor stopped for a short time at Aegeae on the road from Cilicia to Syria and Antioch. The town issued coins of a *neokoria* type to celebrate his visit.[76]

Upon reaching Antioch, Alexander Severus again offered a diplomatic settlement to Ardashir. It is likely that this move was highly unpopular with the rank and file, who had just undertaken an arduous march and seen Rome's Eastern provinces looted and soldiers killed. They would have wanted a satisfactory restoration of Roman honour that could only have been achieved at the point of a sword. However, the emperor and his advisors well understood the risks of war. Defeat would undermine the credentials of the emperor to rule and no doubt lead to further revolts. The loyalty of the Praetorians and soldiers from Pannonia remained problematic, whilst the situation in Mesopotamia itself had not been restored, with a number of claimants to the imperial throne still at large. An embassy was sent to Ardashir, suggesting a little optimistically a 'friendly alliance'. The emperor hoped that the size of the army he had brought to the East would intimidate his foe. He was sadly mistaken; the Roman embassy returned to Antioch empty-handed. Not long afterwards, a Sassanid embassy arrived, composed of 400 of Ardashir's tallest warriors bedecked in gold and all the finery of the Sassanid court. They came not to offer peace or alliance, but to demand from Alexander Severus the return of all Roman provinces that had once been part of the Persian Empire to their rightful owner, Ardashir. The Romans would be allowed to retain their territories on the European side of the Hellespont. The audacity of the Sassanid ruler is breathtaking. Understandably, the emperor realised that any offers of peace would fall on deaf ears. The sacred and sacrosanct rules of ancient diplomacy prevented the emperor from executing the ambassadors; instead they were arrested and forcibly settled on land in Phrygia. Despite all his efforts, war could no longer be refused.[77]

The emperor advanced into Mesopotamia and relieved Nisibis. This city must have been the subject of several sieges, as it could not have survived a prolonged siege lasting a number of years. In all probability, the fortress city was besieged from the start to end of each campaigning season, with Sassanid forces withdrawing each autumn. The approach of the emperor's considerable army forced Taurinus to throw himself in the Euphrates, whilst Uranius, attempting to defend his actions in a cloak of legitimacy, was brought before the emperor, who passed a sentence of death. Enemy forces either withdrew or were ejected from Rome's provinces.[78]

Despite the lateness of the year, the emperor planned an offensive into Sassanid territory beyond the Tigris. Not much could have been achieved at this stage, but it would help to raise morale in the army. However, his plans were thrown into disarray by a rebellion: '[T]he emperor prepared to cross the rivers and invade barbarian territory with his army. But some of the Egyptian-based troops joined by some of the Syrians, mutinied in an attempt to cause a change of emperor.'[79] Many of these men probably resented the prolonged absence of the emperor from the war zone, which they interpreted as evidence of cowardice. The *Legio II Traiana* were the only Egyptian troops we are aware of as taking part in the campaign. The enigmatic Syrians who joined the revolt were probably legionaries from the *Gallica III* of Syria Phoenice. A significant number of inscriptions have been found with the legion's name chiselled out. Removal from the historical records was the usual response to betrayal.[80] The *IV Scythica* was transferred from Syria Palaestina to Alexandria by the emperor. It is highly unlikely that Alexander Severus would transfer a rebellious legion to such a vital province. The *IV Scythica* was moved to Egypt to take the place of the *II Traiana*. This coincides with the appointment of a *dux* to the province, no doubt with instructions to suppress any signs of revolt amongst the Egyptian soldiers left behind, veterans of the *II Traiana* or their families.

The *Historia Augusta* appears to add more detail to this insurrection. The soldiers had become increasingly ill-disciplined, many taking full advantage of the facilities and entertainment offered by Antioch and Daphne, the pleasure capital of the East. The soldiers took to 'whoring and drinking and bathing'. The bathing might be seen as a positive choice; however, they probably chose to frequent these establishments at times laid down for women only, or went to female baths. The baths were themselves centres of iniquity, and it appears the soldiers embraced the opportunities they offered. Discipline was collapsing, so the emperor ordered the arrest of those who had infringed regulations. This precipitated a mutiny in the legions, whose comrades now faced military punishment. The legion was mustered and the imprisoned soldiers brought out in chains to stand before the emperor and the assembled ranks of infantry. The emperor, dressed in his military finery, then harangued the legionaries. The speech in the *Historia Augusta* is fictional, but the author goes on to describe a scene of seething resentment. The emperor's life was clearly at risk. Instead of listening in respectful silence, the soldiers broke into shouting and raised their battle cry. It was outrageous to interrupt the imperial speech. Tacitus described a similar scene where the legionaries verged on mutiny. The tumult increased and swords were drawn. Then the emperor discharged the whole legion, who were made to leave their weapons and withdrew into the city rather than returning to their camp.[81]

The historical context and detail in the account does suggest it is based, at least in part, on fact. Herodian also refers to this revolt and the transfer of the *IV Scythica* to Alexandria at this time, and the unique appointment of a *dux* to the home province of this legion does suggest the account of the *Historia Augusta* should not be dismissed lightly. A number of late sources state that Alexander Severus did cashier legions. However, the *Historia Augusta* dubiously adds that after thirty days the emperor was persuaded to re-enlist this legion, which subsequently proved itself in the war against Ardashir.[82] Herodian mentions nothing of an entire legion being dismissed, but rather stipulates that the leaders of the revolt were quickly caught and punished, while Alexander Severus 'transferred some of the army to other countries where he thought there was more gainful employment for them in checking barbarian raids'.[83] The sudden ending of the revolt in the *Historia Augusta* is clearly suspect. The idealized description of the emperor's haranguing and brave resilience winning the day, the rebellious legionaries meekly laying down their weapons on the emperor's command and withdrawing to the city, seems far-fetched. Then, the account continues, even more remarkably, these dishonoured soldiers are re-enlisted a month later. In such circumstances, it is highly unlikely they would have fought with the 'prowess' so described in the *Historia Augusta*. Such soldiers would surely become even more disaffected.[84]

The difficulty Alexander Severus experienced in disciplining these troops does appear believable, especially as the account casts the emperor in a poor light, struggling to assert his authority upon the massed ranks of legionaries. The biographer, who idealizes Alexander Severus' reign, has to end these passages with the emperor reasserting his authority, hence the fictional ending. Herodian probably preserves the actual outcome of this revolt, stating that these soldiers were not only seditious, as described by the *Historia Augusta*, but actually mutinied in an attempt to replace Alexander Severus. The fact the rebels were quickly punished suggests the vast majority of the army, and in particular the Praetorians, remained loyal. Perhaps these rough and ready Pannonian and Thracian soldiers who filled the ranks of the imperial guard felt little affinity with their Egyptian and Syrian comrades. The *Historia Augusta* might allude to this when it has the emperor condemn the ill-disciplined soldiers of the *II Traiana* as 'conducting themselves in the manner of the Greeks'.[85] Of course this is purely conjecture, but what is evident is that the emperor faced a serious revolt which was quickly crushed, resulting in the postponement of his plans to take the offensive against Rome's Sassanid enemy.

The number of edicts passed by Modestinus and Paul suggest disciplinary issues continued to concern the emperor. The laws they reaffirmed or laid down to counter ill-discipline are draconian and clearly meant to act as a deterrent rather than serve the ideals of justice. Desertion was severely punished: those caught were to be punished with death, and those caught with the intention of joining the enemy were to be tortured before being fed to the beasts in the arena. Loss of weapons was confirmed as another capital offence, as was insubordination, the failure to follow commands, the striking of an officer or vacating of a post. The penalty for insubordination by whole units was in theory its dishonourable discharge. Soldiers caught stealing from the baths were also to be dishonourably discharged. These laws stipulated that such men lost the privileges that usually accrued to veterans, including their entitlement to land at the end of their period of service. It appears that upon his arrival in the East, the emperor was met by an army in the process of disintegration. There can be little surprise that rebellious units would have attempted to raise a pretender to the throne in order to escape punishment.[86]

Surprisingly, the emperor intended to take advantage of the end of the campaigning season to make a personal visit to Egypt. An imperial tour of this province would help to stabilize the volatile situation and guarantee the supply of grain to his army encamped over the winter months around Apamea. A papyrus dated to AD 232/233 from the Prefect of Egypt to one of his senior officials shows preparations were well advanced:

> '[T]o the *strategoi* and *basilikoi* of the seven *nomes* and Arsinote greetings, … necessary preparations being made ready for the imperial visit of our Lord imperator Marcus Aurelius Severus Alexander, … and if Julia Mamaea, … take good care, you the *basilikoi*, having received the schedule of requisitions [?] have been made fairly and justly, … and you the *strategoi*, when you now have all this collected together … taking care of the provisioning, both that for the present imperial visit [?] and that for … to exact only contributions that are fitting; and knowing that, if I find that you have disobeyed these instructions, … your life will be at stake.'[87]

The added incentive at the end of the instructions reflects the stress the Prefect was under to ensure the visit went well. For an unknown reason, the visit appears not to have taken place, probably to the great relief of all the officials and provincials tasked with providing the provisions of the large party of courtiers, soldiers and bureaucrats who were expected. It was perhaps for this visit that a large marble statue in Memphis was reused with stucco additions to resemble the young emperor.[88] However, the emperor and his mother spent the winter months in the imperial palace at Antioch. Julia Mamaea used this opportunity to enhance her understanding of Christianity. The Church historian Eusebius records that Origen was summoned to an audience with the Augusta and was provided with the honour of an escort of imperial guard. According to Eusebius, the imperial household contained many Christians, which is entirely believable considering the open attitude of the emperor to the kaleidoscope of religious beliefs of the age, coupled with Mamaea's intellectual curiosity. There is, however, no validity in the claim that she converted to Christianity.[89] Origen's new home, Caesarea, was elevated to the status of a *metropolis* by Alexander Severus, and it is tempting to link the Christian theologian's extended stay at court with the reason for this award.[90]

There is a strange story in the *Historia Augusta* set at an undetermined time, where Egyptians, Alexandrians and Antiochenes abused the emperor at some kind of festival, calling him the Syrian *archisynogogos*, or Jewish high priest. The imperial family's toleration for Judaism and their Syrian heritage was well known. It has been suggested that the correctness of the term *archisynogogos*, which fits into an accurate historical context, might indicate some validity to this event.[91]

It is quite conceivable that the close proximity of thousands of soldiers wintering around Antioch in the autumn and winter of AD 232/233 would have driven up the price of grain, so increasing the populace's hostility towards their ruler. The Antiochenes would have considered themselves Greek rather than Syrian. The presence of Egyptians, and more specifically Alexandrians, is more puzzling. Perhaps, if there is any truth to this account, they were the families and camp followers of the *II Traiana*. While mere conjecture, this is indicative of the volatile situation facing the imperial party on its arrival in the East.

These autumn and winter months would have been spent planning for the coming campaign and building diplomatic ties. The trading centre of Palmyra was Rome's natural ally, especially since Ardashir had captured Spasinu Charax at the head of the Persian Gulf, depriving the city of vital trade routes and cutting its links with India. The ruling family had added Julii Aurelii Septimii to their name, reflecting not only their close alliance with Rome, but also with its imperial house. Armenia had more pressing reasons to side with Rome. Its ruling family, who were Arsacids, had made common cause with the Parthian royal family in order to overthrow Ardashir. Their aggressive invasion of Sassanid territory resulted in an equivalent invasion of their own lands. A Roman army would march unhindered through their territory, suggesting this had been agreed in negotiations over the preceding months. Herodian refers to 'Armenian archers, some of whom were there as subjects and others under terms of a friendly alliance', that served in the Roman army on the Rhine in AD 234. They were joined by Parthians, whose influence would be extremely useful in winning over local support in Media. However, the jewel in these diplomatic manoeuvres was the addition of the great fortress city of Hatra into Rome's alliance. Both Trajan and Septimius Severus had attempted to capture the city but failed, situated as it was in the middle of arid desert and surrounded by near-impregnable double walls 4 miles in length. It lay 60 miles from the Roman frontier that ran along the Jebel Sinjar. This great trading metropolis controlled the caravan routes through central Mesopotamia to Singara, Zeugma and the Euphrates, but it was now threatened by the rise of the centralizing Sassanid state. Its Arsacid rulers rejected Ardashir and looked to its old enemy Rome for salvation, especially after the Sassanid attempt to capture the city. Alexander Severus looked to integrate Hatra into the Roman defensive system and extend his control from northern to central Mesopotamia, threatening Ctesiphon itself. The emperor needed to secure this position and establish Roman control over this strategically important city.[92]

As well as raising local troops from these territories, as evidenced by the massive open fort built at Ain Sinu, the Romans extended their road repair programme to Mesopotamia, now freed of Sassanid forces. Milestones dated to AD 232 show repairs to communication routes around Singara and the Tigris.[93] Significantly, another repair to the Sinjar to Khabur road is dated to AD 233, at the height of the war between Alexander Severus and Ardashir. These repairs suggest the road was a vital communication route, as a significant body of soldiers would have to be deployed for this construction in the war zone. The road also linked Hatra to Roman territory. The road was clearly reconstructed to facilitate the movement of Roman forces to support their new ally. Some of the statues of Sanatruk II, the last king of Hatra, portray him wearing a breastplate decorated with Hercules, the divine protector of the imperial families. His coins also bear the legend SC (*Senatus Consulta*) surrounded by an eagle with its wings outstretched. One of his sons, M'n', appears to have held some control over 'Arabia of W'I', which is identified as the region of Sumatar Arabesi found to the south-east of Edessa. The Arab writer Adi ibn Zayd of the eleventh century, who recounts the rise and fall of Hatra decries: 'Where is the man of Hadr [Hatra], he who built this citadel and who received the tribute of the lands washed by the Tigris and the Khabur?' Arab tradition combines the power and deeds of Sanatruk II with those of his ancestor Sanatruk I, in the form of the legendary figure of Satirun. The territory of Sanatruk II stretched over vast areas of land between the Tigris and Euphrates, and appears to have encompassed some areas within the Roman province of Mesopotamia. His alliance with Rome probably granted him suzerainty over the nomadic Arab communities in these areas rather than control of the cities, towns and forts in the province and along the Euphrates. However, through him, Roman power was now exerted into central Mesopotamia. Diplomacy and a common foe had now attached both Armenia and Hatra to Rome, kingdoms that previous, more illustrious emperors had attempted to subdue but had now been acquired without the loss of a single drop of Roman blood. The aim of the campaign of AD 233 appears to have been to add further allies to Rome and feed the fires of revolt against Ardashir.[94]

It was a bold and ambitious plan which, according to Herodian, was drawn up with the advice of the emperor's council. This would in all probability be the *concilium principis*, made up of the emperor's most trusted military advisors. The suggestions of men with military skill and experience was imperative. The senatorial council, made up of a cumbersome collection of senators with little or no military background, would not have been an appropriate consultative body. Age would also have necessitated that many of these eminent aristocrats remained in Rome. The most influential *amici* travelling with the court was Rutilius Crispinus. Another laudatory inscription from Palmyra honouring a leading citizen declares: 'Statue of Julius Zabdilah, son of Malko, son of Malko, son of Nassum, who was *strategos* [general] of [Palmyra] at the time of the coming of the divine emperor Alexander, who assisted Rutilius Crispinus, the general in chief, during his stay here, and when he brought his legions here on numerous occasions.' The absence of any reference to Mamaea in these inscriptions or in these discussions is significant. The presence of the Augusta would have been mentioned by Herodian if she had made any significant contribution to a campaign that would go spectacularly wrong.[95]

Herodian, in his account of the war, quite unusually discards his frustrating generalizations and describes the campaign in lavish detail. Rome's forces were divided into three separate armies. The first army, probably setting out well before the second and third, headed north towards Armenia, travelling in all likelihood along the Amaseia to Melitene road, entering the territory of Rome's ally from Cappadocia.[96] This was a mixed force of infantry drawn from the Danubian legions and a large body of cavalry. If the Armenian historians are to be trusted, they were there joined by significant numbers of allied troops: 'There quickly arrived in support great numbers of brave and strong cavalry detachments. Nevertheless Khosrov [Tiridates II] took the vast numbers of his army, plus whatever lancers had arrived to support him in the war.' It is likely Arsacid exiles also joined the invasion force, their target being the Parthian heartland of Media. The staggered start would draw Sassanid forces away from the target areas of the second and third columns.[97]

Clearly, it was hoped that the attack on Media through Armenia would result in a Parthian uprising in support of the Arsacid dynasty. Moses of Khoren refers to the 'disobedience' of the princely Karen family, which is contrasted to the loyalty demonstrated by the Aspahbed and Suren to Ardashir. Perhaps Tiridates II and Alexander Severus hoped that the presence of a large force in Media would persuade the Karen to join them. If so, they were to be disappointed, as the Karen appear at the top of the list of court officials under Ardashir's son and successor, Shapor. There may have been a second reason for the targeting of this province. Ardashir had closely associated his rule with the Zoroastrian religion, in particular its religious leaders or *Magi*. Agathias comments: 'This man [Ardashir] was bound by the rights of the *Magi* and a practitioner of secrets. So it was that the tribe of the *Magi* also grew powerful and lordly as a result of him … It had never been so honoured or enjoyed so much freedom … and public affairs are conducted at their wish and instigation.'[98] All Sassanid rulers dated the commencement of their reign in 'fires' rather than years, referring to the fire temples founded by each ruler at their accession or coronation.[99]

Ardashir founded a fire temple at Adur Gushnasp at the very start of his reign. Its importance is demonstrated by the fact Ardashir went on a pilgrimage on foot to this temple and to no other. Archaeology has identified the location of this site as Takht-e Suleiman in Iranian Azerbaijan. The temple was attached to the warrior class to which the kings belonged, and so was considered the sacred fire of the royal family. This temple was probably founded to spread Zoroastrianism throughout Media and neighbouring Azerbaijan, and from there into Armenia.

An inscription from the time of Ardashir records how the 'fires and the *Magi*' were spread throughout the region, including Armenia and Albania, due to the efforts of the *Magi* Kirder, who rose to the position of high priest, exerting great power and influence under Ardashir and his successor. In the inscription, Kirder openly admits to persecuting other religions in order to spread belief in the divine Ahura Mazda and his earthly representative, Ardashir. The destruction of this temple by the Romans would undermine Ardashir's claims of divine support as Ahura Mazda's champion on earth in the war against evil. The seventh-century Byzantine Emperor Heraclius burnt the fire temple to the ground for the same reason. At this time, the Parthian capital of Azerbaijan, Phraaspa, was abandoned and moved to Ganzak, near to the fire temple of Adur Gushnasp. A later rock relief at Salmas has been interpreted as showing governors of Azerbaijan standing before Ardashir and Shapor I in acknowledgment of their loyalty. This suggests some kind of acknowledgement that their loyalty may have come under pressure. However, if the fire temple was destroyed at this time by the Romans, and Phraaspa sacked or rebelled, the Roman sources fail to refer to it and Sassanid ones would have little reason to do so.[100]

The second and third armies, after a delayed start to allow the northern army to enter Armenia and draw away Sassanid forces, gathered at Palmyra. Inscriptions record the presence of Alexander Severus and Rutilius Crispinus. Here the armies probably divided. The southern army would have followed the Euphrates southward, past the last Roman fortress at Kifrin and into Sassanid territory. The proximity of the Euphrates allowed these troops to be supplied by the flotilla commanded by the newly created *Dux Ripae*. The objective of this force was the Parthian provinces of Mesene and Anthemusia at the confluence of the Tigris and Euphrates, located at the head of the Persian Gulf. These areas had probably remained hostile to the Sassanids despite the fall of Spasinu Charax in c. AD 225. The army's purpose, like in Azerbaijan and Media, was to foment revolt against Ardashir. From the marshland of this area, the Romans were able to enter the arid landscape of Elymais, which had been a vassal kingdom under the Parthians until the centralizing Sassanids had ended their autonomy.[101] It was never the intention for this army to engage with the main Sassanid army, but it had to be strong enough to defeat local forces. Herodian describes its objectives as 'to spy out the eastern marches of the barbarian territory, where reports say the Rivers Tigris and Euphrates at their confluence drain into extensive marshes', and it was expecting little resistance as 'Alexander with the third column [which was the strongest and biggest group] had invaded the central sector of the barbarians, and because the enemy were being diverted to the trouble spot all the time, it would leave them easier and safer to advance'.[102]

The third and central army, commanded by the emperor himself, was described by Herodian as the 'strongest and biggest armies' and 'the cream of the army'.[103]

This would have consisted of the majority of the central reserve at Rome and vex-illations from the units on the Rhine and Danube, supplemented by the recently recruited levies who knew the region well. Their initial objective appears to have been Hatra. The Ninth cohort of Moors was present in the city in AD 235, as evi-denced by three Latin inscriptions. Numerous Roman *castella* were also built to the east of the city, facing the probable route of a Sassanid advance. A sizeable Roman army had clearly been needed to construct these fortifications and guard against an enemy attack. A march across the desert from Palmyra to Hatra involved crossing 450 miles of open desert. This would have destroyed the Roman army, especially if it was expected to then engage with Ardashir. A more likely route is a march up the Euphrates to Zeugma, where it could cross the river and journey on to Edessa, Resaina, Nisibis and then Singara, and from there to Hatra, using the Singara-Khabur road as its supply line. The Roman forces would have been well provisioned as they marched across Roman territory, and then they would cross land controlled by their new allies, Hatra. With the allegiance and security of Hatra assured, this central force was to link up with the northern army, which would use the protection of the Zagros Mountains to avoid contact with the Sassanid heavy cavalry.[104]

The usual Roman objective in an invasion of Mesopotamia was to capture enemy cities and sack the capital, Ctesiphon. However, the Romans could not con-struct alliances with Arsacid rebels and opponents to the Sassanids on the one hand, and then sack their ancient capital. Alexander Severus' strategy was clearly to fan the flames of Arsacid rebellion and destroy the Sassanid army piecemeal as Ardashir attempted to counter the multiple invasions of Media and Azerbaijan in the north, Mesene and Anthemusia in the south and the old Parthian heartland of Mesopotamia with its capital. Herodian alludes to this in his explanation of the emperor's strategic aims: 'He reckoned that by these different lines of advance he would catch the enemy off their guard when they were not expecting him. Also the Persian force would be constantly split facing the numerous invading forces, and thus be weaker and make it more difficult to co-ordinate.'[105]

This central arm of the Roman attack was commanded by the emperor in per-son. However, our sources fail to identify the commanders of the northern and southern armies. The governor of Cappadocia, Q. Julius Proculeianus, may have commanded the former. He would have been responsible for clearing his province of Sassanid raiders, and the Roman army entering Armenia would probably have to pass through his province as well as being supplied from it. This, however, is pure conjecture. It has been suggested that Rutilius Crispinus commanded the southern arm. This is unlikely, as he continued to have an illustrious career after this force met its disastrous fate. He later become the governor of Achaiae and held a *suffect* consulship in AD 235/236, which was followed by the lead military role in the senatorial revolt of the 'Council of Twenty', who gave him the joint responsibility of organizing the defence of Aquileia against Maximinus Thrax in AD 238. The southern arm was utterly destroyed and its commander, even if he survived, could not have preserved the prestige and military reputation that Rutilius Crispinus retained, even after the fall of Alexander Severus. More likely, this important figure, described as 'commander in chief' in the admiring inscription from Palmyra, served as the emperor's advisor in the campaign in central Mesopotamia.[106]

The campaign started well. The northern army entered Armenia and fell upon Sassanid-controlled Media and Azerbaijan. Herodian describes how the Roman force 'devastated the country, burning and plundering many settlements'. Ardashir's main army marched north to counter this invasion, but he would have left a sizeable force in central Mesopotamia. Herodian continues:

> 'The Persian king was kept informed and resisted as forcibly as he could, but was not really able to block them because the terrain was broken. This provided firm and easy going for infantry movement, but the barbarian horses were stopped by the rough mountainous ground from galloping, and so prevented from making any cavalry attacks and charges.'[107]

Perhaps Phraaspa either fell or rebelled. This would certainly provide a historical context for the movement of the capital of Azerbaijan to Ganzak. The Romans avoided the open Iranian plateau and instead negated the Sassanid cavalry through keeping to the high mountainous ranges.

News then reached Ardashir of further Roman invasions that were 'sweeping through territory'. Herodian describes this attack as occurring in 'eastern Parthia'.[108] The lands of central and southern Mesopotamia were considered the traditional Parthian heartland, as its capital, Ctesiphon, was located there. Herodian's use of geographical terms are often generalized. The following passage makes clear that he is referring to the southern army that was now invading Mesene and Anthemusia and threatening Elymais, which neighbours the Sassanid heartland in southern Iran:

> 'Fearing that the Romans, after devastating the Parthian lands without difficulty, would invade Persia, the king left behind what he considered an adequate force to defend Media and hurried off to the eastern districts at the head of his entire army.'

Significantly, Herodian makes a distinction between 'Parthian lands', which Aradshir appears to be willing to sacrifice to the advancing Roman armies, and those of 'Persia', in other words his home province of Pars. These lands constituted the rich estates of his Sassanid nobles; to allow these to be ravaged and destroyed would be both politically and militarily disastrous. Furthermore, Roman attacks by the northern army on Parthian towns and villages in Medea only made it less likely that these areas would rebel, although they do appear to have demonstrated little will to resist.[109]

Ardashir may also have heard of the misfortune now affecting the central army, led by the emperor. Herodian describes how the emperor's 'whole army was suffering from sickness, but particularly the Illyrian troops, who were seriously ill and dying because they were used to a healthy, wintry climate and normally ate more food'. The emperor himself had also become seriously ill, with his life threatened. In the summer months, the temperature is often above 40° centigrade, with dust storms common. The Praetorians and *II Parthica*, as well as many legionary vexillations, would have found the heat and scorching sand almost unbearable, especially as these soldiers were natives of the cooler northern provinces. The weight of their armour would have added to their difficulties, as well as the heat, when they had to wear it. Sand in their clothes and armour would have caused further discomfort. The ringed chain mail weighed 14kg, and the shield a further 8kg. Heat exhaustion would have been a major problem. Herodian also alludes to a reduction in their rations, no doubt a result of the extended supply lines. The historian later adds that their emperor, after falling ill, later returned to health on his return to Antioch with its 'refreshing atmosphere' and 'its plentiful water supply', in contrast to the 'arid drought of Mesopotamia'. Alexander Severus would, unlike Caracalla, have not shared the burdens of the common soldiers, so their health is likely to have deteriorated at a faster rate in the inhospitable conditions. Hatra is situated on a desert oasis, but the huge demands of a massive army may have led to rationing. Most importantly, Herodian refers to the soldiers succumbing to a sickness. Dysentery was the destroyer of many armies, especially those encamped for a prolonged period of time, the sanitary conditions rapidly worsening as attempts to deal with the disposal of sewage are overwhelmed.[110]

We can imagine this central army encamped around Hatra, incapacitated by disease and dehydration. As more and more soldiers fell sick, its ability to successfully engage the Sassanid forces in battle was dramatically reduced. Ardashir's spies would have informed him of the battle-effectiveness of this force, and he came to the conclusion that it could now be ignored. The main Sassanid army now rapidly advanced towards the unsuspecting southern army. Alexander Severus was probably so ill that he was in no position to make decisions. His mother and the *consilium principis* now had a difficult decision to make. The plan envisaged them advancing to meet Ardashir's force before it reached the southern army, but with so many soldiers ill, such a confrontation would have probably resulted in a Roman defeat. As the emperor was in theory still commander-in-chief, his military prestige would never recover. Understandably, the decision was to remain where they were. There can be no doubt that messengers were sent to warn their comrades in the south and north, but subsequent events show they failed to arrive before Ardashir struck. Herodian accuses Alexander Severus, and in particular Mamaea, of cowardice in not keeping to the plan. However, their caution probably saved the main army from total defeat. Chance and misfortune had cancelled Alexander Severus' meticulous preparations and planning. He would never recover from the loss of prestige.[111]

The full force of the Sassanid army now fell upon the southern army. Their own commander clearly made mistakes in not scouting the surrounding territory, advancing blindly in the naïve assumption that Ardashir's main force was hundreds of miles away. Herodian provides a detailed account of the slaughter, suggesting some managed to escape to tell the tale:

'The Persian king attacked with his entire force, catching them by surprise and surrounding them in a trap. Under fire from all sides, the Roman troops were destroyed, because they were unable to stand up to the superior numbers and were continually having to shield with their weapons their exposed sides that formed a target for the enemy. Under the circumstances saving one's skin was preferable to fighting. In the end they were all driven into a huddle and fought behind a wall of shields, as though they were in a siege. Bombarded from every angle and suffering casualties, they held out bravely for as long as they could. But finally they were all destroyed. This terrible disaster, which no one likes to remember, was a set-back to the Romans, since a vast army, matching anything in earlier generations for courage and toughness, had been destroyed.'[112]

In these circumstances, retreating soldiers sought cover and height. There appears to have been none, suggesting the battle took place on the flat plains of Elymais. The design of the *Niedermormter* helmet, with its extended neck-guard, prevented the soldiers from looking upwards to try to avoid incoming missiles. Nor would they have been able to assume their normal defensive position of crouching low behind their shields, as this would have made them vulnerable to a cavalry charge. Each soldier would also have sought to protect their exposed right-hand sides by moving right in order to seek the coverage of their comrade's shield that he held on his left. This would have prevented the men from using their swords as they bunched together in an attempt to evade the hail of arrows. Death for many would have been unseen and sudden. It is likely this southern army included troops from Palmyra. The arid conditions around Dura Europas have preserved a morning report from the ninth month of AD 233 of a unit of Palmyrene cavalry who formed part of the garrison. Only 120 men were present; half are missing. It would be expected that in a time of war, the unit would be at full complement, unless the missing soldiers were dead. Yet a significant number, if they were with the southern army, managed to survive the massacre. The late Roman military historian Vegetius describes the Roman army's standard deployment when marching. At the head was positioned the bulk of the cavalry, the baggage train was positioned in the centre, with infantry deployed on either side, and light cavalry and skirmishers bringing up the rear. This arrangement may have allowed the Palmyrene cavalry units to avoid encirclement and break the enemy lines before the main force was surrounded. The Sassanids did not have everything their own way. As Herodian later admits, they suffered heavy losses and many more wounded.[113]

When news reached the commanders of the central army of this defeat, the order was given to retreat. Ardashir and the Sassanids were emboldened by their victory, and Herodian describes him as being fired with greater ambition. The poor condition of the main Roman army meant it was incapable of successfully fighting a battle. Herodian states that many of the soldiers had died and morale had collapsed.[114] Hatra was now well defended, but the northern army would now be unable to descend from the Zagros Mountains to join up with the emperor's forces. If they had attempted to cross the open plains of Mesopotamia, they would have suffered the same fate as the southern army. Herodian is clear that the retreat was ordered only after news of the defeat in the south, and not before. Yet the emperor was accused of cowardice by the soldiers for retreating and leaving their comrades in Elymais vulnerable to attack. However, by the time the central army marched back to Antioch, the southern army had ceased to exist. It was now late autumn, and the northern army was forced to retreat across the Zagros and the mountain ranges of Armenia in the winter months. This victorious army now suffered grievously from the cold:

'Very few of the many soldiers in this army survived the return trip, most of them dying in the mountains and several suffering mutilation of the hands and feet from the wintry conditions of the country.'[115]

Alexander Severus and his army returned to their winter quarters around Antioch, where the emperor gradually made a full physical recovery, as in all probability did most of his army. However, he suffered greatly from depression. His men were 'absolutely furious with Alexander because the invading army had been betrayed by his deception and failure to keep to the plan'. His reputation had sunk to its lowest point. He stood accused of wanting to avoid risking his own life, in contrast to his men who risked theirs every day. His mother's own female 'timidity' and 'excessive love for her son' had 'blunted Alexander's efforts to behave bravely'. She is reported to have told him that it was not his job to get involved in battle.

These were the rumours and slurs that circulated the Roman camps and forts, probably repeated by Herodian as facts. The historian summarizes these misfortunes as being a consequence of the emperor's poor judgement and poor luck.[116] Luck had certainly failed him, but the Roman plan and preparations were not at fault. The two mistakes that can be levelled at the emperor and his advisors include firstly the failure to understand how seriously Ardashir would perceive the threat to his southern homeland. The southern army should have been stronger, in order to potentially confront the Sassanid king's main army if necessary, and have had a more competent commander appointed. The second error was the protracted absence of the emperor from the Eastern provinces when they were suffering repeated invasions by Sassanid forces from late AD 228 until the late summer of AD 232. This delay was due to the need to recruit and then train large numbers of soldiers to bring units up to strength. The short-sightedness of attempting to restrict expenditure by reducing the costs of the army by keeping units understrength had severely limited the emperor's ability to rapidly respond to a military crisis. If the emperor had led depleted forces into battle, he would probably have been defeated, which would certainly have led to his overthrow. Instead, commanders were appointed to the Eastern provinces to try to contain Sassanid incursions and buy time for units to be brought up to their full complement of men. This, however, took time, leading to further accusations of timidity and cowardice being levelled at Alexander Severus or claims that he was dominated by the supposed female weaknesses of his mother.

What is difficult to understand is why Ardashir did not take full advantage of the military situation. One Roman army had been utterly destroyed, another was in retreat – beset by disease and a collapse of morale – while the northern army was now retreating back into Armenia. The losses to this army were not, according to our sources, due to enemy action but from cold and hunger, so Sassanid forces were not used to harry their retreat. The failure of this army to retreat across the plains of Mesopotamia seems to suggest that Ardashir was advancing up the Tigris. Hatra, thanks to the work of the central army, was now a virtual fortress. Attempting to capture this city would entail a prolonged siege and the relinquishing of the opportunity to make the Romans pay. So where was the Sassanid main force now deployed? The obvious target was Roman Mesopotamia, whose governor was possibly Maximinus Thrax. Our fragmentary sources provide some brief glimpses of the ensuing conflict. The speech in Herodian, previously mentioned, supposedly made by Maximinus Thrax in AD 238 to his legionaries, makes reference to his role as 'commander of legions on the frontier banks of the river'. The river must be the Euphrates. He also makes reference to 'The Persians, after their invasion of Mesopotamia some time ago'.[117] This has been taken to mean the Sassanid invasions of the provinces

from AD 228–232, whilst Alexander Severus was making his elaborate preparations in Rome for the Eastern campaign. More likely, Maximinus Thrax is made
in the speech to refer to an invasion he himself faced when commander of the
legions in AD 233, with these same veterans now arrayed before him in AD 238.
There was a tradition retained in the *Getica*, written by the sixth-century historian Jordanes, that Maximinus 'fought with marvellous success against the
Parthians under Alexander'.[118] This reference in itself cannot be relied upon,
but it is supported to some extent by other, admittedly late, sources.

John Malalas, a sixth-century Greek chronicler from Antioch, also makes reference to the defence of Roman Mesopotamia by Maximinus Thrax, but in less
flattering terms:

> 'He [Alexander Severus] made an expedition with his mother against
> the Persians, and in Antioch appointed Maximinus as general. The latter
> fought a battle against the Persians but was defeated, and the Emperor
> grew angry with him.'[119]

Contextually, this account fits the situation in late AD 233. However, Malalas'
work is often coloured by imperial propaganda, although his knowledge of the
history of his native city might be more reliable for local events. The presence
of the emperor at Antioch is certainly true, but it does not make clear whether
Maximinus' appointment as general was before the campaign of AD 232 or after.
The fact he refers to Maximinus as general, rather than governor, might suggest
he was appointed to his post in response to the retreat from Hatra and the need
to defend Roman Mesopotamia from the advancing Sassanid forces. Whoever was
in charge did a remarkable job, as the province stood firm against a numerous and
victorious enemy. No cities are recorded as being captured at this time. This might
suggest that the reference to a defeat suffered by Maximinus, which is contradicted
in Herodian, could reflect imperial propaganda. All our sources, bar Malalas, agree
that the military reputation of Maximinus Thrax was beyond reproach; a defeat
would not fit with his standing. Jordanes' *Getica* states that Maximinus fought
with marvellous success against the 'Parthians'. If Maximinus Thrax did hold
the province, in sharp contrast to the retreat of the emperor's forces, the victorious general would become a serious threat. An excuse would have to be found to
detach him from his admiring soldiers. In AD 234, Maximinus was appointed to
the post of *Praefectus Tironibus* with responsibility for recruiting soldiers for the
emperor's German campaign. This was nothing less than a demotion. The anger
of Maximinus Thrax's later *damnatio memoriae* against Alexander Severus and
Mamaea, and the sustained attacks on the temples of Jupiter Dolichenus, surely
reflect this.[120]

In order to improve morale and attempt to restore waning loyalty, the army received a distribution of money. Coins of late AD 233 carry the legend '*liberalitas*'. Preparations were also made for another campaign into Sassanid territory. A bronze medallion produced at the same time depicts victory crowning the emperor, who stands on two river gods, probably representing the Tigris and Euphrates. This seems to suggest that Roman losses were not as great as Herodian would have us believe. A significant defeat would have necessitated a defensive strategy, but clearly the emperor planned once more to go on the offensive. Indeed, the historian contradicts himself, stating:

'Even though the barbarians seemed to have emerged the victors by some superior force, yet they had been damaged by the frequent skirmishes in Media and the battle in Parthia, because of the heavy list of losses and even greater number of wounded. The Romans, far from having retreated ignominiously, had in some cases actually inflicted serious damage too on the enemy, and had only been destroyed in so far as they were fewer in number. Practically the same number of soldiers fell on each side, making the barbarian survivors appear to have won by force of numbers and not sturdiness. Fairly clear evidence of the damage to the barbarians lies in the fact that for three or four years they remained quiet without resorting to arms.'

What Herodian is referring to by the 'battle in Parthia' is unclear. Clearly it was a separate event to the Roman attacks in Media. By Parthia, going on our previous assertion that the historian means Mesopotamia, could he be alluding to the destruction of the southern army, as this is the only battle he previously mentions? Or was there another battle, perhaps fought by the central army of Alexander Severus or by Maximinus Thrax in the defence of Roman Mesopotamia? No conclusions can be drawn.[121]

In the winter of AD 233/234, Ardashir had disbanded his army, as they were not a professional standing force like the Romans but composed mainly of farmers, supplemented by the heavily armoured aristocratic cavalry. Zonoras, though, adds another detail:

'A great scourge broke out in the Persian camp and many Romans died not so much by the hand of the enemy but from the march home through the mountains of Armenia. It was freezing cold for the feet of the travellers, while some men were so unfortunate as to have their hands blacken and go frostbitten from the cold. For this misfortune the Romans held Alexander accountable. Accordingly, either from discouragement or a conjunction of the humours he fell very ill.'

The majority of this passage is clearly derived from Herodian, but the spread of disease to the Sassanid forces is an additional piece of information. This outbreak in the Sassanid army would account for the dismissal of their army. In this way Ardashir preserved his forces for future campaigns. However, Merv seems to have been the focus of Ardashir's attention the following year and he was not to return to his western frontier until at least AD 238. Alexander Severus was never to return. In the spring of AD 234, news reached him in Antioch from his governors on the Rhine and Danube that a vast army of Germans had invaded the empire and were now threatening Italy itself. The war in the East was put on hold, which allowed the emperor the opportunity to now march west.[122]

It is striking that the usually triumphalist Sassanids carved no reliefs to celebrate this supposed victory. In stark contrast, Roman propaganda hailed the campaign as a great victory. In Galatia, milestones hail the emperor as 'Parthico Max' and 'Persico Max'. Other inscriptions record the Roman victory, whilst coin issues proclaim 'Victoria Augusti.' The Hatrans were in no doubt, an inscription recording dedications made for the victory with the words *domita Midia*. This appears to be an example of astute political awareness on the part of Hatra in ignoring the defeat of the southern army whilst celebrating the success of the northern.[123]

Historians, both ancient and modern, have argued over the outcome of the campaign. Like Herodian, those ancient historians who wrote in Greek depict it as a defeat. This tradition is found in the Byzantine historian Credenus, who describes how Alexander Severus 'campaigned against the Persians and was overwhelmed in defeat'. Latin sources, including the *Historia Augusta* and Eutropius, portray it as an overwhelming Roman victory. These later accounts are probably based on a now lost earlier source, termed the *Kaisergeschicte*, which in turn appears to have been heavily influenced by the imperial propaganda. For example, Eutropius, in his brief summary of Roman history, records that the emperor 'undertook a war against the Persians and defeated their king Xerxes [Ardashir], with a great victory'. This is reflected in *De Caesaribus* and Festus. Zosimus, Zonaras and Syncellus are unfortunately non-committal in their accounts of the campaign.[124]

In truth, the war ended in a stalemate. Both sides lost an inordinate amount of men. The invading Roman armies had caused an immense amount of damage to Sassanid territory, but the southern arm had suffered a crushing defeat. Yet strategically, the Roman Empire was in a far stronger position in central Mesopotamia than it had ever been, with Hatra a threat to the Sassanid capital of Ctesiphon. Roman Mesopotamia continued to act as a bulwark to the vital Syrian provinces, whilst Armenia, now a committed ally, protected Cappadocia and Asia Minor from attack. However, the campaign had fatally damaged the emperor's martial prestige. Many soldiers could not forgive him for, in their eyes, abandoning the northern and southern armies to their fate. The chronology of events leading to the destruction of the southern army would be blurred by rumours and invective. However, the emperor, as commander-in-chief, was held responsible. The presence of his mother only inflamed the situation. The soldiers had lost confidence in the military abilities of their emperor and his advisors.[125] His fate was sealed from this point. Just as the massive losses at the Battle of Nisibis had led to a collapse of morale and confidence in Macrinus, just so with Alexander Severus. The news from the Rhine only added to the soldiers' anger.

Chapter 9

War in the West AD 234–235

'but when by eastern roads he hastens forth to look on Italy, smitten by
burning iron and all exposed, he will fall, hated for his mother's sake.'
(Sibylline Oracle X (XII), 353–356)

T he severity and extent of the barbarian invasion across the Rhine and
Danube has been much disputed by historians, who point to the emper-
or's slow response to this crisis.[1] However, this is clearly contradicted by
both our ancient sources and archaeological evidence. There was a real emergency
that the depleted garrisons on Rome's northern frontier lacked the manpower to
counter. Herodian describes the arrival of messengers from the governors of the
Illyrian provinces, by which he must mean the Pannonias, Raetia and Noricum,
urgently requesting the return of the emperor and his army. Hordes of barbarians
had crossed both the Rhine and Danube, destroyed garrisons, cities and villages,
slaughtering and pillaging as they went. According to the *Historia Augusta*, the
raids extended into Gaul. The security of Italy was threatened. What is even more
significant is the reaction of the soldiers from these provinces, who had been reluc-
tantly enlisted into the emperor's grand army that he had taken to the East:

> 'This news dismayed Alexander and caused distress to the soldiers
> transferred from Illyricum. They felt they had suffered a double trag-
> edy, first in their misfortunes of the Persian war and then in the reports
> they received individually about the destruction of their families by the
> Germans. They turned their anger on Alexander, blaming him for his
> betrayal of their cause in the East through his negligence or cowardice
> and his hesitant procrastination over the northern crisis.'[2]

We can imagine the soldiers, many slowly recovering from frostbite, exhaustion,
wounds or disease, receiving the letters from home that they hoped would alleviate
their present condition with some good news from their loved ones. Their morale
was low, having lost many comrades and friends, and many grieved for the total
destruction of the southern army. Sat in their tents in the temporary camps that
would have covered the countryside around Antioch and Apamea, they would have
read these letters, sent by comrades and veterans from home rather than wives and

girlfriends, thereby learning of the murder and loss of their family. Many would have resented being taken to the East by their emperor, their previous worries at the prospect of leaving their loved ones vulnerable to the raids of the barbarians being fully justified. Their desire for revenge on the German tribes would burn strong and their emperor, who had weakened the defences on the Rhine and Danube, would be sorely blamed.

Forts at Waaldurn, Osterburken, Butzbach, Holzhausen, Biriciana, Zugmantel, Saalburg, Echzell, Pfunz, Regensberg, Bahming and Lauriacum were destroyed, and that at Altenstadt can probably be added to the list. Some of these forts were subsequently rebuilt, but others completely abandoned. Construction work at the forts at Butzbach, Kapersburg and Kleiner Feldberg initiated by Maximinus Thrax indicates they were also damaged in the invasions. An inscription records the restoration of an important building at Ohringen-Ost at this time. Zugmantal received a new defensive wall under Alexander Severus, and the work was continued under Maximinus Thrax. Saalburg's reconstruction had to wait until the reign of his successor, when it was briefly reoccupied but abandoned permanently c. AD 260. Its garrison in AD 233 was the *Cohors II Raetorum civium romanorum*, a part-mounted auxiliary regiment. This unit appears to have been destroyed in the barbarian attack. The bath house at the small fort at Walldurn had only just been constructed, but a burnt layer shows that both the bath house outside the fort and the fort itself were destroyed. The fact that soldiers had been building outside the walls rather than strengthening the walls themselves suggests that there had been no warning or indication of a concentration of Alamanni. A dual fort had been constructed by Commodus at Osterburken housing an auxiliary unit from Aquitania, and a *numerus* in a smaller adjacent fortlet. Excavations in its ditch protecting the western wall revealed pottery and the skulls of two adults who had clearly died a violent death. Archaeologists discovered a burnt layer inside the fort, followed by a brief period of reoccupation, then a second burnt layer. The first layer was tentatively dated to AD 234. The fort of Biriciana (mod. Weissenberg) was badly damaged in AD 233/234 and rebuilt by Maximinus Thrax. Thirty kilometres to the east is the fortress at Pfunz, Roman Vetiniana. Its fall would have been a major blow, as it was built to guard the military road from Biriciana to Kosching. It was held by the *Cohors I Breucorum civium Romanorum equitata*, a unit whose name suggests all members of the unit were at some point granted citizenship, probably for a significant act of bravery. It appears to have been taken in a surprise attack in AD 233. Archaeologists excavating the southern tower of the fortress discovered the skeletons of its guards without their shields. The attackers were utterly ruthless. A prisoner, chained to the wall of his cell in the headquarters building (*principia*), was found butchered. The settlement that served the soldiers of the fort and housed their families, the *vicus*, was burnt to the ground, as was the Temple of

Jupiter Dolichenus. Fifty kilometres east of Vetiniana lay the legionary fortress of Castra Regina (Regensberg/Ratisbon), holding the *III Italica*. The commander of this legion was also the governor of Raetia, whose official residence lay to the south at Augusta Vindelicorum (Augsburg). Both fortress and city suffered immense damage. The neighbouring province of Noricum also suffered. Lauriacum, the provincial capital garrisoned by the *II Italica* and seat of the governor, was burnt down. It would be immediately rebuilt, only to be levelled again and again in a series of disasters throughout the century.[3]

A significant number of coin hordes dated between AD 229–235 in Upper Germany and Raetia are testimony to the panic these raids engendered. The fact that some of these hordes were buried before the barbarian invasions may have been the result of the military unrest caused by the deployment of vexillations to the East by the emperor. Further coin hordes have been discovered at Kirchmatting, Wiggensbach and Niederaschau dated to AD 231, 233 and 235 respectively. Many of the unprotected settlements surrounding the forts were completely abandoned after AD 233. It is entirely understandable that civilians would bury their earthly wealth in the face of such a crisis, hoping to be able to return some time with their life secured and their homes restored. That they never did suggests they suffered an untimely end. Even the members of the garrisons along the rivers appear to have despaired for their lives. The auxiliary fort at Sorviodurum held a detachment of Syrian archers. Immediately to the west, a rather unusual but stunning horde has been discovered in the grounds of a villa. Hidden within was discovered a large bronze basin, perhaps buried by the commander of the local garrison, in addition to a sumptuous collection of cavalry parade armour, seven helmets and four ceremonial masks ornamented with wavy Grecian-style hair or curled hair reflecting oriental influences. There were also a number of cuirasses, greaves and barbing that would be attached to a horse. This officer, if that was the occupation of the man who had hoped to preserve this valuable and unique collection of military equipment, clearly felt that placing this assemblage in the strong room at the fort was not the safest location. Like so many others, he failed to return and recover his prized possessions. The attack clearly extended into Noricum, where a number of coin hordes have been discovered, including one buried on the northern shore of Lake Attersee near Seewalchen in Upper Austria and a concentration of others around Vindobona.[4]

The barbarian attack must have involved thousands of men. The trail of devastation shows that they fell firstly on the Agri Decumates, a plain bordered by the Rhine and Danube, and the Taunus mountains to the north. The area had been conquered by Domitian between AD 82–87 in order to shorten the communication route from Raetia to the German provinces and protect Gaul from invasion. The series of forts constructed in the area were augmented by an integrated system of military roads, wooden palisades, watchtowers and ditches termed *limes*. The Chatti had held the area in the time of Domitian; however, this tribe appears to have joined with neighbouring ones to form a larger confederation called the Alamanni. This was probably in response to the barrier of the Roman military frontier in front and the pressure of migratory tribes to their rear. They had no central leader, but were led by kings of separate groups who joined together under a single leader in times of crisis or opportunity, as existed in AD 233/234. To these warriors, war was the only true test of valour. A study of grave goods from the early third century shows wealth was gradually concentrated into the hands of fewer individuals. These elites monopolized the economic and political structure of Germanic society. Valour and riches were used to establish their position as they provided gifts to their followers, which attracted more warriors, so creating larger war bands and enabling these leaders to capture more land which could also be distributed to minor rulers. Rome had long since nurtured these leaders through diplomacy, providing gold in return for alliance. This had further helped these elite to consolidate their position until their military power became a threat to the security of the frontier. Caracalla had attacked and defeated them in AD 213. As a consequence, the German frontier had been peaceful for two decades. However, there was regular interaction and trade across the border. These 'princelings' developed a taste for oil, wine, ornate precious bowls and weapons. It would have been obvious through these trading contacts that garrisons along the Rhine and Danube had been depleted and weakened due to the war in the East. The reduction of the Rhine garrison was an opportunity to plunder the rich and fertile lands of the Taunus Wetterau region. The Alamanni leaders could establish a reputation for military prowess and amass wealth beyond imagining from the rich and fertile lands of the empire. The attack appears to have been sudden and well prepared. This is surprising, as the Romans had specialized units of soldiers termed *exploratores* whose job it was to reconnoitre barbarian territory to discover any threats, including a build-up of enemy forces. It was a task they clearly failed to perform.[5] It was perhaps for this reason that the governor of Germania Superior, Sextus Catius Clementinus Priscillianus, appears to have been replaced in AD 234. As the commander of the province opposite Alamanni territory, he was probably held accountable for the failure of intelligence to provide warning of the impending attacks.

The Alamanni had few cavalry but did have large numbers of infantry. However, only their kings and chiefs wore body armour or helmets, which were indicators of wealth and status. Most soldiers carried a shield with a central circular boss and a two-edged long sword, the *spatha*, used increasingly by the Roman infantry. Some had bows, but they were increasingly armed with an axe that could be used for throwing or in close combat. They were not proficient in siege warfare, lacking the engineering skills to construct siege equipment and the logistics to provide the provisions for a prolonged siege. Instead, attacks on fortified positions relied upon surprise and weight of numbers. It appears the depleted garrisons along the Rhine and Upper Danube were simply overwhelmed. Their attack was initially focused upon the Agri Decumates, then, using the Roman roads, they headed east as they fell upon the forts along the banks of the rivers, destroying any rural settlements along the way before looting the prosperous towns that serviced the garrisons, slaughtering the families of the soldiers. They advanced into Raetia, where excavations at Straubing have revealed a destruction level containing horse stripping, weapons and smashed statues dated to AD 233. The destruction of Kunzing has also been dated to AD 233 AD, or possibly AD 242. Archaeologists here revealed the last desperate attempts by its garrison to save themselves and their families. At the first news of the barbarian invasion, repairs were made to the defensive walls and the five separate ditches surrounding the fort were amalgamated into one. After weapons were distributed to all those able to fight, the surplus equipment was buried to the east of the headquarters building where they had been stored. The commander evidently feared the worst. In the event of the fort's capture, these weapons at least would not be used by the poorly equipped Alamanni. The weapons were never recovered, and a fire started in the headquarters building was so intense that it melted bronze parade armour, helmets and greaves that had been left in the building's western rooms.[6]

Alexander Severus' position was extremely vulnerable. His Eastern army had suffered grievously in a war whose outcome was disputed. These losses would have to be replaced and his men allowed time to recover. The defences of the Eastern provinces needed strengthening, and Ardashir had not been defeated or asked for peace. The whereabouts of the Sassanid king probably remained unknown. At the same time, any delay in marching to relieve the beleaguered army and provinces on the Rhine and Danube would only further inflame the resentment of the soldiers. The invasion of Raetia made Italy vulnerable. Emperors were always blamed for military reverses, and armies in areas endangered by enemy incursions looked, in the absence of the imperial presence, to appoint their own emperor to command the resources needed to resist the offensive. This is what happened in Mesopotamia from AD 228–232, and there was a distinct possibility that the army on the Rhine would revolt.[7]

The governors of these threatened provinces would have come under pressure from two directions. Firstly, groups of discontented soldiers would have considered possible candidates to raise to the imperial purple, whilst the emperor would have reminded them of their loyalty and past honours and appointments they had received from his hand. According to the *Historia Augusta*, these legions were in mutinous mood by the time Alexander Severus arrived on the Rhine in late

AD 234.[8] Sextus Catius Clementinus Priscillianus was replaced that year, when the emperor and his army could enforce his decision without fear that the dismissed governor would become the imperial candidate the discontented soldiers were looking for. His next post was governor of Cappadocia, an appointment made by Maximinus Thrax. An inscription also records the presence alongside him of Maximinus's young son. Alexander Severus' successor clearly trusted him, something he would only have done if his loyalty to Alexander Severus was known to be suspect.[9]

Alexander Severus made an extraordinary appointment to Germania Inferior, with the consular senator Flavius Julius Latronianus replaced by the equestrian Furius Sabinius Aquila Timesitheus. The latter had clearly performed well in his post as *Procurator provinciae Syriae Palaestinae ibi Exactor Reliquorum Annonae Sacrae Expeditionis*. This office had provided him with the necessary powers to collect the food and other resources for the war against Ardashir. His reward was a similar role on the Rhine, which combined the powers of a senatorial governor as acting governor of Germania Inferior in conjunction with the resources of the procurator for all imperial estates in Beligica and the two Germanys, an office carrying the imposingly worded title of *vice procuratoris patrimoni provinciarum Belgicae et duarum Germaniarum, ibi vice praesidis provinciae Germaniae inferioris*. This allowed him the power to gather supplies from these provinces with the equivalent rank as the governors of Germania Superior and Belgica, but he also had command over the two legions in his senatorial province, the *XXX Ulpia Victrix* and *I Minervia*. Senatorial sentiment was of secondary importance to the necessities of war. However, in a sop to the Senate, and with his task completed and peace negotiations in full swing, Timesitheus was replaced in late AD 234 or early AD 235 by the illustrious senator Caius Messius Quintus Lucius Decius Valerianus, better known as the future Emperor Decius.[10]

Another prominent figure on the Rhine was Titius Quartinus. He is described by Herodian as 'one of Alexander's consular friends'. Upon the emperor's murder he was dismissed from his post, but appears to have remained in the area and been raised to the purple, despite his professed reluctance, by Macedo, the commander of the Osrhoenian archers. The Eastern unit remained loyal to the memory of the deceased Syrian emperor and wished to overthrow his successor. Macedo then proceeded to murder his protégé and Quartinus' name was erased by Maximinus Thrax when the conspiracy was crushed. It has been suggested that 'Quartinus' is the erased name on an inscription erected sometime after AD 225 who was a commander of the *I Minervia*, making this man governor of Germania Inferior in AD 235. However, firm epigraphic evidence supports the tenures of Timesitheus and Decius at this time. What Herodian does make clear is that it was an official post held by Quartinus rather than the informal membership of the *consilium principis.* He was also prestigious enough to be called an *amicus* of the emperor, as well as be considered by the troops as a potential emperor. The strongest possibility is he replaced Sextus Catius Clementinus Priscillianus as governor of Germania Superior in AD 234.[11]

Another recruitment campaign was started across the empire in late AD 233 and early AD 234 to replace the recent losses. A large component of the annihilated southern army was probably from Palmyra, which contributed troops to units across the empire. Inscriptions made by soldiers from a *numeri* of Palmyrenes at El Katara and El Gahra in the province of Numidia bear Eastern names until this time, when three dedications to the god Melagbel are made by men with African names, who were likely to be local recruits. This is probably because it was impossible to enlist men from their native city due to the urgent need to fill the ranks of local Palmryene units in the East.[12]

The northern legions also required a new draft to supplement their depleted ranks. Maximinus Thrax was given the task of training these new levies as *praefectus tironibus*, a task he was given because of his 'military experience'. However, this post was clearly a demotion from the governorship of Mesopotamia. He had probably needed to be removed from the soldiers he had commanded in the province, their loyalty now being suspect. In these circumstances, Septimius Severus had promoted successful commanders to the Senate, permanently divorcing them from potential supporters in the ranks. This was a lesson Alexander Severus and his advisors failed to appreciate, and they would pay dearly for their mistake. There can be little doubt that Maximinus Thrax burned with anger and resentment. Herodian describes him as performing his responsibilities

'extremely conscientiously, earning great popularity among the troops because he did not confine himself only to teaching them what to do but also took a lead in all the tasks. As a result they were not just pupils but copied his examples of courage. He also won their allegiance still more by awarding them prizes and all kinds of honours. So the young men, of whom the greater majority were Pannonians, admired Maximinus' courage and despised Alexander.'

The office allowed him a freedom of movement and latitude that he would utilize to the full. An inscription records some of his recruits repairing a road near Aquileia.[13] He would have travelled to different training camps and taken his men, for that is what they were, on marches to different forts, using this opportunity to build connections and support. He was pushing against an open door.

Alexander Severus gathered together a huge army for the campaign on the Rhine and reinforced the defences of the Eastern provinces: 'A large force was left behind, sufficiently large in his opinion, to defend the Roman side of the river; the camps and outposts were given more efficient defences and their full complement of soldiers.'[14] The transfer of the *VI Ferrata* from Palestine to Syria Phoenice and *III Gallica* to protect the approaches to Palmyra may be attributed to this reorganization or earlier. It is likely that soldiers withdrawn from local garrisons for the offensives into Sassanid territory were now redeployed, and losses replaced by local levies. All this had taken time, and he could only have left the East once he was assured that the Sassanids would not continue their attacks on Rome's provinces.[15]

The vexillations from the legions on the Rhine and Danube would return with the emperor, along with the Praetorians, *equites singulares*, urban cohorts and *II Parthica*. Herodian also mentions that Alexander Severus incorporated African and eastern troops in this force, including Moroccans and a 'huge force of archers', including soldiers from Osrhoene, Parthian 'deserters' and 'mercenaries'. The Mauritanian units were picked out by the historian as being particularly useful, as their long-range javelins and ability to engage the enemy and quickly withdraw would be highly effective against the massed ranks of the Alamanni, who lacked the protection of armour and helmets. Large numbers of Armenian archers were retained as part of the alliance with Rome. Prisoners of war were also used, but their reliability and esprit de corps must have been suspect. Inscriptions record the presence of these troops on the Rhine. One inscription has the name of the Osrhoenians erased, probably on the orders of Maximinus Thrax in retribution for their failed revolt. Inscriptions from the German provinces record the presence of Praetorians, the *II Parthica*, the *IV Flavia Firma* from Moesia Superior and an '*ala nova firma Milliaria Catafractaria*'. The latter unit of heavy cavalry would be devastating in close contact with the ranks of badly equipped Alamanni. They were probably organized as *numeri*. Other Syrian units appear to have been transferred to both Pannonias. This seems to have taken place late in the reign. A significant number of inscriptions have been discovered dedicated to both the emperor and his mother, made 'to the health of our Lord Alexander Augustus'. It was only after AD 231 that the emperor dropped 'Severus' from his title, hoping to associate himself with the great Macedonian conqueror. These dedications were made by members of an Emesene cohort, probably offering thanks for the emperor's recovery from the illness he suffered on campaign. Twenty-three tombstones have been discovered from Eastern units in the Pannonias, showing many came from Oshroene, Samosata and Apamea, but the names of their wives show they married local women. Their loyalty to their Syrian emperor was unquestioned, their presence amongst the restive northern legions on the Danube could help stabilize the volatile situation or they could be relied upon to help suppress sedition. More positively, the *X Gemina* from Pannonia Superior had regained its honorary title 'Alexandriana' in AD 234. This may have been awarded in response to distinguished service in the war against Ardashir or an attempt to restore its loyalty to the regime. The other legions in the Pannonias conspicuously failed to have this epithet restored. Zosimus confirms the tenuous hold the emperor retained over the loyalty of these legions: '[T]he armies in Pannonia and Moesia, which were far from respecting him previously, now became more disposed to revolt.'[16]

Herodian describes the return west as one made in haste. The army would probably have set off from Antioch in the spring, presupposing the military settlement of the East and the necessary logistical support for the long march home did not delay the departure. The winter snows would have to have cleared, so a departure in April would have led to his arrival on the Rhine in the August of AD 234. The campaign against the Alamanni must thus have been limited to two months at most. The emperor was accompanied by his mother and advisors. Rutilius Crispinus, his chief military advisor, must have been one of these. The inscription recording his *cursus honorum* indicates that at some point he was honoured with a *suffect* consulship, followed by appointment to the governorship of Achaea in Greece. This would be highly surprising now, as the emperor required the services of men of military experience at this time more than any other. The likeliest date for his consulship would be in AD 234, an office served at the side of the emperor. The governorship of Achaea would fall in mid to late AD 235, an appointment made by Maximinus Thrax to effectively banish a powerful supporter of his predecessor to a province lacking a strong military presence; nor would he be in a position to influence senatorial politics in the capital.[17]

The *Historia Augusta* provides a vivid and detailed description of the emperor's triumph in Rome at this time. This also occurs in the late fourth-century historian Festus, who states: 'At Rome, he [Alexander Severus] celebrated with remarkable pomp a triumph over the Persians.' Both probably used a common source. Herodian, however, explicitly states Alexander Severus proceeded directly to the Rhine, which implicitly precludes a visit to Rome. A triumph would have been a significant event, so it is very surprising that it does not appear in his account. It is highly questionable whether this triumph ever took place, but it has been accepted by some historians. The coin issues of AD 233/234 have been used as evidence to support the credibility of these passages. These, as noted, show the emperor crowned by Victory astride the Tigris and Euphrates. Furthermore, coins of Mamaea from this time carry the legend '*Fortuna Redux*'. Another coin issue used to support the case of a triumph shows Alexander Severus holding a branch, accompanied by Victory, in a chariot with horses led by two soldiers either side. This clearly contradicts the account in the *Historia Augusta*, which explicitly states the triumphal chariot was drawn by elephants. The image itself may be symbolic of a triumph over Rome's enemies. These coins are not in themselves firm evidence that the emperor held a triumph. No coin or inscription celebrates the emperor being hailed as 'imperator' by his troops, which would have occurred had he held a triumph. Similar coins were issued before the Eastern campaign in the expectation of victory, and a number of issues were made to propagate the claim of victory but cannot be used as firm proof of a triumph. Coins celebrating the return of fortune could just as easily be celebrating the safe return of the army from the East rather than the actual return of the imperial family to Rome. For example, in Pannonia, Julius Caninus erected an altar to Hercules 'in honour of the safety and return of the Emperor Alexander Severus'. The speech the emperor gave to the Senate in the *Historia Augusta* on his supposed return is claimed by the biographer to be taken from the official records, but this, like all such speeches in the biographies, are dismissed as pure fiction. However, largesse was distributed to the people, referred to on coins as 'LIBERALITAS AUG. QUINTA' and, according to the *Historia Augusta*, the *Mameanae and Mameani* was created, although it is more likely that it was initiated to celebrate the emperor's *decennalia*.[18]

There was little time for a triumph if the emperor had set off west in AD 234. However, some historians believe his army returned west at the end of the campaigning season of AD 233. This appears extremely doubtful. Herodian is clear that the army and the emperor needed an extended period of recovery after being overcome by disease and the rigours of the marches through the Mesopotamian desert and mountains of Armenia. 'On his return to Antioch Alexander made an easy return to health in the refreshing atmosphere of the city with its plentiful water supply after the arid droughts of Mesopotamia.'[19] He also had time to prepare his army for another offensive against Ardashir before hearing of the enemy's demobilization. Upon hearing this welcome news, the emperor reorganized and strengthened the defences in the East, trained his army in preparation for the war against the Germans and re-provisioned the supply depots for his return journey. A single legion of 4,800 men required 7,500kg of grain a day, and the army of Alexander Severus was many times larger. Much of the food would have been concentrated in Syria for the coming campaign rather than along the army's line of march or in the German provinces, whose lands had been devastated by the barbarian invasion. It is difficult to see how there was enough time for all these events to occur between the end of the campaigning season around September in AD 233 and his return to Rome the same year before the winter set in. Herodian continues that even after the 'unofficial peace' had been established with the Sassanids, 'Alexander also stayed in Antioch and devoted himself to the pleasures of the city, growing more cheerful as his worries about the war relaxed'.[20]

C.R. Whittaker, in his notes in the Loeb edition of Herodian, and Brian Campbell, in the Cambridge Ancient History, believe he set off for Rome in the autumn of AD 233 but stayed over the winter in Rome, where he celebrated his triumph before setting off for the war zone in the spring of AD 234.[21] Yet this scenario places the account in the suspect *Historia Augusta* above that of the more reliable Herodian, who explicitly states that the emperor and his army marched directly against the Germans 'at great speed'. It is also difficult to see how the emperor would make such a cardinal error as celebrating a triumph in Rome with soldiers whose families were being slaughtered at the same time by the barbarians in the under-defended German provinces.[22]

Upon his arrival on the banks of the Rhine, the emperor ordered the construction of a bridge of boats, which could have been done rapidly as the boats were lashed together and a rudimentary wooden walkway placed across them. Herodian does not mention this, but it is shown on a coin issue from early AD 235 that celebrated the events of the campaign of the preceding year. The emperor is depicted crossing the bridge of boats over the Rhine, preceded by Victory and followed by his soldiers, one of whom carries the legionary eagle. The reverse shows both the emperor and his mother.[23] This bridge was probably built near his headquarters at Moguntiacum (mod. Mainz). Such a bridge would not have been required if he intended to advance into the Agri Decumates in order to expel the barbarian invaders and recover the province. He clearly intended to attack their heartland, drawing the enemy forces into combat in order to defend their own homes and families. The normal tactic of theses warriors was to engage in guerrilla-style warfare, slipping into the swamps and forests that covered the region. The Roman strategy appears to have been entirely successful, as the Alamanni were forced to offer battle to defend their lands. The emperor took the offensive and advanced into enemy territory. His tactic appears to have been to avoid close combat, destroying the closely packed ranks of soldiers at a distance using the archers and skirmishers armed with javelins. The Alamanni suffered grievously from these missiles as the majority lacked armour, being merely protected by wooden or flimsy wicker shields. When the Germans charged to try to engage their tormentors in close combat, the Roman skirmishers would withdraw and then the archers would find their mark from behind the wall of Roman shields.[24]

The onset of autumn brought an end to the campaign. The heavy rains at this time of year would have strengthened the currents in the Rhine, increasing the likelihood of trees or a heavy torrent destroying the bridge and leaving the army stranded in enemy territory. The bridge itself appears to have been dismantled, as Maximinus Thrax had to reconstruct it when he advanced across the river the following year. This in itself would not have been an onerous or time-consuming task. But now the emperor and his advisors made a fatal misjudgement that all our sources confirm sparked open revolt amongst the Roman army. The emperor opened negotiations with the Alamanni by despatching an embassy offering peace and a subsidy of gold.[25] The terms were probably the same offered by Caracalla, who also appears to have included a subsidy in his offer of peace with this confederation. Herodian describes this as an 'effective bargaining counter'. It was a well-established component of Roman diplomacy. The gold could be used to establish an allied king in a position of authority, who then relied on this subsidy to secure his position. It also removed the necessity to plunder this wealth from Roman territory. An agreement is likely to have been concluded, as the Alamanni had planted crops in their fields, which they would not have done if they expected Roman soldiers to be invading their land.[26]

According to the *Historia Augusta*, the emperor had to face another mutinous situation upon his arrival on the Rhine: '[O]n his arrival he found that there also the legions were ready to mutiny, and accordingly he ordered them to be disbanded.' This is also supported by Aurelius Victor who claims he had to put down many mutinies in 'Gaul'. By Gaul, the historian is referring to the German provinces. Coins bearing the legend '*Fides Militum*' were produced in ever-increasing numbers at this time, a sure sign that the loyalty of the soldiers was suspect.[27] It is likely that the absence of the emperor during this crisis would have resulted in the soldiers looking to a strong leader from the areas under threat to organize resistance to the invasion or a man willing to exploit their fears and resentment in order to further his own ambitions.[28] This is what happened in the East whilst the emperor made his elaborate preparations for war in Rome. However, both sources are late and unreliable, and clearly rely on a common lost source called the *Kaisergeschicte* by historians. However, the claims that Alexander Severus dismissed whole legions have to be rejected. There is no epigraphic evidence to support this, which appears to be an attempt by these historians to erroneously explain the inclusion in the emperor's name of Severus, meaning severe. This is echoed in Eutropius, who asserts that Alexander Severus 'enforced military discipline very severely, cashiering some entire legions which were rebelling'.[29]

There had been no widespread rebellion amongst the soldiers whilst they campaigned successfully against the Alamanni. The emperor may have felt that Roman honour had been restored. The threat to the frontier was not limited to the Rhine, however. The situation in Raetia and Noricum had not been restored, leaving Italy vulnerable to invasion. Furthermore, the campaigns of Maximinus Thrax in Pannonia and against the Sarmatians and free Dacians between AD 236–238 demonstrate that the whole of the Danubian frontier was volatile and unstable. This strategic understanding of the military situation was not a primary concern of many soldiers on the Rhine, even if it greatly concerned their emperor and his advisors. Their blood lust and desire for revenge had not been sated. The Alamanni may have lost many men in battle, but they still had their families, homes and land. Many of the Roman soldiers had lost some, if not all of these. In their eyes, justice had not been served, and now the emperor appeared to be rewarding the very people who had slaughtered their loved ones. Maximinus Thrax understood the situation. Upon his invasion in Alamannic territory, he allowed his men free rein to exact their revenge:

> 'He devastated all the countryside, particularly the ripening corn, and set fire to the villages, which he allowed his army to plunder … Maximinus advanced a long way, acting as described, carrying off plunder and giving the flocks they came across to the soldiers.'[30]

Alexander Severus and his advisors misjudged the mood of his army. They would pay the ultimate price. The rebellion began amongst the newly raised Pannonian recruits. These men, raised from the semi-Romanized inhabitants of this frontier province, had little or no concept of a Roman state or loyalty to a distant emperor. However, they saw their commander, Maximinus Thrax, sharing their burdens, eating their food, sharing combat drills and marching alongside them. This was a well thought out stratagem to raise his own army loyal to him alone. Herodian, almost naively, describes Maximinus Thrax as

> 'discharging his trust [his responsibilities in raising and training new recruits] extremely conscientiously, earning great popularity among the troops because he did not confine himself only to teaching them what to do but also took the lead in all the tasks. As a result they were not just pupils but copied his example of courage. He also won their allegiance still more by awarding them prizes and all kinds of honours. So the young men, of whom the greater majority were Pannonians, admired Maximinus' courage and despised Alexander for being under his mother's control and for the fact that business was conducted on the authority and advice of a woman, while he himself presented a picture of negligence and cowardice in his conduct of war. They reminded themselves of the eastern disasters due to his procrastination and how he had shown no sign of bravery or enthusiasm when he came to Germany.'[31]

These men had not fought in the East, nor in Germany, and certainly had little understanding of the complexities of the imperial government and the supposed influence of Mamaea. This is clearly the propaganda that Maximinus Thrax fed his men, and they lapped it up. Just as Caracalla had presented himself as one of his 'fellow soldiers', sleeping on a soldier's bed, digging ditches and marching on foot, so too did Maximinus. The problem for an emperor was the need to win the support and loyalty of the Senate through *nobilitas* and *dignitas*, demonstrating the bearing, education and lineage of an aristocrat, whilst at the same time earning the loyalty of the common soldier through demonstrations of bravery, *virtus*, courage and military skill.[32] Amongst the latter can be ranked Commodus, Caracalla and Maximinus Thrax, whilst Alexander Severus had spent much of his time mollifying the senatorial class. The supposedly 'good' emperors had managed to find a happy medium between these two opposites: Trajan and Marcus Aurelius amongst them.

The origins of an emperor also influenced the loyalty of soldiers from their native regions. The Severans, and in particular Alexander Severus, relied on the unquestioning loyalty of 'Syrian' soldiers, especially those from Emesa. Units of these men were scattered across the Pannonias in a futile attempt to secure the loyalty of Pannonian units that surrounded them. Soldiers raised in Osrhoene 'bitterly regretted Alexander's death' and rose in revolt against his murderer.[33] Maximinus, whose full official name was Gaius Julius Verus Maximinus, was given the addition 'Thrax', or Thracian, as he was born to a peasant family in the semi-Romanized interior of this province around AD 172. This has been taken to mean that he was born in the tract of territory that bordered the Danube, probably near the Roman colonies of Ratiaria and Oescus. The popularity of Maximinus Thrax amongst his native Thracians, Moesians and Pannonians is reflected in inscriptions. A statue base from Odiavum in Pannonia, raised to honour his son Maximus Caesar, wrongly gives him the title *imperator* in its enthusiastic, laudatory praise. This support for Maximinus Thrax is also found in five statue bases from the Thracian city of Philippopolis. Professions of loyalty recorded on the statue bases are to be expected, but what is surprising is that these honours came from 'excess funds' at a time when the costs of the wars along the Rhine and Danube had forced the emperor to increase taxes on the propertied classes, as well as remove from temples any offerings that were made in precious metals. These wealthy individuals would have been subject to the same vigorous financial constraints, but they were clearly willing to support their Thracian emperor in any way possible.[34]

Many Thracian and Pannonian soldiers are found in the ranks of all the legions along the Rhine, Danube and amongst the 'central reserve' army of the Guard units and *II Parthica* normally based at Rome. Many tombstones around Apamea, where this legion was regularly based during the reigns of Caracalla, Macrinus, Elagabalus and Alexander Severus, carry Thracian names.[35]

Since Septimius Severus, Pannonians also dominated the Praetorian Guard, many of whom were promoted to posts as centurions in the northern legions and commanders of *numeri*, many of whom garrisoned forts along the Rhine. An inscription dated to between AD 215–225 from Monte Sacro on outskirts of Rome provides the full names of fifteen Praetorians, of whom twelve come from Pannonia, Dacia, Moesia and Thrace. A petition was presented to Gordian III (AD 238–244) by a Praetorian, on behalf of his native village of Skaptopara in Thrace, who probably served under Alexander Severus. Soldiers from the provinces of Britain are also well represented. Other inscriptions from the Rhine frontier record the presence of *numeri Brittonum* in a number of forts in Upper Germany, including Odenwald, whilst another from AD 232 from Walldurn was dedicated by the *Brit(tones) gentiles (et) officiales Bri(ttanorum) et deditic(iorum) Alexandrianorum*, a unit of native soldiers from Britain and Germany. A second inscription from the same year identifies their commanding officer as Titus Flavius Romanus, a centurion of the *Legio XXII Primigenia* from Moguntiacum. Another large garrison of two *numeri* stationed at Niederbieber was also commanded by a prefect from Moguntiacum. Vexillations from this legion had served in the East, with many of its legionaries raised along the Danube as well as the hinterland around their base. A further recently discovered tablet records the *diploma* of a legionary from the *Legio XXII Primigenia*. A native of Plotinopolis in Thrace, M. Aurelius Aulusanus was recruited by Caracalla, probably as his army passed through the province, on 28 February AD 215. As he carries the name 'Aurelius', he no doubt gained Roman citizenship through the Antonine Constitution. He would have served under Caracalla, Macrinus and Elagabalus in the East, and then returned to the legionary base at Moguntiacum. He may then have been a member of a vexillation of this legion that accompanied Alexander Severus in his Persian campaign. He will have been a witness to the murder of his emperor, who had his headquarters near the city. What is striking is the fact that all the witnesses to this discharge certificate are veterans from Thrace. These were the military units that were stationed in close proximity to the imperial headquarters.[36]

A detailed study of inscriptions discovered in the two Germanias suggests that 45 per cent of recruits were from the settlements that grew outside the legionary bases at Moguntiacum, Bonna and Argentoratum, the very areas that had suffered most in the Alamanni invasion. Of thirty inscriptions made by centurions from the two German provinces, the origins of thirteen can be ascertained from their names. Three came from either Germania Superior or Inferior, four from veteran colonies in the Pannonias, one from Gaul and six from the East.[37] The imperial army gathered on the Rhine was dominated by soldiers and officers from the northern provinces who had a plethora of reasons to resent their emperor and look to an alternative. Maximinus Thrax appears to have been ordered to base his Pannonian recruits 'not far away' from the emperor's headquarters. This is to some extent supported by the *Historia Augusta*, which states that 'for when he [Maximinus Thrax] was in Gaul [the author considered the two German provinces to be part of the geographical area of Roman Gaul], and had pitched camp not far from a certain city [Moguntiacum], of a sudden the soldiers were incited against him [Alexander Severus], some say by Maximinus, others say by the barbarian tribunes'. The author must be referring to the Pannonians as 'barbarian'. The biographer had the use of a number of sources for the revolt and clearly suspects that the coup was not a spontaneous event, as Maximinus' propaganda would have us believe.[38] This is described in more detail by Herodian, as the recruits

> 'gathered in the open, wearing their armour as though for their usual training, and, as Maximinus came forward to supervise them, they threw the purple, imperial cloak over him and proclaimed him emperor, though it is not clear whether Maximinus himself was aware of what was happening or whether he had planned this secretly. His first reaction was to refuse and throw off the purple cloak, but when they insisted at the point of the sword, threatening to kill him, he preferred to avoid the immediate danger rather than one in the future, and accepting the honour ... He addressed his soldiers and advised them that, although he accepted under protest in spite of himself, because he bowed to their desire, they must back up their decisions by action. They must get hold of their arms and quickly over-power Alexander before the news arrived, while he was still in the dark.'[39]

Both sources are sceptical of Maximinus' feigned ignorance of the planned revolt. His own actions, described in detail by Herodian, clearly demonstrate that it had been prepared long before. His ostentatious reluctance to accept the throne was partly to ascertain the strength of support amongst the recruits and attempt to justify his actions to the supporters of the legitimate emperor once he was in power, especially the senatorial class.[40]

There are some suggestions that the flames of revolt were already burning before Maximinus Thrax made his play. Zosimus' account, which may have been based upon the mid-third-century Athenian historian Dexippus, is in part confused and garbled. The Athenian historian, not appreciating that Maximinus Thrax was already in the vicinity of Moguntiacum, thought that as a commander of Pannonians, he must have raised the revolt somewhere in the two Pannonian provinces. He then has the usurper marching to Rome, where he kills the emperor, whom he initially correctly places on the Rhine before he heads off to confront the army of Maximinus in Italy. Despite this clearly erroneous account, Zosimus' preceding passage appears factually correct and does fit into the historical context. Here he states that 'the armies in Pannonia and Moesia, which were far from respecting him previously, now became more disposed to revolt, and being therefore determined on an innovation, raised to the empire Maximinus, the captain of a Pannonian troop.' He may be referring to vexillations of those armies which had accompanied Alexander Severus to the Rhine. This would make more sense, especially as Maximinus Thrax led a force of Pannonians.[41]

That some form of unrest had already occurred before the revolt is inferred from Maximinus' own actions. In order to win widespread support, the usurper made a public pronouncement that he would double army pay and provide an 'enormous bonus of cash and kind, and cancelled all punishments and marks of disgrace against them'.[42] According to Herodian, the soldiers had become increasingly disaffected with the current regime, as it had become 'unprofitable now that all his munificence had dried up'. Our sources repeatedly accuse Mamaea, and to a lesser extent the emperor, of avarice.[43] The finances of the empire were in a precarious situation before the outbreak of war. For this reason there had been no rise in army pay, although it was wisely decided not to repeat the mistake of Macrinus by reducing it. It is clear, however, that units had been kept under-strength, necessitating the extensive recruitment drive from AD 228 onwards. Now, however, these additional soldiers recruited since AD 229 had to be paid for, as did the road repairs across a large number of provinces, and finances had to be procured to pay for the food and other provisions for the war against the Sassanids and Alamanni. The army had, however, received a distribution of largesse in celebration of the tenth anniversary of the emperor's accession and at the conclusion of the war in the East. Yet the soldiers clearly expected more after the pay rises of Septimius Severus and Caracalla. In times of peace, it would have been difficult to justify these increases, but now, in the minds of the soldiers, it was warranted because they had been constantly fighting since arriving at Antioch in AD 232. These expectations had not been met, leading to accusations of avarice. Furthermore, Maximinus' public amnesty for those soldiers and units that had suffered punishment suggests there was widespread unrest. These men cannot have been his recent recruits, as they would not have served long enough, so this action was directed against units that already served along the Rhine and Danube. This message would have been taken to all the units in the local vicinity and then further afield.

It is extremely doubtful that this experienced and skilful commander would have thought his own recruits, no matter how well trained, could have successfully faced the elite soldiers that constituted the Praetorian Guard. He must have made contact with sympathetic officers in the Guard, the *Legio XXII Primigenia* and *II Parthica* to gauge their level of support for Alexander Severus and likelihood of joining him. The emperor could either face him in open battle or wait for additional support behind the walls of Moguntiacum. Situated as it was behind the Agri Decumates, its walls had not been replaced with stone, as many had along the frontier itself, but were still constructed from wood. They were still strong enough to escape destruction during the Alamannic attacks. The city itself was large. Its amphitheatre, the largest north of the Alps, had capacity for 10,000 people. A number of impressive stone constructions would have dominated its sky line. A large temple to Jupiter, built at the time of Nero, was covered in reliefs of a pantheon of gods and goddess, including Juno, Mars, Neptune, Apollo, Diana, Hercules and Fortuna, surmounted by a bronze statue of Jupiter with a thunderbolt. The emperor, his mother and the imperial court would have worshipped here over the winter months. Another temple to Isis close by supported a ceiling representing the stars, dedicated to Vespasian on the day of his accession to the throne. The *praetorium* which the emperor would have used for his meetings was itself dominated by a triumphal arch raised to celebrate Domitian's defeat of the Chatti. Although employing a more provincial rather than classical style, it showed a legionary holding a spear about to be thrust into the exposed abdomen of a prone barbarian, with two chained prisoners alongside a weeping representation of Germania, distraught at the overwhelming victory of Rome. Many soldiers in the army of Alexander Severus, who had lost all to the Alamanni, must have passed it and wished for a return to those days. The emperor's camp was probably situated in close vicinity to the city. The *Historia Augusta* and Aurelius Victor state that it was located near a village called Sicilia, which is described by Aurelius Victor as a *vicus Britanniae*. A large number of soldiers recruited from Britain garrisoned many of the forts in the Agri Decumates, and it is conceivable that veterans from these units were settled in this area.[44]

Maximinus Thrax acted decisively and with speed. He immediately marched towards the emperor's forces at Moguntiacum. The *Legio XXII Primigenia* garrisoned the city itself, whilst the Praetorians and *Equites Singularii* were probably encamped in close vicinity. This would have been a suicidal act by Maximinus Thrax unless he knew that the emperor's troops were likely to betray him. No doubt the emperor sent despatch riders to summon surrounding units, yet no source mentions any reinforcements arriving to support their emperor. Surprise was a contributory factor, but many of the local forts garrisoned by units of *numeri* were commanded by centurions from the *Legio XXII Primigenia*, which also significantly failed to support the emperor. Furthermore, many of the forts in the Agri Decumates had been destroyed. As peace was being negotiated with the Alamanni, we can expect the majority of his army had been dispersed across the two German provinces and Raetia. The legionary garrisons at Regensberg and Strasbourg were too far away. Herodian's account of the revolt indicates that Maximinus had marched for a day and probably most of the preceding night before arriving at dawn before the emperor's camp.[45]

Herodian gives a graphic description of the reaction of Alexander Severus to news of the revolt. He had clearly assembled the Praetorians on the parade ground after

'rushing out of the imperial tent like a man possessed, weeping and trembling and raving against Maximinus for being unfaithful and ungrateful, recounting all the favours that he had showered upon him. He blamed the recruits for daring to do such a rash thing in violation of their oaths of allegiance; he promised he would give them anything they wanted and put right any complaint. All that day Alexander's own soldiers stood by him with expressions of loyalty and promising they would protect him with all their strength.'[46]

How much of this extraordinary picture can be trusted? Firstly, we can understand the emperor showering the usurper with insults. However, Maximinus had only received imperial favour up to a point. He had been granted the honour of commanding a significant army in the East, perhaps as governor of Mesopotamia. But then he had clearly fallen from favour, being demoted to the post of *praefectus tironibus* with the task of training recruits. The emperor also makes reference to complaints that fit into the historical context. In Herodian's account, the importance of the oath of allegiance which the recruits would have taken around a month after their enlistment does hold true. Such an oath to defend the emperor was sacred, made before the gods. A man who broke this oath invited divine retribution.[47]

That night, the emperor must have slept little. No units came to support him. Nor is there any mention of the *Legio XXII Primigenia* coming to the aid of their emperor. The cover of darkness probably also allowed the agents of Maximinus Thrax to do their work. The first rays of dawn revealed the dust cloud of the approaching forces. As they drew nearer, their battle cries carried to the imperial camp. The Praetorians were once more assembled before the tribunal to be addressed by their emperor. However, Alexander Severus was soon made aware that the wheel of fortune had turned. Discipline and respect demanded that the assembled ranks listen to the emperor's address in silence, only shouting out support at the direction of their centurions. Alexander Severus reminded his Guard of its duty to defend their emperor, a duty they had performed since he was a child. For fourteen years, they had been rewarded and enjoyed a privileged position, and now was the time for them to repay him. Imperial speeches, the *adlocutio*, were meant to be uplifting, confident, heralding an expectation of victory. Yet Herodian describes the tone and content of Alexander Severus' speech as 'begging', a desperate attempt to invoke the sympathy and pity of the assembled soldiers.[48]

Many of these men were Pannonians and Thracians, recruited from the semi-Romanized interiors of the empire's frontier provinces. Many, as the emperor states, would have served throughout his long reign. They had been regularly bribed and bought by Mamaea, and helped raise her son to the throne by murdering his cousin, Elagabalus. Their resultant indiscipline had led to the appointment of Ulpian, tasked with restoring order. They had fought Rome's populace on the streets of the capital and nearly burnt the city to the ground, and then their swords had brutally cut down their Prefect as he sought sanctuary with the emperor and his mother. Their punishments: none. Their Caesar, Seius Sallustius, had vainly sought their support in a coup against the imperial family. Then they had threatened the life of Dio, honoured by their emperor with a second consulship; an office he could not come to Rome to fulfil for fear of being murdered by the Guard. Their ranks had been thinned by the heat and disease of Mesopotamia, but they remained a formidable fighting force. They admired *virtus* more than *nobilitas*. Their emperor was their commander-in-chief, whose martial abilities would dictate success in battle, and ultimately, on his decisions and commands, they either lived or died. This was nothing new. It had been evident to the historian Tacitus, who wrote in the first century AD, that: 'The quality of a good general was the emperor's virtue [*virtus*].'[49] After the huge loss of life in the war against Ardashir, they no longer had any confidence in Alexander Severus' ability as a military commander. Despite his assertions, he was no Septimius Severus or Caracalla. In times of peace, they were willing to accept the claims of imperial propaganda that he was the illegitimate son of their beloved Caracalla. War had changed that. With the emperor's biological legitimacy and martial ability questioned, his position was increasingly threatened by the greater prestige of a successful general. So who had these qualities that the soldiers so valued? None other than Maximinus Thrax.

As the emperor delivered his address, the rebel army appeared on the horizon. The speech was not well received. Instead of respectful silence, shouts could be heard from the ranks. The order issued to collect their weapons was ignored, and instead demands were shouted out. Some demanded the execution of the 'military prefect', others wanted the death of those advisors responsible for the retreat of the central army in the Persian campaign. Amongst these would be the Praetorian Prefect who had accompanied the emperor on campaign and his *amici* who formed the *concilium principis*. Herodian's language is vague, but it is likely the soldiers were referring to the Praetorian Prefect who at this time was possibly M. Attius Cornelianus, who is recorded on an inscription as holding this office in AD 234. According to Zosimus, both Praetorian Prefects died alongside their emperor. As the emperor had been incapacitated by illness, these were the people the Praetorians identified as being responsible for the reverses they had experienced in Mesopotamia. Significantly, his mother was not included in this list of military advisors. However, Mamaea did become the target of their rage. She was accused of 'rapacity and miserliness' over money. As a result of this parsimonious attitude and reluctance to distribute largesse, Alexander was hated. Thus the soldiers remained where they were for some time, shouting out different complaints. The *Historia Augusta* repeats some of the complaints included in Herodian: 'For they hurled many insults at him, speaking of him as a child and his mother as greedy and covetous.' The biographer does refer to an additional rumour that the *amici* of Maximinus spread, suggesting that Mamaea wished to abandon the war against the Germans in order to return with the army to the East. This is described by the biographer as a fiction, but it may have been used as a clever rouse to ferment the northern soldiers' indignation at the ending of the war against the Alamanni without their desire for revenge being satisfied. The added threat of a return to the East, leaving their remaining family and property yet again insecure and vulnerable, would have further fanned the flames of rebellion. Cleverly, this was rumoured to be Mamaea's idea, a person the soldiers despised and were led to believe had an overbearing control over her son.[50]

The forces of Maximinus Thrax were now deployed close to the imperial camp. His followers called out to the Praetorians still assembled behind the ramparts. They urged them to desert, comparing the prestige and military bearing of their leader to the lack of *virtus* exhibited by the emperor. These men were probably sent close to the walls to engage their opponents in a dialogue in order to undermine the last vestiges of loyalty that constrained then. The same tactic had been used by the rebellious legionaries of Maesa and Elagabalus as they shouted down from the walls of Raphanaea to the soldiers of Macrinus' Praetorian Prefect, Julianus, who were assaulting their walls. Alexander Severus was insulted as a 'mean little sissy' or a 'timid little lad tied to his mother's apron strings', in contrast to Maximinus Thrax, who was 'brave and moderate, always their companion in battle and devoted to a life of military action'. The Guard abandoned their emperor and their oath and joined Maximinus Thrax, who they acclaimed emperor. Perhaps by not murdering their emperor themselves, they believed the gods would forgive them.[51]

Alexander Severus had fled to his tent and there awaited his fate, along with his mother and close advisors. Herodian's account drips with pathos, but its authenticity is questionable. The historian readily admits that it was based on 'reports'. All those associated with the emperor were murdered. It was not in his successor's interests to publicize a stoic, final end to the last of the Severans. Herodian describes the young emperor trembling and terrified as he awaited his executioners,

'clinging to his mother and weeping and blaming her for all his misfortunes. After Maximinus had been hailed with the title of Augustus by the whole army, he sent a tribune with some centurions to kill Alexander and his mother and any of his entourage that showed resistance. On arrival they burst into the tent and slaughtered the emperor, his mother and all those thought to be his friends or favourites. Some of them managed to escape or hide for a brief time, but Maximinus soon caught up with them and killed them all.'[52]

This account of his death is in part reflected in the *Historia Augusta*, where the emperor was awoken in his tent but his assassin, losing heart, fled, whereupon his comrades waiting outside rushed in and killed the emperor's companions as they attempted to defend him, and then fell upon the emperor himself, stabbing him many times.[53] The *Epitome De Caesaribus* offers a contrasting account, where the emperor firstly blames his mother for his death and then offers his neck to the soldier so he could end his life swiftly with one blow.[54] It is pointless to conjecture on the last moments of Alexander Severus. What can be said is that instead of attempting to flee in one last frantic and desperate attempt to escape his fate, he waited in his tent with his mother, whom he clearly loved and trusted beyond measure. He was still a young man, 26 years old, and the last of his line. Legitimacy would no longer be based upon the noble blood of the imperial family flowing in the veins of an aspiring emperor, but instead be forged in the fire of battle.

No source specifies the exact date for the death of Alexander Severus. The consensus is that he died around 22 March, based upon the length of his reign cited in Herodian.[55] The large number of coins of Alexander Severus from AD 235 would support this date and undermine the argument of certain historians who suggest the emperor was killed on 8 January. Their premise is based upon an Egyptian papyrus that appears to refer to the Emperor Maximinus Thrax on 25 February. Taking into account the delay in the spread of the news of the assassination from the Rhine to the other side of the empire, they calculate the accession of Maximinus to a date in January. However, the line in the document that this convoluted argument is based upon is missing and is based upon a contested reconstruction. Epigraphic and documentary evidence demonstrates that news of the demise of Alexander Severus had reached Rome on 25 March, where an inscription records the co-option of Maximinus Thrax into the *sodales antoniniani*, and Numidia by 3 May. However, parts of Egypt had still not recorded Maximinus Thrax as emperor on 4 April, and in Dura Europas on 21 June. A date in early January would not sit well with this chronology.[56]

The reign of Alexander Severus was, to most wealthy inhabitants of the empire, a time of political stability and economic prosperity. However, it was increasingly an empire in flux, undergoing great social, cultural and religious change. The poor, the *humiliores*, had less and less of a stake in this society and the economic and political status quo. The Antonine Constitution had little impact on their lives and the emperor remained a distant figure. It was the army that served as both their escape route, through service in the ranks, and also their oppressor. Ever-decreasing resources meant the soldiers increasingly used coercion to gather the food, transport and supplies they needed, whilst the state resorted to austerity measures and increased efficiency in the gathering of taxes and other contributions, including goods in kind, the *annona*. The assassination of the last of the Severans was the tipping point. The regime had faced constant threats to its existence from the Praetorians, and then, after AD 228, from commanders of the army in areas under threat. Yet it had survived for over thirteen years. The decades after AD 235 brought almost constant civil war and barbarian invasions. The two factors are clearly interlinked, and in many ways Alexander Severus was lucky in that he faced no external threats from the commencement of his reign to AD 228. Even after this date, he survived insurrections and revolts for another six years. In such circumstances, the question that needs to be asked is not why the emperor was overthrown, but how did the regime survive so long?

Epilogue

'May you be even more fortunate than Augustus, and even better than
Trajan.'
(Eutropius, 8.5.3, referring to the ritual acclamation of an emperor in
the Senate)

There was no official *damnatio memoriae* issued by the Senate against Alexander Severus and Mamaea. However, their deaths unleashed a frenzied attack upon their images, probably encouraged by Maximinus Thrax. They were later deified by Gordian III, but many of their statues and inscriptions have been deliberately damaged, especially those of Mamaea. Three portraits in the Capitoline Museum and Bochum show evidence of attack. One of the fragmentary statues of Alexander Severus in the Capitoline has been split in half by repeated blows, whilst the other in Bochum has been attacked with a pick axe. A bust in the Louvre has its eyes, brows, nose, mouth and chin mutilated, and another from Ostia was attacked in the same manner using a square hammer. A bronze portrait in the *Museo Nazionale Romano delle Terme* has been vandalized and was then thrown into the River Tiber where it was discovered near the *Ponte Sisto*. This was a deliberate attempt to remove the reign of Alexander Severus from the official record. Most pagans had no concept of an afterlife, and so, in their minds, they only lived on in the memory and records of their deeds. The destruction of the eyes, ears and mouth represents a symbolic attempt to negate the power of the emperor and his mother to communicate with the living from beyond the grave. The attacks on these images were as much a condemnation of the previous regime as an assertion of loyalty to the new one. That Mamaea, like Soamias before her, was such a focus of this violence, perhaps reflects resentment of the power and influence wielded by imperial women in a male-centred world. An attack on her image represented an attack on the empress herself.[1]

The vast majority of the army clearly supported the overthrow of Alexander Severus. His reputation had been initially destroyed by the losses incurred in the East. In this way, military support for Macrinus was undermined by the losses the Romans incurred at the Battle of Nisibis. Even Septimius Severus struggled to contain the resentment of his army after many had been killed or badly injured before the walls of Hatra. Added to this was the devastation caused by the invasion of the Alamanni that left many soldiers from the Rhine burning for revenge for the loss of loved ones and their property. The emperor's decision to seek an accommodation with these invaders before the soldiers' blood lust had been satisfied was the catalyst for the final coup. The Praetorians, however, had never been brought under control. Their proximity to the emperor and his family provided them with immense power and influence. Caracalla had given these soldiers free rein. Alexander Severus appointed Ulpian to restore the discipline that had been undermined by the repeated bribery of Maesa and Mamaea in their attempt to undermine the Guard's loyalty to Elagabalus. Many guardsmen would have considered that the emperor owed his position to their support in AD 222 and their murder of his adopted imperial father. Ulpian, a legal expert with little military experience, was not the right man for such a responsibility, but he was loyal, and he paid a heavy price for his loyalty. It was to the Praetorians that the Caesar, Seius Sallustius, turned in his last desperate throw of the dice in his attempt to gain the honours and prestige he felt his office deserved. The Praetorians retained close links with their comrades in the northern legions, especially Pannonia and Moesia, leading to their threats to murder Dio, another loyal *amicus* appointed to restore order in the legions. Yet the emperor survived, until the Guards' resentment at what they had suffered from heat and disease in the Persian campaign reached boiling point.

J.B. Campbell asserts that Alexander Severus was the first emperor to be overthrown by purely military discontent on a wide scale due to the failure of his military duties. This is not entirely accurate, as the revolt against Macrinus was in part due to the damage incurred to his military reputation. Yet Alexander Severus' demise was primarily due to this reason. The soldiers considered their emperor as first and foremost their commander-in-chief. They wanted a strong leader who not only guaranteed their privileges and pay, but most importantly would not endanger their lives, or those of their loved ones, through poor decision-making or a lack of martial courage (*virtus*). Essentially, they considered that Alexander Severus had made serious mistakes, either through inexperience, cowardice or the supposed overbearing influence of his mother. As the emperor remained for the majority of his reign in Rome, distant from the concentration of military forces at the periphery of the empire, most soldiers only learned of their emperor through the propaganda messages on their coins, imperial proclamations and gossip.[2] That rumours and gossip spread like a disease through the army pervades our sources. Alexander Severus was said to be a 'sissy', a boy 'tied to his mother's apron strings'. Gossip is not based on fact. The revolts in Mesopotamia were a direct result of the prolonged absence of the emperor from the point of crisis. However, he was also accused of retreating from Mesopotamia, allowing the southern army to be annihilated by Ardashir. The facts, however, clearly show that he fell back only after receiving the news of the defeat of the southern arm of his invasion forces. Once again, rumour and invective appear to have distorted the true chronology of events in the minds of the soldiers. The regime was also accused of avarice and greed, despite largesse distributed by the emperor before his departure from Rome to celebrate the tenth anniversary of his accession to the throne, and again after the conclusion of the Eastern war. No doubt much of this was black propaganda spread by Maximinus Thrax before his revolt and distributed more widely upon his seizure of the throne. Had the reign of Alexander Severus been blessed with peace, as it had between AD 223–228, he might have survived into middle age. However, he was not more fortunate than Augustus, nor a better general than Trajan.

Yet an emperor cannot survive for more than thirteen years without a foundation of support and control. That came from the senatorial and equestrian elite. Commodus and Caracalla had been murdered by those with greatest access to them – members of the courtly circle. Such a threat never appears to have been a concern to Alexander Severus. The plot of the aristocratic senator Camillus in the *Historia Augusta* has been dismissed as pure fiction.[3] The aristocracy were given the access to the emperor they craved and the imperial *beneficia* they desired, such as the great offices of state that enhanced their *dignitas* and prestige. This was the key to the stability of the regime until the outbreak of war. Those aristocratic families who had been alienated by Caracalla, Macrinus and Elagabalus were invited back into the courtly circle, provided with imperial access and honours. Seneca describes these bonds of patronage in terms of *amicitiae* (friendship). In a practice that dated back to C. Gracchus in the second century BC, *amici*, or friends, were divided into three groups for the morning *salutatio* (greeting). Those of lesser status who were treated as social inferiors were termed clients and were admitted to their patron's presence en masse. They would often be the last group admitted to the large entrance hall, the *atrium*, of the prestigious houses of the wealthy. Due to their numbers, they were unlikely to be granted the opportunity to pass on their requests and petitions personally. The second group were the 'lesser *amici*', who would be granted an audience in small groups. The most prestigious group were the *amici*, who were treated, at least superficially, as equals. These were received in private on a one-to-one basis, and so had time and opportunity to present their requests in surroundings that were more conducive for success. The emperor's *amici* would also increase their own network of *amici* and clients through access to the emperor. They were called upon for advice and served on the *concilium principis*, calling themselves *amici Caesaris*, the friends of the emperor. The problem for the emperor was that only a few aristocrats could be granted this honour. The imaginative solution of Mamaea was to create the senatorial council, which further extended imperial *beneficia* to a significant proportion of the leading senators. All our sources agree that political power rested solely with the emperor, and earlier in the reign his mother and grandmother, with the council, when summoned, merely being consulted for advice. Its function was to provide a wider opportunity to enhance the *dignitas* and honours available to more members of the aristocratic elite. It did not, in any way, represent a dilution of the powers of the emperor.[4]

It is no surprise that the influence and power of imperial freedmen was greatly reduced, as this caused considerable friction with the elite. Imperial propaganda proclaimed a restoration of the Augustan settlement, where, in theory at least, the *Princeps* held power at the legal acquiescence of the Senate. The term *Princeps* was itself an attempt to hide the real power of the emperor, casting himself merely as the 'first among equals'. This fictional facade of equality between the emperor and the senatorial elite was a part played to perfection by the supposed 'good' emperors, including Augustus and Marcus Aurelius. This role was also well played by Alexander Severus. The aristocracy mourned his loss. Upon his death, an equestrian held the throne. The prolonged presence of Maximinus Thrax on the Rhine and Danube denied the aristocracy access to him. He was equally suspicious of their loyalty, Herodian describing him as being 'afraid' of the Senate. The new emperor

'immediately disposed of all friends accompanying Alexander, members of the council selected by the Senate; some were sent to Rome, others he removed from the administration on some excuse. He wanted to be left on his own surrounded by his army, without anyone being near him who had the advantage of being aware of their own nobility. ... The entire serving staff, who had been with Alexander for many years, were dismissed from court. Most of them were executed on suspicion of treason since Maximinus knew they mourned the loss of Alexander.'[5]

Loss of influence led a number of the *amici* of Alexander Severus to revolt. Titius Quartinus, probably the governor of Germania Superior, was involved in a failed plot by Osrhoenian archers. He is described as 'one of Alexander's consular friends'.[6] Another conspiracy was formed by 'A man called Magnus, a patrician consular, [who] was accused of gathering together a group round himself and prompting some soldiers to transfer power to himself.' He planned to trap Maximinus Thrax in enemy territory by destroying the bridge across the Rhine once the army had crossed it. Clearly a senator of noble lineage, he has been tentatively identified as C. Petronius Magnus, who was a praetor under Caracalla and appears at number fourteen in the rankings for the patrons of Canusium in AD 223.[7] Maximinus Thrax would eventually be overthrown in AD 238 by revolts in Africa and Rome, initiated by many senators who had served under Alexander Severus, including M. Antonius Gordianus Sempronianus, a *suffect* consul in AD 222,[8] and

the military commander in the East, Rutilius Pudens Crispinus.[9] Other aristocrats involved in the coup include Appius Claudius Julianus, the Prefect of Rome
in AD 233 and head of the list of patrons of Canusium in that year, L. Bruttius
Crispinus (ordinary consul in AD 224), C. Bruttius Praesens (ordinary consul in
AD 217), L. Didius Marinus, who had married Commodus' sister, Cornificia, and
as the probable Prefect of the Annona in AD 223 was a member of the imperial
concilium, as well as Alexander Severus' old Praetorian Prefects *adlected* into the
Senate, L. Aedinius Julianus and L. Domitius Honoratus. The two men appointed
by the Senate to replace Maximinus Thrax on the imperial throne had held a number of posts under Alexander Severus. M. Clodius Pupienus Maximus had been
honoured with a proconsular governorship of Asia and a second consulship in
AD 234, followed by the prefecture of Rome in the same year. Whilst the details of
D. Caelius Calvius Balbinus' career are now lost, he probably held a second consulship in AD 213. Another member of the twenty aristocratic senators appointed by
that body to organize resistance to Maximinus Thrax was L. Caseonius Lucillus
Macer Rufinianus, who was a *comes* of the emperor. This strata of society clearly
had much invested in the Alexandrian regime and provided it with political
stability.[10]

Many senators were also from the East, like their emperor himself, as well as
many of the equestrian administrators, including Ulpian. These senators and officials retained close links to their provinces and cities of origin. Often, like Cassius
Dio, they kept vast estates in their native lands and became patrons of its towns
and cities. The Greeks saw themselves as the true embodiment of the Classical
tradition, the exercise of the mind in terms of philosophical and rhetorical thought.
The aristocratic elite considered education and training in rhetoric, grammar and
philosophy as a necessity for all those who belonged to the elite. This cultural and
intellectual ideal was termed *paideia* and was personified in the figure of the great
philosopher emperor Marcus Aurelius.[11] In stark contrast to Elagabalus, Mamaea
conscientiously had her son educated in the classics, courting the support of Rome's
nobility. The empress and the emperor both continued to encourage the late flowering of Greek culture, as embodied in the Second Sophist movement which ended
with their deaths. An intellectual and theological openness prevailed throughout
the empire, to the extent that a Christian theologian was invited to court, which
according to the Church historian Eusebius, already consisted of many Christians.

There is a significant lack of images that depict the emperor in military attire.
His sculptures show him with the short military haircut, but he carries a serene
and calm expression, in contrast to the intense and forceful images of Caracalla and
Maximinus Thrax. Emphasis is placed upon the emperor's senatorial and constitutional role.[12] Only after c. AD 229 does an increase in martial themes occur, especially
in the propaganda images and legends on coin issues.[13] The increased militarization

in the regime's coinage is mirrored by the intensive preparations for the war against Ardashir. An issue of AD 229 shows Jupiter, now increasingly found on coins, clothed in armour, with the emperor similarly dressed in military garb receiving an orb from the god; behind stands a soldier and Mars leaning on a shield. The legend betrays increasing popular concern over the outcome of the forthcoming campaign, but also hints at their resentment at the increased exactions by the state to fund and resource the great armies on the move: FELICITATI POPULI ROMANI (the happiness of the Roman people).[14] The appearance of Jupiter emphasizes divine confirmation of the legitimacy of Alexander Severus' claim to the throne. This coin reflects the emperor's understanding of the threats to his rule at this time: his lack of military experience in the eyes of both the army and civilians; his contrived legitimacy based on the dubious claim to be the illegitimate son of Caracalla, and the limited nature of resources the state was able to draw upon in this time of crisis.

The effects of the Antonine plague continued to echo throughout the early third century. Increased taxation on the wealthy land-owning elite would have undermined their support for the regime, which had been constructed over the preceding seven years. Instead, state officials and officers placed larger demands on the provincials. The socio-economic gap between rich and poor grew ever wider, with the state increasingly serving the interests of the upper strata of society whilst the poor were reduced in both social and legal terms to a status little better than slaves. This change is reflected in the increase in brigandage throughout the third century and the multitude of legal distinctions between the *humiliores* as opposed to the property-owning *honestiores*. The heavy demands made on the monetary supply and a refusal to reduce the amount of precious metal in the coinage led to an increased reliance on payment in kind, the military *annona*. This inevitably led to further conflict with the rural peasantry. Appeals to the emperor and an array of imperial edicts on this issue reflect the extent of this conflict. The soldiers took what they felt they required, or more likely believed they deserved, but accusations of avarice levelled against the emperor and his mother may reflect the soldiers' resentment at their remuneration in this manner. Puzzlingly, Herodian twice describes the emperor making a 'generous distribution of money' to the soldiers, the first just before their departure from Rome and the second on his return to Antioch in AD 233.[15] It therefore seems surprising that accusations of avarice can be levelled against him and his mother. Their grievance may have lain in them receiving part of their pay in the form of food, or they could have resented the fact that many units before AD 228 appear to have been retained at less than full strength. This was a short-sighted money-saving measure that demoralized the soldiers serving in under-strength units, with its potential effect on combat effectiveness. At the same time, soldiers were increasingly being used to enforce edicts, act as police, collect provisions and combat brigands.

In the times of peace from AD 222–228, Alexander Severus cleverly developed his role as *Princeps* that made him acceptable to the senatorial class, but failed to combine this role with that of the 'fellow soldier'.[16] Few emperors managed to combine these roles well, yet some did: Trajan and Marcus Aurelius among them. The Praetorians' ties to his family, in particular his claims to be the son of Caracalla, may have served to mollify their unruly behaviours. However, such claims had not saved Elagabalus. What many of the disenchanted and embittered probably lacked for the majority of his reign was a suitable imperial alternative and a situation that could be readily exploited. When Seius Sallustius paraded himself before the Guard in AD 227, the Praetorians remained loyal. A wealthy senator from a noble family was clearly not the type of candidate they felt was deserving of their support. We know little of his background, save the fact he was from a patrician family.[17] Whatever military experience he had, if any, clearly failed to impress the Praetorians. Significantly, Seius Sallustius did not direct his criticisms at Alexander Severus himself, yet there can be little doubt that he would have done if it had served his purpose. The Praetorians had ample opportunity to murder the emperor, the first occasion when Ulpian was slaughtered in the imperial presence and then upon the attempted coup of Seius Sallustius. His attempt to use antagonisms towards Mamaea hints at desperation and a benevolent attachment to the 'son' of Caracalla. Alexander Severus' military qualities had also yet to be tested. The coup failed as Seius Sallustius was perceived to lack the necessary qualities and experience in the eyes of the soldiers. This would also be the undoing of the emperor himself.

War regularly provided the soldiers with men who had the opportunity to prove themselves in the eyes of their armies. Avidius Cassius, the successful general of Lucius Verus in the Parthian War (AD 162–166), had used his military renown to raise the standard of revolt in AD 175 against Marcus Aurelius. The majority of the Eastern legions that had fought under him acclaimed him emperor. The early revolts against Elagabalus were led by men of military experience such as Verus and Castinus. At the start of Alexander Severus' reign, the Praetorian Prefects Chrestus and Flavianus were considered a real and considerable threat due to their proven *virtus* and admiration they inspired in their men. Their rapid execution reflects this, whereas Ulpian, whose loyalty was without question, lacked any significant military record and so engendered such hostility in the ranks of the Praetorians.

The absence of the emperor at a time of crisis often led to the soldiers turning to a leader closer to hand. The usurpers Taurinus and Uranius were raised to the purple by soldiers and civilians in Mesopotamia and Syria in response to the pressure of Ardashir. Yet these men lacked widespread support, and the eventual arrival of the vast army of Alexander Severus led to their downfall. Maximinus Thrax was a military man, the first of the 'soldier emperors'. He was clearly seen as a man with extensive military experience, but the details of that career are based on conjecture due to the problematic nature of our sources. According to Herodian, he started his career in the cavalry and then, under Septimius Severus, may have been transferred into the *equites singulares*, the Guard cavalry, based upon a suspect passage in the *Historia Augusta*. At some point he gained his citizenship, perhaps as a reward for bravery on the field of battle. He then served in the legions, probably initially as a centurion, rising to the post of *primus pilius*, the foremost legionary centurion. He was then promoted to the equestrian class and pursued a career as an officer. He perhaps served in Egypt in AD 232 as *praefectus legionis II Traianae* or as *praefectus castrorum*.[18] The appointment of such an equestrian officer with extensive military experience to the governorship of the strategic province of Mesopotamia is entirely feasible. If he successfully held this province against the incursions of Ardashir as the sick emperor and his debilitated army, racked as it was by disease and heat exhaustion, made its retreat to Antioch, his reputation would have constituted a real and viable threat to the emperor. Here was a man whose *virtus* eclipsed the damaged martial image of Alexander Severus. The appointment to the post of *praefectus tironibus* with responsibility for recruitment was clearly a demotion, yet it provided Maximinus Thrax with an opportunity that he seized with both hands.

The war against Ardashir and the devastation caused by the Alamannic invasion across the Rhine damaged the military standing of Alexander Severus, and his advisors, so completely that an army revolt was almost inevitable. The coup was not based around a few units or legions, but was so widespread that his position as a leader in times of war had become untenable. The army was not concerned in times of conflict with the legal niceties of an emperor descended from the imperial house. Nor did the Roman soldier consider their emperor's right to rule coming from a senatorial decree.[19] The emperor, in times of crisis, was their *imperator*, their commander-in-chief, and as such the throne had to be occupied by a man of proven military ability and *virtus*. Alexander Severus' generous distributions of money were ineffective, as they questioned his ability as a general and his bravery. To a soldier, money was of no use when you were dead. Much of the army believed, incorrectly, that their emperor's decisions had cost them the lives of many of their comrades in the East and their families on the Rhine. Moreover, an alternative was readily available, a proven general, who would not risk their lives unnecessarily. He was the embodiment of a 'fellow soldier'.

The senatorial historian Dio describes the Roman army as little more than a rabble, with soldiers more willing to desert than fight, who 'indulge in such wantonness, licence and lack of discipline' that whole provinces fell to the invader.[20] This picture has been coloured by his own experiences in Pannonia and his humiliation in not being able to hold his consulship in Rome alongside the emperor.

Yet the Roman army remained a formidable fighting force. Ardashir had been unable to make any significant gains, and his possessions in central and southern Mesopotamia were left strategically vulnerable due to the Roman occupation of Hatra. Furthermore, the Sassanids had lost a similar amount of soldiers as the Romans. Although the southern army had been completely destroyed, this was primarily due to the over-confidence and negligence of its commander rather than a lack of fortitude or bravery on the part of the soldiers themselves. Rome's alliance with Armenia also opened up further attacks on Media. Ardashir sought to redress this disadvantageous strategic situation during the reigns of Maximinus Thrax and Gordian III. The army of Alexander Severus that Maximinus Thrax now led across the Rhine also left a path of devastation through and beyond the territory of the Alamanni. Herodian describes how the Romans 'advanced deep into the country'.[21]

A recent archaeological discovery has shown this campaign in another light. Since 2008, German archaeologists have been excavating a Roman battle site littered with the debris of war, including arrow heads, bolts from the *scorpio* or *Cheiroballistra*, nails from Roman boots and chain mail. Artefacts from Roman carts suggest these were used to transport the artillery or were the remains of wagons from the baggage train destroyed in the initial attack. A number of coins were excavated from the reigns of Elagabalus and Alexander Severus. As there are no historical records of a Roman attack into Germany during the reign of Alexander Severus' predecessor, and Alexander Severus only had time for a brief attack on enemy territory in AD 234, the battle has been dated to the campaign of Maximinus Thrax in AD 235. A Roman column numbering around 1,000 soldiers had been campaigning deep in *barbaricum*, hundreds of miles from the Roman frontier. They were a small component of a larger force that had advanced along a wide front. The army was returning home when this column appears to have been ambushed as it passed into a narrow valley between two ridges near Harzhorn hill in the modern state of Lower Saxony. The concentration of bolts and arrow heads suggests the Romans initially concentrated their fire at the incline above the pass, which was defended by a shield wall. These bolts, however, can easily pass through wooden shields, so the Germans no doubt incurred considerable losses. The Romans then charged the shield wall, marked by the discovery of a large number of hob nails from the soldiers' boots, and after a brief struggle the Germans retreated to the top of the ridge. This allowed the Romans to manoeuvre through the pass and attack the hill from both north and south. A second concentration of arrows found along the top of the ridge was fired from both the enemy's front and rear. It is estimated the battle was over within an hour.[22] This suggests that the Roman army remained a highly effective and disciplined fighting machine.

Herodian describes this war as one of skirmishes until the Germans chose to engage the main army. Maximinus Thrax was lured into a swamp where, isolated, he fought with great bravery. His example inspired his men, who had been reluctant to enter the water until this point, and they rallied and charged into the waters to support him. Casualties were heavy but the Germans were overcome.[23] The imperial headquarters were then moved to Sirmium on the Danube, where victorious campaigns were fought against the Sarmatians and free Dacians. The facts appear to contradict Dio's contemptuous dismissal of the quality of the Roman army. However, as with all armies, it needed to be well led and its soldiers needed to have confidence in their commander. The military leadership of Alexander Severus was sound and, as his preparations for the Eastern campaign demonstrate, he was thorough but ponderous and uninspiring.

The empire was increasingly faced with attacks on a number of fronts, each requiring the presence of the emperor. This problem was initially solved by the emperor appointing a Caesar, normally a close family member or son, to represent the central imperial authority. However, as the crises along Rome's borders multiplied, with numerous incursions, even this solution proved unsatisfactory. The establishment of the tetrarchy under Diocletian in the late third century stabilized the situation. It is far too simplistic to point to failures in military discipline or question the loyalty of the soldiers as a primary reason for the third-century crisis. This age of insurrection was born from the military, political and social stresses resulting from the massive migrations beyond and then through Rome's borders. Like many of his predecessors, Alexander Severus and his advisors looked to restore a supposed golden age that existed in a different, more tranquil time, when the emperor resided in Rome, governing a peaceful and stable realm, predominantly for the benefit of the wealthy landowning elite. It has to be said that the emperor had the ability to provide the honours, offices and symbols of status that kept this social elite satisfied and loyal, more so than Domitian, Commodus or Caracalla. However, war placed greater power into the hands of the army as the emperor's physical proximity to the legions led to the soldiers' ever-increasing leverage in the power politics of the third century. This was Alexander Severus' failing. He had never truly courted the loyalty of the Roman soldier, born in the semi-Romanized fringes of empire where life was, in the words of Thomas Hobbs, 'nasty, brutish and short'.[24] Alexander Severus may have been their *imperator*, their commander-in-chief, but he was never their 'fellow soldier'.

End Notes

Chapter 1: Murderers and Usurpers AD 192–211

1. Suetonius, *Life of Domitian*, 21.
2. Jones, B.W., *The Emperor Domitian* (Routledge, 1993), pp.193–96.
3. Dio (Loeb, trans. Earnest Cary), 73.22.6.
4. Herodian (Loeb, trans. C.R. Whittaker), 1.5.5.
5. Norena, Carlos F., *Imperial Ideas in the Roman West: Representation, Circulation, Power* (Cambridge, 2011), p.232, n.134, 135; Herodian (Loeb), 1.5.5, p.25 n.4, citing ILS 398.
6. Dio, 74.3.1.
7. Herodian, 2.3.3.
8. Dio, 74.3.4.
9. Dio, *74.11.1-6;* Herodian, *2.6.5-13;* Historia Augusta, *Didius Julianus*, 2.6.
10. HA, *Didius Julianus*, 2.7.
11. Tacitus, *The Histories*, 1.4.
12. HA, *Clodius Albinus*, 1.3; Herodian, 1.10.3, 2.7.5, 2.15.1; Dio, 72.8.1.
13. Herodian, 2.9.12; Birley, A., *The African Emperor Septimius Severus*, (B.T. Batsford Ltd, 1988), p.97; www.Roman-Britain.org, citing RIB 591 (Ribchester) and RIB 1151 (Corbridge).
14. Herodian, 2.7.7-8.
15. Herodian (Loeb), p.187 n.2.
16. Herodian 2.7.1-6; Dio 74.14.1, 16.5, 17.2; HA, *Didius Julianus*, 2.6.
17. Herodian (Loeb), p.181 n.2.
18. Dio, 74.16.2.
19. Herodian, 2.7.2-5.
20. Dio, 74.13.4-5; hand signal, Dio, 61.32.1; rhythmic swing of acclaim in amphitheatre, Dio, 74.2.3; HA, *Didius Julianus*, 4.7-10; Aulus Gellius, *Attic Nights*, 5.14.19; Whittaker, C.R., 'The Revolt of Papirius Dionysius AD 191', *Historia: Zeitschrift für Alte Geschichte Bd.13*, H.3 (July 1964), pp.348–69, published by Franz Steiner Verlag; use of clients as agents to stir up unrest, see Africa, Thomas W., 'Urban Violence in Ancient Rome', *The Journal of Interdisciplinary History*, Vol 2 No 1 (summer 1971), pp.3–21, published by The MIT Press.
21. Dio, 74.15.2; Herodian, 2.7.6.
22. Herodian, 2.7.5, p.184–85 n.2, n.3.
23. Dio, 75.6.2; Herodian, 2.7.5.

24. HA, *Niger*, 6.8-9; McHugh, J., *The Emperor Commodus: God and Gladiator* (Pen and Sword, 2015), pp.66, 132, 157, 172, 208, 230–31, 245–46.
25. Dio, 75.9.2-4.
26. Dio, 75.6.1; Birley, *The African Emperor Septimius Severus*, pp.108, 212, 241 n.12.
27. Herodian, 2.7.8.
28. Syme, R., *The Roman Revolution* (Oxford University Press, 1979), p.386; Saller, R.P., *Personal Patronage under the Early Empire* (Cambridge University Press, 2002), pp.29, 50; Winterling, Aloys, *Politics and Society in Imperial Rome* (Wiley-Blackwell, 2009), pp.28–33; Ste Croix, G.E.M. de, 'Suffragum', *British Journal of Sociology*, 5, 1954, pp.33, 40; Pliny, *Letters*, 2.9.2, 10.5, 10.6, 10.58.7-9, HA, *Septimius Severus*, 1.5.
29. HA, *Septimius Severus*, 5.2.
30. Vegetius, *Epitoma Rei Militaris*, c.383, in Campbell, J.B., *The Emperor and the Roman Army 31 BC-235 AD* (Clarendon Press Oxford, 1984), p.23.
31. Epictetus, 1.14.15.
32. Philostratus, *Life of Apollonius of Tyana*, 5.35.
33. Tertullian, *Apolegeticus*, 16.8; Campbell, *The Emperor and the Roman Army 31 BC-235 AD*, pp.97–99.
34. Seneca, *Letters*, 95.35.
35. HA, *Septimius Severus*, 5.4, 'he was universally regarded as the avenger of Pertinax'.
36. Campbell, *The Emperor and the Roman Army*, p.198.
37. Tacitus, *Annals*, 1.6.
38. Dio, 75.8.4; Herodian, 2.7.9-10, p.188 n.1.
39. Herodian, 2.9.9, 3.2.3; Ando, Clifford, '*Imperial Rome AD 193 to 284: The Critical Century* (Edinburgh University Press, 2012), p.31.
40. HA, *Septimius Severus*, 5; HA, *Didius Julianus*, 6–7; Herodian, 2.12.1-13.2; Dio, 74.16.1-17.6.
41. Dio, 75.1.1-2; Herodian, 2.13 2–12; HA, *Septimius Severus*, 7.1-2.
42. HA, *Septimius Severus*, 7.2.
43. Herodian, 2.2.3, 8.6.7; Whittaker, C.R., 'The Revolt of Papirius Dionysius AD 191', pp.348–69.
44. Dio, 75.2.3; HA, *Septimius Severus*, 7.3.
45. Elliot, Paul, *Legions In Crisis: transformation of the Roman Soldier AD 192–284* (Fonthill, 2014) pp.23, 62–63, 151–53.
46. Oliva, Pavel, 'Pannonia and the Onset of Crisis in the Roman Empire', in *Nakladatelstvi Ceskovenske*, akademie ved Praha, 1962, pp.166–67, 256, 303–04 n.139, 345, 348–49.
47. Bingham, Sandra, *The Praetorian Guard: A History of Rome's Special Forces* (I.B. Taurus, 2013), pp.17, 56.
48. Dio, 75.2.6.
49. Dio, 74.8.1; Herodian, 2.4.1, 2.4.4; Juvenal, 5.16.10-13.

50. Dio, 77.15.2-3, 75.2.3.
51. Watson, G.R., *The Roman Soldier*, (Thames and Hudson, 1981), pp.91, 98–99.
52. Smith, R.E., 'The Army Reforms of Septimius Severus', *Historia Bd.*, 21, H.3 (3rd Qtr 1972), pp.481–500.
53. Herodian, 3.8.4-5, p.309 n.4; de Blois, Lukas, 'The Third Century Crisis and the Greek Elite in the Roman Empire', *Historia Bd.*, 33, H.3 (3rd Qtr, 1984), p.373; Spiedel, M. Alexander, 'Roman Army Pay Scales', *The Journal of Roman Studies*, Vol. 82 (1992), pp.87–106, published by Society for the Promotion of Roman Studies; Hekster, Oliver, *Rome and its Empire* AD *193–284* (Edinburgh University Press, 2008), p.39; Smith, 'The Army Reforms of Septimius Severus', pp.481–500; MacMullen, R., *Soldier and Civilian in the Later Roman Empire* (Harvard University Press, 1963), p.116, comments on difficulty of recruiting soldiers from the end of the second century.
54. Birley, *The African Emperor Septimius Severus*, pp.108–10; Campbell, *The Emperor and the Roman Army*, p.6; Herodian, 3.2.1-3, p.186 n.1, p.253 n.2; Dio, 75.6.4-6, 75.7.3-8.5.
55. Birley, *The African Emperor Septimius Severus*, pp.117–18.
56. Ando, *Imperial Rome* AD *193 to 284*, p.37, quoting ILS 418.
57. Herodian, 3.5.2-8.
58. Dio ,76.7.1-3.
59. Dio, 76.8.1-4; Herodian, 3.8.3.
60. HA, *Septimius Severus*, 12.4, n.1 in Herodian, Loeb edition, p.306.
61. Birley, *The African Emperor Septimius Severus*, pp.129–32; Dignas, Beate, & Winter, Englebert, *Rome and Persia in Late Antiquity: Neighbours and Rivals* (Cambridge University Press, 2008) p.15.
62. Dio, 76.9.3.
63. Herodian, 3.9.3.
64. Herodian, p.320, n.1; Ando, *Imperial Rome* AD *193 to 284*, p.1; Mennen, Inge, *Power and Status in the Roman Empire* AD *193–284* (Brill, 2011), pp.213–15.
65. Herodian, 3.9.5.
66. Campbell, *The Emperor and the Roman Army*, pp.6–7; Birley, *The African Emperor Septimius Severus*, p.131; Dio, 76.10.1-12.5; HA, *Septimius Severus*, 16.5.
67. Aurelius Victor, *De Ceasaribus*, 20.29.

Chapter 2: Conspiracy AD 211–217

1. Birley, A., *Septimius Severus*, pp.177, 221 n.36; HA, *Alexander Severus*, 1.3; Dio, 79.30.3; Herodian, 5.3.3, 5.7.4, n.3 p.19.
2. Cleve, Robert L., 'Some Male relatives of the Severan Women', *Historia* Bd 37, H.2 (2nd Qtr 1988), pp.196–206; Ertel, Andrea Beverly, 'The Life of Severus Alexander', Thesis for MA, McMaster University 1984, University of British

Columbia 1986 (UBC_1986_A8 E77 Turinus) pp.17–19; Williams, Mary Gilmore, 'Studies in the Lives of Roman Empresses: Julia Mamaea', *Roman Historical Sources and Institutions*, H.A. Sanders (ed.) (New York, 1904), p.68; Birley, A, *Septimius Severus*, p.222 n.37, both citing Digest 1.19.12; Dio, 79.31.4. HA, *Maximinus Thrax*, 29, refers to a further daughter, Theoclia, but this is entirely fictitious, having no other ancient or epigraphical sources to support it.

3. Dio, 79.30.3; Herodian, 5.3.2.

4. Levick, Barbara, *Julia Domna: Syrian Empress* (Routledge, 2007), pp.9–10,13–14, 171 n.60. Epitome Caesaribus, 21.1, probably using the work of the contemporary historian Marius Maximus; Birley, A., *Septimius Severus*, pp.221–24 n34–50; Cleve, Robert L., 'Some Male relatives of the Severan Women', pp.196–99; Herodian, 5.7.3, p58–59 n.1–2.

5. Herodian, 5.3.3.

6. Levick, Barbara, *Julia Domna*, p.93, citing IGR 4, 1287.

7. Herodian, 5.3.3, n.4 p.19, 5.3.6.

8. Herodian, 5.3.4; Levick, Barbara, *Julia Domna*, pp.15–16 & Fig.1.2 showing Emesene coinage carrying image of Julia Domna on obverse and altar on reverse (BMC Galatica, p.253 no.9), p.21, coin showing bust of Caracalla on obverse with image of temple on reverse; Butcher, Kevin, *Roman Syria and the Near East* (The British Museum Press, 2003), pp.338–44; Turcan, Robert, *The Cults of the Roman Empire* (Blackwell, 1996), pp.176–77.

9. Herodian, 5.3.8; Butcher, Kevin, *Roman Syria and the Near East*, p.347.

10. Herodian, 5.3.5.

11. Turcan, Robert, *The Cults of the Roman Empire*, pp.177–78; Ando, Clifford, *Imperial Rome* AD *193 to 284*, p. 112. Dio, 78.3.2.

13. Dio, 78.13.1; Campbell, J.B., *The Emperor and the Roman Army*, pp.13–18, 93.

14. Ando, Clifford, *Imperial Rome* AD *193 to 284*, pp.56–57; Bowman, Alan K., Garnsey, Peter, and Cameron, Averil, *The Cambridge Ancient History: The Crisis of Empire* AD *193–337, Volume XII* (Cambridge University Press, 2007), p.18; Campbell, J.B., *The Emperor and the Roman Army*, pp.162, 170–71.

15. Honore, Tony, *Ulpian: Pioneer of Human Rights* (Oxford University Press, 2002), pp.23–27.

16. Honore, Tony, *Ulpian: Pioneer of Human Rights*, p.5.

17. Dio, 77.15.2; HA, *Septimius Severus*, 15.4-6.

18. Mennen, Inge, Power *and Status in the Roman Empire*, p.215.

19. Dio, 78.12.3.

20. Dio, 78.23.2-24.1.1; HA, *Caracalla*, 6.2-4; Herodian, 4.9.4-8.

21. Herodian, 4.11.1-6; Dio, 79.1.1.

22. Dio, 79.4.1-5.5, 79.13.4; HA, *Caracalla*, 6.4-7.2, n.2-7 pp.18-19; Herodian, 4.12-13.

23. Dio, 79.5.2-5; Herodian, 4.13.3-7.

24. Herodian, 4.13.7.
25. Dio, 79.11.5; Ando, Clifford, *Imperial Rome* AD *193 to 284*, p.64.
26. Ando, Clifford, *Imperial Rome* AD *193 to 284*, pp.7–8.
27. Levick, B., *Julia Domna*, p.105; HA, *Caracalla*, 11.5; HA, *Macrinus*, 11.5.
28. HA, *Macrinus*, 5.4.
29. Levick, B., *Julia Domna*, p.106; Dio, 79.23.1-4; Herodian, 4.13.8.
30. Dio, 79.23.6.
31. HA, *Macrinus*, 9.1-2; Herodian, 5.3.2-3.
32. Herodian, 5.3.2-4.
33. Herodian, 5.7.3; Dio, 79.30.3, 34.1; Cleve, Robert L., 'Some Male Relatives of the Severan Women', pp.196–206; Birley, A., *Septimius Severus*, pp.221–24. The supposed career of Gaius Julius Avitus Alexianus is constructed by Robert Cleve purely from inscriptions. He suggests he is a relative of Maesa's husband, but is more likely that they are one and the same. Birley, A., *Septimius Severus*, p.221 n.35 suggests that a M. Julius Gessius Bassianus, identified in the list of 'Arval Brethren' in AD 214, is not to be identified with the future emperor but a possible elder brother. However, he does not appear in any of our surviving sources, nor did he participate in the revolt of AD 218 by his family, suggesting he had died before then.
34. Dio, 79.7.4-5, 8.1-3.
35. Dio, 79.20.1-4.
36. Dio, 79.21.1-5; HA, *Macrinus*, 12.9.
37. HA, *Caracalla*, 3.1; Mennen, Inge, *Power and Status in the Roman Empire* AD *193–284*, pp.95–96.
38. Epitome de Caesaribus, 20.6; Dio, 79.21.2, 80.5.1-4; Mennen, Inge, *Power and Status in the Roman Empire* AD *193–284*, pp.119–120.
39. Dio, 79.20.4; Herodian, 4.8.3, n.6 p.415.
40. Dio, 79.20.3.
41. Millar, Fergus, *A Study of Cassius Dio* (Oxford University Press, 1964), pp.11–14.
42. Dio, 79.11.5.
43. Dio, 79.26.2-3.
44. Millar, Fergus, *A Study of Cassius Dio*, p.165; Herodian, 4.13.6-14.4, n.2 p.437, n.2 p.451.
45. Dio, 79.26.5; Herodian, 4.15.1.
46. Herodian, 3.3.5, 4.15.1,n.2 p.461; Dio. 79.32.1-2; ILS, 1356, refers to regiments of Moorish foot soldiers and cavalry in Herodian, 5.4.3, n.1 pp.28–29; Elliot, Paul, *Legions in Crisis: Transformation of the Roman Soldier* AD *192–284*, pp.97–98.
47. Elliot, Paul, *Legions in Crisis*, p.98
48. Elliot, Paul, *Legions in Crisis*, pp.71–78.
49. Herodian, 4.15.1-3.
50. Herodian, 4.15.4.

51. Dio, 79.26.5-7.
52. Dio 79.27.1, 28.2; Millar, Fergus, *A Study of Cassius Dio*, p.165; HA, *Macrinus*, 8.4.
53. Herodian, 4.15.7-8; Dio, 79.26.8-27.4
54. Herodian, Vol.1 n.1 p.465; Dio, 79.27.3.
55. Herodian, 5.2.3.
56. Watson, G.R., *The Roman Soldier*, pp.91–99; Campbell, J.B., *The Emperor and the Roman Army*, pp.162–70.
57. Dio, 79.28.1-4, 36.1-3.
58. Dio, 79.28.3.
59. Herodian, 5.2.6.
60. Herodian, Loeb edition, p.15 n.1, citing BMC V.494, 497, 505.
61. Herodian, 8.6.4.
62. Campbell, J.B., *The Emperor and the Roman Army*, p.368.

Chapter 3: Revolt AD 217–218

1. Herodian, 5.2 3-3.1.
2. Dio, 79.27.4.
3. Dio, 79.25.1-5.
4. Levick, Barbara, *Julia Domna*, p.147, citing CREBM 5 ccxxi; 522f no 129f., 130, 135 and coins carrying legend 'FIDES MILITUM' in CREBM 5 494 no.1; 497 nos 13–15; 505 no64f; Bowman, Alan, Garnsey, Peter & Cameron, Averil, *The Cambridge Ancient History: The Crisis of Empire* AD *193–337'*, *Volume XII*, p.20.
5. Dio, 79.20.4.
6. O'Hanlon, Bernard Michael, *The Army of Severus Alexander*, ch.1, n.1,310, location 12,392 in Kindle edition. P. Dura 55= RMR 90 letter demanding restoration of discipline linked to disorder leading to removal of Macrinus. The regiment later provided escort for Elagabalus' journey to Rome. P. DURA 100 =RMR 1.
7. Herodian, 5.2.4.
8. Plutarch, *Life of Marius*, 7.4-5; Campbell, J.B., *The Emperor and the Roman Army*, pp.13, 18, 28.
9. HA, *Macrinus*, 5.7, 8.3-4, 9.5-6, 10.3, 12.1-9, 14.1.
10. Herodian, 5.3.1-2.
11. Herodian, 5.3.2-3.
12. Dio, 79.31.1; Levick, Barbara, *Julia Domna*, p.41.
13. Herodian, 5.3.2-7; Dio, 79.31.1-4, 80.6.1-2.
14. Dio, 79.31.1, 32.4; Herodian, Loeb edition, pp.22–23 n.2 suggests Herodian, who does not identify Gannys by name, had him in mind when referring to Maesa's influential clients, 5.3.9. Some historians have identified Gannys with Eutychianus, but a lack of evidence precludes any conclusions in this matter; Levick, Barbara,

Julia Domna, p.147, refers to disputed role of Eutychianus, see Xiph, 344.22, and Dio, 78/79.31.1, who has him as a freedman and separately refers to Gannys, perhaps Elagabalus' guardian, as a '*prostates*', which is a tutor or legal guardian but also referred to as a '*tropheus*' or nurse.

15. Dio, 79.31.3.

16. Ando, Clifford Ando, *Imperial Rome AD 193 to 284*, pp.64–65; Levick, Barbara, *Julia Domna*, p.99; Dio, 79.33.3; Herodian, 5.3.10; Eutropius, *Breviarium*, 8.22; HA, *Macrinus*, 9.4; HA, *Elagabalus*, 2.1; PIR I, 169; Herodian, Loeb edition, p.24 n.1 referring to AE (1932) 70.

17. Herodian, 5.3.11, 5.4.4; Dio, 79.31.3; Butcher, Kevin, *Roman Syria and the Near East*, p.347.

18. Dio, 79.31.3-4; Herodian, 5.3.10-12; Turton, Godfrey, *The Syrian Princesses: The Women Who Ruled Rome AD 193–235*, (American Council of Learned Societies, Cassell and Company, 1974), p.140; Herodian, Loeb edition, p.22 n.1.

19. Dio, 79.31.4, 33.2.

20. Dio, 79.31.4-32.4; Herodian, 5.4.3; HA, *Macrinus*, 9.5-6.

21. HA, *Elagabalus*, 3.2, Herodian, Loeb edition, p.23 n.3, citing ILS III 292, and p.25 n.2; Bowman, Alan, Garnsey, Peter, & Cameron, Averil, *The Cambridge Ancient History: The Crisis of Empire AD 193–337, Volume XII*, pp.20–21; Icks, Martijn, *The Crimes of Elagabalus: the Life and Legacy of Rome's Decadent Emperor* (I.B. Taurus, 2011), pp.11–12; Ando, Clifford, *Imperial Rome AD 193 to 284*, p.65.

22. Dio, 79.33.2.

23. HA, *Macrinus*, 10.1; Syme, Ronald, 'The Son of the Emperor Macrinus', *Phoenix*, vol.26, No.3 (Autumn 1972), published by the Classical Association of Canada, pp.275–91.

24. Batty, Jean Ch., 'Apamea in Syria in the Second and Third Centuries AD', *JRS*, 1988, vol.78, pp.91–104; Dando-Collins, Stephen, *Legions of Rome: The Definitive History of Every Roman Legion* (Quercus, 2010), pp.113, 130–31, 168, 171.

25. Hobbes, Thomas, *Leviathan* (Oxford World's Classics, 2008), ch.12.

26. Dio, 79.27.5.

27. Dio, 79.34.1-8, 37.6, 40.4; Herodian, Loeb edition, p.30 n.1, for date of rebellion of II *Parthica* based on the '*fratres Arvales*' in honour of Maesa and Elagabalus on CIL VI. 2104 b. 23 and distribution of *congiaria* in Antioch, p.37 n.2 ; Batty, Jean Ch., 'Apamea in Syria in the Second and Third Centuries AD', pp.91–104.

28. Dio, 80.4.1-2; Icks, Martijn, *The Crimes of Elagabalus: the Life and Legacy of Rome's Decadent Emperor*, p.13; Mennen, Inge, *Power and Status in the Roman Empire AD 193–284*, p.168; Turton, Godfrey, *The Syrian Princesses: The Women Who Ruled Rome AD 193–235*, p.142.

29. Dio, 79.38.1; Talbert, Richard J.A., *The Senate of Imperial Rome* (Princeton University Press, 1984), p.356; Levick, Barbara, Julia Domna, p.148.

30. Dio, 79.35.1-3; Saller, R.P., *Personal Patronage under the Early Empire*, pp.10–21.

31. Dio, 79.38.3–39.3; Herodian, 5.4.5–8; HA, *Macrinus*, 10.3; Batty, Jean Ch., 'Apamea in Syria in the Second and Third Centuries AD, pp.91–104; Baillie Reynolds, P.K., 'The Troops Quartered in the Castra Peregrinorum,' *Journal of Roman Studies*, vol.13 (1923), pp.168–89.

32. Dio, 79.39.2.

33. Whittaker, C.R., 'The Revolt of Papirius Dionysius AD 190', *Historia*, pp.348–69.

34. Dio, 79.40.1–2; Herodian, 5.4.12; HA, *Macrinus*, 10.6; Icks, Martijn, *The Crimes of Elagabalus: the Life and Legacy of Rome's Decadent Emperor*, pp.16, 21–22.

35. Icks, Martijn, *The Crimes of Elagabalus: the Life and Legacy of Rome's Decadent Emperor*, p.15, referring to BMC V Elagabalus no.10–15, nos.274–76.

36. Dio, 79.39.3–40.3, 80.3.1, 80.4.3; Herodian, 5.4.10–12 & n.1 pp34–35; HA, *Macrinus*, 10.3.

37. Butcher, Kevin, *Roman Syria and the Near East*, p.49; Finegan, Jack, *The Archaeology of the New Testament: The Mediterranean World of the Early Christian Apostles* (Routledge, 1981), pp.65–66.

38. Levick, Barbara, *Julia Domna*, p.148; Icks, Martijn, *The Crimes of Elagabalus: the Life and Legacy of Rome's Decadent Emperor*, pp.14–16, citing CIL VI, 31776a, 31776b, 31875; Salway, B.P.M., 'A Fragment of Severan History: The unusual career of …atus, praetorian prefect of Elagabalus,' *Chiron*, 27 (1997) pp.127–54', and for *damnatio memoriae* of Verus ILS 2657, 5865, 9198 (p.228); Syme, Ronald, 'The Son of the emperor Macrinus', pp.275–91; Dio, 80.7.3.

39. Butcher, Kevin, *Roman Syria and the Near East*, pp.102, 190, 229.

40. Dio, 80.4.3.

41. Birley, Anthony, *The African Emperor Septimius Severus*, pp.215–17; Mennen, Inge, *Power and Status in the Roman Empire AD 193–284*, pp.200, 207.

42. Dio, 80.4.4–6, 7.3–4; Herodian, 5.5.5–6; HA, *Elagabalus*, 5.1; Southern, Pat, *The Roman Empire from Severus to Constantine* (Routledge, 2001), p.56.

43. Dio, 79.13.2, 80.3.1.

44. Dio, 80.4.5.

45. Dio, 80.3.1, 6.3; Herodian, 5.4.6, 5.5.6–8.

46. Dio, 80.3.1.

47. Dio, 80.4.3; HA, *Caracalla*, 6.7; Boteva, Dilyana, 'On the Cursus Honorum of P. Fu. Pontianus (PIR2 F 496), Provincial Governor of Lower Moesia', *Zeitschrift für Papyrologie und Epigraphik* 51. Bd. 110 (1996), pp.248–52; Mocsy, Andras, *Pannonia and Upper Moesia: a History of the Danube Provinces of the Roman Empire* (Routledge Revivals, 2015), p.158.

48. *Dio, 80.4.6.*

49. *Bennett, Julian, Trajan: Optimus Princeps* (Routledge, 1997), p.p45–46.

50. Ando, Clifford, *Imperial Rome AD 193 to 284*, pp.7, 66.

Chapter 4: A Palace Coup AD 218–222

1. Ando, Clifford Ando, *Imperial Rome* AD *193 to 284*, p.66; Turcan, Robert, *The Cults of the Roman Empire*, pp.179–81, 184 & plate 23.
2. HA, *Elagabalus*, p.110 n.3.
3. Gottfried, Mader, 'History as Carnival, or Method and Madness in the *Vita Heliogabali*', *Classical Antiquity* 2005, Vol.24 (1), pp.131–72; Turcan, Robert, *The Cults of the Roman Empire*, pp.179–80.
4. Dio, 80.11.1.
5. Gottfried, Mader, 'History as Carnival, or Method and Madness in the *Vita Heliogabali*', pp.131–72.
6. Herodian, 5.5.7.
7. Herodian, 5.5.8—0.
8. Gottfried, Mader, 'History as Carnival, or Method and Madness in the *Vita Heliogabali*', pp.131–72; Herodian, Loeb edition, p.45 n.3, 5.6.6; Ando, Clifford, *Imperial Rome* AD *193 to 284*, p.66; Icks, Martijn, *The Crimes of Elagabalus*, pp.27–31, 72–77.
9. Dio, 80.11.1.
10. Herodian, 5.6.1-2; Dio, 80.9.3.
11. Dio, 80.9.3-4.
12. Herodian, 5.6.2.
13. Turcan, Robert, *The Cults of the Roman Empire*, p.180; Herodian, 5.6.5.
14. HA, *Elagabalus*, 3.4, 7.1, 7.5-6, 11.6-7.
15. Herodian, 5.6.6-9.
16. Herodian, Loeb, p.53 n.2; Icks, Martijn, *The Crimes of Elagabalus*, pp.29–30; HA, *Elagabalus*, 7.4.
17. Winterling, Aloys, *Politics and Society in Imperial Rome*, pp.20, 31; Dio, 60.19.2; Herodian, 5.6.10, p.57 n.2; Syme, Ronald, *The Roman Revolution*, pp.48, 209.
18. Cicero, *Tusculan Disputations*, Loeb 1945, 2.47-48.
19. Williams, Craig, *Roman Homosexuality* (Oxford University Press, 2010), pp.146–47; Earl, Donald, *The Moral and Political Tradition of Rome* (Cornell University Press, 1967), pp.20–21; Herodian, Loeb edition, p.67 n.1; Dio, 80.16.1.
20. Dio, 80.14.4, 80.15.4, 80.16.1-2; Earl, Donald, *The Moral and Political Tradition of Rome* (Thames and Hudson, 1967), pp.31, 73.
21. Winterling, Alloys, *Politics and Society in Imperial Rome*, p.147.
22. Mader, Gottfried 'History as Carnival, or method and madness in the *Vita Heliogabali*', pp.131–72; according to Dio, 80.15.1, he was named Gordius, although the less reliable *Historia Augusta* identifies him as Cordius in *Elagabalus*, 6.3, 15.2.
23. Dio, 80.15.1-4, 16.6; HA, *Elagabalus*, 6.5.
24. Dio, 80.5.1-2.
25. HA, *Elagabalus*, 11.1-12.3.

26. HA, *Elagabalus*, 10.2-6; Herodian, 5.7.6, n.3 p.63, Loeb edition, citing CIL XIV 3553.

27. Ando, Clifford, *Imperial Rome* AD *193 to 284*, p.67; Saller, R.P., *Personal Patronage under the early Empire*, pp.41–59, 77 ; Syme, Ronald, *The Roman Revolution*, p.386.

28. Mennen, Inge, *Power and Status in the Roman Empire*, pp.98–99, 118–21.

29. Mennen, Inge, *Power and Status in the Roman Empire*, pp.86–89: Q Annius Faustinus of the powerful Anicii, had been suffect consul in 198 but Septimius Severus refused to allow him to stand for further senatorial proconsular provinces after holding the governorship of Moesia Superior at some point between AD 202–205. The reason for this is unknown but his career was resurrected by Macrinus, to whom he would owe a debt of gratitude. Consequently his loyalty to Elagabalus would have been questionable at the very least.

30. Mennen, Inge, *Power and Status in the Roman Empire*, pp.89–90.

31. Mennen, Inge, *Power and Status in the Roman Empire*, pp.109–12; HA, *Elagabalus*, 11.6.

32. Mennen, Inge, *Power and Status in the Roman Empire*, pp.104–05; Dio, 80.21.1-2.

33. Icks, Martijn, *The Crimes of Elagabalus*, p.23. His first consulship is dated to AD 192. His daughter Tineia married the son of the future Emperor Pupienus.

34. Mennen, Inge, *Power and Status in the Roman Empire*, pp.112–15, 127–28.

35. Epictetus, *Discourses*, 4.148; Pliny, *Panegyrics*, 23.3; Icks, Martijn, *The Crimes of Elagabalus*, pp.16, 21–22. The career of '...atus' is only preserved on an inscription found in CIL VI, 31776a, 31776b, 31875; Salway, B.P.M., 'A Fragment of Severan History', *Chiron* 27, 1997. This records that he was both a '*comes*', companion, and '*amicus fidissimus*', most loyal friend, of Elagabalus due to unknown services to the emperor. The inscription records that he was appointed Prefect of the Grain Supply (the annona), Pontifex Minor and then Praetorian Prefect.

36. Herodian, 5.7.1; Dio, 80.16.1; HA, *Elagabalus*, 15.1-2; Mennen, Inge, *Power and Status in the Roman Empire*, p.258; Peacock, Phoebe, 'Usurpers under Elagabalus', in *De Imperatoribus Romanis*; Gilliam, J.F., 'The Governors of Syria Coele from Severus to Diocletian', *American Journal of Philology* vol.79 (no.3) 1958, p.230.

37. Herodian, 5.7.2.

38. Dušanić, Slobodan, '*Nobilissimus Caesar imperii et sacerdotis*', *Zeitschrift für Papyrologie und ... Epigraphik* Bd. 37 (1980), pp.117–20, published by Dr Rudolf Habelt GmbH.Bonn (Germany). The Caesar's title is based upon CIL VI 2001, referring to the Fasti sodalium Antoninianorum dated to 10 July AD 221 and from an inscription from Chester's Roman fort: CIL VII 585 dated to 30 October AD 221 carrying the inscription '(nobiliss..) Caesar imper(i) ... '. A fragment of a Praetorian diploma (CIL XVI 140) with the inscription 'nobilissimus Caes. ... (sace)rdotis'. A copy of a military diploma from 7 January AD 222 from Planinica supports this interpretation, giving the full title as 'Nobilisimus Caesar imperi et sacerdotis'. Coinage referring to 'Indulgentia Aug' in BMC R Emp V p.264f no.452; Herodian (Loeb, trans. C.R. Whittaker) p.60 n.1, citing AE (1964) 269, CIL XVI

135, 140, 141, Dusanic, Hist, 13 (1964) 490. The existence of Alexander Severus' name on laws published before the death of Elagabalus is suggested to be a later addition when the codex was being compiled (Cod. Just, 9.1.3, 4.44.1, 8.44.6); Ando, Clifford, *Imperial Rome AD 193 to 284*, p.151; Dušanić, Slobodan, 'Severus Alexander as Elagabalus' Associate', *Historia: Zeitschrift für Alte Geschichte*, Bd. 13, H. 4 (Oct. 1964), published by Franz Steiner Verlag, p.494; Full inscription of Praetorian diplomata of 7 January AD 222 AD: '…Imper(ator) Caes(ar) M(arci) Aurelli Antonini Pii Felici(s) Aug(usti) fil(ius) divi Antonini Magni nep(os) divi Severi Pii pron(epos) M(arcus) Aurelius Alexander nobilissimus Caesar imperi et sacerdotis co(n)s(ul)', (CIL XVI 140, 141; AE (1964) 269) found in 1984 MA thesis 'The Life of Severus Alexander' by Andrea Beverly Ertel.

39. Dio 80.17.2-3, 18.1-3; Ertel, Andrea Beverly, 'The Life of Severus Alexander', p.20; Talbert, Richard J.A., *The Senate of Imperial Rome*, p.122.

40. Rea, John, 'A Letter of the Emperor Elagabalus', *Zeitschrift für Papyrologie und Epigraphik* Bd. 96 (1993), pp.127–32, published by Dr Rudolf Habelt, GmbH. Bonn (Germany); the *Historia Augusta, Alexander Severus*, 1.2, erroneously places Alexander Severus' adoption after the death of Macrinus. This mistake possibly originates with Aurelius Victor, *Epitome de Caesaribus*, 23.3, which the author of the *Historia Augusta* used as a source; Ertel, Andrea Beverly, 'The Life of Severus Alexander', p.19, asserts the date he was made Caesar, aged 12, is taken from Alexander's induction into '*solades Antoniniani*' on 10 July AD 221. However, CIL VI 3069, dated 1 July AD 221, is dedicated to Antoninus and Alexander as '*imperatores*', suggesting he was made Caesar earlier, i.e. 26 June.

41. Herodian, 5.7.3, n.2 p.59, Loeb edition; HA, *Alexander Severus*, 5.1, suggests Alexander was born on the same day Alexander the Great died, and this was the reason why he chose this name. However, Alexander Severus was born on 1 October AD 208, according to the Calendar of Philocalus (CIL I2· p.274), whilst Alexander the Great died in June; Everitt, Anthony, *The First Emperor: Caesar Augustus and the Triumph of Rome* (John Murray, 2006), p.312; Dio, 80.17.3, on Elagabalus' choice of 'Alexander'.

42. According to Herodian 5.7.4, Alexander Severus was 'in his twelfth year' at the time of his adoption, but 9 at the time of the revolt against Macrinus, 5.3.3; Icks, Martijn, *The Crimes of Elagabalus*, p.37, citing ILS 9058, 483, 2009, 4340, 5854. It was only during his sole rule that Alexander Severus would officially claim to be son of Caracalla.

43. Herodian, 5.7.4, p.58 n.1 Loeb edition.

44. Rea, John, 'A letter of the Emperor Elagabalus', pp.127–32.

45. Eutropius, *Breviarium* (Liverpool University Press, 1993), 8.23; Hammond, Mason, 'The Transmission of Powers of the Roman Emperor from the Death of Nero in AD 68 to that of Alexander Severus in AD 235', *Memoirs of the American Academy in Rome*, Vol. 24 (1956), published by the University of Michigan Press

for the American Academy in Rome, pp.121–22; Hopkins, Richard, The Life of Alexander Severus (Forgotten Books, 2012, originally published 1907), pp.34–35.

46. Herodian, 5.6.2; Dio, 80.5.3-5; Rea, John, 'A letter of the Emperor Elagabalus', pp.127–32.

47. Herodian, p72, Loeb edition, citing AE (1954) 28, referring to Soamias as '*mater Augusti*', '*consors imperii*' AE (1936) 39, '*mater senatus*' AE (1956) 144; Herodian, 5.8.8; Dio, 80.17.2; on coinage they are called 'Augusta', HA Vol.2, p.106, citing Cohen IV, pp.387–89.

48. Herodian, 5.7.1-2.

49. Dio, 80.11.2, 80.13.1, 80.16.5, 80.17.1, 80.18.4 etc.

50. Herodian, 5.7.5.

51. HA, *Alexander Severus*, 3.1-5; Syme, Ronald, *The* Historia Augusta: *A Call of Clarity* (Rudolf Habelt Verlag GmbH Bonn, 1971), p.107; Champlin, Edward, 'Serenus Sammonicus', *Harvard Studies in Classical Philology*, Vol.85 (1981), pp.189–212.

52. HA, *Alexander Severus*, 3.1; Herodian, 5.7.5.

53. Herodian, 5.3.3-4.

54. HA, *Life of Elagabalus*, 16.4.

55. Herodian, 5.7.6; Codex Just,. 4.56.4.1; Syme, Ronald, 'Lawyers in Government: The Case of Ulpian', *Proceedings of the American Philosophical Society*, Vol.116, No.5 (13 Oct. 1972), pp.406–09; Syme, Ronald, *Emperors and Biography: Studies in the* Historia Augusta (Oxford University Press, 1971), pp.147–51; Oliver, James H., 'On the Edict of Alexander Severus (P. Fayum 20)', *American Journal of Philology*, Vol.99, No.4 (1978), published by John Hopkins University Press, pp.474–85.

56. Honoré, Tony, *Ulpian: Pioneer of Human Rights* (Oxford University Press, 2002), pp.1–4, 7, 14, 17–18; Digest, 1.9.1; Levick, Barbara, *Julia Domna: Syrian Empress*, pp.113–15.

57. HA, *Life of Elagabalus*, 16.4; Herodian, 5.7.5.

58. Mennen, Inge, *Power and Status in the Roman Empire*, p.9.

59. Herodian, 5.7.6.

60. Herodian, 5.7.5-6, 8.1-2.

61. Icks, Martijn, *The Crimes of Elagabalus*, p.39.

62. Herodian, 5.8.2.

63. Herodian, 5.8.1.

64. Herodian, 5.7.6, n.3 p.63; Dio, 80.18.4.

65. Mennen, Inge, *Power and Status in the Roman Empire*, pp.109–12.

66. HA, *Life of Elagabalus*, 13.2-4.

67. Ando, Clifford, *Imperial Rome* AD *193 to 284*, pp.7–8.

68. HA, *Life of Elagabalus*, Loeb edition, n.1 p.132, edited by David Magie, suggests that sections 13–17 form a coherent account in contrast to other sections, and are taken from another source that was more detailed and clearer than those

accounts in Herodian and Dio. Dio was not present in Rome during the reign of Elagabalus. Gottfried, Mader, 'History as Carnival or Method and Madness in the *Vita Heliogabali*', *Classical Antiquity 2005*, Vol.24, pp.131–72, suggests the first half of the *Life*, from 1.4 to 18.3, can be considered reasonably accurate, although after these sections, fiction, fantasy and fact are mixed together. Unusually, the death of Elagabalus is described twice, firstly at 16.5–17.1 and then again at the end of 33.2–8 of a mainly unreliable digression detailing the sexual and luxurious excesses of the emperor. Syme, Ronald, *The* Historia Augusta: *A Call of Clarity* (Rudolf Habelt Verlag GmbH Bonn, 1971), pp.12, 26, 28, 95, identifies two main sources for the *Historia Augusta* up to the *Life of Elagabalus*. He feels a significant source was the work of Marius Maximus, who, following the biographies of Suetonius, wrote accounts of the lives of twelve Caesars, from Nerva to Elagabalus. However, Syme considers that the author of the *Historia Augusta* drew mostly from a lost work by an unknown historian, whom he names 'Ignotus'. This work was written after AD 217 and based on 'Nine Vitae' up to Caracalla. Significantly for the author of the *Historia Augusta*, his two main sources end c. AD 222, accounting for the reliable nature of the *Life of Alexander Severus*. Jardé, A., *Etudes critiques sur la vie et le règne de Sévère Alexandre* (E. De Boccard Editeur, 1925), pp.10–17, also concurs that this section of the life contains an accurate account of the palace intrigues.

69. Claridge, Amanda, *Rome, An Oxford Archaeological Guide* (Oxford University Press, 2010), pp.377–81.
70. HA, *Life of Elagabalus*, 13.4-14.5; Herodian, 5.8.3-4.
71. HA, *Life of Elagabalus*, 14.5-8.
72. Mennen, Inge, *Power and Status in the Roman Empire*, p.264.
73. Campbell, J.B., *The Emperor and the Roman Army 31 BC - 235 AD*, pp.23–29, citing Epictetus, 1.14.15; Herodian, 2.13.8.
74. Dio, 80.9.4.
75. Dio, 80.20.1; Herodian, 5.8.2.
76. HA, *Life of Elagabalus*, 15.1-6.
77. Herodian, 5.8.2; HA, *Life of Elagabalus*, 15.4-5.
78. Herodian, 5.8.4; Dio, 80.20.2.
79. HA, *Life of Elagabalus*, 15.5-7; Herodian, 5.8.4, n.2 p.69, citing BMCV ccxli, 614–15, nos 453, 456; Talbert, Richard J.A., *The Senate of Imperial Rome*, p.191; Icks, Martijn, *The Crimes of Elagabalus*, p.41, citing BMC V Elagabalus, nos 452, 453, 456.
80. Dio, 80.19.1; Icks, Martijn, *The Crimes of Elagabalus*, p.41.
81. Icks, Martijn, *The Crimes of Elagabalus*, p.41.
82. HA, *Life of Elagabalus*, 16.1-4; Mennen, Inge, *Power and Status in the Roman Empire AD 193–284*, pp.93–95; Turton, Godfrey, *The Syrian Princesses: The Women Who Ruled Rome AD 193–235*, p.163.

83. Icks, Martijn, *The Crimes of Elagabalus*, p.41, n.86 p.231, citing CIL XVI 140, AE 1964, no.269; Birley, Anthony, *The African Emperor Septimius Severus*, p.194.
84. Herodian, 5.8.5-7, n.1–2, pp.70–71.
85. Herodian, 5.8.7.
86. Herodian, 5.8.7-8; Dio, 80.20.1-2.
87. Herodian, 5.8.8; Dio, 80.21.1.
88. HA, *Life of Elagabalus*, 16.5-17.1.
89. Aurelius Victor, *De Caesaribus*, XXIII; *Epitome de Caesaribus*, 157; Eutropius, *Breviarium*, 8.22.
90. Icks, Martijn, *The Crimes of Elagabalus*, p.43; Syme, R., *Emperors and Biography*, p.118; Syme, R., *The Historia Augusta: a Call of Clarity*, pp.39–40; H.W. Bird translation and commentary of Eutropius, *Breviarium*, p.132 n.65.
91. Herodian, 5.8.9; Dio, 80.20.2; HA, *Life of Elagabalus*, 17.1-3; Zosimus, 1.11.
92. Varner, Eric R., Punishment after death: Mutilation of images and corpse abuse in ancient Rome', in *Mortality: Promoting the interdisciplinary study of death and dying*, 6:1, published by Emory University, USA (2001), pp.45–64.
93. H.W. Bird translation and commentary of Eutropius, *Breviarium*, p.132 n.65.
94. Turton, Godfrey, *The Syrian Princesses: The Women Who Ruled Rome* AD *193–235*, p.156.
95. Dio, 75.2.6; Campbell, J.B., The Emperor and the Roman Army, p.13.
96. Herodian, 5.8.8.
97. Tacitus, *Annals*, 11.35; Campbell, J.B., *The Emperor and the Roman Army*, pp.72–76.
98. Herodian, 5.8.10.

Chapter 5: Regency AD 222–223

1. Hammond, Mason, 'The Transmission of the Powers of the Roman Emperor from the Death of Nero in AD 68 to That of Alexander Severus in AD 235', p.122; Herodian, 5.8.10 and n.1 & 2 p.74–752; *Feriale Duranum* extract taken from Hekster, Oliver, Rome and its Empire AD 193–284, Debates and Documents in Ancient History, p.127; Dušanić, Slobodan, 'Severus Alexander as Elagabalus' Associate', *Historia: Zeitschrift für Alte Geschichte*, Bd. 13, H. 4 (Oct. 1964), pp.487–98, published by Franz Steiner Verlag; Eutropius, *Breviarium*, 23; O'Hanlon, Bernard Michael, *The Army of Severus Alexander* AD *222–235*, loc. 630.
2. Dušanić, Slobodan, 'Severus Alexander as Elagabalus' Associate', p.494.
3. Herodian, 6.1.2; O'Hanlon, Bernard Michael, *The Army of Severus Alexander*, loc. 3586, 10524, n.749, 759, for *Legio I Minervia* in lower Germany dated to 25 April AD 222, a month after death of Elagabalus, given the title 'Alexandriana', citing CIL XIII.8035 Bonn 222 in Fitz, p.136.
4. HA, *Life of Severus Alexander*, 1.2-3.
5. HA, *Life of Severus Alexander*, 5.1-5; Ertel, Andrea Beverly, 'The Life of Severus Alexander', pp.31–32, citing CIL VIII 866 and 23995: '*Aureliae Dionysiae, Aurelli Dionysi patroni filiae, municipes municipii Aurelli Alexandriani Augusti Magni Guifitani.*'

6. HA, *Life of Elagabalus*, 18.1-4; Varner, Eric R. 'Punishment after death: Mutilation of images and corpse abuse in ancient Rome', pp.45–64; Varner, Eric R., 'Portraits, Plots, and Politics: "*Damnatio memoriae*" and the Images of Public Women', *Memoirs of the American Academy in Rome Volume 46* (2001), published by University of Michigan, pp.41–93; AE (1954), p.28, for example of erased named of Soamias along with her title of '*mater Augusti*' (mother of the emperor). For Elagabalus, see ILS 468 in Ertel, Andrea Beverly, 'The Life of Severus Alexander', pp.27–28; Van Sickle, C.E., 'The Headings of Rescripts of the Severi in the Justinian Code', *Classical Philology* Vol.23 no.3 (July 1928), University of Chicago Press, pp.270–77.

7. Icks, Martijn Icks, *The Crimes of Elagabalus*, p.81.

8. Potter, David S., *The Roman Empire at Bay* AD *180–395* (Routledge, 2004), p.164, citing P. Oxy 3298i.2

9. Icks, Martijn, *The Crimes of Elagabalus*, p.87.

10. Icks, Martijn, *The Crimes of Elagabalus*, p.37, citing ILS 9058, 483, 2009, 4340, 5854 and p.43; Dmitrev, Sviatoslav, 'Traditions and Innovations in the Reign of Aurelian', *The Classical Quarterly*, Vol.54, no.2 (Dec. 2004), pp.568–78, citing CJ 9.51.6, which refers to the '*indulgentia*' of Alexander Severus in issuing his amnesty; Honoré, Tony, *Ulpian*, p.165, citing CJ 6.54.6 dated 8 January AD 225, referring to Book 52 of Ulpian's *On the Edict*; Turton, Godfrey, *The Syrian Princesses*, p.168.

11. HA, *Life of Elagabalus*, 18.3-4. See Dio, 80.17.2, and HA, *Elagabalus*, 4.1, 12.3, for attendance of Soamias and Maesa at senatorial meetings.

12. Bowman, Alan K., et al, *The Cambridge Ancient History: The Crisis of Empire* AD *193–337*,' p.140; HA, *Severus Alexander*, 1.3; Talbert, Richard J.A., *The Senate of Imperial Rome*, pp.165–66, 450.

13. Zonaras, 12.15, in Loeb edition of Dio Cassius, p.488–89.

14. HA, *Severus Alexander*, 12.2.

15. Levick, Barbara, *Julia Domna: Syrian Princess*, p.213 n.63; Benario, Herbert W., 'The Titulature of Julia Soaemias and Julia Mamaea: two notes', *Transactions and Proceedings of the American Philological Association* Vol.90 (1959), published by John Hopkins University Press, pp.9–14, cites the restored inscription which is reconstructed as:
    [M. Aureliurn An]toninu[rn August]urn Pi[urn Felicern et Iuliarn SoaeJrniadern [et Iuliarn] Marna[earn Augustas ArisJtaenetu[s et .... s. lib. preocc. (AE, 1933, 281)

16. Icks, Martijn, The Crimes of Elagabalus, p.19; Levick, Barbara, *Julia Domna: Syrian Princess*, p.213, citing AE (1967), 573.

17. Zonaras, 12.15, in Loeb edition of Dio Cassius, pp.488–89; Herodian, 6.1.4-7, n.4 p.85.

18. Herodian, 5.3.3, n.3 p.19, 5.7.4, n.2 pp.60–61, 6.1.1, n.1 p.78.

19. Herodian, 6.1.1-2.

20. Herodian, Loeb edition, p.78 n.2, citing AE (1912), 155; Turton, Godfrey, *The Syrian Princesses*, p.168; Levick,Barbara, *Julia Domna: Syrian Princess*, p.152.

21. Herodian, 6.1.6, 6.1.10; HA, *Severus Alexander*, 60.2, 66.1.

22. HA, *Life of Elagabalus*, 2.1; Levick, Barbara, *Julia Domna: Syrian Princess*, p.152.

23. Levick, Barbara, *Julia Domna: Syrian Princess*, p.162, fig.9.6, sourced from CREM 6, p.119, no.43; p.154, citing CREM 5,435 (Domna), 540n and 577 no.297.

24. Levick, Barbara, *Julia Domna: Syrian Princess*, p.162, fig.9.5, sourced from CREM 6, p.115, no.1.

25. Silver denarius RIC IV 5, BMCRE VI 13. RSC III 204.

26. Dio, 80.21.2; Herodian, 6.1.3, n.2 pp.80–81; O'Hanlon, Bernard Michael *The Army of Severus Alexander*, ch.3 loc. 1502; Shotter, David, 'Gods, Emperors, and Coins', *Greece and Rome*, 1979, Vol.26 (1), Cambridge University Press, pp.48–57; 'Thirty Ninth General Meeting of the Archaeological Institute of America', *American Journal of Archaeology*, Vol.42, no.1 (Jan.–March 1938), p.129.

27. Dio, 80.21.3; HA, *Severus Alexander*, 15.1-2.

28. Icks, Martijn, *The Crimes Of Elagabalus*, pp.21–22, citing CIL XIV 3553; O'Hanlon, Bernard Michael, *The Army of Severus Alexander*, ch.3, loc. 565; Herodian, 5.7.6; Mennen, Inge, *Power and Status in the Roman Empire* AD *193–284*, p.168; Syme, Ronald, 'Fiction about Roman Jurists', *Roman Papers*, Vol.3, ed. Anthony Birley (Oxford, 1984), p.1,405, and for Ulpian as *'praefectus annonae'* citing CJ viii 37, 4; iv 65, 4 until first day of December AD 222, when he was placed in charge of the two Praetorian Prefects; Salway, B., 'Prefects, Patroni and Decurions: A New Perspective on the Album of Canusium', *Bulletin of the Institute of Classical Studies* (University of London, 2000), p.115.

29. Saller, R.P., *Personal Patronage under the Early Empire*, pp.10–15, 69; Syme, Ronald, *The Roman Revolution*, pp.73, 386; Birley, A., *Britain and Rome*, p.56ff., as cited in Herodian, Loeb edition, pp.180–83 n.1; Honoré, Tony, *Ulpian*, p.28, citing CJ 9.1.3, CJ 4.44.1.

30. Mennen, Inge, *Power and Status in the Roman Empire* AD *193–284*, pp.109–11, 112–15.

31. Dio, 80.1.2-3; Millar, Fergus, *Cassius Dio*, pp.25–27.

32. Levick, Barbara, *Julia Domna: Syrian Princess*, pp.113–14.

33. Epitome of Dio in Zonoras, 12.15, in Loeb edition of Dio Cassius, pp.488–489; Crook, J.A., Concilium Principis, *Imperial Councils and Councillors from Augustus to Diocletian* (Cambridge, 1955), considers this council genuine, pp.86–91, but it is dismissed as a fictional creation by Herodian to support his assertion that Alexander Severus instituted an 'aristocratic' style of government, Salway, B., 'Prefects, Patroni and Decurions', p.115. This rather tenuous conclusion is based upon the fact Zonoras' account, probably based on Herodian as the council does not appear in the summarized and brief account of the reign in Dio, states it was Mamaea who created this council. Due to the role of Mamaea in consolidating the position of

her son, this is entirely reasonable. Furthermore, we don't have the full account of Dio, who himself readily admits his account lacks accuracy due to his absences from Rome (Dio, 80.1.2). Although Herodian's work is at times frustratingly generalized, there is very little evidence he deliberately distorted the facts to suit a theme. For general pardon issued by Alexander Severus, see CJ 9.51.5, 9.51.6.

34. Herodian, 6.1.2.
35. Herodian, 7.1.3.
36. HA, *Severus Alexander*, 16.1-3, n.1 p.208, citing Codex Theodosianus vi.4,9.
37. Crook, John, Concilium Principis*: Imperial Councils and Councillors from Augustus to Diocletain*, pp.86–91; Winterling, Aloys, *Politics and Society in Imperial Rome*, pp.80–82; Millar, Fergus, *The Emperor in the Roman World* (Duckworth, 1977), pp.39, 94–95; Honoré, Tony, *Ulpian: Pioneer of Human Rights*, pp.16, 29.
38. Herodian, 6.1.4: 'All civil and legal business and administration was put in the charge of men with the highest reputation and legal skill.'
39. Victor, *De Caesaribus*, 24; Herodian, 5.6.1, n.3 p.47, citing PIR J 660, but discounts the relationship; Honoré, Tony, *Ulpian: Pioneer of Human Rights*, p.29, citing both Syme, Ronald, The Fiction About Roman Jurists, SZ 97.78-104 (1980), and Liebs, D., 'Jurisprudenz', in HLL 4 (1997), pp.410–31, who suggest the connection between Julia Paulus and Paul is possible.
40. HA, *Severus Alexander*, 26.5, but assertion that Paul was a Praetorian Prefect is doubted; HA, *Pescinius Niger*, 7.4; Mennen, Inge, *Power and Status in the Roman Empire*, p.152, n.68, citing Digest 4.4.38, 14.5.8, 32.27.1, and p.151; Millar, Fergus, *The Emperor in the Roman World*, pp.94, 96–97; Honoré, Tony, *Ulpian: Pioneer of Human Rights*, p.29.
41. Dio, 52.33.5.
42. Mennen, Inge, *Power and Status in the Roman Empire*, p.149.
43. Millar, Fergus, *The Emperor in the Roman World*, pp.122–31.
44. Millar, Fergus, *The Emperor in the Roman World*, pp.88–97.
45. Dio, 69.3.5, 71.22.2, comments on Avidius Heliodorus, who became Hadrian's '*ab epistulis Graecis*' due to his rhetorical skill, but his abilities were questioned by the sophist Dionysius, who commented that: 'The emperor can give you money and honour, but he cannot make you an orator.'; Townend, G.B., 'The Post of Ab Epistulis in the Second Century', *Historia* Bd 10 H 3 (July 1961), pp.375–81.
46. In a letter from Commodus to Athens in AD 186, the '*a rationibus*' Julius Candidus is described as 'my friend'. AE 1952 6.II.18–19.
47. Philo, *On the Embassy to Gaius*, Loeb Vol.X (1989), 27.175.
48. Millar, Fergus, *The Emperor in the Roman World*, pp.80–81.
49. Herodian, 6.1.3.
50. Herodian, 6.1.2; O'Hanlon, Bernard Michael, The Army of Severus Alexander, ch.3 loc. 565; Cambridge Ancient History, *The Crisis of Empire* AD *193–337*, Vol.12, p.23; Millar, Fergus, *A Study of Cassius Dio*, p.107.

51. For examples of Maesa making decisions, see Herodian, 6.1.4 (by implication). For examples of Mamaea's role in the decision-making process: Herodian, 6.1.4-6, 6.1.8-10, 6.9.4; Dio in Zonoras, 12.15 (Loeb edition of Dio, pp.488–89); Zosimus, *New History*, 1.10. Examples of Ulpian's role: Dio, 80.1.1, 80.2.2; Zosimus, *New History*, 1.10. Examples of the primacy of Alexander Severus in the decision-making process: Herodian, 6.1.6-7, 6.2.1, 6.2.3, 6.3.1-4, 6.5.1-4, 6.6.2, 6.6.4, 6.7.1, 6.7.5, 6.7.9; Zosimus, *New History*, 1.10; Festus, 22; O'Hanlon, Bernard Michael, The Army of Severus Alexander, loc. 8,555, citing RIC vol.4 part II, p.63.

52. Herodian, 6.2.3.

53. Zonoras, 12.15 (Loeb edition of Dio, pp.488–89); O'Hanlon, Bernard Michael, *The Army of Severus Alexander*, ch.3 loc. 588.

54. Herodian, 6.1.5.

55. Herodian, 6.1.2.

56. Millar, Fergus, *Cassius Dio*, pp.102–08; Bleicken, J., 'Der politische Standpunkt Dios gegenuber der Monarchie', *Hermes* 90 (1962), p.444, assumes that the speech was written in the reign of Alexander Severus but agrees with the interpretation of Millar.

57. Dio, 78.17.3-4.

58. Millar, Fergus, *Cassius Dio*, pp.23–25.

59. Dio, 52.15.1-2.

60. Dio 52.15.3-4.

61. Saller, R.P., *Personal Patronage under the Early Empire*, p.50.

62. Tacitus, *Annals*, 4.1, 13.20-22; Pliny, *Panegyrics*, 23.3; Syme, R., The Roman Revolution, pp.73, 386; Saller, R.P., *Personal Patronage under the Early Empire*, pp.61, 78.

63. Suetonius, *Vespasian*, 2.3; HA, *Severus Alexander*, 4.3, 18.2; Millar, Fergus, *The Emperor in the Roman World*, p.20; Saller, R.P., *Personal Patronage under the Early Empire*, p.11, citing Seneca, *De Beneficiis*, 6.33.3-8; Talbert, Richard J., *The Senate of Imperial Rome*, p.69, citing Dio, 79.14.4, and ILS1078.

64. McHugh, John, *The Emperor Commodus: God and Gladiator'*, pp.44–46.

65. Millar, Fergus, *The Emperor in the Roman World*, pp.39, 94–95.

66. Honoré, Tony, *Ulpian*, p.29.

67. Lewis, Naphtali, & Rienhold, Meyer (ed. and notes), *Roman Civilisation: source-book 2: The Empire* (Harper Tourchbooks, 1966), pp.444–45; Fayum Papyrus No.20 (= Select Papyri, No.216; rev. ed. in 'Archiv für Papyrusforschung', XIV (1941), pp44–59; Millar, Fergus, *The Emperor in the Roman World*, p.142.

68. McHugh, John, *The Emperor Commodus: God and Gladiator*, pp.118–21.

69. Herodian, 6.1.8. Also Herodian 6.8.2, 6.9.4-5 and 8; HA, *Severus Alexander*, 65.3.

70. Ando, Clifford, *Imperial Rome* AD *193 to 284*, pp.69–70.

71. Oliver, James H., 'On the Edict of Alexander Severus', pp.474–85.

72. Lewis, Naphtali, & Rienhold, Meyer (ed. and notes), *Roman Civilisation: Sourcebook 2: The Empire*, p.439; Giessen Papyrus No.40, col.1, lines 16–29.

73. O'Hanlon, Bernard Michael, *The Army of Severus Alexander*, loc. 8501 n.154; Barnes, J.W.B., 'A Letter of Alexander Severus', *Journal of Egyptian Archaeology*, LII/1966, pp.141–46, but no evidence visit took place, but J.D. Thomas and W. Clarysse propose a projected visit of Severus Alexander to Egypt after the Persian War in AD 232/233, *Ancient Society* VIII/1977, pp.195–207. However, this is highly unlikely as the emperor had to rapidly return to the Rhine, where barbarians had made a large-scale incursion into Roman territory; Lehmann, Clayton Miles, '*Epigraphica Caesariensia*', *Classical Philology* Vol.79 No.1 (Jan. 1984), pp.45–52; Mârghitan, Liviu, & Petolescu, Constantin, '*Vota pro Salute Imperatoris* in an Inscription at Ulpia Traiana Sarmizegetusa', *Journal of Roman Studies* Vol.66 (1976), pp.84–86.

74. McHugh, John, *The Emperor Commodus: God and Gladiator*, pp.145–57.

75. MacMullen, Ramsey, *The Corruption and Decline of Rome* (Yale University Press, 1988), p.69; Honoré, Tony, *Ulpian*, p.29, citing CJ 4.65.4.1 (1 December AD 222) and CJ 7.66.2 (3 December AD 222).

76. Dio, 80.1.1, p.479, in Loeb edition; Herodian, 6.1.4.

77. Zonoras, The *History of Zonoras: From Alexander Severus to Theodosius the Great*, trans. Thomas M. Banchich and Eugene N. Lane (Routledge, 2009), 12.18.

78. HA, *Severus Alexander*, 67.2, 68.1.

79. Zosimus, 1.10; Mennen, Inge, *Power and Status in the Roman Empire*, pp.164, 168, 265

80. Millar, Fergus, *The Emperor in the Roman World*, pp.122–31.

81. This might be reflected in an inscription found at Coptus in Egypt from 12 October AD 222 regarding the safety and victory of the emperor. See Todd, Marcus N., 'Greek Inscriptions (1931–1932)', *The Journal of Egyptian Archaeology* Vol.19, Nos3/4 (November 1933), pp.185–88.

82. Syme, R., 'Lawyers in Government: The Case of Ulpian', *Procedures of the American Philosophical Society* Vol.116 No.5 (1972), pp.406–09; Salway, B., 'Prefects, Patroni and Decurions: A New Perspective on the Album of Canusium', p.115; Mennen, Inge, *Power and Status in the Roman Empire*, pp.89–91; Saller, R.P., *Personal Patronage under the Early Empire*, pp.69–71; Mennen, Inge, *Power and Status in the Roman Empire*, p.168; Nicols, Jon, *Civic Patronage in the Roman Empire* (Brill, 2013), pp.289–301, citing Digest 31.87.3.

83. Dio, 79.39.1, 40.1; Potter, David S., *The Roman Empire at Bay* AD *180–395*, p.165.

84. Salway, B., 'Prefects, Patroni and Decurions: A New Perspective on the Album of Canusium', p.115, citing PIR C 1428; Mennen, Inge, *Praetorian Prefects' Power and Senatorial Status in the Third Century: Re-evaluation the* Historia Augusta, Vita Alexandri *21.5* (Universiteit van Amsterdam, Faculteit der Geesteswetenschappen, Spuistraat 134, 1012 VB Amsterdam, The Netherlands 2010); O'Hanlon, Bernard Michael, *The Army of Severus Alexander*, ch.3 loc. 656; Honoré, Tony, *Ulpian*, p.7.

85. HA, *Severus Alexander*, 19.1, 21.3; Cambridge Ancient History, *The Crisis of Empire* AD *193–337*,Vol.12, p.23; Mennen, Inge, *Power and Status in the Roman Empire*, p.180.
86. HA, *Severus Alexander*, 51.4.
87. Honoré, Tony, Ulpian, pp.11, 33, citing AE 1988.1051; Mennen, Inge, *Power and Status in the Roman Empire*, p.153; Millar, Fergus, 'The Greek East and Roman Law: The dossier of M. Cn. Licinius Rufinus', *Journal of Roman Studies* 89, pp.90–108; Gordon, Richard, & Reynolds, Joyce, 'Roman Inscriptions 1995–2000', *Journal of Roman Studies* Vol.93 (Nov. 2003), pp.212–94.
88. Honoré, Tony, *Ulpian*, pp.33–35, supported by Syme, R., 'Fiction about Roman Jurists', online loc. 1,397, 1,406.
89. Millar, Fergus, 'The Greek East and Roman Law: The Dossier of M. Cn. Licinius Rufinus', pp.90–108; Honoré, Tony, *Ulpian*, p.89.
90. Dio, 80.1.1, p.479, in Loeb edition.
91. Athenaeus, *Deipnosophistae* (*Sophists at Dinner*), translation found online at LacusCurtius; Honoré, Tony, *Ulpian*, pp.11–14, discounting the identification, in contrast to Künkel, W., *Herkunft und soziale stellung der römischen Juristen*, (1967), pp.248–54, who believes they are one and the same; Whitmarsh, Tim, 'Prose Literature and the Severan Dynasty', in *Severan Culture* (ed. Simon Swain, Stephen Harrison and Jaś Elsner) (Cambridge University Press, 2007), pp.47–48; Trapp, Michael, 'Philosophy, scholarship, and the world of learning in the Severan period', in *Severan Culture*, pp.470–71.
92. Dio, 80.2.2.
93. Herodian, 6.1.3.
94. HA, *Severus Alexander*, 15.1-2.
95. Honoré, Tony, *Ulpian*, p.34, citing CJ 9.8.1.
96. Herodian, 6.1.7.
97. Millar, Fergus, *The Emperor in the Roman World*, pp.122–31; O'Hanlon, Bernard Michael, *The Army of Severus Alexander*, loc. 4658, citing AE 1949.108 and ILS 9074; Mennen, Inge, *Power and Status in the Roman Empire*, pp.159–77; CJ, 4.65.4.1; Philostratus, *Lives of the Sophists*, 2.32; Zosimus, 1.11.2; Honoré, Tony, *Ulpian*, p.16, citing CIL XI 6337, where Praetorian Prefect's advisors appear to have been chosen by the emperor personally as he was dispensing justice on emperor's behalf.
98. Cambridge Ancient History, Vol.12, p.24, citing CJ 9.8.1, 6.23.3; Honoré, Tony, *Ulpian*, p.34, citing CJ, 9.8.1; Digest, 1.4.1.1, 4.1.4 (*Ulpian*).
99. Dio, 80.2.2; Zonoras, 12.15; Zosimus, 1.10.
100. Dio, 75.2.6, 80.2.2; Zonoras, 12.15; Campbell, J.B., *The Emperor and the Roman Army*, pp.8, 117; Bingham, Sandra, *The Praetorian Guard: A History of Rome's Special Forces*, p.47; Honoré, Tony, *Ulpian*, p.32; Whittaker, C.R., 'The Revolt of Papirius Dionysius AD 190', pp.348–69.
101. Dio, 80.2.4.

102. McHugh, John, *The Emperor Commodus*, pp.145–57; Whittaker, C.R., 'The Revolt of Papirius Dionysius AD 190', pp.348–69.

103. HA, *Severus Alexander*, 22.7.

104. Cedrenus, in Dodgeon, M., & Lieu, S.N., *The Roman Eastern Frontier and the Persian Wars AD 226–363* (Routledge, 1991), p.28, mentions famine in Rome during reign of Alexander Severus.

105. HA, *Severus Alexander*, 21.9.

106. Robathan, Dorothy M., 'A Reconstruction of Roman Topography in the *Historia Augusta*', *Transactions and Proceedings of the American Philological Association* Vol.70 (1939), pp.527–28; Levick, Barbara, *Julia Domna*, p.154: ABUNDANTIA AUG = CREBM 6,172f. nos591–94, also TEMPORUM 174f, nos610f.

107. HA, *Severus Alexander*, 39.3.

108. Dio, 80.2.2; Zosimus, 1.10; Zonoras, 12.15; Herodian, 7.11.6. The 'Chronicon Paschale' 223 seems to record disturbances lasting three days and nights in AD 223.

109. Herodian, 7.12.5-6.

110. Herodian, 1.12.8, n.1 pp.80–81.

111. Dio, 80.2.3; Zonoras, 12.15; Zosimus 1.10; Honoré, Tony, *Ulpian*, p.7.

112. Honoré, Tony, *Ulpian*, p.32, citing P. Oxy 2565.

113. Honoré, Tony, *Ulpian*, p.32. 'Album of Canusium' of Oct. AD 223 CIL IX 338; Salway, B., 'Prefects, Patroni and Decurions: A New Perspective on the Album of Canusium', p.168, mentions amongst the city's senatorial patrons T. Lorenius Celsus, M. Aedinius Julianus, L. Didius Marinus and L. Domitius Honoratus. Ulpian is not referred to so it is likely he was dead. Salway suggests these were chosen as persons able and willing to advance the interests of Canusium and listed in order of precedence on Alexander Severus' council. Millar, Fergus, *A Study of Cassius Dio*, pp.25–27.

114. Dio, 80.4.2.

115. Honoré, Tony, *Ulpian*, p.33; Millar, Fergus, *A Study of Cassius Dio*, p.23.

116. Gold aureus c. AD 224/225 RIC 139, Sear 7808; Emperor in military dress RIC IV 433 and 434.

117. Herodian, 5.3.3.

Chapter 6: Restoring the 'Golden Age' AD 224–228

1. Ertel, Andrea Beverly, 'The Life of Severus Alexander', pp.112–13, citing P. Mich 3627, a letter addressed to *strategoi* and *basilikoi* of the Seven Nomes and the Arsinoite giving instructions for a visit of Alexander and his mother; Thomas, J.D., & Clarysse, W., 'A Projected Visit of Severus Alexander to Egypt', *Ancient Society* 8 (1977), pp.195–207. Thomas and Clarysse suggest AD 233 for the date of the proposed visit, pointing to another papyrus P.Lond. III 944 dated to 10 Feb. AD 233 which mentions payments for Annona, perhaps when Alexander Severus departed Antioch for Rome.

2. Lewis, Naphtali, & Reinhold, Meyer (Ed. ad notes), *Roman Civilization Sourcebook II: the Empire* (1955), p.445, citing inscription from Thorigny CIL XIII no.3162 = Abbott–Johnson no.140; Claudius Paulinus as governor of Lugdunensis Gaul PIR C 955; Levick, Barbara, The Government of the Roman Empire: A Sourcebook (Routledge Sourcebooks for the Ancient World, 2000), p.450; On PIR A 113 Marcus Aedinius Julianus described as legate on inscription but more likely acting governor of Lugdunensis Gaul. MacMullen, Ramsey, *The Corruption and Decline of Rome*, pp.106–07.

3. Ste Croix, G.E.M. de, 'Suffragium', pp.33, 40; Gellner, E., *Patrons and Clients* in 'Patrons and Clients', edited by E. Gellner and J. Waterbury, Chapter 1; Kaufman, Robert R., 'The Patron-Client Concept and Macro-Politics: Prospects and Problems' (June 2009), in *Comparative Study of Society and History* (1974), pp.284–308.

4. Salway, B., 'Prefects, Patroni and Decurions: A New Perspective on the Album of Canusium', p.115; Mennen, Inge, *Power and Status in the Roman Empire*, pp.89–90, 254, 260–61; Nicols, John, Civic Patronage of the Roman Empire, pp.289–301.

5. Salway, B., 'Prefects, Patroni and Decurions: A New Perspective on the Album of Canusium', p.115; Mennen, Inge, *Power and Status in the Roman Empire*, p.168; Nicols, John, *Civic Patronage of the Roman Empire*, pp.289–301. Saller, R.P., *Personal Patronage under the Early Empire*, p.48.

6. Salway, B., 'Prefects, Patroni and Decurions: A New Perspective on the Album of Canusium', p.115.

7. Salway, B., 'Prefects, Patroni and Decurions: A New Perspective on the Album of Canusium', p.115, dates Honoatus' Prefecture of Egypt as AD 226. However, Mennen, Inge, *Power and Status in the Roman Empire*, p.168, and Brunt, P.A., 'The Administrators of Roman Egypt', *Journal of Roman Studies* Vol.65 (1975), pp.124–47, both date his Egyptian Prefecture to AD 222 and Praetorian Prefecture to AD 223. Nicols, John, *Civic Patronage of the Roman Empire*, pp.289–301, cites both points of view without drawing a conclusion.

8. Saller, R.P., *Personal Patronage under the Early Empire*, pp.59–61; Barnes, T.D., 'Who Were the Nobility of the Roman Empire?', *Phoenix* Vol.28 (Winter 1984), pp.444–49.

9. Nicols, John, *Civic Patronage of the Roman Empire*, pp.289–301.

10. Nicols, John, *Civic Patronage of the Roman Empire*, pp.289–301; Davenport, Caillan, 'Cassius Dio and Caracalla', *The Classical Quarterly* 2012, Vol.62, pp.796–815; Dio, 78.21.3-5.

11. Nicols, John, *Civic Patronage of the Roman Empire*, pp.289–301; Mennen, Inge, *Power and Status in the Roman Empire*, pp.89–90.

12. Nicols, John, *Civic Patronage of the Roman Empire*, pp.289–301, citing Digest 22.3.20 for date of his praetorship; Herodian, 7.1.4-7, n.2 pp.152–53 in Loeb edition.

13. HA, *Severus Alexander*, 25.3-9.

14. Marvin, Miranda, 'Freestanding Structures From the Baths of Caracalla', *American Journal of Archaeology* Vol.87, no.3 (July 1983), pp.347–84; Claridge, Amanda, *Rome: An Oxford Archaeological Guide*, pp.357–65.

15. Claridge, Amanda, *Rome: An Oxford Archaeological Guide*, pp.233–34; Hopkins, Richard, *The Life of Alexander Severus*, p.173, citing Cohen, 'Alexander', nos 102-04, 297-98, 483-84.

16. Claridge, Amanda, *Rome: An Oxford Archaeological Guide*, p.61.

17. Fabio, Barry, 'The Mouth of Truth and the Forum Boarium: Oceanus, Hercules and Hadrian', *The Art Bulletin* (2011), pp.7–37; Claridge, Amanda, *Rome: An Oxford Archaeological Guide*, p.333; Lusnia, Susann S., 'Urban Planning and Structural Display in Severan Rome: Reconstructing the Septizodium and its Role in Dynastic Policies', *American Journal of Archaeology* Vol.108, no.4 (October 2004), pp.517–44: Karmon, D.E., *The Ruin of the Eternal City: Antiquity and Preservation in Renaissance Rome* (Oxford University Press, 2011), ch.6; Grisanti, G. Tedeschi, *Trofei di Mario: Il Ninfeo dell' Acqua Giulia sull' Esquilino* (Monumenti Romani VII) (Rome Instituto Di Studi Romani, 1977) refers to quarry marks dated to AD 84–96; HA, *Severus Alexander*, 25.3.

18. Claridge, Amanda, *Rome: An Oxford Archaeological Guide*, pp.158–59.

19. Lusnia, Susann S., 'Urban Planning and Structural Display in Severan Rome: Reconstructing the Septizodium and its Role in Dynastic Policies', pp.517–44; MacMullen, Ramsey, 'Roman Imperial Building in the Provinces', *Harvard Studies in Classical Philology* (26) Vol.64 (1959), pp.207–35, citing Annee epigr 1942–3 no.93 for construction of aqueduct by *III Augusta*; Claridge, Amanda, *Rome: An Oxford Archaeological Guide*, pp.203–04, 233; HA, *Severus Alexander*, 26.8-11.

20. Albertson, Fred C., 'Zenodorus "Colossus of Nero"', *Memoirs of the American Academy in Rome* Vol.46 (2001), pp.95–118, citing BMCRE 6:128, nos 156–58; gold aureus RIC 33cf, Sear 7825, Cohen 247; Sesterces, RIC 410.

21. Claridge, Amanda, *Rome: An Oxford Archaeological Guide*, pp.307, 312–13; Hopkins, Richard, *The Life of Alexander Severus*, p.175, citing Eph.Epigr. IV. 745 for inscription found near the fourth-century Arch of Constantine that stands next to the Meta Sudens.

22. Robathan, Dorothy M., 'A Reconsideration of Roman Topography in the Historia Augusta', pp.518, 524; HA, *Severus Alexander*, 44.7-8; Hermansen, G., 'The Population of Imperial Rome: The Regionaries', *Historia* Bd. 27. H.1 (1st Qtr. 1978), pp.129–68, suggests that the Theatre of Marcellus had fallen into disrepair, and in the following century its Travertine blocks were used to repair the Pons Caestius; Hopkins, Richard, *The Life of Alexander Severus*, p.174, citing CIL vi 1083; Claridge, Amanda, *Rome: An Oxford Archaeological Guide*, pp.307, 379, on Sessorium and the imperial gardens at 'Old Hope'; Hartswick, K.J., *The Gardens of Sallust: A Changing Landscape* (Austin, University of Texas Press, 2004), pp.233–36.

23. Gergel, Richard A., 'The Tel Shalem Hadrian Reconsidered', *American Journal of Archaeology*, Vol.95, no.2 (April 1991), pp.231–51; Zanker, P., 'Klassizistische Statuen: Studien zur Veränderung des Kunstgeschmacks', *Römischen Kaiserzeit* (1974), p.10; Vermeule, Cornelius C., 'Egyptian Contributions to Late Roman Imperial Portraiture', *Journal of American Research Centre in Egypt* Vol.1 (1962), pp.63–68; Lee, Kevin S., 'Priest, Pater and Patron: A thematic Analysis of the Building Programs of Elagabalus and Alexander Severus', CLST 519 The Art and Architecture of the Severan Period (December 2014) at academia.edu.

24. RIC IV 569; Cohn, 123. Also RIC 0567.cf, Cohen 0122 cf, Banti 0037.

25. Brunt, P.A., 'Free Labour and Public Works at Rome', *Journal of Roman Studies* Vol.70 (1980), pp.81–100.

26. HA, *Severus Alexander*, 44.4; MacMullen, Ramsey, 'Roman Imperial Building in the Provinces', pp.207–35; Africa, Thomas W., 'Urban Violence in Imperial Rome', pp.3–21.

27. HA, *Severus Alexander*, 39.3; Potter, David S., & Mattingly, D.J. (eds), *Life, Death, and Entertainment in the Roman Empire* (University of Michigan Press, 1999), p.180.

28. Robathan, Dorothy M., 'A Reconsideration of Roman Topography in the Historia Augusta', pp.527–28; 'Georgius Cedrenus' in Dodgeon, M. & Lieu, S.N., *The Roman Eastern Frontier and the Persian Wars* AD *226–363*, p.28.

29. Palmer, R.E.A., 'Customs on Market Goods Imported into the City of Rome', *Memoirs of the American Academy in Rome* Vol.36, in *The Seaborne Commerce of Ancient Rome: Studies in Archaeology and History* (1980), pp.217–33.

30. HA, *Severus Alexander*, 22.1.

31. Claridge, Amanda, *Rome: An Oxford Archaeological Guide*, p.365; Lo Cascio, Elio, 'The Emperor and his Administration', *Cambridge Ancient History*, Vol.12 (Cambridge University Press, 2005), pp.163–64.

32. HA, *Severus Alexander*, 22.4.

33. Wilson, Andrew, 'The Water-Mills on the Janiculum', *Memoirs of the American Academy in Rome*, Vol.45 (2000), pp.219–46.

34. HA, *Severus Alexander*, 22.2.

35. Broekaert, Wim, 'Oil for Rome During the Second and Third Century AD: A Confrontation of the Archaeological Records and the Historia Augusta', *Mnemosyne: A Journal of Classical Studies* 64 (2011), pp.591–623.

36. Blázquez, J.M., 'The Latest Work on the Export of Baetican Olive Oil to Rome and the Army', *Greece and Rome*, Vol.39, Issue 2 (October 1992), pp.173–88; HA, *Severus Alexander*, 22.1. According to HA, *Severus Alexander*, 32.2, the emperor also remitted the customs tax and obligation to present a crown of gold on the anniversary of his accession. However, there is no collaborating evidence for this.

37. HA, *Severus Alexander*, 66.1.

38. Bertrand-Dagenbach, C., Alexandre Sévere et l' 'Histiore Auguste' (Collections Latomus 208 Brussels, 1990), pp.216–19.
39. Herodian, 6.1.5-6, 6.1.10, 6.3.1, 6.5.9, 6.9.5-8.
40. Barnes, J.W.B., 'A Letter of Severus Alexander', pp.141–46.
41. Oliva, Pavel, *Pannonia and the Onset of Crisis in the Roman Empire* (Nakladatelstvi Ceskovenske Academia ved Praha 1962), p.81; Herodian, 6.1.8.
42. Dio, 80.5.1-2.
43. Levick, Barbara, *Julia Domna*, p.152, citing AE 1912, 155.
44. Levick, Barbara, *Julia Domna*, pp.152–54, citing AE 1967, 573; CIL 3, 7970 from Balkans; AE 1942–3,7; IGBulg.1827 from Hadrianoplis in Thrace; and SEG 12,517 Anazarbus in Cilicia and both referred to by subjects as 'my Lords'.
45. Levick, Barbara, *Julia Domna*, pp.153, 213, n.63–68, citing J. Fitz, Les Syriens a Intercisa, Collection Latomus 122, Brussels (1972: 223n3); CIL 2, 2664; Goddard King, Georgina, 'Some Reliefs at Budapest', *American Journal of Archaeology*, Vol.37, no.1 (Jan–Mar 1933), pp.64–76.
46. Levick, Barbara, *Julia Domna*, p.213, n.68 ,citing AE 1940, 148; SEG 3, 537 =Merlat (1951: 11–13 no.8); Merlat 327–31 no.338 = Schwertheim (1974: 64f, no.56c); Renberg, Gil H., 'Public and Private Places of Worship in the Cult of Asclepius at Rome', *Memoirs of the American Academy in Rome*, Vol.51/52 (2006/2007), pp.87–172.
47. Nash-Williams, V.E., 'Iuppiter Dolichenus', *Greece and Rome* 1952, Vol.21 (62), Cambridge University Press, pp.72–77; Peppers, Jeanne, 'Four Roman Votive Bronzes in the Getty Museum', *The J. Paul Getty Museum Journal*, Vol. 8 (1980), pp.173–80.
48. Herodian, 7.3.5; Toth, I., The Destruction of the Sanctuaries of Jupiter Dolichenus in the Rhine and Danube Regions 235–238 (Acta Arch. Hung. XXV/1973), pp.107–14 (Najdenova, 1989a), p.1,380; Jeno, Fitz, Religions and Cults in Pannonia (A Szent István Király Múzeum Közleményei Bulletin Du Musée Roi Saint-étienne, A.sorozat 33.szám/Série A.No.33. Published by the Fejer Megyei Muzeumok Igazgatosaga), p.123; O'Hanlon, Bernard Michael, *The Army of Severus Alexander*, Loc. 5,144, citing V. Najdenova, *The Cult of Jupiter Dolichenus in Lower Moesia and Thrace* (Aufsteig U Niedergang D Roemwelt II 2/1989), p.1,368.
49. O'Hanlon, Bernard Michael, *The Army of Severus Alexander*, Loc. 2,248: Festus is mentioned on inscriptions, along with Orbiana, placing his governorship c. AD 226.
50. Robinson, E.S.G., 'Department of Coins and Medals', *The British Museum Quarterly*, Vol.15 (1941–1950), pp.48–55. For one further coin, see Mattingly, H.,. Sydenham, E.A., & Sutherland, C.H.V., *The Roman Imperial Coinage*, IV, 2 (London, 1938), no.310 under Alexander Severus: obverse, IMP. C. M. AVR [S] EV. ALEXAND. AVG, and reverse, MAISI AVG; Benario, Herbert W., 'The Date of the "Feriale Duranum"', pp.192–96.
51. Herodian, 5.8.2, and 6.1.9.

52. Herodian, 6.1.4.
53. Herodian, 6.1.6; O'Hanlon, Bernard Michael, *The Army of Severus Alexander*, n.270, citing AE 1967, 573 from Numidia; Millar, Fergus, *The Emperor in the Roman World*, pp.244–46, citing CIL VIII 10570 and 14464 = ILS 6870.
54. Millar, Fergus, *The Emperor in the Roman World*, pp.276, 514, 545, citing CJ XII1.1;V.4.10;V.54.1; Digest, 1.16.6.2; Dig 31.87.3; Dig 49.1.25 + P. Oxy.2104.
55. HA, *Severus Alexander*, 31.1.
56. Honoré, Tony, *Ulpian*, pp.32–33; Syme, R., *Fiction about Roman Jurists*, p.1,411, citing CIL vi 266 for appointment of Modestinus to the Prefecture of the Vigiles. For Marcianus, see Honoré, Tony, *Ulpian*, pp.22–23, 80–83, 212 and CJ 2.13.6; Millar, Fergus, 'The Greek East and Roman Law: The Dossier of M. Cn. Licinius Rufinus', pp.90–108.
57. McGinn, Thomas A.J., 'Concubinage and the *Lex Iulia* on Adultery', *Transactions of the American Philological Association*, Vol.121 (1991), pp.335–75, citing Digest (Paul) 27.7.5 and HA, *Severus Alexander*, 42.4; Millar, Fergus, 'The Greek East and Roman Law: The Dossier of M. Cn. Licinius Rufinus', pp.90–108, citing Dig. 40.13.4.
58. Herodian, 6.1.9, n.1 p.86; O'Hanlon, Bernard Michael, *The Army of Severus Alexander*, n.271, citing BMC 308; RIC 675 (Alexander Severus); Heil, Matthäus, *Severus Alexander und Orbiana. Eine Kaiserehe* (Zeitschrift für Papyrologie und Epigraphik, Bd. 135, 2001), pp.233–48, citing CIL VIII 9371 = ILS 1355. Also O'Hanlon, Bernard Michael, *The Army of Severus Alexander*, n.569, citing PIR S 252 and Jardé, p.72, suggests Orbiana was a descendant of Herennius Nepos (PIR H 113) executed by Septimius Severus in HA, *Septimius Severus*, 13.7; A special marriage issue in all denominations BMC 278–307.
59. Sear, 7810; Cohen IV 488 Orbiane no.8.
60. HA, *Severus Alexander*, 57.7.
61. Ramsey, Hazel G., 'Government Relief during the Roman Empire', *The Classical Journal*, Vol.31, no.8 (May 1936), pp.479–88.
62. HA, *Severus Alexander*, 20.3, 49.3.
63. Heil, Matthäus, *Severus Alexander und Orbiana. Eine Kaiserehe*, p.240; O'Hanlon, Bernard Michael, *The Army of Severus Alexander*, Loc.1,069, citing CIL VIII 15524 = 15525, cf VIII.1486, refers to a Caesar but the name is lost.
64. O'Hanlon, Bernard Michael, *The Army of Severus Alexander*, Loc.1,069; Fink, Robert O., 'Lucius Seius Caesar, Socer Augusti', *The American Journal of Philology*, Vol60, no.3 (1939), pp.326–32.
65. Mennen, Inge, *Power and Status in the Roman Empire*, pp.56–59, 99.
66. Millar, Fergus, *A Study of Cassius Dio*, pp.23–24; O'Hanlon, Bernard Michael, *The Army of Severus Alexander*, Loc.171.
67. O'Hanlon, Bernard Michael, *The Army of Severus Alexander*, Loc.6,438.
68. Dio, 80.4.2, which is translated as the Praetorians complaining to Ulpian. However, he was certainly dead by this time and so perhaps the passage should be interpreted

as the Praetorians complained at the imposition of harsh discipline in the manner Ulpian attempted to impose on them.

69. Benefiel, Rebecca R.J., *A New Praetorian Laterculus from Rome* (Zeitschrift für Papyrologie und Epigraphik, Bd. 134, 2001), pp.221–32; Elliot, Paul, *Legions in Crisis: Transformation of the Roman Soldier*, pp.23, 63–64; Smith, R.E., 'The Army Reforms of Septimius Severus', *Historia*, Bd. 21, H. 3 (3rd Quarter, 1972), pp.481–500; Campbell, J.B., *The Emperor and the Roman Army*, p.8.

70. Campbell, J.B., *The Emperor and the Roman Army*, p.296, citing CJ, 12.35.3.

71. Campbell, J.B., *The Emperor and the Roman Army*, pp.215–16, citing Paul, 29.1.38.1.

72. Campbell, J.B., The Emperor and the Roman Army, pp.310–11, citing Paul, 16.16.1, and Modestinus, 3.20; Grunewald, Thomas, *Bandits in the Roman Empire, Myth and Reality* (Routledge, 2004), pp.124–25; McHugh, J.S., *The Emperor Commodus, God and Gladiator*, pp.95–96.

73. Campbell, J.B., *The Emperor and the Roman Army*, pp.303–04, 307–08, 311, citing Digest, 49.16.3-4 (Modestinus), 49.16.12, 13, 16.3.7 (Modestinus), 16.3.10 (Modestinus), 16.3.13 (Modestinus), 16.3.5 (Modestinus), 16.3.7 (Modestinus), 16.3.21 (Modestinus), 16.14.1 (Paul), Paul, 14.1.

74. Millar, Fergus, *The Emperor in the Roman World*, p.543.

75. Herodian, 6.1.5-6, 6.9.4, 6.9.8; Zosimus, 1.11; O'Hanlon, Bernard Michael, *The Army of Severus Alexander*, Loc.3,108.

76. Herodian, 6.1.1; Dio, 52.33.1.

77. Herodian, 6.1.8.

78. Herodian, 6.1.7.

79. Millar, Fergus, *A Study of Cassius Dio*, pp.73–74; Bleicken, J., 'Der politische Standpunkt Dios gegenuber der Monarchie', p.444, confirms interpretation in Millar and dates composition of the history to the reign of Alexander Severus.

80. Dio, 52.28.1-8; Millar, Fergus, *A Study of Cassius Dio*, pp.109–11; Corbier, Mireille, 'Coinage and Taxation: the State's Point of View, AD 193–337', *Cambridge Ancient History* Vol.12, 'The Crisis of Empire AD 193–337' (Cambridge University Press, 2008), Ch.11, p.364.

81. Lo Cascio, Elio, 'The Emperor and his Administration', p.155; Corbier, Mireille, 'Coinage and Taxation: the State's Point of View, AD 193–337', Ch.11, pp.333–34; Buttrey, T.V., 'Dio, Zonoras and the Value of the Roman Aureus', *Journal of Roman Studies* Vol.51 (1961), pp.40–45; Ertel, Andrea Beverly, 'The Life of Severus Alexander', pp.67–69, citing BMC, Severus Alexander, 546–50.

82. Herodian, 6.1.8; Burton, Graham P., *The Roman Imperial State, Provincial Governors and Imperial Finances of Provincial Cities, 27 BC–235 AD* (Historia Bd.53 H.3, 2004) pp.311–42, citing Philostratus, *The Lives of the Sophists*, 548, Pliny, *Letters*, 10.39.

83. Keay, S.J., *Roman Spain* (British Museum Publications, 1988), pp.100–01; Blázquez, J.M., 'The Latest Work on the Export of Baetican Olive Oil to Rome

and the Army', pp.173–88; O'Hanlon, Bernard Michael, *The Army of Severus Alexander*, Loc.2,628; Herodian, 6.3.1, 6.9.4-5, 7.7.5.

84. Lo Cascio, Elio, 'The Emperor and his Administration', p.164; Millar, Fergus, *A Study of Cassius Dio*, p.23, citing Dio, 79.7.4; Stylow, Armin U., Páez, Rafael Atencia, Fernández, Julián González, Pascual, Ruppert, Monika, & Schmidt, Manfred G., 'Corpus Inscriptionum Latinarum. II: Inscriptiones Hispaniae Latinae. Editio Altera. Pars V. Conventus Astigitanus' *(CIL II²/5)* 5, pp.492–93, revising II.1532-3; Jacques, François, Le Privilège de liberté. Politique impériale et autonomie municipale dans les cités de l'Occident romain (161–244) (Ecole fran-caise de Rome, 1984): to the period up to the reign of Marcus Aurelius there are eight equestrians recorded as curatores to six senators; however, from the reign of Marcus Aurelius to Alexander Severus there are thirty-four senators recorded in such posts, compared to ten equites; Burton, Graham P., 'The Roman Imperial State, Provincial Governors and Imperial Finances of Provincial Cities, 27 BC–235 AD', pp.311–42, citing CJ 4.31.3 (223); De Blois, Lukas, 'The Third Century Crisis and the Greek Elite in the Roman Empire', pp.358–77; Millar, Fergus, 'The Development of Jurisdiction by Imperial Procurators; Further Evidence', *Historia* Bd.14 H3 (July 1965), pp.362–67, citing Digest I.19.3, CJ IX.47.2, Digest XLIV. 1.25 = P.Oxy 2104.

85. Corbier, Mireille, 'Coinage and Taxation: the State's Point of View, AD 193–337', Ch.11, p.374, citing AE 1946.180; De Blois, L., Erdkamp, P.,Hekster, O., De Kleijn, G., & Mols, S., 'The Representation and Perception of Roman Imperial Power. Proceedings of the Third Workshop of the International Network Impact of Empire (Roman Empire c200 BC –AD 476)', *Netherlands Institute in Rome* (20–23 March 2002, Amsterdam): Gieben, J.C., 2003, p.Xiv, 565.

86. Corbier, Mireille, 'Coinage and Taxation: the State's Point of View, AD 193–337', Ch.11 p.374; Miller, Millar, 'Empire and City, Augustus to Julian: Obligations, Excuses and Status', *Journal of Roman Studies* Vol.73 (1983), pp.76–96, citing Dig, Ulpian, 50.1.27.1, Modestinus 'Exemptions', Dig, 50.1.35; Skeat, T.C., & Wegener, E.P., 'A Trial before the Prefect of Egypt Appius Sabinus c250 AD', *Journal of Egyptian Archaeology* 21 (1935), p.224.

87. Zuiderhoek, Arjan, 'Government Centralisation in the Late Second and Early Third Centuries AD, A Working Hypothesis', *The Classical World* Vol.103 no.1 (Fall 2009), pp.39–51, citing IGR IV 598=CIL III 14191.

88. Millar, Fergus, 'Empire and City, Augustus to Julian: Obligations, Excuses and Status', pp.76–96, citing Dig, 50.5.8 (Papinian), and CJ, 10.52.1 (Alexander Severus); Wilson, Andrew, 'Urban Development in the Severan Empire', *Severan Culture* (ed. Simon Swain, Stephen Harrison and Jaś Elsner) (Cambridge University Press, 2007), p.307.

89. Millar, Fergus, 'Empire and City, Augustus to Julian: Obligations, Excuses and Status', pp.76–96, citing Dig, 27.1.6.1 (Modestinus) and 27.1.6.9 (Modestinus).

90. Millar, Fergus, 'Empire and City, Augustus to Julian: Obligations, Excuses and Status', pp.76–96, citing Dig, 49.18.5.2, and CJ, 10.44.1.

91. Millar, Fergus, 'Empire and City, Augustus to Julian: Obligations, Excuses and Status', pp.76–96, citing Dig (Modestinus) XLIV, 18.4.

92. Elliot, Paul, *Legions in Crisis*, p.109; Speidel, M. Alexander, 'Roman Army Pay Scales', pp.87–106.

93. O'Hanlon, Bernard Michael, The *Army of Severus Alexander*, Loc.11877, citing AE, 1977.171, from Fiuminino, Italy, and P.Dura, 61= RMR, 101, from the Cohors XX Palmyrenorum; Sinnigen, William G. 'The Origins of the "Frumentarii"', *Memoirs of the American Academy in Rome* Vol.27 (1962), pp.211, 213, 224.

94. Zuiderhoek, Arjan, 'Government Centralisation in the Late Second and Early Third Centuries AD, A Working Hypothesis', pp.39–51, citing Abbott, F.F., & Johnson, A.C., *Municipal Administration in the Roman Empire* (Princeton, 1926), nos 142, 143, 144, and TAM V.1. 149, 154, 611.

95. CIL, 3.12336, translated in Hekster, Oliver, *Rome and its Empire* AD *193–284*, pp.119–20.

96. Translated in Hekster, Oliver, *Rome and its Empire* AD *193*–284, pp.121–22. The inscription refers to the 'most holy emperors', indicating a date during the reigns of Septimius Severus and Caracalla, the short joint rule of Caracalla and Geta or that of Philip and his son.

97. Ando, Clifford, *Imperial Rome* AD *193 to 284*, pp.180–86; Aemilius Macer, *De publicis iudi*ciis, Book II fr.39 = Dig, 48.19.10; Dig, *Ulpian*, 47.10.35 and *De omnibus tribunalibus*, bk 3 fr.2265; Lo Cascio, Elio, 'The Emperor and his Administration', Ch.6, p.149.

98. Zuiderhoek, Arjan, 'Government Centralisation in the Late Second and Third Century AD, A Working Hypothesis', pp.39–51; Dig, 32.5.89; Cod Just, 4.62.1.

99. Scheidel, Walter, *Roman Well-being and the Economic Consequences of the Antonine Plague* (Princeton/Stanford University Press, 2010), pp.15–21; Littman, R.J. & M.L., 'Galen and the Antonine Plague', *The American Journal of Philology* 94, no.3, pp.243–55; Zuiderhoek, Arjan, 'Government Centralisation in the Late Second and Third Century AD: A Working Hypothesis', pp.39–51; Bruun, Christer, 'The Antonine Plague and the "Third-Century Crisis"', in Hekster, Oliver, de Kleijn, Gerda, & Slootjes, Danielle (eds), *Crises and the Roman Empire: Proceedings of the Seventh Workshop of the International Network Impact of Empire, Nijmegen, June 20–24, 2006* (Leiden/Boston: Brill, 2007), pp.201–18; Dio, 73.14.4.

100. Blanchard, Philippe, Castex, Dominique, Coquerelle, Michaël, Giuliani, Raffaella, & Ricciardi, Monica, *A Mass Grave from the Catacomb of Saints Peter and Marcellinus in Rome Second-Third Centuries* AD (Antiquity, 2007), pp.989–98.

101. Pontius of Carthage, *Life of Cyprian*, trans. Ernest Wallis, c. 1885, online at Christian Classics Ethereal Library.

102. Stathakopoulos, Dionysios Ch. *Famine and Pestilence in the Late Roman and Early Byzantine Empire* (Birmingham Byzantine and Ottoman Monographs) (Ashgate Publishing Limited, 2004), p.95.

103. Hekster, Oliver, *Rome and its Empire AD 193–284*, pp.32–33.

104. Herodian, 6.1.9.

105. Herodian, 1.8.4.

106. HA, *Severus Alexander*, 20.3, 49.4-5.

107. Jardé, A., *Etudes Critiques sur la vie et le règne de Sévère Alexandre*, pp.67–73.

108. Fink, Robert O., 'Lucius Seius Caesar, Socer Augusti', pp.326–32, citing Suetonius, *Galba*, 3.4.

109. Heil, Matthäus, *Severus Alexander und Orbiana. Eine Kaiserehe*, pp.233–48; Levick, Barbara, *Julia Domna*, p.152.

110. Herodian, 6.1.7.

111. Herodian, 6.1.8, 6.1.10; Sidebottom, Harry, 'Roman Imperialism: The Changed Outward Trajectory of the Roman Empire', *Historia* Bd.54 H.3 (2005), pp.315–30.

112. Dio, 49.36.4; Millar, Fergus, A Study of Cassius Dio, pp.26, 209.

113. Dio, 80.5.2.

114. Gergel, Richard A., 'The Tel Shalem Hadrian Reconsidered', pp.231–51; Yegül, Fikret K., 'The Termo-Mineral Complex at Baiae and De Balneis Puteolanis', *The Art Bulletin* Vol.78, no.1 (March 1996), pp.137–61; Dio, 80.5.2-3.

Chapter 7: The Empire of Alexander Severus AD 222–235

1. Cyprian, 'To Demetrianus' Treatise, 5.3.

2. Fowden, Garth, 'Late Polytheism: The World View', *Cambridge Ancient History* Vol.12, ch.17 (Cambridge University Press), p.556, citing Pighi (1965), 142, tr. Lane Fox, *Pagans and Christians*, p.464.

3. Hekster, Oliver, *Rome and its Empire AD 193–284*, pp.78–80; Turcan, Robert, *The Cults of the Roman Empire*, pp.231–32, 296; Segal, J.B., 'Four Syriac Inscriptions', Bulletin *of the School of Oriental and African Studies*, Vol.30, 02 (June 1967), pp.293–304; HA, *Severus Alexander*, 29.2

4. Edwards, Mark, 'Severan Christianity', *Severan Culture* (Cambridge University Press, 2007), pp.40506.

5. Newby, Zahra, 'Art at the Crossroads? Themes and Styles in Severan Art', *Severan Culture*, (Cambridge University Press, 2007), p.240.

6. Newby, Zahra, 'Art at the Crossroads?', *Severan Culture*, p.245; Tuck, Steven L., *A History of Roman Art* (Wiley Blackwell, 2015), pp.317–18; Rodenwaldt, G., *The Transition to Late Classical Art* (CAH), p.553; O'Hanlon, Bernard Michael, *The Army of Severus Alexander*, Loc.4,713, dating the sarcophagus depicting the myth of Adonis to c. AD 220, sarcophagus with lion hunt to c. AD 230–235, Borghese sarcophagus to AD 235–240 and Ludovisi Battle sarcophagus to AD 225–230.

7. Eusebius, *History of the Church*, 6.28.

8. Whitmarsh, Tim, 'Prose Literature and the Severan Dynasty', *Severan Culture*, pp.31, 50, citing P. Oxy, 3.412, and Syncellus, *Chronicle*, 439; Trapp, Michael, 'Philosophy, Scholarship and the World of Learning in the Severan Period', *Severan Culture*, p.470.

9. Eusebius, *History of the Church*, 6.2.13–17.

10. Eusebius, *History of the Church*, 6.26; Trapp, Michael, 'Philosophy, Scholarship and the World of Learning in the Severan Period', *Severan Culture*, p.486.

11. Trapp, Michael, 'Philosophy, Scholarship and the World of Learning in the Severan Period', *Severan Culture*, p.484; Edwards, Mark, 'Severan Christianity', *Severan Culture*, p.409; Clarke, Graeme, 'Christianity in the First Three Centuries: Chapter 18 Third Century Christianity', *Cambridge Ancient History* Vol.12 (Cambridge University Press, 2008), p.622; Clarke, Graeme, 'Some Victims of the Persecution of Maximinus Thrax', *Historia* Bd 15, H.4 (November 1966), pp.445–53; Dunbar, David G., 'The Delay of the Parousia in Hippolytus', *Vigiliae Christianae* Vol.37, no.4 (Brill, December 1983), pp.313–27.

12. Clarke, Graeme, 'Christianity in the First Three Centuries: Chapter 18B Third Century Christianity', *Cambridge Ancient History* Vol.12, pp.597–98, citing Tertullian, *ad Scapulam*, 2.10, *Apologeticus*, 37.2; Cyprian, *Letters*, 59.10.1; Thomas, Edmund, 'Metaphor and Identity in Severan Architecture', *Severan Culture*, p.402.

13. Newton, Tim, *The Forgotten Gospels: A New Translation* (Constable London, 2009), p.54, 'Gospel of Thomas'.

14. Edwards, Mark, 'Severan Christianity', *Severan Culture*, pp.407–08.

15. Borg, Barbara, *Crisis and Ambition: Tombs and Burial Customs in Third Century CE Rome* (Oxford University Press, October 2013), pp.112–15; Newby, Zahra, 'Art at the Crossroads?', *Severan Culture*, pp.277–83; Logan, Alistair, The Gnostics: Identifying an Early Christian Cult (A and C Black, 2006), p.115.

16. Philostratus, *Lives of the Sophists*, 268, 625; Potter, David, *The Roman Empire at Bay* AD *180–395*, p.78; Smith, Steven D., *Man and Animal in Severan Rome: The Literary Imagination of Claudius Aelianus* (Cambridge University Press, 2014), p.72; Trapp, Michael, 'Philosophy, Scholarship and the World of Learning in the Severan Period', *Severan Culture*, p.479; HA, *Severus Alexander*, 44.4.

17. Whitmarsh, Tim, 'Prose Literature and the Severan Dynasty', *Severan Culture*, pp.48–49.

18. Armstrong, A.H., Cambridge *History of Later Greek and Medieval Philosophy* (Cambridge, 1967), pp.196–200; Fowden, Garth, 'Late Polytheism: The World View', *Cambridge Ancient History* Vol.12, p.525; Trapp, Michael, 'Philosophy, Scholarship and the World of Learning in the Severan Period', in *Severan Culture*, p.472.

19. Fowden, Garth, 'Late Polytheism: The World View', *Cambridge Ancient History* Vol.12, p.526.

20. Levick, Barbara, *Julia Domna*, pp.117–19.
21. Whitmarsh, Tim, 'Prose Literature and the Severan Dynasty', *Severan Culture*, p.61.
22. Levick, Barbara, *Julia Domna*, p.199 n.29; Jones, Christopher P., 'Philostratus' Heroikos and Its Setting in Reality', *The Journal of Hellenic Studies*, Vol.121 (2001), pp.141–49; Philostratus, *Lives of the Sophists*, 408.
23. Whitmarsh, Tim, 'Prose Literature and the Severan Dynasty', *Severan Culture*, p.40.
24. Avotins, Ivars, 'Prosopographical and Chronological Notes on Some Greek Sophists of the Empire', *California Studies in Classical Antiquity*, Vol.4 (1971), pp.67–80; Philostratus, *Lives of the Sophists*, 628.
25. Sidebottom, Harry, 'Severan Historiography: Evidence, Patterns and Arguments', *Severan Culture*, pp.58–59; Trapp, Michael, 'Philosophy, Scholarship and the World of Learning in the Severan Period', *Severan Culture*, pp.472–78, citing Suda M46, Heath (2004), p.62; Philostratus, 2.26, 30; Suda, A4204.
26. Oliver, James H., 'Athenian Citizenship of Roman Emperors', *Hesperia: The Journal of the American School of Classical Studies at Athens*, Vol.20 no.4 (October–December 1951), pp.346–49.
27. Trapp, Michael, 'Philosophy, Scholarship and the World of Learning in the Severan Period', *Severan Culture*, p.472. Conversely, according to Porphyry, Plotinus was disappointed with the quality of intellectual debate until he arrived at the Alexandrian school of Ammonius: Porphyry, *Life of Plotinus*, 3.
28. Sidebottom, Harry, 'Severan Historiography: Evidence, Patterns and Arguments', *Severan Culture*, pp.57–58; Millar, Fergus, *A Study of Cassius Dio*, pp.38–40.
29. Syme, Ronald, *Emperors and Biography*, pp.30–53; Barnes, T.D., *The Sources of the Historia Augusta* (Brussels, 1978), pp.98–107; Sidebottom, Harry, 'Severan Historiography: Evidence, Patterns and Arguments', *Severan Culture*, p.58.
30. Honoré, Tony, *Ulpian*, pp.17, 122–23, 207–08, 211–13; D 1.25.16 (Marcianus); Millar, Fergus, 'The Greek East and Roman Law', *Journal of Roman Studies*, pp.90–108; de Cascio, Elio, 'The Emperor and His Administration: General Developments', *Cambridge Ancient History*, Vol.12, ch.6, p.146; McGinn, Thomas A.J., 'Concubinage and the Lex Julia on Adultery', *Transactions of the American Philological Association*, pp.335–75.
31. Honoré, Tony, *Ulpian*, p.78.
32. Scheiber, Alexander, 'Jews at Intercisa in Pannonia', *The Jewish Quarterly Review*, Vol.45, no.3 (January 1955), pp.189–97; Moore Cross, Frank, 'The Hebrew Inscriptions from Sardis', *Harvard Theological Review*, Vol.95, issue 01 (January 2002), pp.3–19; HA, *Severus Alexander*, 28.7.
33. Oliva, Pavel, *Pannonia and the Onset of Crisis in the Roman Empire*, pp.81, 88–89, 102, 115–17, 136, 166–67, 171, 179–81, 256, 303–05, 312–14, 318; Goddard King, Georgina, 'Some Reliefs at Budapest', *American Journal of Archaeology*, pp.64–76.
34. Oliva, Pavel, *Pannonia and the Onset of Crisis in the Roman Empire*, pp.325–28, 333–34, citing CIL III 10481 description of Aquincum as 'a most glorious colony';

Goddard King, Georgina, 'Some Reliefs at Budapest', *American Journal of Archaeology*, pp.64–76.

35. Oliva, Pavel, *Pannonia and the Onset of Crisis in the Roman Empire*, pp.325–28, 331–32, 343–45.

36. Salway, Peter, *A History of Roman Britain* (Oxford University Press, 1997), pp.183–94, 199; MacMullen,Ramsey, 'Roman Imperial Building in the Provinces', *Harvard Studies in Classical Philology*, pp.207–35; Baker, Philip, *The Empire Stops Here* (Pimlico, 2009), pp.30, 58, 61.

37. Richmond, I.A., 'Five Town-Walls in Hispania Citerior', *The Journal of Roman Studies*, Vol.21 (1931), pp86–100.

38. MacMullen, Ramsey, *The Corruption and Decline of Rome*, pp.11–13, 23.

39. Broekaert, Wim, 'Oil for Rome During the Second and Third Century AD: A Confrontation of the Archaeological Records and the Historia Augusta', *Mnemosyne: A Journal of Classical Studies*, pp.591–623; Blázquez, J.M., 'The Latest Work on the Export of Baetican Olive Oil to Rome and the Army', *Greece and Rome*, pp.173–88; Keay, S.J., *Roman Spain*, pp.100–01; Stylow, Armin U. Páez, Rafael Atencia, Fernández, Julián González, Román, Cristóbal González, Muñoz, Mauricio Pastor, Oliva, Pedro Rodríguez, Pascual, Helena Gimeno, Ruppert, Monika, & Schmidt, Manfred G., '*Corpus Inscriptionum Latinarum. II: Inscriptiones Hispaniae Latinae*', *Editors Altera. Pars V. Conventus Astigitanus (CIL II²/5)* citing 5.492-93 revising II.1532-3; Corbier, Mireille, 'Coinage and Taxation: The State's Point of View, AD 193–337', *Cambridge Ancient History*, p.403.

40. Richard, I.A., 'Five Town-Walls in Hispania Citerior', *The Journal of Roman Studies*, Vol.21 (1931), pp.86–100.

41. McHugh, John S., *The Emperor Commodus*, p.95; Herodian, 1.10.1.

42. Grunewald, Thomas, *Bandits in the Roman Empire; Myth and Reality*, pp.111–19.

43. Oliva, Pavel, 'Pannonia and the Onset of Crisis in the Roman Empire', pp.115–17, citing Digest, *Ulpian*, 1.18.13, Dig V. 1.61.1, Paul V.3.4, V.22.1.

44. MacMullen, Ramsey, *The Corruption and Decline of Rome*, p.29; Corbier, Mireille, 'Coinage and Taxation: The State's Point of View, AD 193–337', *Cambridge Ancient History*, pp.408–10; Fowden, Garth, 'Late Polytheism: The World View', *Cambridge Ancient History*, p.567; Hekster, Oliver, *Rome and its Empire AD 193–284*, p.34; Gibbins, David, 'A Roman Ship Wreck of c. AD 200 at Plemmirio, Sicily: Evidence for North African Amphora Production During the Severan Period', *World Archaeology*, 32:3, pp.311–34; Townsend, Prescott W., 'The Significance of the Arch of the Severi at Lepcis', *American Journal of Archaeology*, Vol.42, no.4 (October–December 1938), pp.512–24; Tertullian, *De anima*, 30.3-4, *de Pallio*, 2.7.

45. Newby, Zahra, 'Art at the Crossroads?, *Severan Culture*, pp.304, 307, 310, 311–12, citing CIL 8.2659, CIL 8.2658, CIL 8.23991=ILS 5776, CIL 8.23991=ILS 5776, CIL 8.2659, 8.2658, IRT 448, IRT 449, 450, AE 1913, 120; Lusnia, Susann S., 'Urban Planning and structural display in Severan Rome', *American Journal*

of Archaeology, pp.517–44; O'Hanlon, Bernard, *The Army of Severus Alexander*, Loc.11909, refers to Titus Licinius Hierocles who raised an altar in AD 227 after the suppression of some form of armed conflict, CIL 8.9354, AE 1966.597, AE 1966.593/594, also from Tunisia AE 1917/18.68, AE 1946.52 from Volubilis in Mauretania: '*antea habuit aramque statuit*'; HA, *Severus Alexander*, 58.1; O'Hanlon, Bernard, *The Army of Severus Alexander*, Loc.10775, citing AE 1966. 597 dated to c. AD 225 for unit of Moors and 'burgum', IRT 895 at Wadi Zemzem with vexillation from *III Augusta*; Ertel, Andrea Beverly, 'The Life of Alexander Severus', p.82; Parker, Philip, The Empire Stops Here: *A Journey Along the Frontiers of the Roman World* (Pimlico, 2010), p.496; Whittaker, C.R., in *Herodian*, Loeb edition, p.92 n.1, citing BMC VI.60, 61, Jardé, *Sévère Alexandre*, p.76n.

46. Vickers, M.J., & Reynolds, J.M., 'Cyrenaica, 1962–72', *Archaeological Reports*, no.18 (1971–1972), pp.27–47.

47. Vermeule, Cornelius C., 'Egyptian Contributions to Late Roman Imperial Portraiture', *Journal of American Research Center in Egypt*, pp.62–68; Ferguson, John, *The Religions of the Roman Empire* (Thames and Hudson, 1982), p.36.

48. MacMullen, Ramsey, *Corruption and Decline of Rome*, p.31; Braunert, Horst, *Die Binnenwanderung. Studien zur Sozialgeschichte Ägyptens in der Ptolemäer- und Kaiserzeit* (Bonn Ludwig Rohrscheid Verlag, 1964), pp.165–68, 186–89.

49. Hekster, Oliver, *Rome and its Empire AD 193–284*, p.54; Oliver, J.H., 'Gerusiae and the Augustales', *Historia* Bd. 7, H 4 (October 1958), pp.472–96; Millar, Fergus, 'Empire and city, Augustus to Julian: Obligations, Excuses and Status', *Journal of Roman Studies*, pp.76–96, citing Skeat, T.C., & Wegener, E.P., 'A Trial before the Prefect of Egypt Appius Sabinus c250', *JEA*, p.224.

50. Corbier, Mireille, 'Coinage and Taxation: The State's Point of View, AD 193–337', *Cambridge Ancient History*, p.425.

51. Brunt, P.A., 'The Administrators of Roman Egypt', Journal of Roman Studies, pp.124–47, citing P Oxy, 2565; Butcher, Kevin, *Roman Syria and the Near East*, p.412.

52. Birley, A., *The African Emperor Septimius Severus*, p.132; Lehmann, Clayton Miles, 'Epigraphica Caesariensis', *Classical Philology*, pp.45–52, inscription preserved on the sarcophagus AE 1971 476; O'Hanlon, Bernard Michael, *The Army of Severus Alexander*, Loc. 2127; Foerster, Gideon, 'The Early History of Caesarea', *Bulletin of the American Schools of Oriental Research*, Supplementary Studies, no.19, 'The Joint Expedition to Caesarea Maritima', Vol.1, *Studies in the History of Caesarea Maritima* (1975), pp.9–22, citing the Palestinian Talmud Kila'im IX, 32c.

53. Hammond, Mason, 'Composition of the Senate, AD 68–235', *Journal of Roman Studies*, Vol.47 (1957), pp.74–81; Butcher, Kevin, *Roman Syria and the Near East*, pp.114, 139, 232, 257, 324–25; Corbier, Mireille, 'Coinage and Taxation: The State's Point of View, AD 193–337', *Cambridge Ancient History*, pp.408–09; Mennen, Inge, *Power and Status in the Roman Empire*, p.31; Borg-Witschel, B.C.,

Veranderungen im Reprasentationsverhalten der romischen Eliten wahrend des 3. Jhs.n. Chr. (2001), p.61; Duncan-Jones, R.P., 'Economic Change and the transition to Late Antiquity', in S. Swain and M. Edwards (eds), *Approaching Late Antiquity: The Transformation from Early to Late Empire* (Oxford, 2004), pp.20–52; Alfody, G., and Panciera, S. (eds), *Inschriftliche Denkmaler als Medien der Selbstdarstellung in der romischen welt* (Stuttgart, 2001), pp.47–120, assert that not only Syria but Africa and Pamphylia prospered throughout the third century; Tome, I., *Les Campagnes Pe La Syrie Pu Nord Du Ile Au Vlle Siecle. Un Exemple d'Expansion Demographique Et Economique A La Fin D'Antiquite* (Institut francais d'archeologie du proche-orient, Bibliotheque archeologique et historique), Paris: Librairie orientaliste Paul Geuthner (1992), demonstrates that the prosperity of Syria was based upon an agricultural diversity lasting until the second half of the third century.

54. Butcher, Kevin, *Roman Syria and the Near East*, pp.146, 351; Rostovtzeff, M., 'Vexillum and Victory', *Journal of Roman Studies*, Vol.32, parts 1–2 (1942), pp.92–106.

55. Butcher, Kevin, *Roman Syria and the Near East*, p.325.

56. Clarke, Graeme, 'Christianity in the First Three Centuries: Third Century Christianity', *Cambridge Ancient History*, p.603; Eusebius refers to the 'many rulers of country churches' possibly near Caesarea (Eusebius, *Mart.Pal*, 1.3) and describing the situation in the early third century he mentions 'bishops administering the churches round Jerusalem' (Eusebius, *Church History*, vi.11.2). Another reference is to a confessor bishop 'in a small city in Palestine' (Epiph.Panarion ixiii, 2.4).

57. MacMullen, Ramsey, *The Corruption and Decline of Rome*, p.5.

58. Zuiderhoek, Arjan, 'Government Centralization in the Late Second and Early Third Centuries AD: A Working hypothesis', *The Classical World*, pp.39–51.

59. Ando, Clifford, *Imperial Rome AD 193 to 238*, pp.189–90; Frend, W.H.C., 'A Third Century Inscription Relating to Anagareia in Phrygia', *Journal of Roman Studies* 46 (1956), pp.46–56.

60. Jones, Christopher P., 'Philostratus' Heroikos and its Setting in Reality', *The Journal of Hellenic Studies*, pp.141–49; HA, *Severus Alexander*, 40.6.

61. Hekster, Oliver, *Rome and its Empire AD 193–284*, p.34.

62. Millar, Fergus, *A Study of Cassius Dio*, pp.10–11; Mennon, Inge, *Power and Status in the Roman Empire*, p.64; Talbert, Richard J.A., *The Senate of Imperial Rome*, p.56; Digest, 50.1.22.4.

63. Mennon, Inge, *Power and Status in the Roman Empire*, p.53: families identified are the Acilii (Glabriones and Aviolae); Anicii; Bruttii; Caesonii; Catii; Claudii Pompeiani; Claudii Severi; Egnatii; Fulvii Aemiliani; Hedii Lolliani; Marii; Nummii; Pollieni; Pomponii; Postumii; Valerii; Vettii; and Virii. Other families appear to belong to this elite group but fail to meet the criteria, for example the Ragonii: L. Ragonius Urinatus Tuscenius, *suffect* consul c. AD 210, and L. Ragonius Venustus, ordinary consul AD 240. Also the Aufidii from Pisaurum: Aufidius Fronto, ordinary consul, AD 199, and Aufidius Victorinus, ordinary consul, AD 200, were related but it is

unclear if C. Aufidius Marcellus, proconsul of Asia in AD 220/221 and ordinary consul for the second time in AD 226, were related.

64. Mennon, Inge, *Power and Status in the Roman Empire*, pp.64–66.
65. Mennon, Inge, *Power and Status in the Roman Empire*, pp.72–78.
66. Mennon, Inge, *Power and Status in the Roman Empire*, pp.123–24; Dio, 78.5.5.
67. Mennon, Inge, *Power and Status in the Roman Empire*, pp.98–99, 118–21; Dio, 80.5.1.
68. Mennon, Inge, *Power and Status in the Roman Empire*, pp.100–03; Bray, J., *Gallienus: A Study in Reformist and Sexual Politics* (Wakefield Press, 1997), p.20.
69. Mennon, Inge, *Power and Status in the Roman Empire*, pp.112–15.
70. Mennon, Inge, *Power and Status in the Roman Empire*, pp.109–12, n.123.
71. Inge Mennon 'Power and Status in the Roman Empire' p129 note 219,130–1.
72. Lo Cascio, Elio, 'The Emperor and his Administration: General Developments', *Cambridge Ancient History*, p.150.
73. Birley, Anthony, *The African Emperor Septimius Severus*, p.128.
74. Carroll, Maureen, 'Vagnari: Is This the Winery of Rome's Greatest Landowner?', *World Archaeology* 76, April/May 2016, pp.30–33.
75. MacMullen, Ramsey, *The Corruption and Decline of Rome*, p.15.

Chapter 8: War in the East AD 228–233

1. Dio, 78.3.1; Millar, Fergus, 'Emperors, Frontiers and Foreign Relations, 31 BC to AD 378', *Britannia*, Vol. 13 (1982), pp.1–23; Dignas, Beate, & Winter, Engelbert, *Rome and Persia in Late Antiquity: Neighbours and Rivals*, p.16.
2. Whittaker, C.R., *Herodian*, Loeb edition, p.89 n.2, citing a relief raised by Artabanus to commemorate his victory over his brother in September AD 221. The coinage of Vologases VI in Babylonia comes to a sudden end in AD 222/223, suggesting the area was captured by either Artabanus V or Ardashir.
3. Taqizadeh, S.H., 'The Early Sasanians, Some Chronological Points Which Possibly Call for Revision', *Bulletin of the School of Oriental and African Studies*, 1943, Vol.11 (1), pp.6–51.
4. Cameron, Averil, *Agathias on the Sassanids*, Dumbarton Oaks Papers, Vol.23/24 (1969/1970), published by Dumbarton Oaks, trustees for Harvard University, pp.67–183, citing Agathias, 121.19B; Taqizadeh, S.H., 'The Early Sasanians, Some Chronological Points Which Possibly Call for Revision', *Bulletin of the School of Oriental and African Studies*, pp.6–51, for Agathias' access to Sassanid court archives, citing Agathias, *Sassanid Chronicle*, IV.24.
5. Ando, Clifford, *Imperial Rome AD 193 to 284*, p.72.
6. Taqizadeh, S.H., 'The Early Sasanians, Some Chronological Points Which Possibly Call for Revision', *Bulletin of the School of Oriental and African Studies*, pp.6–51.
7. Edwell, Peter, *Between Rome and Persia: The Middle Euphrates, Mesopotamia and Palmyra Under Roman Control* (Routledge, 2010), p156; Potter, David S., *The Roman Empire at Bay AD 180–395*, p.166.

8. Taqizadeh, S.H., 'The Early Sasanians, Some Chronological Points Which Possibly Call for Revision', *Bulletin of the School of Oriental and African Studies*, pp.6–51.

9. Taqizadeh, S.H., 'The Early Sasanians, Some Chronological Points Which Possibly Call for Revision', *Bulletin of the School of Oriental and African Studies*, pp.6–51.

10. Edwell, Peter, *Between Rome and Persia: The Middle Euphrates, Mesopotamia and Palmyra Under Roman Control*, p.156; Agathangelos, *History of St Gregory and the Conversion of Armenia*, part 1 (internet download); Dignas, Beate, & Winter, Engelbert, *Rome and Persia in Late Antiquity: Neighbours and Rivals*, p.174.

11. Dio, 80.3.2-4; Millar, Fergus, *A Study of Cassius Dio*, p.171.

12. Herodian, 6.2.1-2, 6.2.5; Zonoras, 12.15; Syncellus, 1.674; Potter, David S., *The Roman Empire at Bay* AD *180–395*, p.166, supports the view that there were two invasions of Roman Mesopotamia and Syria in AD 229 and 230; Butcher, Kevin, *Roman Syria and the Near East*, p.52.

13. Alram, Michael, 'Ardashir's Eastern Campaign and the Numismatic Evidence', in Cribb, Joe, & Herrman, Georgina (eds), *After Alexander: Central Asia Before Islam* (Vienna British Academy, 2007), ch.10; O'Hanlon, Bernard Michael, *The Army of Severus Alexander*, Loc.11,948, n.1,189.

14. O'Hanlon, Bernard Michael, *The Army of Severus Alexander*, ch.3, Loc.1,271, 1,298, 1,507, 'Fides' denarii RIC 193, 194; Whittaker, C.R., *Herodian*, p.92, n.1, citing AE (1899), 7.

15. Sinclair, T.A., *Eastern Turkey: An Architectural and Archaeological Survey*, Vol.III (The Pindar Press, 1989), p.365; Dodgeon, M, & Lieu, S.N., *The Roman Eastern Frontier and the Persian Wars* AD *226–363*; Dignas, Beate, & Winter, Engelbert, *Rome and Persia in Late Antiquity: Neighbours and Rivals*, p.19.

16. Mennen, Inge, *Power and Status in the Roman Empire* AD *193–284*, p.30.

17. Herodian, 6.2.1; Zonoras, 12.15; Syncellus, 1.674. There may have been a second unsuccessful attack on Hatra at this time, as described in Adversus Paganos VII, 18.7, and Syncellus, 1.674; Butcher, Kevin, *Roman Syria and the Near East*, p.54; Dignas, Beate, & Winter, Engelbert, *Rome and Persia in Late Antiquity: Neighbours and Rivals*, p.19.

18. Edwell, Peter, *Between Rome and Persia: The Middle Euphrates, Mesopotamia and Palmyra Under Rome*, p.161; Campbell, Brian, 'The Army', *Cambridge Ancient History*, p.114; MacMullen, Ramsey, *The Corruption and Decline of Rome*, pp.214–15; Elliot, Paul, *Legions In Crisis: Transformation of the Roman Soldier* AD *192–284*, p.151; Kennedy, D.L., 'Ti. Claudius Subatianus Aquila, First Prefect of Mesopotamia', *Historia* 25 Bd.36 (1979), pp.255–62, points to coins minted at Resaina carrying the name of the *III Parthica*; O'Hanlon, Bernard Michael, *The Army of Severus Alexander*, Loc.6,649–6,690; Butcher, Kevin, *Roman Syria and the Near East*, p.413.

19. Dio, 80.3.1, 80.4.1; O'Hanlon, Bernard Michael, *The Army of Severus Alexander*, Loc.3,453–3,479, citing CIL VIII 2877.

20. *Epitome De Caesaribus*, 157.

21. Zosimus, 1.10–11.

22. Potter, David S., *The Roman Empire at Bay* AD *180–395*, p.166. The throne of Oshroene had been vacant since the removal of Abgar IX in AD 214 by Caracalla. Uranius was associated with invasion by Persians and active around Edessa. Ertel, Andrea Beverly, 'The Life of Severus Alexander', p.80, believes they can be identified as being the same person but she ignores the account of Syncellus. Jardé, A., *Etudes critiques sur la vie et le règne de Sévère Alexandre*, pp.66–67, however, considers the latter a direct descendant of the former.

23. Butcher, Kevin, *Roman Syria and the Near East*, p.55; Ertel, Andrea Beverly, 'The Life of Severus Alexander', p.80, citing PIR J 195 BMC VI Severus Alexander 883; Campbell, J.B., *The Emperor and the Roman Army*, pp.23–28; O'Hanlon, Bernard Michael, *The Army of Severus Alexander*, Loc.3,500, citing PIR I 195 and coinage RIC vol.IV p.205 n.1–9; Levick, Barbara, *Julia Domna*, p.155, citing Vict., *Caes.*, 29.2.

24. Dio, 79.24.1. An epithet dismissed by Barbara Levick in her work on the empress, *Julia Domna: Syrian Princess*, pp.17–18.

25. Syncellus, p.437, 15–25, in Dodgeon, M. & Lieu, S.N. (eds), *The Roman Eastern Frontier and the Persian Wars* AD *226–363*, p.28.

26. Polemius Silvius, 30–31, in O'Hanlon, Bernard Michael, *The Army of Severus Alexander*, Loc.1,507, citing PIR I 154, 3,500; Syme, Ronald, *Emperors and Biography: Studies in the Historia Augusta*, p.159.

27. Campbell, J.B., *The Emperor and the Roman Army*, pp.93, 413; Mennen, Inge, *Power and Status in the Roman Empire* AD *193–284*, p.31.

28. Herodian, 6.2.1, 6.2.3-5, 6.3.1.

29. Herodian, 6.3.1-2, Whittaker, C.R., *Herodian*, p.97, n.3, citing ILS 1173 = CIL X 3856 from Capua.

30. HA, *The Two Maximini*, 5.5.

31. CIL V 7989–90 and AE 1919, 256–7.

32. Mann, J.C., 'A Note on the Legion IV Italica', *Zeitschrift für Papyrologie und Epigraphik*, Bd. 126 (1999), p.228b, citing Notitia Dignitatum. Or. VII, 54: Mann, J.C., 'The Raising of New Legions During the Principate', *Hermes* 91 Bd., H. 4 (1963), pp.483–89; Magie, David, *Historia Augusta*, Vol.II (Loeb edition), p.323, n.2.

33. O'Hanlon, Bernard Michael, *The Army of Severus Alexander*, Loc 12,200, citing Moses of Chorene II.72, Loc.4,328, citing CIL III.99, and Loc.4,407; *Cambridge Ancient History*, Vol.12, p.128; Oates, David & Joan, 'Ain Sinu: A Roman Frontier Post in Northern Iraq', *Iraq*, Vol.21, no.2 (Autumn 1959), published by the British Institute for the Study of Iraq, pp.207–42.

34. Biver, A.D.H., 'Cavalry Equipment and Tactics on the Euphrates Frontier', *Dumbarton Oaks Papers*, Vol.26 (1972), pp.271–91.

35. Heliodorus, *Aethiopica*, IX 15.1-6; Dignas, Beate, & Winter, Engelbert, Rome and Persia in Late Antiquity: Neighbours and Rivals, pp.63–65; O'Hanlon, Bernard Michael, *The Army of Severus Alexander*, Loc.4,274; Herodian, 6.15.2.

36. O'Hanlon, Bernard Michael, The Army of Severus Alexander, Loc.4,281; Kennedy, D.L., 'Ti Claudius Subatianus Aquila, First Prefect of Mesopotamia', *Historia*, Bd.36 (1979), pp.255–62.

37. Elliot, Paul, *Legions in Crisis: Transformation of the Roman* Soldier, pp.72, 82–83.

38. Elliot, Paul, *Legions in Crisis: Transformation of the Roman Soldier*, pp.93–99; Batty, Jean, 'Apamea in Syria in the Second and Third Centuries AD', *Journal of Roman Studies*, pp.91–104.

39. HA, *Severus Alexander*, 50.5; Spawforth, A.J.S., 'Notes on the Third Century AD in Spartan Epigraphy', *The Annual of the British School at Athens*, Vol.79 (1984), pp.263–88, citing IG V.I.130 (SEG xi.603); Herodian, 6.8.2-3. Roth, Jonathan, 'The Size and Organisation of the Roman Imperial Legion Phalanx', *Historia*, Bd.43. H.3 (Third Quarter 1994), pp.346–62, citing Wheeler, E.L., 'The Legion as a Phalanx', *Chron* 9 (1979), p.314, considers Alexander Severus' creation of a 'phalanx' to be based to a certain degree on fact.

40. Campbell, Brian, 'The Army', *Cambridge Ancient History*, pp.111–13; O'Hanlon, Bernard Michael, *The Army of Severus Alexander*, Loc.4,088.

41. Elliot, Paul, *Legions in Crisis: Transformation of the Roman Soldier*, p.29; Smith, R.E., 'The Army Reforms of Septimius Severus', *Historia*, pp.481–500; O'Hanlon, Bernard Michael, *The Army of Severus Alexander*, Loc.4,051, citing CIL VIII 20996.

42. Herodian, 7.11.2.

43. Batty, Jean, 'Apamea in Syria in the Second and Third Centuries AD', *Journal of Roman Studies*, pp.91–104; O'Hanlon, Bernard Michael, *The Army of Severus Alexander*, Loc.3,845, citing AE 1908.272 and IGLS 1375, Loc.5,612, 12,177, 10,557 n.756, citing AE 1977.746, AE 1957.161, AE 1905.163, and for removal of honorary epithets, Loc 359, the *VIII Augusta* CIL XIII.1171, *XXII Primigenia* CIL XIII.6669 (Mogontiacum) and CIL XIII 6592 from (Walldurn), *II Adiutrix* see CIL III.10594 and CIL III.3457, also CIL III.10489=ILS 2456 and CIL III.3427, for *X Gemina* AE 1934, 79, and restoration CIL III.5460; Herodian, 6.4.3, p.106, n.2, for log book of the strategos of the nome of Ombos and Elephantine, Wilcken, chrest. No.41 dated AD 232/233 and AE (1957) 161 for officer of *Legio XXX Ulpia* from Vetera, also for grave of a soldier from *Legio VII Claudia* in Moesia Superior records him as interfectus in expeditione Partica et Ar(meniaca) JOAI 8 (1905), 19 no.58; cf Ritterling, RE (legio), 1332.

44. O'Hanlon, Bernard Michael, *The Army of Severus Alexander*, Loc.4,390, citing RIB 1594 Vercovicium and 4407, citing Breeze, D., 'A note on the use of the titles Optio and Magister below the Centurionate during the Principate', *Britannia*, VII/1976, p.130, and CIL VIII 2562 and P. Dura 83.8 = RMR 48.8.

45. Elton, Hugh, *Frontiers of the Roman Empire* (Routledge, 2012), p.67; Butcher, Kevin, *Roman Syria and the Near East*, p.167

46. Mennen, Inge, Power and Status in the Roman Empire AD 193–284, pp.145–46; O'Hanlon, Bernard Michael, *The Army of Severus Alexander*, Loc.4,625, citing AE 1972.624 in Bean, G.E., & Mitford, T.B., 'Journeys in Rough Cilicia', 1970, p.44 n.21, and AE 1972.626, p.38 n.19.

47. Frend, W.H.C., 'A Third Century Inscription Relating to Angareia in Phrygia', *Journal of Roman Studies*, pp.46–56; O'Hanlon, Bernard Michael, *The Army of Severus Alexander*, Loc.4,625, citing Brunt, P.A., 'The Revenues of Rome', *JRS* LXXI/1981, p.170; (Modestinus) Digest XXVI.7.32.6; Corbier, Mireille, 'Coinage and Taxation: The State's Point of View AD 193–337', *Cambridge Ancient History*, p.381.

48. Hopkins, Richard, *The Life of Alexander Severus*, p.180: repairs to lesser roads in Pannonia Inferior: CIL III. 3715, 3719, 3721, 3731, 3738, 3703. Series of repairs to road from Aquincum to Sirmium, CIL III 10628–30, 33, 50–52; from Aquincum to Brigetio, CIL III 10655, 10657; Brigetio, CIL III 10984; road from Emona to Neviodunum, CIL III 11331, 11335; road from Aquincum, CIL III 1349.

49. O'Hanlon, Bernard Michael, *The Army of Severus Alexander*, Loc.1,802, citing PIR I.490; French, David H., Russell, Harry, Mitchell, Stephen, & Payton, Robert, 'The Year's Work', *Anatolian Studies*, Vol.33 (1983), pp.5–11; Hopkins, Richard, *The Life of Alexander Severus*, p.180, citing CIL III 14184, 14120, 14142, 12169, 12211 from Galatia; French, D.H., 'Milestones of Pontus, Galatia, Phrygia and Lycia', *Zeitschrift für Papyrologie und Epigraphik* Bd.43 (1981), pp.149–74; Harper, R.P., 'Roman Senators in Cappadocia', *Anatolian Studies*, Vol.14 (1964), pp.163–68; French, D.H., 'Roman Roads and Milestones of Asia Minor' Vol.3, *British Institute at Ankara* (Electronic Monograph 3, 2012), pp.11–12, 73–74, 86, 88, 98, 100, 127, 131–33, 135, 164, 167, 169, 175, 189, 206, 212–13, 217–18, 220, 227–31, 248–49, 276, 291–93, record a significant number of repairs in AD 235 by Licinnius Serenianus in the reign of Maximinus Thrax. Licinnius Serenianus must have been appointed to the governorship of Cappadocia in AD 234 by Alexander Severus. The extensive repair programme of the following year suggests Sassanid incursions into Mesopotamia and Cappadocia in that year; Harper, Richard P., 'Podandus and the via Tauri', *Anatolian Studies*, Vol.20 (1970), pp.149–53; Dodgeon, M., & Lieu, S.N., *The Roman Eastern Frontier and the Persian Wars AD 226–363*, p.23; Champlin, Edward, 'Serenius Sammonicus', *Harvard Studies in Classical Philology*, pp.189–212, for Paternus as governor of Cappadocia in AD 231.

50. Wilson, D.R., 'Two Milestones from Pontus', *Anatolian Studies*, Vol.10 (1960), pp.133–40, citing Cumont, F., in CRAL 1905, pp.347f., 348 n.i; Reed Stuart, Duane, 'The Reputed Influence of the *Dies Natalis* In Determining the Inscription of Restored Temples', *Transactions and Proceedings of the American Philological Association*, 1 January 1905, Vol.36, pp.52–63; HA, *Severus Alexander*, 26.11.

51. O'Hanlon, Bernard Michael, *The Army of Severus Alexander*, Loc.11,836, n.1,135, 1,136.

52. Herodian, 6.3.2; HA, *Severus Alexander*, 45.2-4, 47.1. Mennen, Inge, *Power and Status in the Roman Empire*, AD *193–284*, p.146, suggests this passage reflects the situation in the late fourth century, although it is likely such preparations would be made. This is supported by archaeological and epigraphical evidence.

53. Mennen, Inge, *Power and Status in the Roman Empire*, AD *193–284*, pp.24, 260.

54. Mennen, Inge, *Power and Status in the Roman Empire*, AD *193–284*, pp.56–60, 91–93; Gilliam, J.F., 'Caesonius Bassus: cos.ord AD 317', *Historia*, Bd.16. H.2 (April 1967), pp.252–54; O'Hanlon, Michael Bernard, *The Army of Severus Alexander*, Loc.1,583: C. Caesonius Macer Rufianus PIR C 210, a patrician decorated by Marcus Aurelius, *suffect* consul AD 207–209, governor of Germania Superior, proconsul of Africa at end of Elagabalus' reign or start of Alexander Severus', 'comes Imperatoris Severi Alexandri'. His son, L. Caesonius Lucillus Macer Rufianus PIR C 209, was an instigator of rebellion against Maximinus Thrax and Urban Prefect AD 239–253.

55. O'Hanlon, Bernard Michael, *The Army of Severus Alexander*, Loc.1,972, citing PIR M 393, PIR C 564, PIR C 1633 and AE 1977.593; Townsend, Prescott W., 'Sextus Catius Clementinus Priscillianus, Governor of Cappadocia in 238 AD', *Classical Philology*, Vol.50, no.1 (Jan, 1955), pp.41–42.

56. O'Hanlon, Bernard Michael, *The Army of Severus Alexander*, Loc.2,016, citing PIR F 297, AE 1932.70, ILS 8841; Mennen, Inge, *Power and Status in the Roman Empire*, AD *193–284*, pp.118, 260.

57. O'Hanlon, Bernard Michael, *The Army of Severus Alexander*, Loc.2,351; Mennen, Inge, *Power and Status in the Roman Empire*, AD *193–284*, pp.69, 100–03.

58. O'Hanlon, Bernard Michael, *The Army of Severus Alexander*, Loc.2,273, citing Numidia AE 1967.573, PIR A 599; Mennen, Inge, *Power and Status in the Roman Empire*, AD *193–284*, pp.86–89.

59. O'Hanlon, Bernard Michael, The Army of Severus Alexander, Loc.2,273, citing PIR E 25, 37; Mennen, Inge, *Power and Status in the Roman Empire*, AD *193–284*, pp.100–03; Bowersock, G.W., *Roman Arabia* (Harvard University Press, 1998), p.162.

60. O'Hanlon, Bernard Michael, *The Army of Severus Alexander*, Loc.1,926, citing for *I Italica* AE 1972.526; Sherk, Robert K., 'A Chronology of the Governors of Galatia AD 122–285', *The American Journal of Philology*, Vol.100, no.1 (Spring 1979), pp.166–75; Bowersock, G.W., *Roman Arabia*, p.162.

61. French, D.H., 'Milestones of Pontus, Galatia, Phrygia and Lycia', *Zeitschrift für Papyrologie und Epigraphik*, pp.149–74, citing Lambaesis CIL VIII 18270=ILS I.1196, AE 1917.18.51; O'Hanlon, Bernard Michael, *The Army of Severus Alexander*, Loc.2,363.

62. Harper, R.P., 'Roman Senators in Cappadocia', *Anatolian Studies*, pp.163–68; French, D.H., 'Roman Roads and Milestones of Asia Minor', *British Institute at Ankara*, pp.11–12.

63. Gilliam, J.F., 'The Governors of Syria Coele from Severus to Diocletian', *The American Journal of Philology*, pp.225–42, citing Cf. P. I. R.2, II, p.250, no.1,030; Barbieri, Guido, '*Albo senatorio da Settimio a Carino*, 193–285', (Roma: A Signorelli, 1952), pp. 202–03. A. McN. G. Little and H. T. Rowell; O'Hanlon, Bernard Michael, *The Army of Severus Alexander*, Loc.1,656, 2,363.

64. O'Hanlon, Bernard Michael, The Army of Severus Alexander, Loc.1,572, 2,363; Whittaker, C.R., *Herodian*, Books 5–8, p.109, n.4, citing IGRR III.1033, pp.172–73, n.2; Herodian, 8.2.5, 8.3.6; Leunissen, Paul M.M., 'Direct Promotions from Proconsul to Consul under the Principate', *Zeitschrift für Papyrologie und Epigraphik*, Bd.89 (1991), pp.217–60; Greenstreet Addison, Charles, *Damascus and Palmyra: A Journey to the East, with a sketch of the state and prospects of Syria under Ibrahim Pasha*, Vol.2 (Filiquarian Legacy Publishing, 2012, first published 1838), pp.318–19; Hopkins, Richard, *The Life of Alexander Severus*, p.242, n.4, citing CIG 4483.

65. Lehmann, Clayton Miles, 'Epigraphica Caesariensia', *Classical Philology*, pp.45–52; Mennen, Inge, *Power and Status in the Roman Empire*, AD *193–284*, pp.42, 138–39; O'Hanlon, Bernard Michael, *The Army of Severus Alexander*, Loc.1,656, citing PIR F.581, Loc.9,496, n.378, citing Keyes, C.W., op cit pp.7ff for large numbers of substitute governors from Alexander Severus' reign onwards, suggests a deliberate policy, as Timestheus' career demonstrates the promotion of equestrians of ability.

66. Isaac, Benjamin, 'The Meaning of the Terms *Limes* and *Limitanei*', *The Journal of Roman Studies*, Vol.78 (1988), pp.125–47; O'Hanlon, Bernard Michael, *The Army of Severus Alexander*, Loc.2,127, for '*Dux Ripae*' falling under jurisdiction of the governor of Syria Coele, Loc.6,007, for Dura Europas papyrus citing P.Dura 3; Gilliam, J.F., 'The *Dux Ripae* at Dura', *Transactions and Proceedings of the American Philological Association*, Vol.72 (1941), pp.157–75, suggests an alternative date as the reign of Gordian III or Philip, with Licinius Pacatanius as the first 'dux' in AD 245.

67. Herodian, 6.8.1, 7.8.4.

68. Zosimus, 1.13; O'Hanlon, Bernard Michael, *The Army of Severus Alexander*, Loc. 2127: Maximinus Thrax full name, C. Julius Verus Maximinus, citing PIR I 619 and Herodian, VI.8.1. Both sources suggest he was first a cavalryman in a career that led to command over legions and provinces. He was probably 'adlected' into equites by Septimius Severus and pursued an equestrian military career: see Zosimus 1.13.1 for Maximinus Thrax as a '*praefectus alae*' in AD 235. Whittaker suggests his career path was through the post of '*primus pilus*' or first centurion of a legion, then a Praetorian Tribune in Rome: see Whitaker II, p.131, n.3. However, Speidel (1994), pp.68–69, based on HA, *The Two Maximini*, 3.5, suggests his

career started in the 'ala' then he was promoted to the '*Equites Singulares Augusti*', perhaps in AD 232 after serving as '*praefectus legionis II Traianae*' in Egypt, see Loc.2,165. This is sometimes described as '*praefectus castrorum*'. A restored papyrus from Egypt dated to c. AD 230 might indicate his presence in the province. This was a common appointment from that of '*primus pilus*'. However, this legion rebelled in AD 231 and this would certainly have ended his career if Maximinus had been in command: see Herodian, VI 4.7. According to O'Hanlon, Maximinus was in Mesopotamia, probably as prefect of this legion, or perhaps in AD 232 with his son. However, the restoration is open to conjecture and debate. His office in Mesopotamia was probably that of '*Praeses Mesopotamiae*', which is supported by PIR I 619. Whittaker suggests Maximinus might have been a '*praefectus castrorum*', but this office has responsibility for only one legion, not the number of legions mentioned in Herodian. The '*praefectus Mesopotamiae*' would be in command of two legions, or perhaps he was given a special command as '*dux ripae*', but this would not include legions: see Whittaker II, p.208, n.2.

69. O'Hanlon, Bernard Michael, *The Army of Severus Alexander*, Loc.1,922, citing for Claudius Masculinus PIR C 932, M. Aurelius Zeno Ianurius V-VIII/AD 231 in PIR A 1638, as Procurator of Mauretania Caesariensis PIR A 1639 and perhaps Praeses Mauretaniae PIR I 193, and for Maevius Honoratianus a diploma dated to AD 232 and AE 1988.598 for promotion to the Egyptian prefecture from prefect of the imperial fleet at Ravenna, a normal step of the promotional ladder. Brunt, P.A, 'The Administrators of Roman Egypt', *Journal of Roman Studies*, pp.124–47.

70. Levick, Barbara, *Julia Domna*, p.152, citing IGBulg.1827 from Hadrianopolis and SEG 12,517 Anazarbus in Cilicia; Whittaker, C.R., *Herodian*, Books 5–8, pp.103–04, n.4; Butcher, Kevin, *Roman Syria and the Near East*, p.332; 'Acquisition Highlights', *Annual Report of the Harvard University Art Museums* (2005–2006), p.11.

71. O'Hanlon, Bernard Michael, *The Army of Severus Alexander*, Loc.1,298, citing BMC 783 for medallion of Salus, BMC 785 for '*Virtus*' type coin. For use se of Romulus on coins: RIC 85, 96, 97, 223, 224, 481, 482, 483, 626; Whittaker, C.R., *Herodian*, Books 5–8, p.92, n.1: in AD 229, Alexander bore the title '*invictus*', e.g. AE (1899) 7, probably to give himself a more martial image in a time of increased military activity.

72. Levick, Barbara, *Julia Domna*, p.152: issue carrying legend 'ADLOCUTIO' have mother and son facing each other on the obverse CREBM 6 187 no.733; O'Hanlon, Michael Bernard, *The Army of Severus Alexander*, Loc.1.401, citing RIC 544, RIC 659=BMC 725; Campbell, J.B., *The Emperor and the Roman Army*, pp.70–72; Levick, Barbara, *Julia Domna*, p.152, citing CREBM 6 187 no.733 showing Alexander Severus and Mamaea face to face. Also Cohen, IV², p.402, nos3–7; p.480, no.1: '*Adlocutio Augusti*'.

73. Herodian, 6.3.2-6.4.3, and Whittaker, C.R., *Herodian*, Books 5–8, p.99, n.2, pp.102–03, n.2–4; Millar, Fergus, 'Emperors, Frontiers and Foreign Relations, 31 BC to AD 378', *Britannia*, pp.1–23; O'Hanlon, Bernard Michael, *The Army of Severus Alexander*, Loc.4,844, citing CIL XIII 8017 for inscription on eve of Persian campaign; Ertel, Andrea Beverly, 'The Life of Severus Alexander', p.85, citing Henzen, W., Acta Fratrum Arvalium (Berlin, 1874), p.217.

74. Fishwick, Duncan, 'Dated Inscriptions and the "Feriale Duranum"', *Institut Francais du Proche-Orient, Syria* T.65 Fasc. 3/4 (1988), pp.349–61, citing CIL 13.8017 from Bonna, Germania Inferior.

75. Hardie. P.R., '*Imago Mundi*, Cosmological and Ideological Aspects of the Shield of Achilles', *The Journal of Hellenic Studies*, Vol.105 (1985), pp.11–31.

76. Peachin, Michael, 'Philip's Progress: From Mesopotamia to Rome in AD 224', *Historia*, Bd.40, H.3 (1991), pp.331–42.

77. Herodian, 6.4.4-7.

78. Epitome de Caesaribus, 22; Zonoras; Zosimus, 1.11.

79. Herodian, 6.4.7.

80. Butcher, Kevin, *Roman Syria and the Near East*, p.412; O'Hanlon, Bernard Michael, *The Army of Severus Alexander*, Loc.3,573, citing ILS 2657, 5865, 9198, CIL III 186, 206, XIV. 385b, 387; IGRR III.1113, 1116, 1128, 1148, 1149, 1183.

81. HA, *Severus Alexander*, 52.2-7; Tacitus, *Annals*, 11.35; Campbell, J.B., The Emperor and the Roman Army, p.72.

82. HA, *Severus Alexander*, 54.7.

83. Herodian, 6.4.7.

84. HA, *Severus Alexander*, 54.7.

85. Herodian, 6.4.7; HA, *Severus Alexander*, 53.7.

86. Campbell, J.B., *The Emperor and The Roman Army*, pp.296–311, citing CJ, 12.35.3 for loss of privileges for soldier dishonourably discharged; stealing from baths, Paul, 47.17.3; Modestinus Dig, 49.16.3-4 for desertion in face of the enemy; Dig, 16.3.12 for desertion to enemy; Dig, 16.3.10 for desertion with intention of joining the enemy; Modestinus Dig, 16.3.13, Paul, 14.1, for loss of weapons; Modestinus Dig, 16.3.5, 16.3.7, Paul, 16.14.1, for distinction between deserter who returned voluntarily to his unit and one returned forcibly; disobedience and insubordination, Paul, 16.16.1, Modestinus, 16.3.21, 3.20.

87. Thomas, J.D., & Clarysse, W., 'A Projected Visit of Severus Alexander to Egypt', *Ancient Society*, pp.195–207; CJ 12.35.3.

88. Ingholt, Harold, & Sanders, John E., 'A Colossal Head from Memphis, Severan or Augustan', *Journal of the American Research Centre in Egypt*, Vol.2 (1963), pp.125–45.

89. Ertel, Andrea Beverly, 'The Life of Severus Alexander', p.91, citing Eusebius, *History of the Church*, 6.21.3, 6.28; Orosius, 7.18.7, Syncellus, *Chron.*, p.358, Cedrenus, *Compendium Historiarum*, p.450 II, 3-12; Glycas Annals, 3, Alexander.

90. Foerster, Gideon, 'The Early History of Caesarea', *Bulletin of the American Schools of Oriental Research*, Supplementary Studies, number 19, pp.9–22.

91. HA, *Severus Alexander*, 28.7; Herodian, 7.2.1; Rajak, Tessa, & Noy, David, 'Archisynagogoi: Office, Title and Social Status in the Greco-Jewish Synagogue', *The Journal of Roman Studies*, Vol.83 (1993), pp.75–93.

92. Dignas, Beate, and Winter, Engelbert, *Rome and Persia in Late Antiquity*, pp.152–58; Birley, A., *Septimius Severus*, pp.132–33.

93. Dodgeon, M., and Lieu, S.N., *The Roman Eastern Frontier and the Persian Wars* AD *226–363*, p.29; O'Hanlon, Bernard Michael, *The Army of Severus Alexander*, Loc.5,724.

94. Oates, David, 'The Roman Frontier in Northern Iraq', *The Geographical Journal*, Vol.122, no.2 (June 1956), pp.190–99. The Arab writer 'Adi ibn Zayd is quoted by Tha'libi (AD 1035), in which he refers to the power of the Hatran kings.

95. Herodian, 6.5.1; O'Hanlon, Bernard Michael, *The Army of Severus Alexander* Loc.10,802, citing CISem II 3932.

96. Herodian, 6.5.1, Whittaker, C.R., (Loeb edition), p.108, n.2, citing AE (1905) 132–33, for the extensive repairs to this road in AD 231.

97. O'Hanlon, Bernard Michael, *The Army of Severus Alexander*, Loc.11,948, n.1,188, citing Agathangelos, *History of the Armenians*, I.18–23, and to support quote: Moses Khorenats'i, *History of Armenia*, II.71–73; Herodian, 6.5.1; Whittaker, C.R., *Herodian*, Books 5–8, n.4, p.103: *legio VII Claudia* in Moesia Superior records him as '*interfectus in expeditione Partica et Ar(meniaca)*', JOAI 8 (1905), 19 no.58; cf Ritterling, R.E., *Legio*, 1,332.

98. Agathias, 121.19B, in Cameron, Averil, 'Agathias on the Sassanians', *Dumbarton Oakes Papers*, pp.67–183; Ghodrat-Dizaji, Mehrdad, 'Administrative Geography of the Early Sasanian Period: The Case of Adurbadagan', *Iran*, Vol.45 (2007), pp.87–93, citing Moses of Khoren, *History of Armenia* 7, trans. G. Nalbandian (1984), pp.171–72.

99. Taqizadeh, S.H., 'The Early Sasanians, Some Chronological Points Which Possibly Call for Revision', Bulletin of the School of Oriental and African Studies, pp.6–51.

100. Rose, Jenny, *Zoroastrianism; An Introduction* (Taurus, 2012), ch. 'Parthian Religious Praxis'; Taqizadeh, S.H., 'The Early Sasanians, Some Chronological Points Which Possibly Call for Revision', Bulletin of the School of Oriental and African Studies, pp.6–51; Kia, Mehrdad, 'The Persian Empire, A Historical Encyclopedia', *ABC-CLIO* (June 2016), p.71.

101. O'Hanlon, Brendon Michael, *The Army of Severus Alexander*, Loc.5,491, 5,790; Pollard, Nigel, Soldiers, Cities and Civilians in Roman Syria (University of Michigan Press, 2000), pp.270–73; Edwell, Peter, 'Between Rome and Persia: The Middle Euphrates, Mesopotamia and Palmyra Under Rome', p.163; Whittaker, C.R., *Herodian*, Books 5–8, p.109, n.3.

102. Herodian, 6 5.2, 7.

103. Herodian, 6.5.2.

104. O'Hanlon, Brendon Michael, *The Army of Severus Alexander*, Loc.5,790; Oates, David, 'The Roman Frontier of Northern Iraq', *The Geographical Journal*, pp.190–99.

105. Herodian, 6.5.2.

106. Whittaker, C.R., *Herodian*, Books 5–8, pp.172–73, n.2; Healey, John F., *Aramaic Inscriptions and Documents of the Roman Period: Text Book of Syrian Semitic Inscriptions*, Vol.IV (Oxford University Press, 2009), pp.155–56.

107. Herodian, 6.5.5.

108. Herodian, 6.5.6.

109. Herodian, 6.5 7; Taqizadeh, S.H., 'The Early Sasanians, Some Chronological Points Which Possibly Call for Revision', *Bulletin of the School of Oriental and African Studies*, pp.6–51.

110. Herodian, 6.6.1-2, 6.1.4; Elliot, Paul, *Legions in Crisis: Transformation of the Roman Soldier* AD *192–284*, p.110.

111. Herodian, 6.5.8, 6.6.1.

112. Herodian, 6.5.9-10.

113. Elliot, Paul, *Legions in Crisis: Transformation of the Roman Soldier* AD *192–284*, pp.82–83, 115; O'Hanlon, Bernard Michael, *The Army of Severus Alexander*, Loc.12,392, n.1,310, citing P. Dura 83 = RMR 48; Herodian, 6.6.5.

114. Herodian, 6.6.3.

115. Herodian, 6.6.2-3.

116. Herodian, 6.5.8, 6.1-3.

117. Herodian, 7.8.4.

118. O'Hanlon, Bernard Michael, *The Army of Severus Alexander*, Loc.2,165, citing Jordanes, *Getica*, LXXXVIII, in Mierow, C.C., *The Gothic History of Jordanes* (1915), LXXXVIII.

119. O'Hanlon, Bernard Michael, *The Army of Severus Alexander*, Loc.2,165, citing Malalas, John, p.XI, (trans.) Jeffreys, Jeffreys, Scott.

120. O'Hanlon, Bernard Michael, *The Army of Severus Alexander*, Loc.2,214; Herodian, 6.8.2; Jordanes, *Getica*, 88.

121. Herodian, 6.6.4-6; O'Hanlon, Bernard Michael, *The Army of Severus Alexander*, Loc.5,527, citing RIC IV, pp.82–83.

122. Herodian, 6.6.7, 6.7.2; Zonoras, 12.

123. O'Hanlon, Bernard Michael, *The Army of Severus Alexander*, Loc. 5,612, citing AE 1968.498 for milestone from Galatia, Jardé, p82, referring to the emperor as 'Parthico Max' and 'Persico Max' but due to erasure after '*damnatio memoriea*' it is not certain they refer to Alexander Severus and might conceivably be in honour of Caracalla. Coins, see Loc.12,140, n.1,221, in O'Hanlon; Oates, David, 'The Roman Frontier of Northern Iraq', The Geographical Journal, pp.190–99.

124. O'Hanlon, Bernard Michael, *The Army of Severus Alexander*, Loc.5,496, 5,563, citing Cedrenus, 1.3-7; Eutropius, *Breviarium*, 8.23; Aurelius Victor, *De Caesaribus*, 24; Festus, 22.

125. Campbell, J.B., *The Emperor and the Roman Army*, p.54.

Chapter 9: War in the West AD 234–235

1. *Cambridge Ancient History*, Vol.12, p29.
2. Herodian, 6.7.2-3; HA, *Severus Alexander*, 59.1.
3. Whittaker, C.R., *Herodian*, Books 5–8, p.122, n.2; King, Anthony, *Roman Gaul and Germany* (British Museum Publications, 1990), p.170; Baker, Philip, *The Empire Stops Here: A Journey Along the Frontiers of the Roman Empire*, pp.133, 136–37, 149–50, 163; Schönberger, H., 'The Roman Frontier in Germany: An Archaeological Survey', *Journal of Roman Studies*, Vol.59, no.1/2 (1969), pp.144–97; Wacher, John, The Roman Empire (J.M. Dent and Sons, 1987), p.42; Southern, Pat, *The Roman Empire from Severus to Constantine*, p.210.
4. Schönberger, H., 'The Roman Frontier in Germany: An Archaeological Survey', *Journal of Roman Studies*, pp.144–97; Noreña, Carlos F., 'The Communication of the Emperor's Virtues', *Journal of Roman Studies*, Vol.91(2001), pp.146–68; Baker, Philip, *The Empire Stops Here: A Journey Along the Frontiers of the Roman Empire*, p.153; Oliva, Pavel, *Pannonia and the Onset of Crisis in the Roman Empire*, p.356, n.161.
5. Baker, Philip, *The Empire Stops Here: A Journey Along the Frontiers of the Roman Empire*, p.75; Southern, Pat, *The Roman Empire from Severus to Constantine*, pp.205–07, 210.
6. O'Hanlon, Bernard Michael, *The Army of Severus Alexander*, Loc.6,075; Todd, Malcolm, *The Northern Barbarians 100 BC–AD 300* (Basil Blackwell Ltd, 1987), pp.156–57; Schönberger, H., 'The Roman Frontier in Germany: An Archaeological Survey', *Journal of Roman Studies*, pp.144–97.
7. De Blois, Lukas, 'The Third Century Crisis and the Greek Elite in the Roman Empire', *Historia*, pp.358–77.
8. HA, *Severus Alexander*, 59.4-5.
9. O'Hanlon, Bernard Michael, *The Army of Severus Alexander*, Loc.1,972, citing PIR C 564, AE 1977.593, for Sextus Clementinus Priscillianus as governor of Germania Superior in AD 231 and as governor of Cappadocia c. AD 235–238, citing PIR C 1633 with '*nobilissimus* Caesar'.
10. O'Hanlon, Bernard Michael, *The Army of Severus Alexander*, Loc.1,656, 2,270; Mennen, Inge, *Power and Status in the Roman Empire AD 193–284*, pp.25, 138–39, 164–65.
11. O'Hanlon, Bernard Michael, *The Army of Severus Alexander*, Loc.1,972, citing CIL XIII 8728; Whittaker, C.R., *Herodian*, Books 5–8, p.157, n.2, citing Albo 1144, PIR C 327; Jardé, A., *Sévère Alexandre*, p.89; Herodian, 7.1.8; HA, *The Two Maximi*, 11.1-6.

12. Southern, Pat, 'The Numeri of the Roman Imperial Army', *Britannia*, Vol.20 (1989), pp.81–140.

13. Herodian, 6.8.2-3, Whittaker, C.R., *Herodian*, Books 5–8, p.134, n.1.

14. Herodian, 6.7.5.

15. Whittaker, C.R., *Herodian*, Books 5–8, p.126, n.1.

16. Herodian, 6.7.8, 7.2.1-3, Whittaker, C.R., *Herodian*, Books 5–8, p.129, n.2, citing CIL XI.3104, n.1, p.160, citing ILS 9148; O'Hanlon, Bernard Michael, *The Army of Severus Alexander*, n.1,383, Loc.12,597, 3,845, 6,100 for *IV Flavia* citing CIL XIII 6104, for Praetorian Guard citing CIL. 6677a at Mogontiacum, for vexillations of *II Parthica* CIL XIII 6231 in Germania Superior and CIL XX 8516 for Germania Inferior. Also Loc.6,328: *cohors I nova Severiana Surorum Milliaria sagittaria* and possibly other Syrian units used to control unreliable units in both Pannonias. The units transferred could also include the *ala II Septimia Syrorum milliaria*, the *cohors I Hemesenorum Milliaria sagittariorum* and *cohors IX Severiana Surorum*; Southern, Pat, 'The Numeri of the Roman Army', *Britannia*, pp.81–140; Goddard King, Georgina, 'Some Reliefs at Budapest', *American Journal of Archaeology*, pp.64–76; Zosimus, 1.11.

17. Herodian, 6.7.6; O'Hanlon, Bernard Michael, *The Army of Severus Alexander*, Loc.1,572.

18. Madar, Gottfried, 'Triumphal Elephants and Political Circus at Plutarch, Pomp. 14.6', *Classical World* (2006), Vol.99.4, pp.397–403; Ando, Clifford, *Imperial Rome* AD *193 to 284*, pp.74–75; O'Hanlon, Bernard Michael, The Army of Severus Alexander, Loc.1,453, citing RIC 499; Hopkins, Richard, *The Life of Alexander Severus*, citing CIL III 3427; HA, *Severus Alexander*, 56.1-57.7, Magie, David, *Historia Augusta*, Vol.II, p.290, n.1, 2, citing Cohen, IV no.446 and IV.30; Ertel, Andrea Beverly, 'The Life of Severus Alexander', p.90; Campbell, J.B., *The Emperor and the Roman Army 31* BC–235 AD, p.124; Festus, 22.1.

19. Ertel, Andrea Beverly, 'The Life of Severus Alexander', p.95; Ando, Clifford, *Imperial Rome* AD *193 to 284*, p.74, who asserts Alexander Severus visited Rome for an 'Impolitic triumph' on his journey to the Rhine; Herodian, 6.6.3.

20. Herodian, 6.6.6, 7.7.8; Elton, Hugh, *Frontiers of the Roman Empire*, p.67.

21. Whittaker, C.R., *Herodian*, Books 5–8, p.125, n.2; Campbell, Brian, 'The Severan Dynasty', in *Cambridge Ancient History*, Vol.12, p.26.

22. Herodian, 6.7.6.

23. Hopkins, Richard, *The Life of Alexander Severus*, citing Eckhel VII 277. Cohen lc no.16 year 235 with legend IMP.ALEXANDER.PIUS.AUG.IULIA.MAMAEA. MATR.AUG.P.M.TR.P.XIIII.COS.III.P.P, see BMC VI Severus Alexander 967.

24. Herodian, 7.7.8; Todd, Malcolm, 'Germanic Peoples and Germanic Society', in *Cambridge Ancient History*, Vol.12, p.452.

25. Herodian, 7.2.2, 7.8.9.

26. Herodian, 6.7.8, 7.2.3; Campbell, Brian, 'The Severan Dynasty', in *Cambridge Ancient History*, p.18.

27. Victor, *De Caes.*, 24.4; HA, *Severus Alexander*, 59.4; O'Hanlon, Bernard Michael, *The Army of Severus Alexander*, Loc.1,435, citing RIC 231, 662.
28. Campbell, J.B., *The Emperor and the Roman Army 31 BC–235 AD*, pp.367–68.
29. Eutropius, 8.23; O'Hanlon, Bernard Michael, *The Army of Severus Alexander*, Loc.3,535.
30. Herodian, 7.2.3-4.
31. Herodian, 6.8.2-3; Elliot, Paul, *Legions In Crisis: Transformation of the Roman Soldier AD 192–284*, pp.104–05.
32. Campbell, J.B., *The Emperor and the Roman Army 31 BC–235 AD*, pp.13–18.
33. Herodian, 7.1.9.
34. Whittaker, C.R., *Herodian*, Books 5–8, p.131, n.3, citing PIR J 407; Syme, Ronald, 'Danubian and Balkan Emperors', *Historia*, pp.310–16; Cooley, Alison E., & Salway, Benet, 'Roman Inscriptions 2006–2010', *Journal of Roman Studies*, Vol.102 (November 2012), pp.172–286.
35. Batty, Jean Ch., 'Apamea in Syria in the Second and Third Centuries', *Journal of Roman Studies*, pp.91–104.
36. Cooley, Alison E., and Salway, Benet, 'Roman Inscriptions 2006–2010', *Journal of Roman Studies*, pp.172–286; Hekster, Oliver, *Rome and its Empire AD 193–284*, p.38; O'Hanlon, Bernard Michael, *The Army of Severus Alexander*, Loc.4,658; Southern, Pat, 'The Numeri of the Roman Imperial Army', *Britannia*, pp.81–140, citing Mainz CIL XIII 6814, Niederbieber CIL XIII 6814, 7054, 11828, and from the fort at Niederbieber the *numerus Brittonum* and *numerus exploratorum Germanicianorum Divitiensium* see CIL XIII 7750, 7751, 7761, 11979: Benefiel, Rebecca R.J., 'A New Praetorian Laterculus from Rome', *Zeitschrift für Papyrologie und Epigraphik*, pp.221–32.
37. Ezov, Amiram, 'The Centurions in the Rhine Legions in the Second and Early Third Century', *Historia*, Bd.56, H.1 (2007), pp.46–81.
38. Herodian, 6.8.8. Also HA, *The Two Maximini*, 7.4.
39. Herodian, 6.8.5-7.
40. Whittaker, C.R., *Herodian*, Books 5–8, p.137, n.3.
41. Zosimus, 1.11; Jardé, A., *Etudes Critiques sur la Vie et le Regne de Severe Alexandre*, p.90 and notes, considers this information derives from Dexippus and so can be considered trustworthy as he was a contemporary.
42. Herodian, 6.8.8.
43. Herodian, 6.8.2, 6.9.8.
44. HA, *Severus Alexander*, 59.6; Aurelius Victor, *De Caesaribus*, 24.4; Baker, Philip, *The Empire Stops Here: A journey Along the Frontiers of the Roman World*, p.109.
45. Southern, Pat, 'The Numeri of the Roman Imperial Army', *Britannia*, pp.81–140; Schönberger, H., 'The Roman Frontier in Germany: An Archaeological Survey', *Journal of Roman Studies*, pp.144–97.
46. Herodian, 6.9.1-2; Whittaker, C.R., *Herodian*, Books 5–8, p.134, n.1.

47. Campbell, J.B., *The Emperor and the Roman Army 31 BC-235 AD*, pp.23–29.

48. Herodian, 6.9.3-4.

49. Tacitus, *Agricola*, 39.2.

50. Herodian, 6.9.4-5; Zosimus, 1.13; HA, *Severus Alexander*, 59.8, 62.5-6; Whittaker, C.R., *Herodian*, Books 5–8, p.143, n.1, citing CIL II.2664 (234).

51. Herodian, 5.4.3, 6.9.5; Dio, 79.34.1, 32.1-3.

52. Herodian, 6.9.7.

53. HA, Severus Alexander, 61.5-6.

54. Epitome de Caesaribus, 24.2-4. See also Victor, *Epit*, 24.4-5, Orosius, 7.18.8.

55. Herodian, 6.9.8; the figure provided in the HA, *Severus Alexander*, 60.1, is clearly incorrect, taking his birthday as 1 October AD 208.

56. Peachin, Michael, 'P.Oxy. VI 912 and the Accession of Maximinus Thrax', Zeitschrift *für Papyrologie und Epigraphik*, Bd.59 (1985), pp.75–78; Thomas, J. David, 'SB XVI 13050 Reconsidered', *Zeitschrift für Papyrologie und Epigraphik*, Bd.88 (1991), pp.121–24; Whittaker, C.R., *Herodian*, Books 5–8, citing P. Oxy.912, CIL VI 2001 (Rome), AE (1948) 209 (Numidia), Stud.pal 20, no.35 (Egypt), Dura Europas, Prelim. Report V 1.298; Rea, J.R., 'O. Leid.144 and the Chronology of AD 238', *Zeitschrift für Papyrologie und Epigraphik*, Bd.9 (1972), pp.1–19; Hammond, Mason, 'The Transmission of the Powers of the Roman Emperor from the Death of Nero in AD 68 to that of Alexander Severus in AD 235', *Memoirs of the American Academy in Rome*, pp.61–63, 124; Van Sickle, C.E., 'The Terminal Dates of the Reign of Alexander Severus', *Classical Philology*, Vol.22 (9 July 1927), pp.315–17.

Epilogue

1. Varner, Eric R., 'Portraits, Plots, and Politics: "Damnatio memoriae" and the Images of Imperial Women', *Memoirs of the American Academy in Rome*, pp.41–93, citing Musee du Louvre MA 3552, Ostia Museo inv 26, Capitoline Museum Magazinne inv 1451 and Bochum, Kunstsammlung der Ruhr-Universitat; Varner, Eric R., 'Punishment after death: Mutilation of images and corpse abuse in ancient Rome', *Mortality*, pp.45–64.

2. Campbell, J.B., *The Emperor and the Roman Army 31 BC-235 AD*, pp.383–86.

3. Herodian, 6.9.5; HA, *Severus Alexander*, 48.1-6.

4. Seneca, *De Beneficia*, 6.33.3-6; Pliny, *Letters*, 2.6.2, 7.3.2; Syme, R., The *Roman Revolution*, p.386; Saller, R.P., *Personal Patronage under the Early Empire*, pp.10–12.

5. Herodian, 7.1.2-4.

6. Herodian, 7.1.9-11.

7. Herodian, 7.1.4-5: Whittaker, C.R., *Herodian*, Books 5–8, pp.152–53, n.2, citing CIL IX. 338=ILS 6121; Digest, 22.3.20; Nicols, Jon, *Civic Patronage in the Roman Empire*, p.298.

8. Whittaker, C.R., *Herodian*, Books 5–8, pp.178–82, n.1.

9. Whittaker, C.R., *Herodian*, Books 5–8, p.172, n.2.

10. Southern, Pat, *The Roman Empire from Severus to Constantine*, p.67; Syme, *Emperors and Biography*, pp.162–65, 176; Whittaker, *Herodian*, Books 5–8, pp.152–53, n.2, 226, n.1, citing ILS 1186, 229, n.2; Jardé, A., *Sévère Alexandre*, pp.123–25; Mennen, Inge, *Power and Status in the Roman Empire*, pp.89–90, 258, 260; Nicols, Jon, *Civic Patronage in the Roman Empire*, pp.289–301; Gilliam, J.F., 'Caesonius Bassus: cos.ord. AD 317', *Historia*, pp.252–54; O'Hanlon, Bernard Michael, *The Army of Severus Alex*ander, Loc.8,555, ch.3.

11. De Blois, Lukas, '*The Third Century Crisis and the Greek Elite in the Roman Empire*', *Historia*, pp.358–77.

12. Herodian, 5.7.5; O'Hanlon, Bernard Michael, *The Army of Severus Alexander*, Loc.8,475, ch.3, citing Wood, S., *Roman Portrait Sculpture* AD *217–260: The Transformation of an Artistic Tradition* (1986), p.60.

13. Carson, R., A Catalogue of the Roman Coins in the British Museum (1962), Vol. VI, p.171.

14. O'Hanlon, Bernard Michael, *The Army of Severus Alexander*, Loc.8,555.

15. Herodian, 6.4.1, 6.6.4.

16. Campbell, J.B., *The Emperor and the Roman Army 31 BC-235 AD*, p.18.

17. Herodian, 6.1.9.

18. Herodian, 6.8.1; Zosimus, 1.13.1; Zonoras, 12.16; HA, *The Two Maximi*, which supposedly drew upon Dexippus, 2.2-3, 3.5, 4.4; C. Julius Verus Maximinus=Maximinus Thrax PIR I 619; Whittaker, C.R., *Herodian*, Books 5–8, pp.131–32, n.3, p.133, n.2, p.134, n.1; O'Hanlon, Bernard Michael, *The Army of Severus Alexander*, Loc.1,802, 2,165.

19. Campbell, J.B., *The Emperor and the Roman Army 31 BC-235 AD*, p.381.

20. Dio, 80.4.1-2.

21. Herodian, 7.2.2; HA, *The Two Maximi*, 12.1, states he marched 30 or 40 Roman miles into hostile territory, although the figure appears to have been amended from 300–400 Roman miles as, until recently, this figure was not believed possible.

22. Spiegel Online, 2008–12=16, 'German Archaeologists Hail New Find: Discovery of Roman Battlefield Poses Historical Riddle'; 'Archaeologists from Freie Universität Berlin Excavate Well Preserved Roman Chain Mail', fu-berlin.de; benedante.blogspot.co.uk.

23. Herodian, 7.2.6-8.

24. Hobbes, Thomas, *Leviathan*, ch.12.

Bibliography

Abbreviations

AE   L'Annee epigraphique (Paris, 1888)

AJPH   American Journal of Philology

BMC   H. Mattingly, *Coins of the Roman Empire in the British Museum V, Pertinax to Elagabalus, and VI, Severus Alexander to Balbinus and Pupienus* (London, 1940)

CIL   Corpus Inscriptionum Latinarum (Berlin, 1867)

CNR   Corpus Nummorum Romanorum, A. Bonti and Z. Simonetti (Firenze, 1972–79)

ILS   Dessau, H., Inscriptiones Latinae Selectae (Berlin, 1892–1916)

PIR   Prosopograhia Imperii Romani (Berlin and Leipzig, 1933)

RIC   Roman Imperial Coinage, H. Mattingly and R. Syndenham etc (London, 1923–67)

RIB   Ribchester Inscriptions

Ancient Sources

Agathangelos, *History of St Gregory and the Conversion of Armenia* (internet download) *History of the Armenians*, trans. Robert W. Thomson (State University of New York Press, June 1974)

Agathias, *Sassanid Chronicle*, (trans. in Averil Cameron, 'Agathias on the Sassanians', *Dumbarton Oakes Papers*, Vol.23/24, 1969/1970)

Athenaeus, *Deiposophistai*, Book on Demand Pod (2011)

Aulus Gellius, *Attic Nights Vol.1, Books 1–5*, trans. John C. Rolfe (Loeb Classical Library no.195)

Carson, R., *A Catalogue of the Roman Coins in the British Museum* (1962, Vol.VI)

Cedrenus, *Compendium Historiarum* (Dodgeon, M. and Lieu, S.N., The *Roman Eastern Frontier and the Persian Wars* AD *226–363*, 1991)

Chronicon Paschale, trans. Michael and Mary Whitby (Liverpool University Press, 1989)

Cicero, *Tusculan Disputations*, trans. J.E. King, Loeb Classical Library (Harvard University Press, 1945)

Cyprian, *To Demetrianus*, notes and edited by Arthur Cleveland Coxe (Kindle edition, by Amazon Media EU S.á r.l.) *Letters*, trans. Rose Bernard Donna (The Catholic University of America Press, December 1992)

Dio, Cassius, *Roman History*, trans. Earnest Cary, Loeb Classical Library (Harvard University Press, 1989)

Epictetus, *Discourses*, trans. W.A. Oldfather, Loeb Classical Library (Harvard University Press, 1989)

Epitome de Caesaribus, online translation at De Imperatoribus Romanis: //www.luc. edu/roman-emperors/epitome.htm.

Eusebius, *The History of the Church*, trans. G.A. Williamson (Penguin Classics, 1989)

Eutropius, *Breviarium*, trans. H.W. Bird (Liverpool University Press, 1993)

Fayum Papyrus No.20 (= select Papyri, No.216; rev.ed. in Archiv für Papyrusforschung, XIV (1941))

Feriale Duranum, extract taken from Oliver Hekster, *Rome and its Empire AD 193–284, Debates and Documents in Ancient History* (Edinburgh University Press, 2008)

Festus, *Breviarium* (trans. from attalus.org)

Heliodorus 'Aethiopica' (Forgotten Books, September 2015)

Herodian, *History of the Empire Books 5–8*, trans. C.R. Whittaker, Loeb Classical Library (Harvard University Press, 1989)

Historia Augusta, *The Lives of Didius Julianus, Pescinius Niger, Clodius Albinus, Septimius Severus, Caracalla, Macrinus, Elagabalus, Severus Alexander, The Two Maximi*, trans. David Magie, Loeb Classical Library (Harvard University Press, 1991)

Hyppolitus, *Philosophoumena*, trans. Patrice Franois Marie Cruice (Saraswasti Press, 2012)

Justinian, *Codex Justinianus*, trans. S.P. Scott (Lee Walker, 2013)

Justinian, *The Digest of Justinian* (University of Pennsylvania Press, 2008)

Juvenal, *The Sixteen Satires*, trans. Peter Green (Penguin Classics, 1998)

Malalas, John, *Chronicle*, Australian Centre of Byzantine Studies (University of Sydney, 1986)

Mattingly, H., *Coins of the Roman Empire in the British Museum V, Pertinax to Elagabalus*, and *VI, Severus Alexander to Balbinus and Pupienus* (London, 1940)

Mattingly, H., Sydenham, E.A., & Sutherland, C.H.V., *The Roman Imperial Coinage, IV, 2* (London, 1938)

Moses of Chorene (Khorenats'i), *History of Armenia*, trans. Robert W. Thompson (Caravan Books, August 2006)

Newton, Tim, *The Forgotten Gospels: A New Translation* (Constable, London, 2009)

Orosius, *Christian History*, The Iberian Fathers: V.3, Fathers of the Church Series (The Catholic University of Americas Press, 1969)

   Adversus Paganos Historiarum Libri Septem, UT Et Apologeticus Contra Pelgium de Arbitrii Lebertate (Kessinger Publishing, September 2010)

Philo, *On the Embassy to Gaius*, trans. F.H. Colson, Loeb Vol X (1989)

Philostratus, *Life of Apollonius of Tyana, Vol.2, books 5–8*, Loeb Classical Library (Harvard University Press, 2005)

Philostratus, *Lives of the Sophists*, Loeb Classical Library (Harvard University Press, 1989)

Pliny, *Letters and Panegyricus*, trans. B. Radice, Loeb Classical Library (Harvard University Press, 1969)

Plutarch, *Life of Marius*, in *Fall of the Roman Republic*, trans. Rex with introduction and notes by Robin Seager (Penguin Classics, 1973)

Pontius of Carthage, *Life of Cyprian*, trans. Ernest Wallis, c. 1885 (online at Christian Classics Ethereal Library)

Porphyry, *Life of Plotinus*, trans. S. Mackenna (Alexandrian Press, US, New edition, December 1984)

Robinson, E.S.G., 'Department of Coins and Medals' (*The British Museum Quarterly*, Vol.15, 1941–1950)

Roman Civilisation: sourcebook 2: The Empire, (dited and notes by Naphtali Lewis and Meyer Rienhold (Harper Torchbooks, 1966)

Stylow, Armin U., Páez, Rafael Atencia, Fernández, Julián González, Pascual, Monika Ruppert, and Schmidt, Manfred G., *Corpus Inscriptionum Latinarum. II: Inscriptiones Hispaniae Latinae* (Editio Altera. Pars V. Conventus Astigitanus. CIL II²/5)

Seneca, *Letters from a Stoic: epistulae Morales ad Lucilium*, trans. Robin Campbell (Penguin Classics, 2004)

Suetonius, *Lives of the Caesars*, trans. Robert Graves (Penguin Classics, 2007)

Syncellus, *Chronicle*, trans. William Adler and Paul Tuffin, *The Chronology of George Synkellos, A Byzantine Chronicle of Universal History from the Creation* (Oxford University Press, August 2002)

Tacitus, *Annals of Imperial Rome*, trans. M. Grant (Penguin Classics, 1996)

Tacitus, *The Histories*, trans. Kenneth Wellesley (Penguin Classics 1982)

Tertullian, *Apologeticus Adversus Gentes Pro Christianis* (Ulan Press, 2012)

   De Pallio, trans. Vincent Hunink (www.tertullian.org)

   De anima, trans. Peter Holmes (www.tertullian.org)

The Government of the Roman Empire: A Sourcebook (Routledge Sourcebooks for the Ancient World, Barbara Levick, 2000)

The Roman Eastern Frontier and the Persian Wars AD *226–363: A Documentary History* (edited by Michael Dodgeon and Samuel N.C. Lieu, Routledge, 1994)

Vegetius, *Epitoma Rei Militaris*, trans. N.P. Milner (Liverpool University Press, 1995)

Victor, Aurelius, *De Caesaribus*, trans. H.W. Bird (University of Liverpool Press, 1994)

Zonaras, *History: From Alexander Severus to the Death of Theodosius the Great*, trans. Thomas Banchich and Eugene Lane (Routledge Classical Translations, 2011)

Zosimus, *New History*, trans. J.J. Buchanan and H.T. Davis (Trinity University Press, 1967)

Modern Sources

Africa, Thomas W., 'Urban Violence in Ancient Rome', *The Journal of Interdisciplinary History*, Vol.2 No.1 (Summer 1971), published by The MIT Press

Alberston, Fred C., 'Zenodorus' "Colossus of Nero"', *Memoirs of the American Academy in Rome*, Vol.46 (2001)

Alfody, G. and Panciera, S. (eds), *Inschriftliche Denkmaler als Medien der Selbstdarstellung in der romischen welt* (Stuttgart, 2001)

Alram, Michael, 'Ardashir's Eastern Campaign and the Numismatic Evidence', in Joe Cribb and Georgina Herrmann (ed.), *After Alexander: Central Asia Before Islam* (Vienna British Academy, 2007)

Ando, Clifford, *Imperial Rome* AD *193 to 284: The Critical Century* (Edinburgh University Press, 2012)

Armstrong, A.H., *Cambridge History of Later Greek and Medieval Philosophy* (Cambridge, 1967)

Avotins, Ivars, 'Prosopographical and Chronological Notes on Some Greek Sophists of the Empire', *California Studies in Classical Antiquity*, Vol.4 (1971)

Baillie Reynolds, P.K., 'The Troops Quartered in the Castra Peregrinorum', *Journal of Roman Studies*, Vol.13 (1923)

Baker, Philip, *The Empire Stops Here: A Journey Along the Frontiers of the Roman World* (Pimlico, 2009)

Barnes, J.W.B., 'A Letter of Alexander Severus', *Journal of Egyptian Archaeology*, LII (1966)

Barnes, T.D., 'Who Were the Nobility of the Roman Empire?', *Phoenix*, Vol.28 (Winter, 1984)

The Sources of the Historia Augusta (Brussels, 1978)

Batty, Jean Ch., 'Apamea in Syria in the Second and Third Centuries AD', *Journal of Roman Studies*, Vol.78 (1988)

Benario, Herbert W., 'The Titulature of Julia Soaemias and Julia Mamaea: two notes', *Transactions and Proceedings of the American Philological Association*, Vol.90 (1959), published by John Hopkins University Press

'The Date of the "Feriale Duranum"', *Historia*, Bd.11, H.2 (April 1962)

Benefiel, Rebecca R.J., 'A New Praetorian Laterculus from Rome', *Zeitschrift für Papyrologie und Epigraphik*, Bd.134 (2001)

Bennett, Julian, *Trajan: Optimus Princeps* (Routledge, 1997)

Bertrand-Dagenbach, C., *Alexandre Sévere et l''Histiore Auguste'* (Collections Latomus 208 Brussels, 1990)

Bingham, Sandra, *The Praetorian Guard: A History of Rome's Special Forces* (I.B. Taurus, 2013)

Birley, A., *The African Emperor Septimius Severus* (B.T. Batsford Ltd, 1988)

Bivar, A.D.H., 'Cavalry Equipment and Tactics on the Euphrates Frontier', *Dumbarton Oaks Papers*, Vol.26 (1972)

Blanchard, Philippe, Castex, Dominique, Coquerelle, Michaël, Giuliani, Raffaella, & Ricciardi, Monica, *A Mass Grave from the Catacomb of Saints Peter and Marcellinus in Rome Second-Third Centuries AD* (Antiquity, 2007)

Blázquez, J.M., 'The Latest Work on the Export of Baetican Olive Oil to Rome and the Army', *Greece and Rome*, Vol.39, Issue 2 (October 1992)

Bleicken, J., *Der politische Standpunkt Dios gegenuber der Monarchie* (Hermes 90, 1962)

Borg, Barbara, *Crisis and Ambition: Tombs and Burial Customs in Third Century CE Rome* (Oxford University Press, October 2013)

Borg-Witschel, B.C., *Veranderungen im Reprasentationsverhalten der romischen Eliten wahrend des 3. Jhs.n. Chr.* (2001)

Boteva, Dilyana, 'On the Cursus Honorum of P. Fu... Pontianus (PIR2 F 496), Provincial Governor of Lower Moesia', *Zeitschrift für Papyrologie und Epigraphik 51*, Bd.110 (1996)

Bowersock, G.W., *Roman Arabia* (Harvard University Press, 1998)

Bowman, Alan K., Garnsey, Peter, and Cameron, Averil, *The Cambridge Ancient History: The Crisis of Empire AD 193–337, Volume XII* (Cambridge University Press, 2007)

Braunert, Horst, *Die Binnenwanderung. Studien zur Sozialgeschichte Ägyptens in der Ptolemäer- und Kaiserzeit* (Bonn: Ludwig Rohrscheid Verlag, 1964)

Bray, J., Gallienus: *A Study in Reformist and Sexual Politics* (Wakefield Press, 1997)

Broekaert, Wim, 'Oil for Rome During the Second and Third Century AD: A Confrontation of the Archaeological Records and the *Historia Augusta*', *Mnemosyne: A Journal of Classical Studies*, 64 (2011)

Brunt, P.A., 'The Administrators of Roman Egypt', *Journal of Roman Studies*, Vol.65 (1975) 'Free Labour and Public Works at Rome', *Journal of Roman Studies*, Vol.70 (1980)

Bruun, Christer, 'The Antonine Plague and the "Third-Century Crisis"', in Olivier Hekster, Gerda de Kleijn and Danielle Slootjes (eds), *Crises and the Roman Empire: Proceedings of the Seventh Workshop of the International Network Impact of Empire, Nijmegen, June 20–24, 2006* (Leiden/Boston: Brill, 2007)

Burton, Graham P., 'The Roman Imperial State, Provincial Governors and Imperial Finances of Provincial Cities, 27 BC–235 AD', *Historia*, Bd.53, H.3 (2004)

Butcher, Kevin, *Roman Syria and the Near East* (The British Museum Press, 2003)

Buttrey, T.V., 'Dio, Zonoras and the Value of the Roman Aureus', *Journal of Roman Studies*, Vol. 51 (1961)

Cameron, Averil, 'Agathias on the Sassanids', *Dumbarton Oaks Papers*, Vol.23/24 (1969/1970) published by Dumbarton Oaks, trustees for Harvard University

Campbell, Brian, 'The Severan Dynasty', in *Cambridge Ancient History volume 12, 'The Crisis of Empire AD 193–337'*, ch.11 (Cambridge University Press, 2008)

Campbell, J.B., *The Emperor and the Roman Army 31 BC–235 AD* (Clarendon Press Oxford, 1984)

Carroll, Maureen, 'Vagnari: Is This the Winery of Rome's Greatest Landowner?', *World Archaeology*, 76 (April/May 2016)

Carson, R., *A Catalogue of the Roman Coins in the British Museum*, Vol.VI (1962)

Champlin, Edward, 'Serenus Sammonicus', *Harvard Studies in Classical Philology*, Vol.85 (1981)

Claridge, Amanda, *Rome, An Oxford Archaeological Guide* (Oxford University Press, 2010)

Clarke, Graeme, 'Christianity in the First Three Centuries: Chapter 18B Third Century Christianity', in *Cambridge Ancient History*, Vol.12 (Cambridge University Press, 2008)
'Some Victims of the Persecution of Maximinus Thrax', *Historia*, Bd.15, H.4 (November 1966)

Cleve, Robert L., 'Some Male Relatives of the Severan Women', *Historia*, Bd.37, H.2 (2nd Qtr, 1988)

Cooley, Alison E. and Salway, Benet, 'Roman Inscriptions 2006–2010', *Journal of Roman Studies*, Vol. (November 2012)

Corbier, Mireille, 'Coinage and Taxation: the State's Point of View, AD 193–337', *Cambridge Ancient History*, Vol.12, 'The Crisis of Empire AD 193–337', ch.11 (Cambridge University Press, 2008)

Crook, J.A., *Concilium Principis, Imperial Councils and Councillors from Augustus to Diocletain* (Cambridge, 1955)

Dando-Collins, Stephen, *Legions of Rome: The Definitive History of Every Roman Legion* (Quercus, 2010)

Davenport, Caillan, 'Cassius Dio and Caracalla', *The Classical Quarterly*, Vol.62 (2012)

De Blois, Lukas, 'The Third Century Crisis and the Greek Elite in the Roman Empire', *Historia*, Bd.33, H.3 (3rd Qtr, 1984)

De Blois, L., Erdkamp, P., Hekster, P., De Kleijn, G. and Mols, S., 'The Representation and Perception of Roman Imperial Power', *Proceedings of the Third Workshop of the International Network Impact of Empire (Roman Empire c.200 BC–AD 476)*, Netherlands Institute in Rome (20–23 March 2002, Amsterdam)

Dignas, Beate, and Winter, Englebert, *Rome and Persia in Late Antiquity: Neighbours and Rivals* (Cambridge University Press, 2008)

Dodgeon, M. and Lieu, S.N., *The Roman Eastern Frontier and the Persian Wars AD 226–363* (Routledge,1991)

Dmitriev, Sviatoslav, 'Traditions and Innovations in the Reign of Aurelian', *The Classical Quarterly*, Vol.54, no.2 (December 2004)

Dunbar, David G., 'The Delay of the Parousia in Hippolytus', *Vigiliae Christianae*, Vol.37, no.4, (December 1983) Brill

Duncan-Jones, R.P., 'Economic Change and the Transition to Late Antiquity', in S. Swain and M. Edwards (eds), *Approaching Late Antiquity: The Transformation from Early to Late Empire* (Oxford, 2004)

Dušanić, Slobodan, 'Nobilissimus Caesar imperii et sacerdotis', *Zeitschrift für Papyrologie und Epigraphik*, Bd.37 (1980)

'Severus Alexander as Elagabalus' Associate', *Historia: Zeitschrift für Alte Geschichte*, Bd.13, H.4 (October 1964)

Earl, Donald, *The Moral and Political Tradition of Rome* (Thames & Hudson, 1967)

Edwards, Mark, 'Severan Christianity', in Swain, Simon, Harrison, Stephen, and Elsner, Jaś (eds), *Severan Culture* (Cambridge University Press, 2007)

Edwell, Peter, *Between Rome and Persia: The Middle Euphrates, Mesopotamia and Palmyra Under Rome* (Routledge, 2010)

Elliot, Paul, *Legions In Crisis: Transformation of the Roman Soldier AD 192–284* (Fonthill, 2014)

Elton, Hugh, *Frontiers of the Roman Empire* (Routledge, 2012)

Ertel, Andrea Beverly, 'The Life of Severus Alexander' (Thesis for MA McMaster University, 1984, University of British Columbia, 1986, UBC_1986_A8 E77 Turinus)

Everitt, Anthony, *The First Emperor: Caesar Augustus and the Triumph of Rome* (John Murray, 2006)

Ezov, Amiram, 'The Centurions in the Rhine Legions in the Second and Early Third Century', *Historia*, Bd.56, H.1 (2007)

Fabio, Barry, 'The Mouth of Truth and the Forum Boarium: Oceanus, Hercules and Hadrian', *The Art Bulletin* (2011)

Ferguson, John, *The Religions of the Roman Empire* (Thames and Hudson, 1982)

Finegan, Jack, *The Archaeology of the New Testament: The Mediterranean World of the Early Christian Apostles* (Routledge, 1981)

Fink, Robert O., 'Lucius Seius Caesar, Socer Augusti', *The American Journal of Philology*, Vol.60, no.3 (1939)

Fishwick, Duncan, 'Dated Inscriptions and the "Feriale Duranum"', *Institut Francais du Proche-Orient, Syria*, T.65 Fasc. 3/4 (1988)

Foerster, Gideon, 'The Early History of Caesarea', *Bulletin of the American Schools of Oriental Research*, Supplementary Studies, No.19, 'The Joint Expedition to Caesarea Maritima. Vol.1, Studies in the *History of Caesarea Maritima*' (1975)

Fowden, Garth, 'Late Polytheism: The World View', *Cambridge Ancient History*, Vol.12, ch.17 (Cambridge University Press, 2005)

French, David H., Russell, Harry, Mitchell, Stephen, and Payton, Robert, 'The Year's Work', *Anatolian Studies*, Vol.33 (1983)

French, D.H., 'Milestones of Pontus, Galatia, Phrygia and Lycia', *Zeitschrift für Papyrologie und Epigraphik*, Bd.43 (1981)
    Roman Roads and Milestones of Asia Minor, Vol.3 (British Institute at Ankara, Electronic Monograph 3, 2012)

Frend, W.H.C., 'A Third Century Inscription Relating to Anagareia in Phrygia', *Journal of Roman Studies*, 46 (1956)

Gellner, E., *Patrons and Clients on Patrons and Clients* (edited by E. Gellner and J. Waterbury, ch.1, Robert R. Kaufman, 'The Patron-Client Concept and Macro-Politics: Prospects and Problems' (June 2009), *Comparative Study of Society and History*

Gergel, Richard A., 'The Tel Shalem Hadrian Reconsidered', *American Journal of Archaeology*, Vol.95, no.2 (April 1991)

Ghodrat-Dizaji, Mehrdad, 'Administrative Geography of the Early Sasanian Period: The Case of Adurbadagan', *Iran*, Vol.45 (2007)

Gibbins, David, 'A Roman Shipwreck of c. AD 200 at Plemmirio, Sicily: Evidence for North African Amphora Production During the Severan Period', *World Archaeology*, 32:3 (2008)

Gilliam, J.F., 'The Dux Ripae at Dura', *Transactions and Proceedings of the American Philological Association*, Vol.72 (1941)
    'Caesonius Bassus: cos.ord AD 317', *Historia*, Bd.16, H.2 (April 1967)
    'The Governors of Syria Coele from Severus to Diocletian', *American Journal of Philology*, Vol.79, no.3 (1958)

Goddard King, Georgina, 'Some Reliefs at Budapest', *American Journal of Archaeology*, Vol.37, no.1 (January–March 1933)

Gordon, Richard, and Reynolds, Joyce, 'Roman Inscriptions 1995–2000', *Journal of Roman Studies*, Vol.93 (November 2003)

Gottfried, Mader, 'History as Carnival, or Method and Madness in the *Vita Heliogabali*', *Classical Antiquity*, Vol.24, 1 (2005)

Greenstreet Addison, Charles, *Damascus and Palmyra: A Journey to the East, with a sketch of the state and prospects of Syria under Ibrahim Pasha*, Vol.2 (Filiquarian Legacy Publishing, 2012; first published 1838)

Grisanti, G. Tedeschi, *Trofei di Mario': Il Ninfeo dell' Acqua Giulia sull' Esquilino* (Monumenti Romani VII Rome Instituto Di Studi Romani, 1977)

Grunewald, Thomas, *Bandits in the Roman Empire; Myth and Reality* (Routledge, 2004)

Hammond, Mason, 'The Transmission of Powers of the Roman Emperor from the Death of Nero in AD 68 to that of Alexander Severus in AD 235', *Memoirs of the American Academy in Rome*, Vol.24 (1956), published by the University of Michigan Press for the American Academy in Rome
'Composition of the Senate, AD 68–235', *Journal of Roman Studies*, Vol.47 (1957)

Hardie, P.R., '*Imago Mundi*, Cosmological and Ideological Aspects of the Shield of Achilles', *The Journal of Hellenic Studies*, Vol.105 (1985)

Harper, R.P., 'Roman Senators in Cappadocia', *Anatolian Studies*, Vol.14 (1964)
'Podandus and the via Tauri', *Anatolian Studies*, Vol.20 (1970)

Hartswick, K.J., *The Gardens of Sallust: A Changing Landscape* (Austin: University of Texas Press, 2004)

Healey, John F., *Aramaic Inscriptions and Documents of the Roman Period: Text Book of Syrian Semitic Inscriptions*, Vol.IV (Oxford University Press, 2009)

Heil, Matthäus, 'Severus Alexander und Orbiana. Eine Kaiserehe', *Zeitschrift für Papyrologie und Epigraphik*, Bd.135 (2001)

Hekster, Oliver, *Rome and its Empire* AD *193–284, Debates and Documents in Ancient History* (Edinburgh University Press, 2008)

Hermansen, G., 'The Population of Imperial Rome: The Regionaries', *Historia*, Bd.27. H.1 (1st Qtr, 1978)

Hobbes, Thomas, *Leviathan* (Oxford World's Classics, 2008)

Honoré, Tony, *Ulpian: Pioneer of Human Rights* (Oxford University Press, 2002)

Hopkins, Richard, *The Life of Alexander Severus* (Forgotten Books, 2012; first published 1907)

Icks, Martijn, *The Crimes of Elagabalus: the Life and Legacy of Rome's Decadent Emperor* (I.B. Taurus, 2011)

Ingholt, Harold, and Sanders, John E., 'A Colossal Head from Memphis, Severan or Augustan', *Journal of the American Research Centre in Egypt*, Vol.2 (1963)

Isaac, Benjamin, 'The Meaning of the Terms *Limes* and *Limitanei*', *The Journal of Roman Studies*, Vol.78 (1988)

Jacques, François, *Le Privilège de liberté. Politique impériale et autonomie municipale dans les cités de l'Occident romain (161–244)* (Ecole francaise de Rome, 1984)

Jardé, A, *Etudes critiques sur la vie et le règne de Sévère Alexandre* (E. De Boccard Editeur, 1925)

Jeno, Fitz, 'Religions and Cults in Pannonia', A *Szent István Király Múzeum Közleményei Bulletin Du Musée Roi Saint-étienne*, A.sorozat 33.szám/Série A. No.33. Published by the Fejer Megyei Muzeumok Igazgatosaga

Jones, B.W., *The Emperor Domitian* (Routledge, 1993)

Jones, Christopher P., 'Philostratus' *Heroikos* and Its Setting in Reality', *The Journal of Hellenic Studies*, Vol.121 (2001)

Karmon, D.E., *The Ruin of the Eternal City: Antiquity and Preservation in Renaissance Rome* (Oxford University Press, 2011)

Kaufman, Robert R., 'The Patron-Client Concept and Macro-Politics: Prospects and Problems' (published online June 2009), in *Comparative Study of Society and History* (1974)

Keay, S.J., *Roman Spain* (British Museum Publications, 1988)

Kennedy, D.L., 'Ti. Claudius Subatianus Aquila, First Prefect of Mesopotamia', *Historia*, 25, Bd.36 (1979)

Kia, Mehrdad, *The Persian Empire, A Historical Encyclopedia* (ABC-CLIO, June 2016)

King, Anthony, *Roman Gaul and Germany* (British Museum Publications, 1990)

Künkel, W., *Herkunft und soziale stellung der römischen Juristen* (1967)

Lee, Kevin S., 'Priest, Pater and Patron: A thematic Analysis of the Building Programs of Elagabalus and Alexander Severus', CLST 519 The Art and Architecture of the Severan Period (December 2014), academia.edu

Lehmann, Clayton Miles, '*Epigraphica Caesariensia*', *Classical Philology*, Vol.79, No.1 (January 1984)

Leunissen, Paul M.M., 'Direct Promotions from Proconsul to Consul under the Principate', *Zeitschrift für Papyrologie und Epigraphik*, Bd.89 (1991)

Levick, Barbara, *Julia Domna: Syrian Empress* (Routledge, 2007)
    The Government of the Roman Empire: A Sourcebook (Routledge Sourcebooks for the Ancient World, 2000)

Lewis, Naphtali, and Rienhold, Meyer, *Roman Civilisation: Sourcebook 2: The Empire* (edited and notes by Harper Torchbooks, 1966)

Littman, R.J. and M.L., 'Galen and the Antonine Plague', *The American Journal of Philology*, 94, no.3 (1973)

Lo Cascio, Elio, 'The Emperor and his Administration', in *Cambridge Ancient History*, Vol.12 (Cambridge University Press, 2005)

Logan, Alistair, *The Gnostics: Identifying an Early Christian Cult* (A and C Black, 2006)

Lusnia, Susann S., 'Urban Planning and Structural Display in Severan Rome: Reconstructing the Septizodium and its Role in Dynastic Policies', *American Journal of Archaeology*, Vol.108, no.4 (October 2004)

MacMullen, Ramsey, 'Roman Imperial Building in the Provinces', *Harvard Studies in Classical Philology*, 26, Vol.64 (1959)
    Soldier and Civilian in the Later Roman Empire (Harvard University Press, 1963)
    The Corruption and Decline of Rome (Yale University, 1990)

Madar, Gottfried, 'Triumphal Elephants and Political Circus at Plutarch, Pomp. 14.6', *Classical World*, Vol.99, 4 (2006)
    'History as Carnival, or Method and Madness in the *Vita Heliogabali*', *Classical Antiquity* Vol.24 (2005)

Mann, J.C., 'The Raising of New Legions During the Principate', *Hermes*, Bd.91, H.4 (1963)
    'A Note on the Legion IV *Italica*', *Zeitschrift für Papyrologie und Epigraphik*, Bd.126 (1999)

Mârghitan, Liviu, and Petolescu, Constantin, '*Vota pro Salvte Imperatoris* in an Inscription at Ulpia Traiana Sarmizegetusa', *Journal of Roman Studies*, Vol.66 (1976)

Marvin, Miranda, 'Freestanding Structures From the Baths of Caracalla', *American Journal of Archaeology*, Vol.87, no.3 (July 1983)

McGinn, Thomas A.J., 'Concubinage and the *Lex Iulia* on Adultery', *Transactions of the American Philological Association*, Vol.121 (1991)

McHugh, J.S., *The Emperor Commodus: God and Gladiator* (Pen and Sword, 2015)

Mennen, Inge, *Power and Status in the Roman Empire* AD *193–284* (Brill, 2011)
    'Praetorian Prefects' Power and Senatorial Status in the Third Century:
    Re-evaluating *Historia Augusta*, *Vita Alexandri* 21.5', *Mnemosyne*, Vol.65, No.4-5
    (2012)

Millar, Fergus, *A Study of Cassius Dio* (Oxford University Press, 1964)
    'The Development of Jurisdiction by Imperial Procurators; Further Evidence',
    Historia, Bd.14, H.3 (July 1965)
    The Emperor in the Roman World (Duckworth, 1977)
    'The Greek East and Roman Law: The dossier of M. Cn. Licinius Rufinus',
    Journal of Roman Studies, Vol.89 (1999)
    'Emperors, Frontiers and Foreign Relations, 31 BC to AD 378', *Britannia*, Vol.13 (1982)
    'Empire and City, Augustus to Julian: Obligations, Excuses and Status', *Journal of
    Roman Studies*, Vol.73 (1983)

Mocsy, Andras, *Pannonia and Upper Moesia: a History of the Danube Provinces of the
    Roman Empire* (Routledge Revivals, 2015)

Moore Cross, Frank, 'The Hebrew Inscriptions from Sardis', *Harvard Theological
    Review*, Vol.95, no.1 (January 2002)

Najdenova, V., *The Cult of Jupiter Dolichenus in Lower Moesia and Thrace* (Aufsteig U
    Niedergang D Roemwelt II 2/1989)

Nash-Williams, V.E., *'Iuppiter Dolichenus'*, *Greece and Rome*, Vol.21, 62, Cambridge
    University Press (1952)

Newby, Zahra, 'Art at the Crossroads', in Swain, Simon, Harrison, Stephen, and
    Elsner, Jaś, (eds) *Severan Culture* (Cambridge University Press, 2007)

Newton, Tim, *The Forgotten Gospels: A New Translation* (Constable, London, 2009)

Nicols, Jon, *Civic Patronage in the Roman Empire* (Brill, 2013)

Noreña , Carlos F., 'The Communication of the Emperor's Virtues', *Journal of Roman
    Studies*, Vol.91 (2001)
    Imperial Ideas in the Roman West: Representation, Circulation, Power (Cambridge,
    2011)

O'Hanlon, Bernard Michael, *The Army of Severus Alexander* (Amazon Media EU S.á
    r.l, Kindle edition, 2015)

Oliva, Pavel, *Pannonia and the Onset of Crisis in the Roman Empire* (Nakladatelstvi
    Ceskovenske akademie ved Praha, 1962)

Oliver, James H., 'Athenian Citizenship of Roman Emperors', *Hesperia: The
    Journal of the American School of Classical Studies at Athens*, Vol.20, no.4
    (October–December 1951)
    'Gerusiae and the *Augustales'*, *Historia*, Bd.7, H.4 (October 1958)
    'On the Edict of Alexander Severus (P. Fayum 20)', *American Journal of Philology*,
    Vol.99, No.4 (1978), published by John Hopkins University Press

Oates, David, 'The Roman Frontier in Northern Iraq', *The Geographical Journal*,
    Vol.122, no.2 (June 1956)

Oates, David, & Oates, Joan, *'Ain Sinu*: A Roman Frontier Post in Northern Iraq', *Iraq*,
    Vol.21, no.2 (Autumn 1959), published by the British Institute for the Study of Iraq

Palmer, R.E.A., 'Customs on Market Goods Imported into the City of Rome', *Memoirs of the American Academy in Rome*, Vol.36, in *The Seaborne Commerce of Ancient Rome: Studies in Archaeology and History* (1980)

Parker, Philip, *The Empire Stops Here: A Journey along the Frontiers of the Roman World* (Pimlico, 2010)

Peachin, Michael, 'P.Oxy. VI 912 and the Accession of Maximinus Thrax', *Zeitschrift für Papyrologie und Epigraphik*, Bd.59 (1985)

'Philip's Progress: From Mesopotamia to Rome in AD 244', *Historia*, Bd.40, H.3 (1991)

Peacock, Phoebe, 'Usurpers under Elagabalus', online at De Imperatoribus Romanis (2002)

Peppers, Jeanne, 'Four Roman Votive Bronzes in the Getty Museum', *The J.Paul Getty Museum Journal*, Vol.8 (1980)

Pollard, Nigel, *Soldiers, Cities, and Civilians in Roman Syria* (University of Michigan Press, 2000)

Potter, David S., *The Roman Empire at Bay* AD *180–395* (Routledge, 2004)

Potter, David S. and Mattingly, D.J. (eds), *Life, Death, and Entertainment in the Roman Empire* (University of Michigan Press, 1999)

Rajak, Tessa, and Noy, David, '*Archisynagogoi*: Office, Title and Social Status in the Greco-Jewish Synagogue', *The Journal of Roman Studies*, Vol.83 (1993)

Ramsey, Hazel G., 'Government Relief during the Roman Empire', *The Classical Journal*, Vol.31, no.8 (May 1936)

Rea, John, 'A Letter of the Emperor Elagabalus', *Zeitschrift für Papyrologie und Epigraphik*, Bd.96 (1993)

Rea, J.R., 'O. Leid.144 and the Chronology of AD 238', *Zeitschrift für Papyrologie und Epigraphik*, Bd.9 (1972)

Reed Stuart, Duane, 'The Reputed Influence of the Dies Natalis In Determining the Inscription of Restored Temples', *Transactions and Proceedings of the American Philological Association*, Vol.36 (1 January 1905)

Renberg, Gil H., 'Public and Private Places of Worship in the Cult of Asclepius at Rome', *Memoirs of the American Academy in Rome*, Vol.51/52 (2006/2007)

Richmond, I.A., 'Five Town-Walls in Hispania Citerior', *The Journal of Roman Studies*, Vol.21 (1931)

Robathan, Dorothy M., 'A Reconsideration of Roman Topography in the *Historia Augusta*', *Transactions and Proceedings of the American Philological Association*, Vol.70 (1939)

Robinson, E.S.G., 'Department of Coins and Medals', *The British Museum Quarterly*, Vol.15 (1941–1950)

Rodenwaldt, G., 'The Transition to Late Classical Art', *CAH*, 12 (1939)

Rose, Jenny, *Zoroastrianism; An Introduction* (Taurus, 2012)

Rostovtzeff, M., '*Vexillum* and Victory', *Journal of Roman Studies*, Vol.32, parts 1–2 (1942)

Roth, Jonathan, 'The Size and Organisation of the Roman Imperial Legion Phalanx', *Historia*, Bd.43, H.3 (3rd Quarter, 1994)

Saller, R.P., *Personal Patronage under the Early Empire* (Cambridge University Press, 2002)

Salway, B.P.M., 'A Fragment of Severan History: The unusual career of …atus, praetorian prefect of Elagabalus,' *Chiron*, 27 (1997)

Salway, B., 'Prefects, *Patroni* and Decurions: A New Perspective on the Album of Canusium', *Bulletin of the Institute of Classical Studies* (University of London, 2000)

Salway, Peter, *A History of Roman Britain* (Oxford University Press, 1997)

Scheiber, Alexander, 'Jews at Intercisa in Pannonia', *The Jewish Quarterly Review*, Vol.45, no.3 (January 1955)

Scheidel, Walter, *Roman Well-being and the Economic Consequences of the Antonine Plague* (Princeton/Stanford University Press, 2010)

Schönberger, H., 'The Roman Frontier in Germany: An Archaeological Survey', *Journal of Roman Studies*, Vol.59, no.1/2 (1969)

Segal, J.B., 'Four Syriac Inscriptions', *Bulletin of the School of Oriental and African Studies*, Vol.30, no.2 (June 1967)

Sherk, Robert K., 'A Chronology of the Governors of Galatia AD 122–285', *The American Journal of Philology*, Vol.100, no.1 (Spring 1979)

Shotter, David, 'Gods, Emperors, and Coins', *Greece and Rome*, Vol.26, 1 (Cambridge University Press, 1979)

Sidebottom, Harry, 'Roman Imperialism: The Changed Outward Trajectory of the Roman Empire', *Historia*, Bd.54, H.3 (2005)

'Severan Historiography: Evidence, Patterns and Arguments', in *Severan Culture* (Cambridge University Press, 2007)

Sinclair, T.A., *Eastern Turkey: An Architectural and Archaeological Survey*, Vol.III (The Pindar Press, 1989)

Sinnigen, William G., 'The Origins of the '*Frumentarii*', *Memoirs of the American Academy in Rome*, Vol.27 (1962)

Skeat, T.C., & Wegener, E.P., 'A Trial before the Prefect of Egypt Appius Sabinus c.250 AD', *Journal of Egyptian Archaeology*, 21 (1935)

Smith, R.E., 'The Army Reforms of Septimius Severus', *Historia*, Bd.21, H.3 (3rd Quarter, 1972)

Smith, Steven D., *Man and Animal in Severan Rome: The Literary Imagination of Claudius Aelianus* (Cambridge University Press, 2014)

Southern, Pat, 'The *Numeri* of the Roman Imperial Army', *Britannia*, Vol.20 (1989)

The Roman Empire from Severus to Constantine (Routledge, 2001)

Spawforth, A.J.S., 'Notes on the Third Century AD in Spartan Epigraphy', *The Annual of the British School at Athens*, Vol.79 (1984)

Speidel, M. Alexander, 'Roman Army Pay Scales', *The Journal of Roman Studies*, Vol.82 (1992)

Stathakopoulos, Dionysios Ch., 'Famine and Pestilence in the Late Roman and Early Byzantine Empire', *Birmingham Byzantine and Ottoman Monographs* (Ashgate Publishing Limited, 2004)

Ste Croix, G.E.M.de, '*Suffragum*', *British Journal of Sociology*, 5 (1954)

Syme, R., *Emperors and Biography: Studies in the* Historia Augusta (Oxford University Press, 1971)

The Historia Augusta*: A Call of Clarity* (Rudolf Habelt Verlag GmbH Bonn, 1971)

'Lawyers in Government: The Case of Ulpian', *Proceedings of the American Philosophical Society*, Vol.116, no.5 (13 October 1972)

'The Son of the Emperor Macrinus', *Phoenix*, Vol.26, no.3 (Autumn 1972), published by the Classical Association of Canada

'Danubian and Balkan Emperors', *Historia*, Bd.22, H.2 (2nd Quarter, 1973)

The Roman Revolution (Oxford University Press, 1979)

'Fiction about Roman Jurists', *Roman Papers*, Vol.3, edited by Anthony Birley (Oxford, 1984)

Talbert, Richard J.A., *The Senate of Imperial Rome* (Princeton University Press, 1984)

Taqizadeh, S.H., 'The Early Sasanians, Some Chronological Points Which Possibly Call for Revision', *Bulletin of the School of Oriental and African Studies*, Vol.11.1 (1943)

Thomas, Edmund, 'Metaphor and Identity in Severan Architecture', in *Severan Culture* (Cambridge University Press, 2007)

Thomas, J.D. and Clarysse, W., 'A Projected Visit of Severus Alexander to Egypt', *Ancient Society*, 8 (1977)

Thomas, J. David, 'SB XVI 13050 Reconsidered', *Zeitschrift für Papyrologie und Epigraphik*, Bd.88 (1991)

Todd, Malcolm, *The Northern Barbarians 100 BC–AD 300* (Basil Blackwell Ltd, 1987)

'Germanic Peoples and Germanic Society', *Cambridge Ancient History*, Vol.12 (Cambridge University Press, 2008)

Todd, Marcus N., 'Greek Inscriptions 1931–1932', *The Journal of Egyptian Archaeology*, Vol.19, no.3/3 (November 1933)

Tome, I., *Les Campagnes Pe La Syrie Pu Nord Du Ile Au Vlle Siecle. Un Exemple d'Expansion Demographique Et Economique A La Fin D'Antiquite*, Institut francais d'archeologie du proche-orient, Bibliotheque archeologique et historique cxxxnr (Paris: Librairie orientaliste Paul Geuthner, 1992)

Toth, I., *The Destruction of the Sanctuaries of Jupiter Dolichenus in the Rhine and Danube Regions 235–238* (Acta Arch. Hung. XXV/1973 Najdenova 1989a)

Townend, G.B., 'The Post of *Ab Epistulis* in the Second Century', *Historia*, Bd.10, H,3 (July 1961)

Townsend, Prescott W., 'The Significance of the Arch of the Severi at Lepcis', *American Journal of Archaeology*, Vol.42, no.4 (October–December 1938)

'Sextus Catius Clementinus Priscillianus, Governor of Cappadocia in 238 AD', *Classical Philology*, Vol.50, no1 (January 1955)

Trapp, Michael, 'Philosophy, Scholarship and the World of Learning in the Severan Period', in *Severan Culture* (Cambridge University Press, 2007)

Tuck, Steven L., *A History of Roman Art* (Wiley Blackwell, 2015)

Turcan, Robert, *The Cults of the Roman Empire* (Blackwell, 1996)

Turton, Godfrey, *The Syrian Princesses: The Women Who Ruled Rome AD 193–235* (American Council of Learned Societies, Cassell and Co, 1974)

Van Sickle, C.E., 'The Terminal Dates of the Reign of Alexander Severus', *Classical Philology*, Vol.22 (July 1927)

'The Headings of Rescripts of the Severi in the Justinian Code', *Classical Philology*, Vol.23, no.3 (University of Chicago Press, July 1928)

Varner, Eric R., 'Punishment after death: Mutilation of images and corpse abuse in ancient Rome', *Mortality: Promoting the interdisciplinary study of death and dying*, 6:1 (Emory University, USA, 2001)

'Portraits, Plots, and Politics: '*Damnatio memoriae*' and the Images of Public Women', *Memoirs of the American Academy in Rome*, Vol.46 (University of Michigan, 2001)

Vermeule, Cornelius C., 'Egyptian Contributions to Late Roman Imperial Portraiture', *Journal of American Research Center in Egypt*, Vol.1 (1962)

Vickers, M.J. and Reynolds, J.M., 'Cyrenaica, 1962–72', *Archaeological Reports*, No.18 (1971–1972)

Wacher, John, *The Roman Empire* (J.M. Dent and Sons, 1987)

Watson, G.R., *The Roman Soldier* (Thames and Hudson, 1981)

Whitmarsh, Tim, 'Prose Literature and the Severan Dynasty', in *Severan Culture* (Cambridge University Press, 2007)

Whittaker, C.R., 'The Revolt of Papirius Dionysius AD 191', *Historia: Zeitschrift für Alte Geschichte*, Bd.13, H.3 (July 1964)

Williams, Craig, *Roman Homosexuality* (Oxford University Press, 2010)

Williams, Mary Gilmore, 'Studies in the Lives of Roman Empresses: Julia Mamaea', in Sanders, H.A. (ed.), *Roman Historical Sources and Institutions* (New York, 1904)

Wilson, Andrew, 'The Water-Mills on the Janiculum', *Memoirs of the American Academy in Rome*, Vol.45 (2000)

'Urban Development in the Severan Empire', in *Severan Culture* (Cambridge University Press, 2007)

Wilson, D.R., 'Two Milestones from Pontus', *Anatolian Studies*, Vol.10 (1960)

Winterling, Aloys, *Politics and Society in Imperial Rome* (Wiley-Blackwell, 2009)

Yegül, Fikret K., 'The Termo-Mineral Complex at Baiae and De Balneis Puteolanis', *The Art Bulletin*, Vol.78, no.1 (March 1996)

Zanker,P., *Klassizistische Statuen: Studien zur Veränderung des Kunstgeschmacks* (Römischen Kaiserzeit, 1974)

Zuiderhoek, Arjan, 'Government Centralisation in the Late Second and Early Third Centuries AD, A Working Hypothesis', *The Classical World*, Vol.103, no.1 (Fall 2009)

Biography of Pictures

Picture Credits and copyright information:

1. By Anagoria - Own work, CC BY 3.0, https://commons.wikimedia.org/w/index.php?curid=31464404 via Wikimedia Commons
2. By shakko - Own work, CC BY 3.0, https://commons.wikimedia.org/w/index.php?curid=3128990 via Wikimedia Commons
3. By Heinz-Joachim Krenzer - http://www.hjkrenzer.de/roemer/_Portraitgalerie.htm, Public Domain, https://commons.wikimedia.org/w/index.php?curid=382455 via Wikimedia Commons
4. By unknown Roman sculptor - own photo in Cologne, RÖMISCH-GERMANISCHES MUSEUM, Public Domain, https://commons.wikimedia.org/w/index.php?curid=3008178 via Wikimedia Commons
5. By Classical Numismatic Group, Inc - CNG coins, through Wildwinds, original upload 8 June 2005 by Panairjdde, Public Domain, https://commons.wikimedia.org/w/index.php?curid=342959 via Wikimedia Commons
6. By shakko - Own work, CC BY 3.0, https://commons.wikimedia.org/w/index.php?curid=3149380 via Wikimedia Commons
7. By Classical Numismatic Group, Inc. http://www.cngcoins.com, CC BY-SA 3.0, https://commons.wikimedia.org/w/index.php?curid=379717 via Wikimedia Commons
8. By G.dallorto assumed (based on copyright claims) - No machine-readable source provided. Own work assumed (based on copyright claims). Attribution, https://commons.wikimedia.org/w/index.php?curid=619774 via Wikimedia Commons
9. By Classical Numismatic Group, Inc. http://www.cngcoins.com, CC BY-SA 3.0, https://commons.wikimedia.org/w/index.php?curid=2520263 via Wikimedia Commons
10. By Philippus Arabs - Own work, CC BY-SA 3.0, https://commons.wikimedia.org/w/index.php?curid=3463127 via Wikimedia Commons
11. By Anonymous - Ophelia2, Public Domain, https://commons.wikimedia.org/w/index.php?curid=14634260 via Wikimedia Commons
12. By © Marie-Lan Nguyen/Wikimedia Commons, CC BY 2.5, https://commons.wikimedia.org/w/index.php?curid=3896776 via Wikimedia Commons.
13. By I, George Shuklin, CC BY 2.5, https://commons.wikimedia.org/w/index.php?curid=2256639 via Wikimedia Commons
14. By User: Bibi Saint-Pol - Own work, Public Domain, https://commons.wikimedia.org/w/index.php?curid=1959457 via Wikimedia Commons
15. By Unknown - Jastrow (2006), Public Domain, https://commons.wikimedia.org/w/index.php?curid=1332351 via Wikimedia Commons
16. By Unknown - Jastrow (2006), Public Domain, https://commons.wikimedia.org/w/index.php?curid=1255008 via Wikimedia Commons

17. By Classical Numismatic Group, Inc. http://www.cngcoins.com, CC BY-SA 2.5, https://commons.wikimedia.org/w/index.php?curid=7142186 via Wikimedia Commons

18. http://www.cngcoins.com/Coin.aspx?CoinID=106212 via Wikimedia Commons

19. http://www.cngcoins.com/Coin.aspx?CoinID=230579 via Wikimedia Commons

20. http://www.cngcoins.com/Coin.aspx?CoinID=230579 via Wikimedia Commons

21. http://www.cngcoins.com/Coin.aspx?CoinID=230579 via Wikimedia Commons

22. Photograph by Lalupa via Wikimedia Commons; Amanda Claridge, Rome, An Archaeological Guide, Oxford University Press, 2010, p.234

23. By Lalupa - Own work, Public Domain, https://commons.wikimedia.org/w/index.php?curid=429424 via Wikimedia Commons; Amanda Claridge, Rome, An Archaeological Guide, Oxford University Press, 2010, p.333

24. By TcfkaPanairjdde - Own work, CC BY-SA 3.0, https://commons.wikimedia.org/w/index.php?curid=5791726 via Wikimedia Commons; Amanda Claridge, Rome, An Archaeological Guide, Oxford University Press, 2010, p.333

25. Photograph by Jérémy-Günther-Heinz Jähnick via Wikimedia Commons. Link: https://fr.wikipedia.org/wiki/User:J%C3%A9r%C3%A9my-G%C3%BCnther-Heinz_J%C3%A4hnick

26. Source - own work. Date=2. & 4. H Januar 2007. Author=Marcus Cyron. Permission=Own work, copyleft: Multi-license with GFDL and Creative Commons CC-BY-SA-2.5 and older versions (2.0 and 1.0) other_versions= self2, GFDL, CC BY, via Wikimedia Commons

27. Photographed at the Palazzo Altemps venue of the National Museum of Rome by Mary Harrsch. Source via Wikimedia Commons

28. Photographed at the Palazzo Altemps venue of the National Museum of Rome by Marie-Lan Nguyen via Wikimedia Commons

29. By Nicholas Gemini - Own work, CC BY-SA 3.0, https://commons.wikimedia.org/w/index.php?curid=35663234 via Wikimedia Commons; Amanda Claridge, Rome, An Archaeological Guide, Oxford University Press, 2010, p.61

30. By Michel-georges Bernard - Own work, CC BY-SA 3.0, https://commons.wikimedia.org/w/index.php?curid=6263951 via Wikimedia Commons

31. By Daviegunn - self-made by David Gunn, Public Domain, https://commons.wikimedia.org/w/index.php?curid=2217744 via Wikimedia Commons

32. By SashaCoachman - Own work, CC BY-SA 3.0, https://commons.wikimedia.org/w/index.php?curid=14640958 via Wikimedia Commons

33. CC BY-SA 3.0, https://commons.wikimedia.org/w/index.php?curid=178512 via Wikimedia Commons; Amanda Claridge, Rome, An Archaeological Guide, Oxford University Press, 2010, pp.363-365

34. By Heretiq - Own work, CC BY-SA 2.5, https://commons.wikimedia.org/w/index.php?curid=434120 via Wikimedia Commons

35. By en: User: Victrav - Own work, Copyrighted free use, https://commons.wikimedia.org/w/index.php?curid=239514 via Wikimedia Commons

36. Classical Numismatic Group, Inc. http://www.cngcoins.com via Wikimedia Commons

37. Photograph taken by Matthias Kabel via Wikimedia Commons
38. Hara1603 via Wikimedia Commons
39. Photograph taken by Ivan Mlinaric from Slovenia via Wikimedia Commons
40. CC BY-SA 3.0, https://commons.wikimedia.org/w/index.php?curid=174651 via Wikimedia Commons

Bibliography of Maps

1. Jniemenmaa from fi [GFDL (http://www.gnu.org/copyleft/fdl.html) or CC-BY-SA-3.0 (http://creativecommons.org/licenses/by-sa/3.0/)], via Wikimedia Commons
2. By Unknown - from the Nordisk familjebok (1916), band 23, artikeln 'Rom' [1], upload to Swedish wikipedia 23.10.2003 by Den fjättrade ankan, Public Domain, https://commons.wikimedia.org/w/index.php?curid=1326053
3. Public Domain, https://commons.wikimedia.org/w/index.php?curid=621374
4. Sketch map drawn by Paul N Pearson based on Birley (1988), taken from *Maximinus Thrax – From Common Soldier to Emperor of Rome* (Pen & Sword Military, 2016). © Paul N Pearson and used with his kind permission
5. Sketch map drawn by Paul N Pearson based on Herodian, taken from *Maximinus Thrax – From Common Soldier to Emperor of Rome* (Pen & Sword Military, 2016). © Paul N Pearson and used with his kind permission

Key Events

AD 193: Septimius Severus declared emperor by the legions on the Danube. He marches on Rome and is recognized by the Senate. The Emperor Didius Julianus is executed. Dismissal of Praetorian Guard, replaced with soldiers from the legions loyal to Septimius Severus.

AD 194: Septimius Severus defeats rival claimant to the throne Pescennius Niger at the Battle of Issus. He claims to be posthumously adopted by Marcus Aurelius.

AD 195: Septimius Severus campaigns against the Parthians.

AD 196: Caracalla declared Caesar and the emperor returns to Rome.

AD 197: Defeat of rival claimant Clodius Albinus at the Battle of Lugdunum and start of the Second Parthian War.

AD 198: Sack of Parthian capital Ctesiphon and victory over Parthia. The province of Roman Mesopotamia added to the empire, with its provincial capital at Nisibis. Failure to capture Hatra. Septimius Severus granted the title 'Parthicus'.

AD 199: Imperial family stay in Egypt and Syria.

AD 200: Imperial family return to Rome.

AD 202: Septimius Severus celebrates his *decennalia* in Rome.

AD 204: The *Ludi Saeculares* celebrated in Rome.

AD 206: War against the bandit leader Felix Bulla in Italy.

Late AD 207/early 208: Departure for Britain of Septimius Severus, Julia Domna, Caracalla and Geta for campaign beyond Hadrian's Wall.

1 October AD 208: Birth of Alexander Severus (Gessius Alexianus Bassianus) in the city of Arca.

4 February AD 211: Death of Septimius Severus at Eboracum (York). Accession of Geta and Caracalla and return of imperial family to Rome.

19 or 26 December AD 211: Murder of Geta by Caracalla.

AD 212: Caracalla issues the Antonine Constitution and announces large increase in army pay.

AD 213: Caracalla campaigns in Germany against the Alamanni until September.

AD 213–214 AD: Army then marches east. Imperial family winter in Nicomedia.

Summer AD 214–215: Imperial family travel to Antioch via Ilium, Pergamum, springs at Thyatira, Prusias ad Hypium, Tyana and Tarsus.

Autumn AD 215: Caracalla travels to Egypt.

December AD 215: Rioting in Alexandria suppressed by massacre of male citizens.

Spring AD **216**: Caracalla returns to Antioch.

AD **216–217**: Caracalla's Parthian campaign and Julia Domna remains at Antioch. Caracalla winters at Edessa.

8 April AD **217**: Murder of Caracalla in a conspiracy led by his Praetorian Prefect, Macrinus.

11 April AD **217**: M. Opellius Macrinus becomes emperor. Julia Maesa and her daughters forced to leave court and retire to their family estates at Emesa.

Summer AD **217**: Death of Julia Domna at Edessa. Macrinus campaigning in Mesopotamia against Parthians.

23 August AD **217**: Lightning bolt starts a fire that destroys entire upper storey of the Colosseum.

October/November AD **217**: The indecisive Battle of Nisibis results in significant losses of Roman soldiers.

AD **217–218**: Macrinus winters in Antioch and peace made with Artabanus V. Reduces pay of new recruits to level introduced by Septimius Severus. Julia Maesa uses her control of the temple of Elagabal to ferment revolt amongst the soldiers who visit the temple and soldiers of the *III Gallica* who garrison the near-by fortress of Raphanaea.

16 May AD **218**: Mutiny at Raphanaea. Elagabalus (Varus Avitus Bassianus) declared emperor by the troops of the *III Gallica*.

8 June AD **218**: Defeat of Macrinus at battle near Imma.

June to October AD **218**: Julia Maesa, Julia Soamias and Elagabalus remain at Antioch

Late October AD **218**: Departure of Elagabalus and Soamias from Antioch for Bithynia via Cappadocia-Galatia. Revolt of Gellius Maximus and Verus in Syria.

Winter AD **218–219**: Imperial family at Nicomedia. Unrest amongst troops in Bithynia led by Castinus and the imperial fleet at Cyzicus. The senator Sulla executed for subverting returning soldiers. Murder of Gannys by Elagabalus.

July/August AD **219**: Imperial party arrive in Rome with the image of the god Elagabal after journey through Thrace, Moesia and the Pannonias.

Late AD **220**: Elagabalus gives greater emphasis to his priestly rather than political role with coins issued carrying the legend '*sacerd(os) dei solis Elagab(ali), summus scarerdos Aug(ustus)*' or '*Invicts Sacredos Aug (ustus)*'.

c. AD **221/early 222**: Revolt of Seleucus?

June AD **221**: Adoption of Alexander Severus as Caesar.

Autumn AD **221**: Elagabalus attempts to murder Alexander Severus, causing the Praetorians to riot. Elagabalus forced to agree to the removal of his *amici*, including Hierocles.

1 January AD **222**: Elagabalus refuses to accompany Alexander Severus in the consular procession.

11/12 March AD **222**: Second attempt by Elagabalus to remove Alexander Severus results in revolt of Praetorian Guard and murder of the emperor and Soamias. Alexander Severus declared Augustus.

By 1 December AD **222**: Ulpian promoted to senior Praetorian Prefect from the Prefecture of the Annona.

AD **223**: Colosseum and Meta Sudens restored.

Autumn AD **223**: Execution of the Praetorian Prefects Flavianus and Chrestus. Praetorians and Rome's populace fight on the streets of the capital. Murder of Ulpian by members of the Guard.

Spring AD **224**: Execution of Epagathus.

April AD **224**: The Parthian ing Artabanus V defeated and killed by the Sassanid Ardashir at the Battle of Hormizdjan.

Late AD **225/Early 226**: Death of Julia Maesa.

c. AD **225**: Marriage of Alexander Severus to Orbiana and adoption of her father, Seius Herennius Sallustius Barbius, as Caesar.

c. AD **226**: Nymphaeum of Alexander Severus completed at the same time as the Alexandrina aqueduct and the rebuilding of the Baths of Nero, which were renamed the Baths of Alexander Severus.

AD **226**: Cassius Dio appointed to the governorship of Pannonia Superior, where he introduces a strict disciplinary regime, resulting in complaints by the soldiers to their comrades in the Praetorian Guard.

AD **227**: Attempt by Seius Caesar to incite the Praetorians into revolt, resulting in his execution and the divorce and exile of his daughter. Ardashir captures Ctesiphon, where he was crowned '*Shahanshah*' or 'King of Kings'.

AD **228**: Ardashir invades Armenia and Adharbaijan from Media and towards the end of the campaigning season marches south through Roman Cappadocia into Mesopotamia.

AD **229**: Sassanid invasion of Mesopotamia precipitates revolts of units of the province's garrison. Flavius Heracleo is murdered by the troops and Taurinius acclaimed emperor by the rebels. Edessa supports claim of Uranius for the throne. The governors of the Eastern provinces demand the presence of the emperor. Hostility of the Praetorians towards Dio prevents him from returning to Rome to hold office with the emperor. Failure of the diplomatic initiative to restrain Sassanid aggression.

AD **230**: Extensive preparations for the war against Ardashir, including recruitment to bring units up to strength, training of the new recruits, road repairs and collection of supplies. Continued Sassanid attacks in Roman Mesopotamia, and Syria threatened.

c. AD **231**: Origen leaves Alexandria to set up a Christian school of theology at Caesarea. Possible unrest in Pannonian legions.

AD **231**: Continued Sassanid attacks on Roman-held Mesopotamia. Carrhae and Nisibis probably besieged.

Spring AD **232**: Alexander Severus departs Rome for the Persian Campaign.

Late summer AD **232**: Arrival of Alexander Severus at Antioch. Rebellions of Taurinus and Uranius crushed. Failure of second diplomatic initiative to secure a peaceful resolution to the war. Offensive against Ardashir delayed by rebellion amongst Egyptian and Syrian soldiers. Siege of Nisibis relieved.

Winter AD **232/233**: Origen summoned to imperial court. Recruitment and training of men raised in the East. Alliances agreed with Hatra and Armenia.

Spring AD **233**: Three-pronged invasion of Sassanid territory. Defeat of southern arm, leading to withdraw of central and northern arms. Roman troops supplement garrison of Hatra. Alamannic invasions of Agri Decumates, Upper Germany, Raetia and Noricum.

AD **234**: Continued Alamannic attacks.

Late summer AD **234**: Arrival of the army of Alexander Severus at Moguntiacum (Mainz), bridging of the Rhine and invasion of Alamannic territory.

Winter AD **234/235**: Negotiations with Alamanni.

March AD **235**: Murder of Alexander Severus, Julia Mamaea and their advisors. Maximinus Thrax declared emperor by the army.

April/May AD **235**: Failed conspiracy of Titius Quartinus and Osrhoenian archers against Maximinus Thrax.

Summer AD **235**: Failed conspiracy of C. Petronius Magnus.

AD **238**: Death of Maximinus Thrax.

Index